S0-BLF-616

55
EASY-TO-BUILD
ELECTRONIC PROJECTS

No. 1999
$21.95

55 EASY-TO-BUILD ELECTRONIC PROJECTS

EDITORS OF ELEMENTARY ELECTRONICS

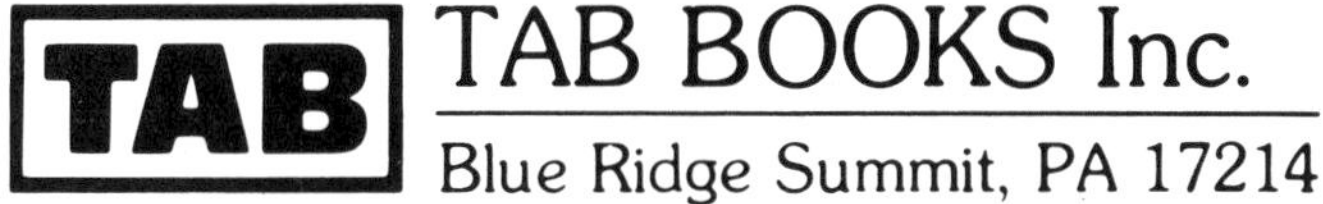

FIRST EDITION
SECOND PRINTING

Library of Congress Cataloging in Publication Data

Main entry under title:

55 easy-to-build electronic projects.

Includes index.
1. Electronics—Amateurs' manuals. I. Elementary electronics. II. Title: Fifty-five easy-to-build electronic projects.
TK9965.A115 1985 621.381'07'8 85-17346
ISBN 0-8306-0999-7
ISBN 0-8306-1999-2 (pbk.)

Contents

Preface vii

Sources of Projects viii

1 Experimenting with Electricity 1

Van de Graaff Generator—1,000,000-Volt Lightning—Build a Midget Motor—Electro-Snoop—The BOTDC Motor—Roto-Stat—Experimenter's Electroscope

2 Science Projects 57

"Windy" the Wind Gauge—Give Your Plants a Voice—Sounds from the Ground—Thermistor Thermometer—Houndog: the Electronic Metal Detector—Grandpa's Whisker—Solar Swinger

3 Digital Projects 113

Chip-Clip—Electronic Pendulum—Dashboard Digital Voltmeter—Maxiclock—SonoPulse Timer—Basic CMOS NAND Oscillator—TTL Logic Probe—Logical Probe—Crystal-Controlled TTL—Basic Pulse Maker—Do-It-Yourself Logic—AND Logic Demonstrator—NAND Logic Demonstrator—OR Logic Demonstrator—NOR Logic Demonstrator

4 Fun 'N Game Projects 151

Blinkey—Elec-Tac-Toe—The New Shell Game—The

Balanced Bridge Game—Winky-Dink—Magic Lamp—Pushie-Button—Sobriety Tester—Jogging Pacesetter—Touch 'N Flip—High Performance Transistor Radio

5 Security Projects 195

Mobile Gas Alarm—Nightlight Blackout Alarm—Light Sensor—Hobbyist's Night Light—Audio Fire Alarm—Black Box Alarm—Foil-A-Burglar Alarm—Intruder Detector—Siren Circuit—Auto Burglar Alarm

6 Power Supply Projects 229

The Smart Power Supply—The Junk Box Special—TTL Power Supply—Dual-Polarity Power Supply—Variable Regulated Power Supply

Index 243

Preface

THIS BOOK IS THE THIRD IN A SERIES OF BOOKS BY THE EDITORS of *Elementary Electronics Magazine*. The first two books in the series are *The Giant Book of Easy-to-Build Electronic Projects* (TAB Book No. 1599) and the *Second Book of Easy-to-Build Electronic Projects* (TAB Book No. 1679). All three of these exciting electronics projects books are published by TAB BOOKS Inc., of Blue Ridge Summit, Pennsylvania. If you don't have copies of the first two books in this series, you can order them at your local bookstore or directly from TAB BOOKS Inc.

Between the covers of this book, you will find 55 of the very best electronics projects ever to appear in *Elementary Electronics Magazine.* All of the projects have been carefully selected to provide hobbyists and do-it-yourselfers with many hours of enjoyable and educational project-building fun. Some of the projects can be completed in a single evening; others will require several evenings or a weekend. The science projects detailed in Chapter 2 should be of special interest. Such projects can be adapted by students for use in local science fairs.

Power for the projects has not been forgotten, either. In the final chapter you will find five power supply projects to help you get these and other electronic projects up and running fast. There is no need to start at the beginning of this book. Simply leaf through the pages until you find a project that interests you and get ready for some pleasant leisure hours!

Sources of Projects

Chapter 1

P1—*Radio & TV Exp.* Fall 1960, P2—*Radio & TV Exp.* June-July 1968, P3—*EE* Spring 1965, P4—*EE* Aug-Sept 1970, P5—*S&E* Dec-Jan 1970, P6—*S&E* June-July 1970, P7—*EE* Mar-Apr 1969.

Chapter 2

P1—*EH* Spr-Sum 1971, P2—*EH* Fall-Win 1974, P3—*EH* Fall-Win 1972, P4—*Radio & TV Exp.* Spring 1963, P5—*EH* 1981 Ed., P6—*EE* Sept-Oct 1978, P7—*EH* Fall-Win 1979.

Chapter 3

P1—*EE* 1980 Ed., P2—*S&E* Mar-Apr 1981, P3—*EH* 1980 Ed., P4—*EE* Mar-Apr 1975, P5—*EE* Jan-Feb 1970, P6—*99 IC Projs.* 1979, P7—*ibid,* P8—*ibid,* P9—*ibid,* P10—*ibid,* P11—*99* IC Projs. 1980, P12—*ibid,* P13—*ibid,* P14—*ibid,* P15—*ibid.*

Chapter 4

P1—*EE* Nov-Dec 1980, P2—*EE* Nov-Dec 1978, P3—*EE* July-Aug 1979, P4—*EE* Jan-Feb 1972, P5—*EE* Summer 1965, P6—*EE* Sept-Oct 1970, P7—*EE* July-Aug 1974, P8—*99 IC Projs.* 1980, P9—*ibid,* P10—*ibid,* P11—*ibid.*

Chapter 5

P1—*EE* Nov-Dec 1974, P2—*EE* Mar-Apr 1974, P3—*EE* Mar-Apr 1972, P4—*EE* May-June 1972, P5—*EE* Spring 1965, P6—*EE* Spring 1965, P7—*EH* Spr-Sum 1975, P8—*EH* Spr-Sum 1975, P9—*EH* Spr-Sum 1979, P10—99 *IC Projs.* 1980.

Chapter 6

P1—*99 IC Projs.* 1980, P2—*ibid,* P3—*ibid,* P4—*ibid,* P5—*ibid.*

"P"—project number

"EE"—Elementary Electronics magazine.

"EH"—Electronics Hobbyist magazine.

"S&E"—Science & Electronics magazine.

"Radio & TV Exp."—Radio & TV Experimeter magazine.

"99 IC Projs."—99 IC Projects magazine.

Chapter 1

Experimenting with Electricity

VAN DE GRAAFF GENERATOR

YOU CAN BUILD A SIMPLIFIED VERSION OF THE ELECTROSTATIC generator developed in 1931 by Dr. Robert J. Van de Graaff that aided in the development of the atomic bomb. The full-size generators produce several million volts on an aluminum sphere at the top of an insulated column.

The small counterpart of these Van de Graaff generators will perform a variety of experiments (Fig. 1-1) and develop up to 380,000 volts under ideal atmospheric conditions. Dampness in the air reduces the efficiency of the unit causing leaks of the static charges from the belt, the column and the sphere to the air. When this unit was tested at the high-voltage laboratory of a large university in dry air, the short-circuit current was 18 microamps at the calculated voltage. (See Fig. 1-2.)

The high voltages generated are not usually dangerous, although you can feel a good sting if sparks jump to your fingertips when held too close to the ball. There is no electrical power supplied to the belt; it picks up charges as the velvet rubs over plastic. Static charges on the surface of the plastic are positive and attract negative charges from the ground through a brush near the bottom end of the belt. These negative charges are carried upward on the moving belt, picked off by one of the two brushes in the top and carried to the surface of the sphere through the corona gap. The other brush is called the charging

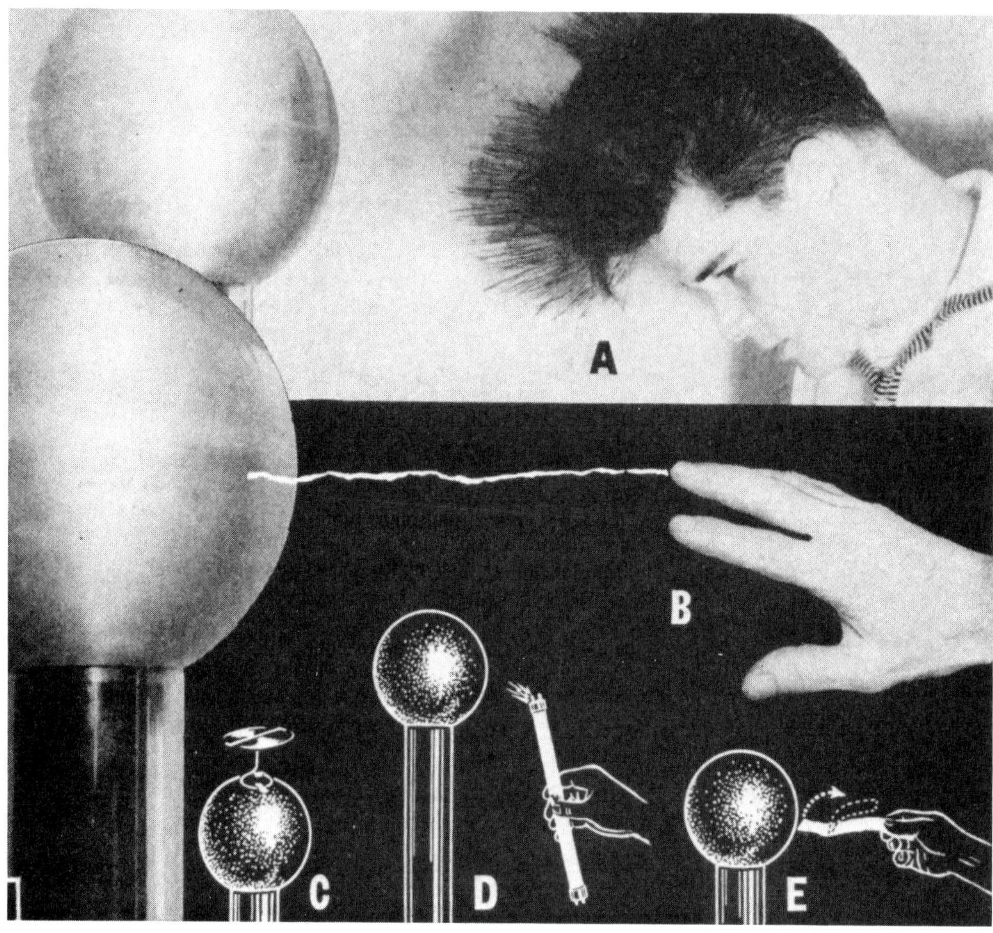

Fig. 1-1. (A) Standing close to the sphere stands your hair on end and charges to tingle your scalp. (B) Blue flashes will jump to your fingers held 12 in. or more away. (C) Corona point discharge from the tips of a wire rotor spins it like a pin wheel. (D) When end of a fluorescent tube is held closely to sphere, small streamers of blue discharges burn from the lamp terminals and lamp lights. (E) Cloth strip shows electrostatic laws of attraction and repulsion. Tossing a strip of cotton cloth at sphere causes it to remain horizontal. When end touches sphere, it becomes charged to its polarity and is violently repelled.

brush because it ensures a positive polarity of the belt on the way down (Figs. 1-3 and 1-4). After a few minutes of operation, voltage builds up on the sphere to the maximum possible with the insulation provided and atmospheric conditions present. The model stands 39 1/2 in. high and only weighs 18 pounds. The only requirement for operating it is a 115-volt ac or dc outlet for the motor.

An inexpensive motor for driving the belt can be salvaged from an old vacuum cleaner. A slide-wire resistor or rheostat controls the speed to around 3000-4000 rpm. These motors are usually available at repair shops for a few dollars and develop about 1/4 hp. Be sure to select one with tight bearings that runs fast, smooth and without excessive sparking. It's a good idea to disassemble the motor, clean out dirt and old oil first. While the armature is out, turn the threaded end of the shaft to a 1/4-in. diameter (Fig. 1-5). To reverse the direction of rotation to drive the velvet belt counterclockwise, reverse the brush leads by soldering on extensions. When you test the reassembled motor on the line with the resistance in series, loosen the two screws securing brush yoke and move to the position that generates maximum torque on the shaft; you can determine this point by holding the shaft in your hand lightly to feel maximum turning force.

A plywood cabinet encloses the motor and the base of the plastic column (Fig. 1-4). The motor mounts on two angle brackets bent up from 3/16 × 3/4-in. mild steel or aluminum. Make a base for the motor from 1/2-in. birch plywood and mount it on large rubber knobs at the four corners to reduce vibration and to allow the belt to be tightened by compressing the rubber. Adjust compression on rubber mounts to align pulley.

A turned hardwood ring with its inside diameter of about 4 7/16 in. should be a tight fit around the Lucite column. Shellac or varnish makes an effective cement to hold the column in the ring. A flat copper wire (salvaged from the field winding of an old automobile starter)

Fig. 1-2. Table-top Van de Graaff throws heavy, noisy discharge to hand electrode up to 5 in. or thinner discharges up to 8 or 10 in. This model simulates the full-size generators that helped in atomic research.

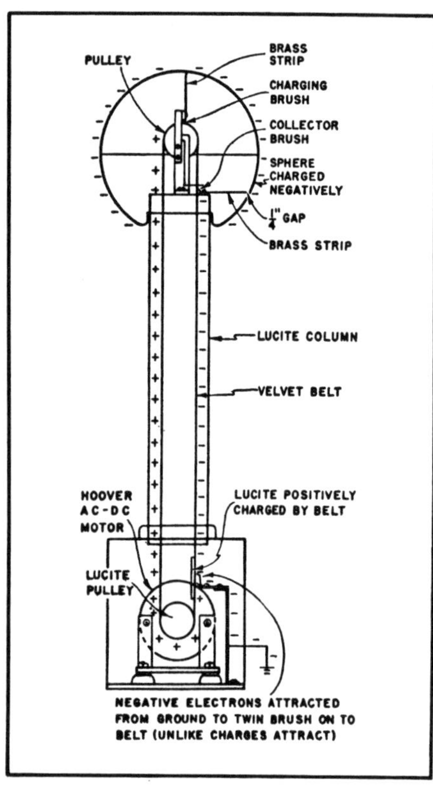

Fig. 1-3. Electrostatic charges.

around the column keeps lower end of unit at ground potential.

The lower belt pulley mounts directly on the end of the motor shaft (Fig. 1-5). Turn a slight crown on the solid Lucite pulley to help keep the belt centered. Turn the center rod parts from brass stock and assemble pulley to the end of the motor shaft with set screw. Turning and center hole boring must be done accurately.

A bent-up piece of .064 aluminum supports the ground inductor brush (Fig. 1-6). Two pieces of copper screening, 1/32-in. mesh, give numerous arcing points and are adjusted with screws to about 1/8 in. from the moving belt after it is in place.

A piece of Lucite sheet must be fitted inside the cabinet so the back of the belt rubs it (Fig. 1-7). Fit the Bakelite supports after the belt is in place.

When you complete the base cabinet, mount the driving motor, lower brush pickup and pulley, you're ready to add the top pulley assembly, make the belt and top sphere. (See Figs. 1-8 and 1-9.)

The top pulley and brush collector assembly inside the aluminum sphere mounts on two chunks of paperbase Bakelite screwed and Pliobond cemented to the inside of the Lucite column (Fig. 1-10). These blocks are curved to fit the column and must be mounted directly opposite each other and centered. The vertical U-supports that hold

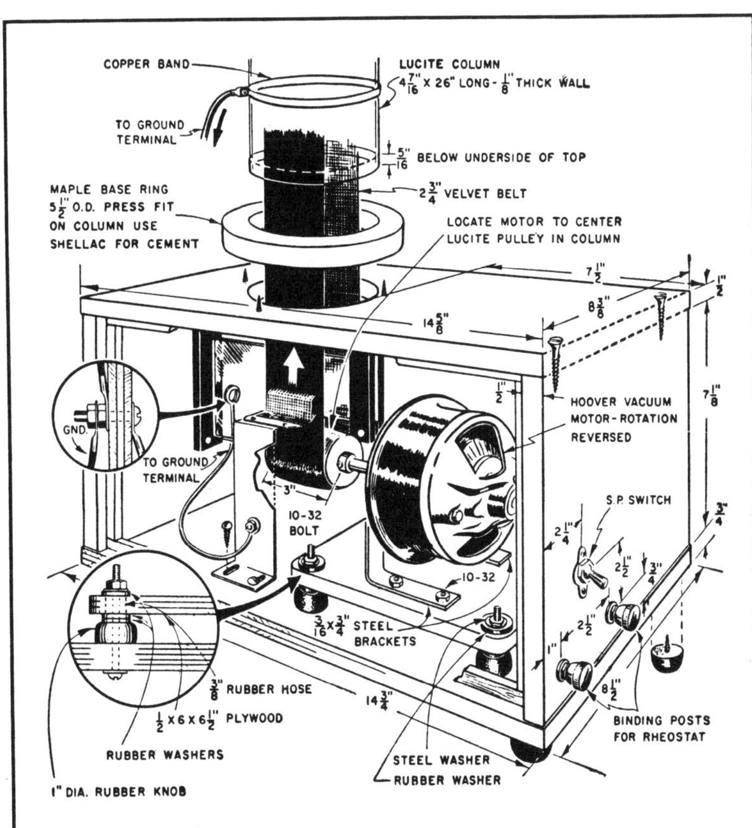

Fig. 1-4. Inside view of generator.

the top pulley must be bored for a press fit with the bearings. Use a 3/4-in. end cutting bit or end mill .0003-.0006 in. undersize in a drill press to bore out for the bearings. Or you may use a single lip type wood boring bit without a threaded center worm in a drill press if well sharpened.

Bore a 1/4-in. center hole about .0003 in. undersize in the piece of 2-in. dia. Lucite to be used for the top pulley for a press fit with the 1/4-in. shaft, or you can drill a full-size 1-4-in. hole and turn a

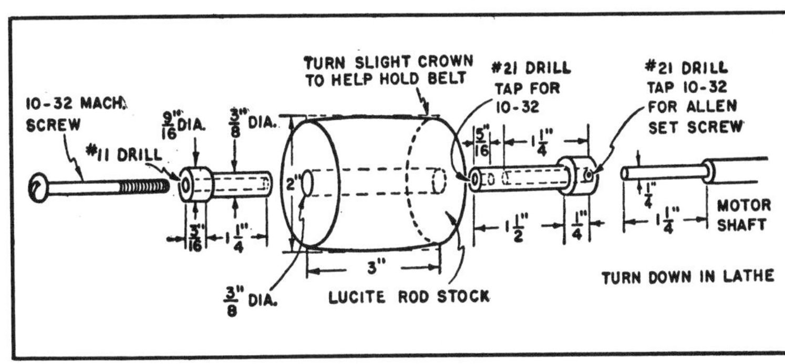

Fig. 1-5. Lower pulley assembly.

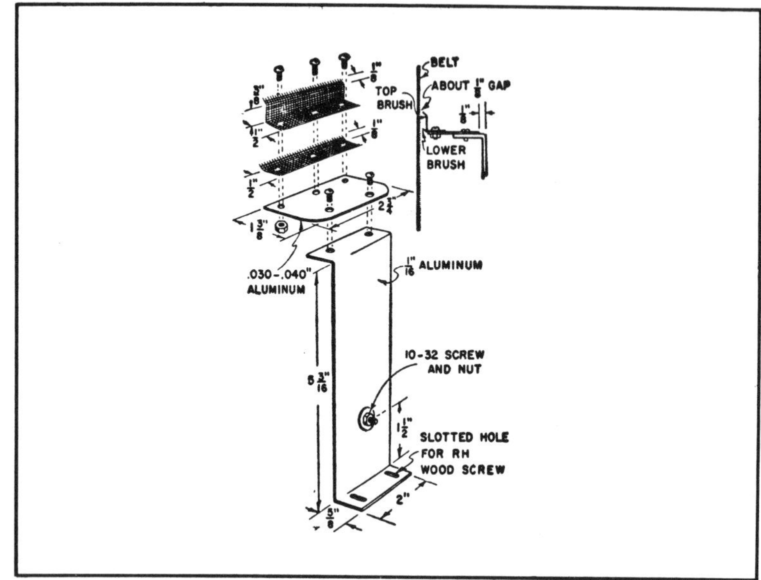

Fig. 1-6. Brush support.

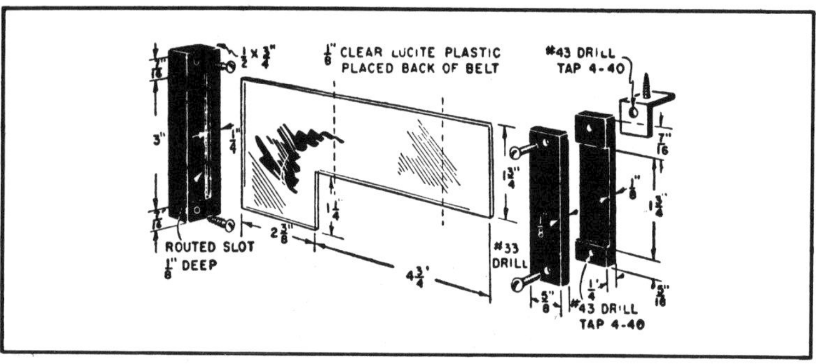

Fig. 1-7. Lucite sheet inside cabinet.

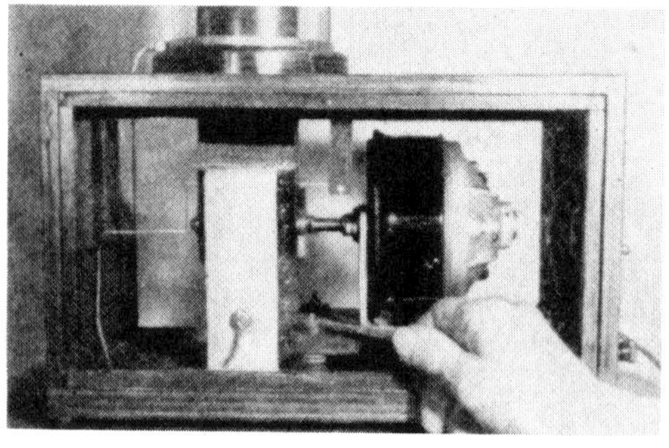

Fig. 1-8. Adjusting compression of rubber mounts helps to align lower pulley to keep belt tracking. Sides can be fitted with masonite panels if desired.

slightly oversize steel shaft for a press fit in the hole (Fig. 1-11). Cut bearing seats on the ends of the shaft for a light press fit in the bearings. Use the lathe cut-off tool to indicate length of the shaft, remove from lathe and remove the excess length; file ends smooth. Now, cut a piece of aluminum foil long enough to wrap around the

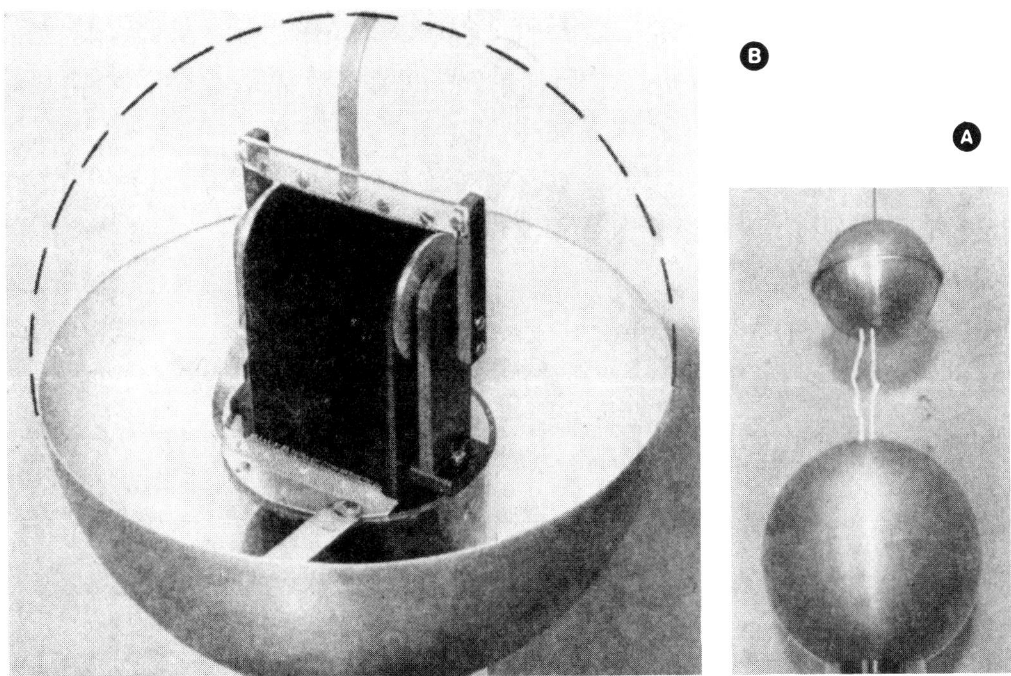

Fig. 1-9. Noisy discharge sparks jump from top to sphere to hand electrode suspended without its handle from ceiling with ground wire. Air space is 5 to 6 in. Interval between sparks depends on atmospheric conditions and speed of belt (A). Pulley, charging brush, collector brush and spark strips at top end of column. Pulley supports are made of Bakelite for strengthened insulation (B).

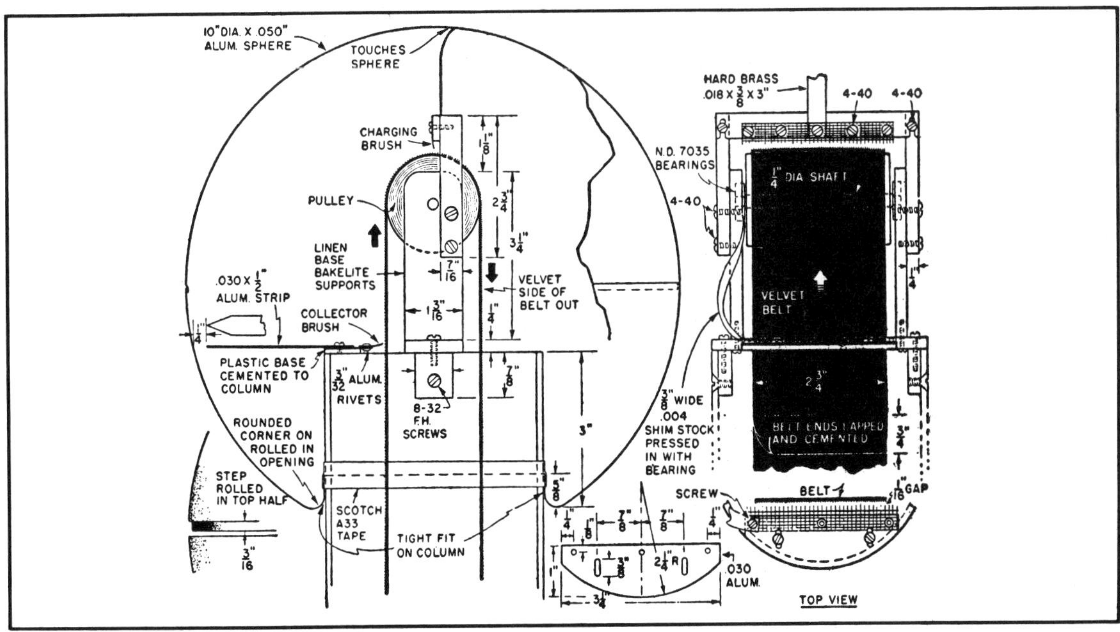

Fig. 1-10. The collector brush assembly.

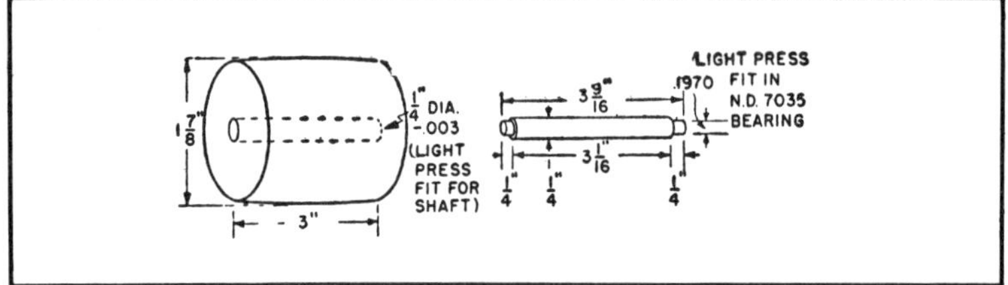

Fig. 1-11. Pulley and shaft.

pulley and lap 1/16 in. Pliobond to pulley.

To assemble the upper pulley unit, press the bearings on the ends of the pulley shaft, then press the Bakelite side supports over the outer race of the bearings. The U-supports and the cross piece must be centered so the pulley is directly over and in alignment with the bottom pulley. A plumb bob or weight on a string helps to align the pulleys vertically, but be sure the bottom assembly is resting level. After locating the U-supports, screw them to the Bakelite cross piece and screw the cross piece to the blocks at the top of the column. The top pulley assembly will be removed later to slip on the belt.

Velvet ribbon for the belt may usually be obtained from a large department store. You'll need about 6 ft. of 2 3/4-in. ribbon of any color. To determine the exact length, run a string over both pulleys and allow about 3/4 in. for lapping at the joint (Fig. 1-10). Apply a generous coating of Pliobond cement to both surfaces to be joined and clamp between two pieces of wood in C-clamps. Be careful not to allow cement outside of the lap area, or it will be difficult to separate from the wood later. Let the lap set overnight.

To install the belt, remove the top pulley assembly at the two #6-32 screws and slip the unit through the loop of the belt. Tightening the base nuts maintains the reasonably tight tension required. When the belt is running straight and true, adjust the plastic piece in the base and fit the ground brush in place.

In case you have difficulty keeping the belt running true, there are several ways to correct misalignment. Thin shims of cardboard under either base end of the top pulley support or tightening front or rear motor bolts allow considerable adjustment. For further adjustment, the holes in the cabinet base can be slotted to permit shifting the motor as required.

The aluminum sphere is a metal spinning made according to Fig. 1-10. You should be able to have a local metal-spinning shop do the job for you, if not, you can get a sphere by mail from the source indicated in Table 1-1. When spinning the turned-in neck that should fit tightly over the top end of the column, avoid any sharp corners or the built-up energy from the sphere will leak away. The seam between the two halves of the sphere should form a smooth joint to eliminate any edges where energy can leak off.

When the bottom half of the sphere is adjusted, fit the brush

Table 1-1. Materials List—Van de Graaff Generator.

Clear Lucite

1 tubing 26″ long × 4 1/2″ dia. × 1/8″ wall. May come about 4 7/16″ diameter actual measurement, column
2 solid rod stock 3″ long × 2″ dia., pulleys

Natural paper base Bakelite

1 1/2 × 3/4 × 3 7/8″ (Friction piece support in base)
1 1/4 × 5/8 × 2 1/2″ (Friction piece support in base)
1 1/8 × 5/8 × 2 1/2″ (Friction piece support in base)
Forest Products Company Inc., 131 Portland St., Cambridge, Mass. will supply the above material postage paid to any part of the U.S.

1 1/16 × 2 × 6 1/2″ alum. brush bracket (base)
1 .032 × 1 3/8 × 2 3/4″ alum. alloy (top of bracket)
2 3/16 × 3/4 × 5 1/2″ mild steel motor angle brackets
1 9/16″ dia. × 1 7/16″ brass lower pulley
1 5/8″ dia. × 1 3/4″ brass lower pulley
1 1/2″ 8 3/8″ × 14 5/8″ birch plywood, cabinet
27 1/8″ × 8 3/8″ birch plywood, cabinet
1 fir plywood 3/4 × 8 1/2 × 14 3/4″ base
8 ft 3/8 × 3/8″ hardwood strip stock

Miscellaneous

4 rubber knobs or feet
4 rubber knobs about 3/4 to 1″ diameter for motor base
1 universal motor from an old Hoover vacuum cleaner
1 3× 4″ copper screening, preferably 1/32″ mesh
1 flat copper wire from the field coil of an old auto starter, about 24″ long, ground band around column

No.	Size and Material	Use
1	1/8 × 1/2 × 4 1/4″ sheet Lucite	top brush strip
1	1/8 × 3/4 × 3 1/4″ sheet Lucite	brush base in top
1	1/4 × 1 3/16 × 4 1/2″ paper base Bakelite	top support
2	1/4 × 7/16 × 2 3/4″ paper base Bakelite	side support
2	1/4 × 3/4 × 7/8″ paper base Bakelite	blocks, top edge of column
2	1/4 × 1 3/16 × 3 1/4″ linen base Bakelite	pulley supports
	(Forest Products Company Inc., 131 Portland St., Cambridge, Mass. will supply the above material postpaid to any part of the U.S.)	
1	1/4 dia × 4 1/2″ cold rolled steel	top pulley shaft
1	.030 × 1 × 3 1/4″ sheet aluminum	side collector brush base
1	.030 × 1/2 × 3″ sheet aluminum	corona gap strip
2	6″ dia mixing bowls aluminum	hand electrode
1	.050 × 1 3/4 × 4 1/4″ sheet aluminum	handle support, hand electrode
1	10″ dia sphere, .050 alum. (available from Robert Towne, 49 Abbott Ave., Everett, Mass., $8.25 ppd. in U.S.)	
1	.018 × 3/8 × 3″ hard brass sheet	connecting strip
1	.003 or .004 × 3/8 × 4″ shim stock	jumper to pulley
1	slide wire resistor or a rheostat 95-100 ohms, 1.5 to 2 amps	
1	S.P.S.T. toggle switch	
1	2 3/4″ wide × 6′ long velvet ribbon	belt
2	New Departure ball bearings #7035 (Available from Bearings Specialty Company, 665 Beacon Street, Boston, Mass.)	
1	3/16 dia × 13″ long steel or brass rod	handle for hand electrode
1	3/16 I.D. × 1/2 O.D. × 12″ long rubber tubing	handle for hand electrode
	mis. wire, stain, shellac, screws, nuts, etc. heavy duty aluminum foil, Pliobond cement	

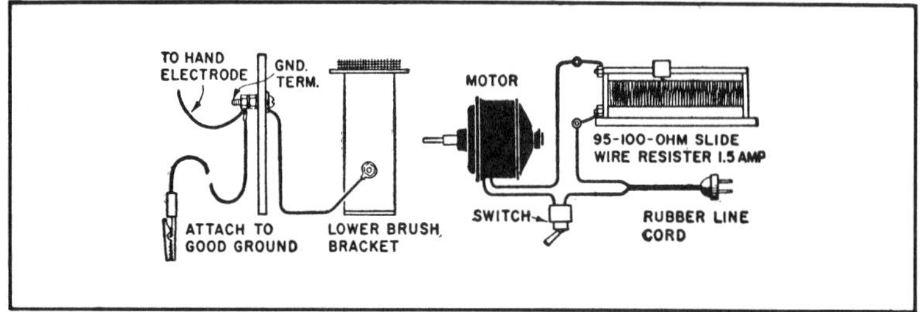

Fig. 1-12. Wiring diagram.

collectors and the spark gap strip at the top (Fig. 1-10). The wiring diagram (Fig. 1-12) shows the necessary connections with the slidewire resistor or rheostat in the circuit to control the motor's speed.

When all parts are assembled and you're ready to make the initial test, run the motor up to about 3000 rpm with the top half of the sphere off. After a few minutes, you should be able to draw short sparks to your finger at the belt in the region between the brushes if the generator is working right. Possible causes for non-operation may be that the plastic sheet in the base is not in full contact with the belt or too much humidity. (See Figs. 1-13 through 1-15.)

A final test is to set the half-sphere on top and connect a dc microammeter between the sphere's surface and the ground terminal. A small chunk of modeling clay will plaster the top lead to the sphere's surface. Start the motor and, after a few moment's operation, you should read 15-20 microamperes, the short-circuit current of the unit.

To test the voltage output of the generator, connect a string of eleven 5000-megohm special high-voltage resistors (Type BBV,

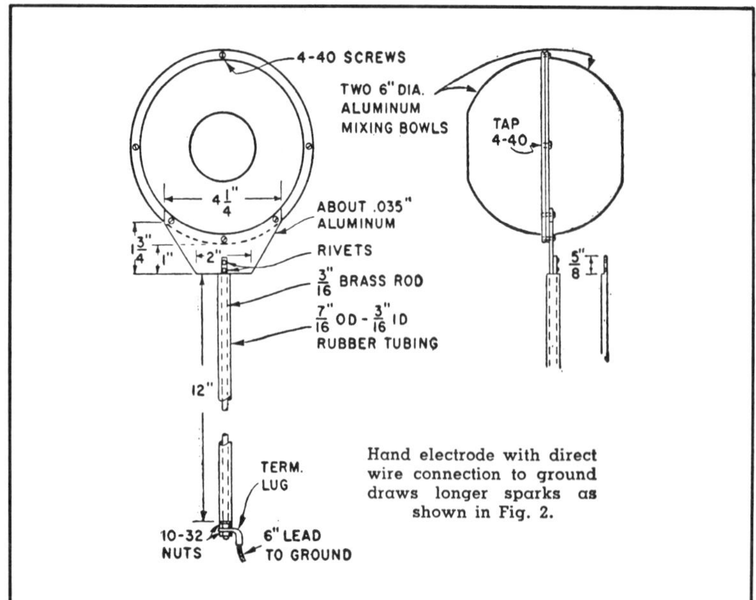

Fig. 1-13. Hand electrode.

Fig. 1-14. Machining shaft to be a light press fit in New Departure ball bearings 7035.

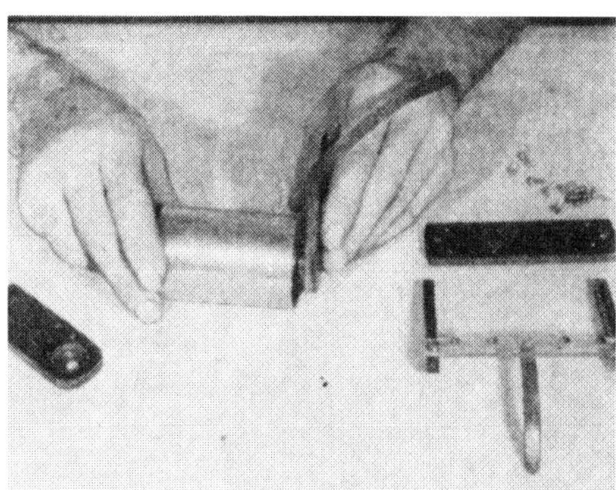

Fig. 1-15. A strip of .003-in. brass shim stock is pressed in with bearing at left side (facing collector brush). After starting the bearings in their holes, an arbor press can be used to seat them. Note other top end parts.

available from Resistance Products Co., Harrisburg, Pa.) by screwing their ends together (Fig. 1-16). Connect the series resistor string to one terminal of a 0-10 dc microammeter away from the generator, using modeling clay to hold it in constant contact with meter terminal. Attach other end of the resistor string to the sphere with clay. Enclose the resistors in a tube of plastic or other insulation. The other terminal

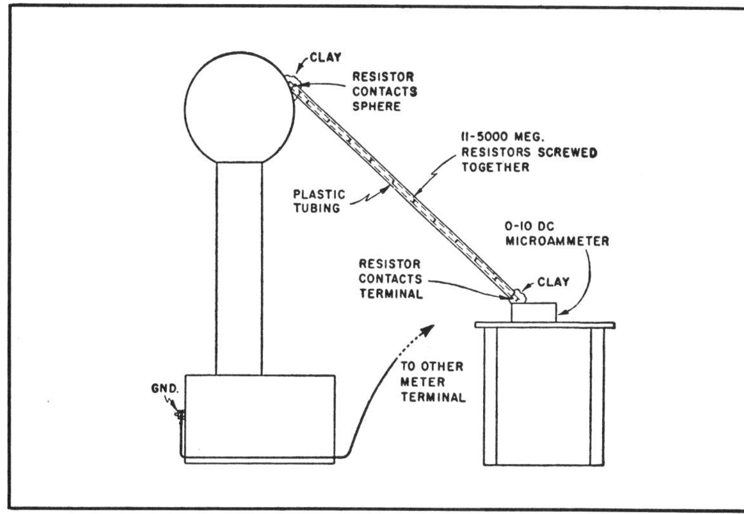

Fig. 1-16. Set up of resistors and microammeter for checking voltage of generator. It will vary with humidity.

of the meter is connected to the ground terminal of the generator. You might be able to test your generator in a nearby university or electrical testing laboratory which would probably have the special resistors and microammeter.

When you complete the voltage test set up, run the motor at about 3000 rpm for a few minutes to allow voltage to build up on the sphere. Depending upon the humidity conditions in your test room, you should be able to read from 6 to 8 microamperes. If the meter's needle fluctuates wildly, it probably indicates the plastic piece is not making full contact with the back of the belt. Good contact between the sphere's surface and the resistor string and at the meter is also important for correct readings.

When you read the current on the meter, calculate the voltage using Ohm's law (E = I × R, where E represents voltage, I the current in amperes and R the resistance in ohms). One microampere is one millionth of an ampere, so 7 microamperes becomes .000007 amperes. One megohm equals 1,000,000 ohms and 55,000 megohms converts to 55,000,000,000 ohms. Completing the calculation shows the voltage at a current reading of 7 microamperes is 385,000 volts.

The hand electrode (Fig. 1-13) capacitor aids in experimenting with the Van de Graaff generator. It should be possible to get satisfactory discharges at speeds as low as 1000 rpm.

1,000,000-VOLT LIGHTNING

EXPERIMENTERS OF EVERY ILK WILL BE TICKLED PINK (THOUGH not too literally, we trust) with the performance of this small-but-potent Lightning Generator. Capable of generating not-so-miniature lightning bolts up to 24-in. long, the device is unusually potent considering its overall simplicity and minimal power requirements.

While in operation, the Lightning Generator spouts a continuous, crackling discharge of gyrating lightning bolts into the air. These waving fingers of electricity will converge and strike any conducting object that comes within range.

A wad of paper placed atop the discharge terminal will burst into flames after a few seconds' operation, and a balloon tossed near the terminal will pop as though shot down by lightning. Though the Generator can inflict a painful shock if a hand gets too close, the current is no more dangerous than that in an automobile ignition system.

Construction

Building the Lightning Generator is relatively simple. (See Figs. 1-17 through 1-21 and Table 1-2.) The cost, depending on your scrounge-ability, will be from $35 to $50.

Start with L2, the secondary coil, which consists of a 36 1/2-in. length of 1 7/8-in. OD cardboard tubing, wound with a single layer of AWG 30 enameled, copper wire. Choose as perfect a tube as possible and make sure that it is not contaminated with paint or other substances. Heat the tube in an oven to drive out moisture and paint it lightly with varnish or plastic spray.

The coil can be wound by hand or chucked in a slow-turning lathe.

Fig. 1-17. Photo shows how author mounted capacitor C1 in home-made, fiberglass-reinforced box.

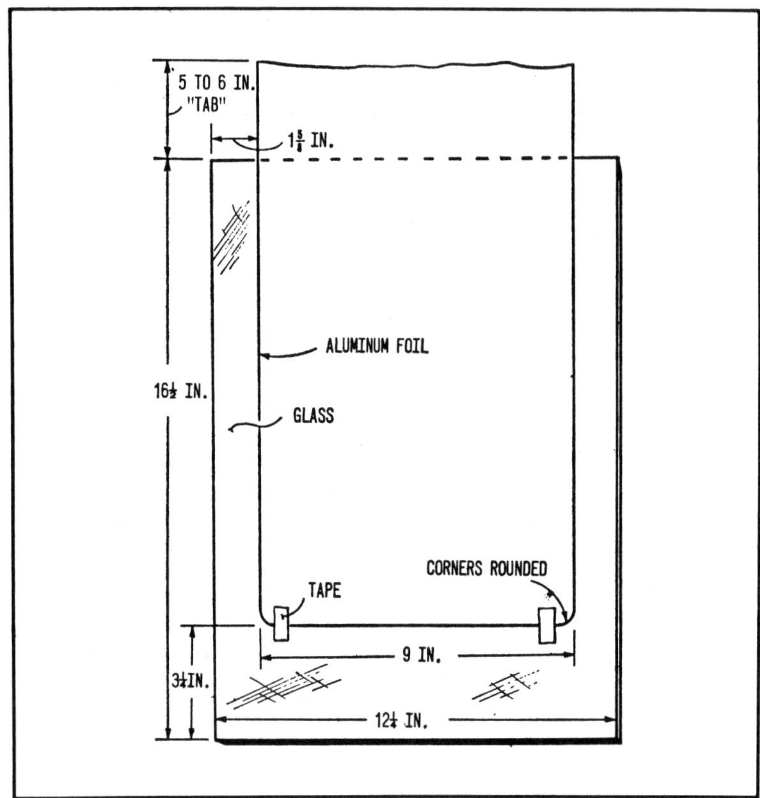

Fig. 1-18. Aluminum foil is taped to the glass foil-side up, with tabs protruding from opposite ends.

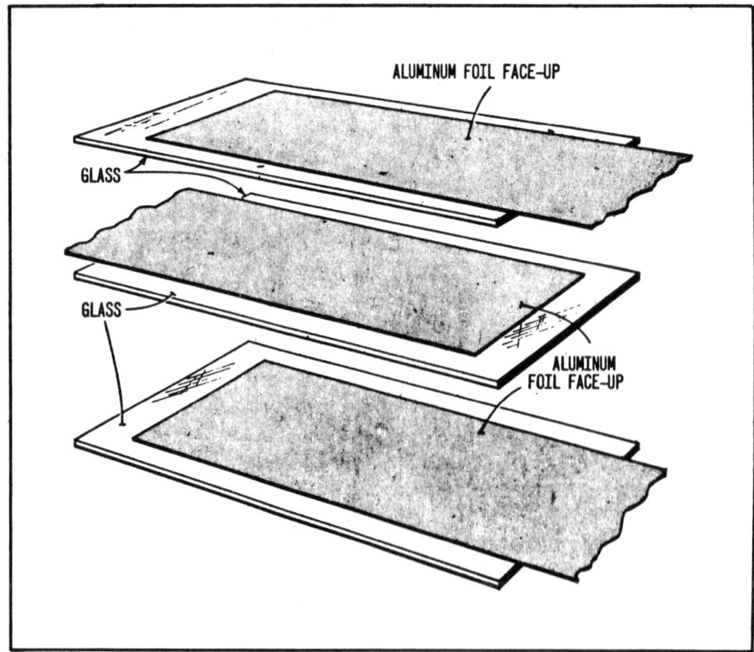

Fig. 1-19. Eight sheets of window glass and seven sheets of heavy-duty aluminum foil form the basis of capacitor C1. Plates are stacked as shown at right, with each layer of foil covered with oil as described in text.

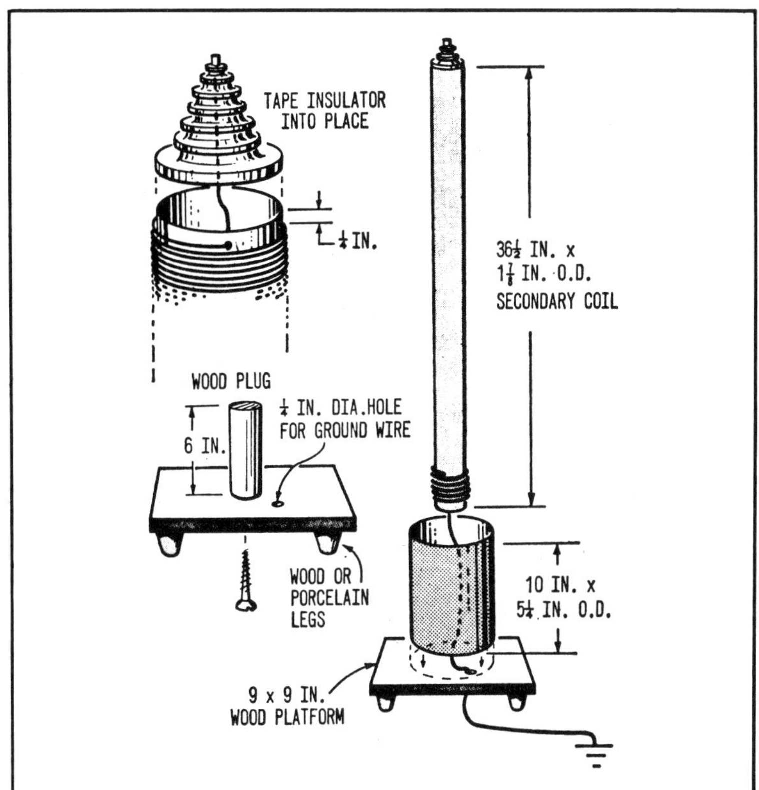

Fig. 1-20. Platform for coil L2 is made from 9 × 9 in. square of 1/2-in. plywood.

Starting 1/4-in. from the end, begin winding clockwise, making all turns as tight and close together as possible. Avoid kinks and overlapping and, if necessary, splice all wire breaks with Western Union splices.

Total number of turns will be about 3350, but there is no need to keep count since the turns are closely spaced. Leave about two feet

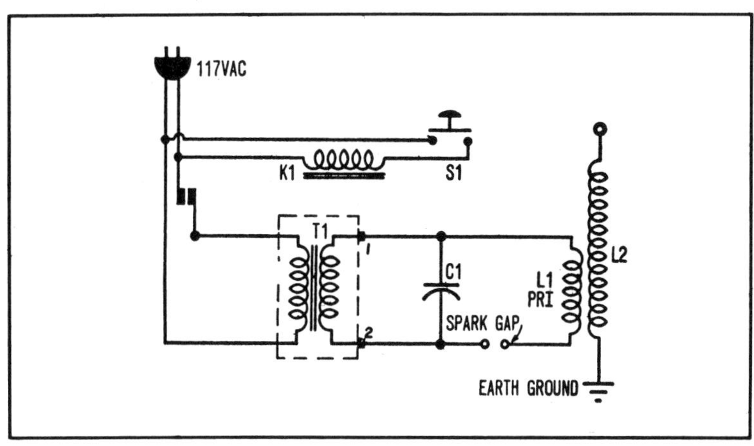

Fig. 1-21. Schematic of Lightning Generator. Biggest single expenditure (roughly $20) is for T1.

Table 1-2. Parts List for Lightning Generator.

K1—5-amp. contact, 120-volt coil relay (Potter & Brumfield type MR3A or equiv.)
L1—38-feet AWG-8 solid insulated wire wound on 5 1/4-in. form.
L2—1650 feet AWG-30 enameled solid copper magnet wire (approximately a 1/2-lb. spool) wound on 1 7/8-in. form.
S1—S.p.s.t. pushbutton switch
T1-15,000-volt, 30-mA. neon-sign transformer
1—Spark gap (see text)
1—16 × 20 × 5-in. deep box (plastic or wood—see text)
1—porcelain insulator for discharge terminal
1—36 1/2 × 1 7/8-in. OD tube (cardboard, phenolic, or other non-conductor)
1—10 × 5 1/4-in. OD tube (cardboard, phenolic, or other non-conductor—see text)
3—SAE-30 motor oil, quart cans
8—12 1/4 × 16 1/2 × 1/4-in. sheets of glass (to fit box above—see text)
Misc.—9 × 9 × 1/2-in. plywood board, switch box, wood screws, hookup wire, solder, insulating varnish or epoxy, tape, etc.

of wire free at the end. Stop winding 1/4 in. from the opposite end of the tube and run a 3-in. length of the wire through a small hole punched in the exposed cardboard.

This end will be the top of the secondary. Apply several coats of varnish or epoxy resin to the windings for protection and insulation.

To make the discharge electrode, fit the top of the secondary with a porcelain, center-fed insulator of any type (length should not exceed 3 in.). Insert a bolt through the center of the insulator and attach the 3-in. coil wire to the bottom end of the bolt. No more than 3/4 in. of the bolt should protrude from the insulator top. Fasten the insulator to the end of the secondary coil with electrical tape.

Make a platform for L2 by cutting a 9-in. square from 1/2-in. plywood and fastening a 6-in. long wooden dowel to the center. Use a 3-in. wood screw to attach the dowel, or glue it in place. The secondary should fit snugly over the dowel.

The 2-ft. length of coil wire from L2 can be brought through a 1/4-in. hole drilled in the platform 1 in. from the dowel. For appearance's sake, add insulator or wooden legs to the platform.

Primary coil L1, which fits at the base of the secondary, consists of 28 closely-spaced turns of AWG 8 insulated copper wire on a 10 × 5 1/4 in. CD Quaker Oats box. In a pinch, ordinary two-conductor line cord can be used, with the ends twisted together to form one conductor. The box should be varnished and it can be reinforced with a few layers of fiberglass cloth and epoxy resin.

To wind L1, secure the first turn at the bottom of the box with a piece of string, then wind clockwise until 28 turns have been made. Do not wind the entire length of the box, but keep the turns as closely spaced as possible. Secure the last winding with electrical tape.

Cut a hole in the bottom of the box and slip the completed L1 over L2, keeping the secondary centered. The exposed cardboard of the primary can be painted with nonconducting enamel or wound with tape.

Low-Leakage Capacitor

A box about 16 × 20 × 5 in. will be needed for capacitor C1. A box can be made of 1/4- or 1/2-in. plywood and reinforced with fiberglass, or a store-bought variety can be had in the form of a plastic refrigerator storage box. Box size is not critical, though the box must be large enough to hold the capacitor about to be described.

Glass dielectric for the capacitor consists of eight sheets of 16 1/2 × 12 1/4 × 1/4-in. window glass. Cost should run about $20. Use extreme care in handling, as the edges are razor sharp.

Cut out seven sheets of 20- × 9-in. heavy-duty aluminum foil and assemble C1 as follows: lay a sheet of glass in the box and place a sheet of 20- × 9-in. aluminum foil on the glass as shown in the drawings. Pour in just enough ASA 30 motor oil to cover the foil. On top of this lay another sheet of glass and aluminum foil, but be sure to reverse the tab or free end of foil to that it protrudes from the opposite side of the glass.

Press all air bubbles from between the glass. This done, pour in more oil and continue the process, always alternating each sheet of foil. Bend the foil tabs together on each side of the capacitor in order that wires from the rest of the circuit can be connected to them. About three quarts of oil will be needed for a 16- × 20-in. box. Wooden blocks can be wedged around the plates as a means of keeping them from shifting.

There are a number of ways to make the spark gap, but the best arrangement consists of two 1/2-in. diameter conductors adjustable from 1/4- to 1-in. separation.

A simple gap can be made by mounting two 1/2-in. diameter bolts through nuts brazed on 1- × 2-in. metal plates. The plates are mounted on a varnished wood block at least 1 3/4-in. thick to prevent arcing around the gap (see our illustrations).

Power for the circuit is supplied by a 15,000-volt, 30 mA neon-sign transformer. New transformers cost about $30 or more—used ones are considerably less. (See Figs. 1-22 through 1-24.)

Wire the circuit with AWG 12 or 14 single-conductor copper wire, as it is stiff enough to be self-supporting. Route all wires separate from each other and other objects, keeping in mind that high voltages will be present throughout most of the circuit. Capacitor C1 is wired into the circuit by attaching wires directly to the aluminum foil tabs. Place components according to drawings.

Operating the Generator

When the circuit is ready for testing, connect the ground wire from the bottom of the secondary to a water pipe or telephone ground

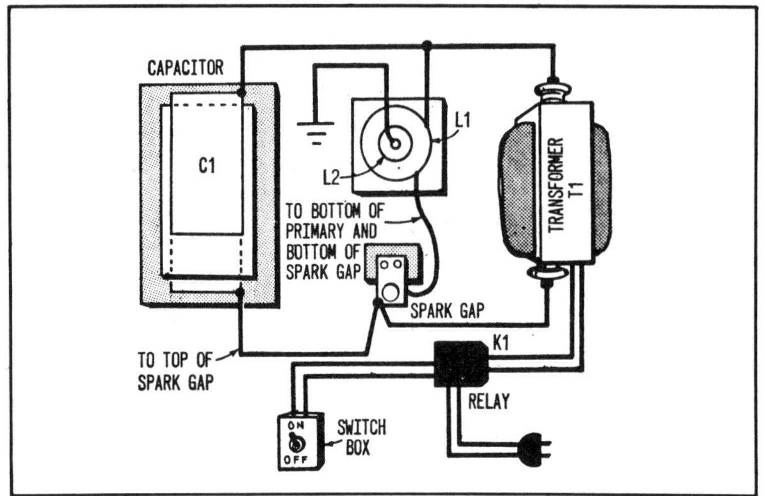

Fig. 1-22. Pictorial diagram of Lightning Generator. Leads are attached directly to tabs on C1.

system. Adjust the spark-gap to about 1/2-in. separation, plug the transformer in, and turn the switch on for a second or two.

A heavy, blue spark should bridge the gap and a visible discharge should show from the tip of L2. Throw the switch on again and watch the capacitor to be sure that it is not arcing around the plates. If no arcing occurs in C1 and the coil seems to be functioning properly, open the gap to 3/4 of an inch and turn the power on again. This time, an 18- to 20-in. discharge should dart from the top of L2. At 1-in. separation the discharge should read a full 24 inches; beyond 1 in. the gap may not fire. Grinding the tips of the bolts (forming the spark gap) into conical points will make it easier for the arc to form. Always keep an eye on the capacitor for arcing—if allowed to occur, the plates may break in time.

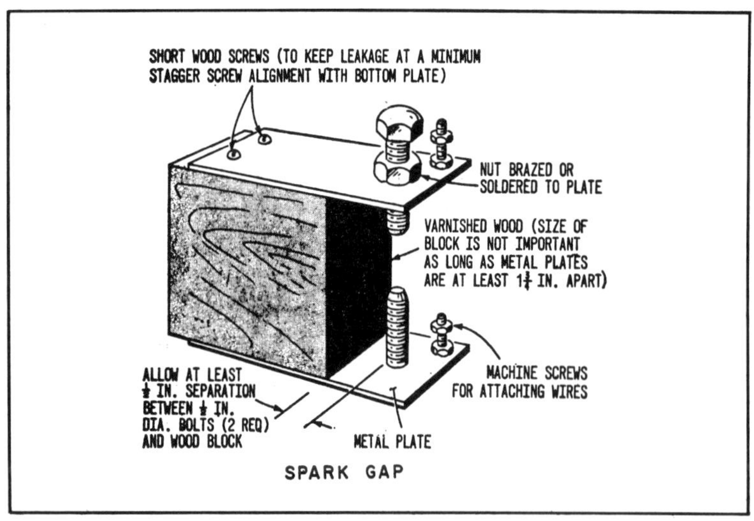

Fig. 1-23. Spark gap can take any number of forms, but this spacing arrangement worked best in author's case. Gap is adjustable from 1/4 to 1-in.

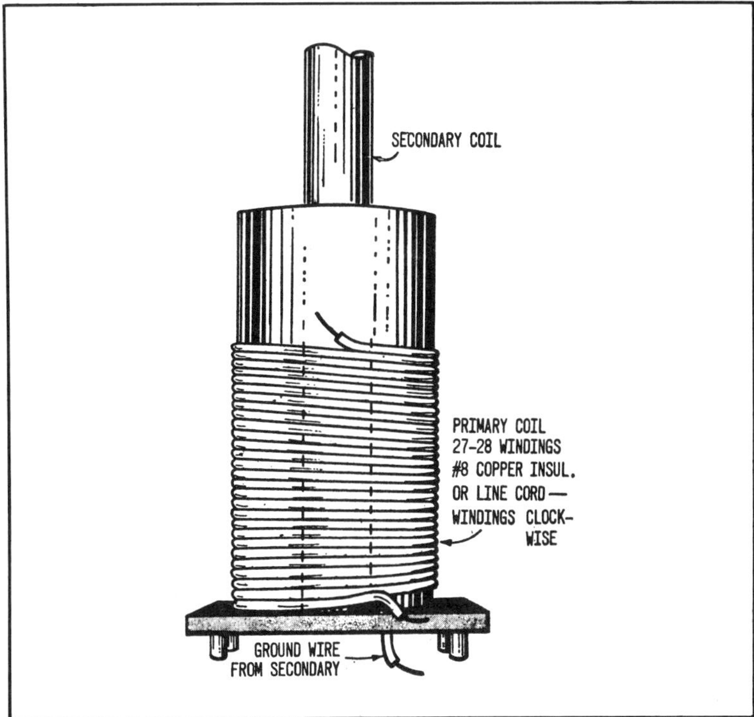

Fig. 1-24. Coil L1 is close-wound with AWG-8 insulated wire. One end of coil connects to spark gap, the other C1 and to T1.

If no spark occurs, double-check the wiring and make sure the plates in the capacitor have been properly assembled. If the transformer is good, a 1 1/2- to 2-in. arc can be drawn between the output terminals 1 and 2 with the L1 and L2 out of the circuit.

Tuning

If the spark-gap is operating, but either a weak discharge or none at all appears at the top of L2, the coil will have to be tuned. This is accomplished by varying the number or size of the aluminum foil sheets in C1 and by varying the effective turns on L1.

It's easier to begin tuning by varying the exposed area of the top sheet of aluminum foil and by "tapping in" a few turns down from the top of the primary. Maximum discharge generally will be reached with a total variation of no more than two or three turns on coil L1 and one full sheet of aluminum foil in C1.

If reducing the number of turns in L1 and changing the number of plates in C1 doesn't help, try adding several turns to L1 by splicing in additional wire. An additional sheet of foil can be added to the capacitor, but another sheet of glass will be needed, too.

It is best not to operate the Generator for more than 15 to 20 seconds continuously without an equal time off, as the oil in the capacitor will start to break down, allowing arcing to occur.

Experiments

Hold a fluorescent light a few feet from the Generator and throw the switch. The light will glow even though not connected to any electrical source. Large, clear light bulbs held near the coil will glow with weird, flowing colors.

Bring a grounded, metal rod within range of the discharge point atop L2 and notice the "bunching" effect as the sparks leave their random pattern and arc to the rod. The discharge will not travel as far to reach a grounded conductor as it will in open air, since the atmosphere itself acts as the opposite electrical pole.

A pinwheel rotor about 6 to 8 in. in diameter can be made from AWG 18 or 20 solid wire and fitted atop the discharge terminal so that it can rotate freely. When the Generator is operating, the rotor will turn from the force of the discharge leaving the ends of the wire.

Place a piece of paper on the terminal and close the switch. In a few seconds, the paper will burst into flames.

Despite the extremely high voltages, the Lightning Generator develops very little current, making a shock from the coil relatively harmless. However, the currents in the rest of the circuit are very dangerous, so they must be treated with respect.

The discharge is virtually impossible to contain. Try inverting a glass tumbler over the discharge electrode; the discharge will pass right through, leaving the glass full of ozone. A heavy, waving arc will easily crackle across a distance of a foot or more to reach a metal rod. To capture the lightning on film, use a camera capable of at least 1/250th sec. shutter speed and try a variety of f-stops.

Balloons can be shot down simply by tossing them at the terminal, and sometimes the effective range of the lightning "anti-aircraft" is surprising.

With reasonable maintenance, the Generator will last indefinitely. And with a little ingenuity you will discover new experiments and gain insight into the fundamentals of tuned circuits with this great-granddaddy of modern radio. (See Fig. 1-25.)

How It Works

The primary coil L1 and capacitor C1 together form a tuned circuit designed to oscillate at a frequency four times the natural resonant frequency of the secondary coil L2. By inducing current at the base of the secondary L2 equal to a quarter of its natural wavelength, the induced voltage will reach a peak, every half-cycle, at the discharge terminal at the top of L2. The voltage generated is determined by the inductance of L1 and how accurately L1 is tuned.

The spark gap, being an open circuit, allows the capacitor to charge to maximum. The spark gap ionizes and the charge stored in the capacitor discharges across the spark gap and most of the charge

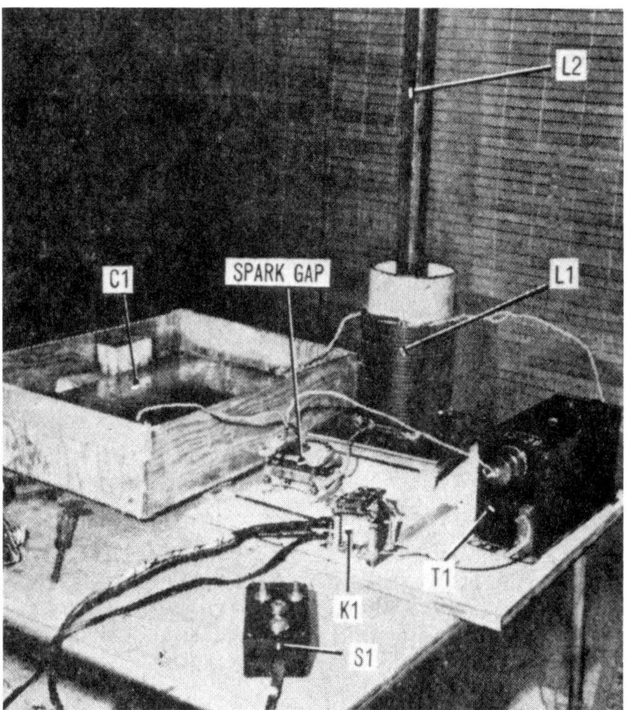

Fig. 1-25. Completed Lightning Generator stands ready to go with all of a million volts! Wiring between components is AWG-12 or 14.

stored in the electrostatic field of the capacitor becomes energy in the magnetic field that builds up around L1 as the discharge current flows through L1. When C1 has discharged to a point where the voltage across C1 will no longer sustain an arc across the spark gap, current stops flowing through L1 and the magnetic field therefore starts to collapse.

When the magnetic field around L1 collapses, it generates a counter EMF (electromotive force) or voltage that is almost as great as the voltage from T1 that originally charged C1. This voltage breaks down the already partially ionized spark gap and C1 begins to charge all over again.

Because of the high inductance and low natural resonant frequency of the secondary winding of T1, this portion of the circuit is effectively nonexistent. Most of the energy pumped into the circuit formed by L1, C1, and the spark gap remains in that portion of the circuit. The secondary of T1 just adds energy every 1/120th of a second. For best results, the oscillation frequency should be some high harmonic (multiple) of this 120—like 120 kHz.

As C1 recharges from the magnetic field around L1, a point is again reached where the spark gap cannot be sustained because all the energy is gone from the winding of L1. This means that the magnetic field has collapsed completely.

Once more C1 discharges, and current flow again reverses through

Fig. 1-26. Lightning-like discharge reaches 24-in. to strike low-hanging ceiling beam, while operator watches from a respectable distance.

the spark gap and a magnetic field builds up around the coil L1. With each cycle of charge and discharge the energy transferred is reduced and would soon die out if energy weren't added by the secondary of T1.

Each buildup and breakdown of the magnetic field induces a voltage in coil L2 which discharges from the tip of L2 in the form of lightning-like flashes and streaks. (See Fig. 1-26.)

BUILD A MIDGET MOTOR

THIS LITTLE MOTOR HAS GOOD TORQUE FOR ITS SIZE AND WILL drive toys such as model cars and boats. The motor's speed can be varied to a wide range of lower speeds by inserting a rheostat in series with one of the armature leads. When connected in series it becomes a universal motor.

The motor has a three-pole armature with a winding, and also a wound field. It is self-starting and operates on 3 to 4 volts dc when connected with the armature and field in shunt. Connected in series it operates on 4 1/2 to 6 volts dc. Two dry cells will produce 3 volts. If connected in series, it will operate on about 12 volts ac via a stepdown transformer. Construction requires a metal-turning lathe, a drill press and metalworking hand tools.

The height of the motor is only 2 3/8 inches. The four terminal posts are 6-32 screws and nuts. They are marked F for field and A for armature (see Fig.1-30, lower left corner). Countersunk flathead machine screws are used at the binding posts and at the points where the motor is attached to the base.

Making the Armature

Since the armature is the most difficult part to build, we'll start with it. A piece of 1/2-inch hexagonal soft steel is used as the center core of the armature; cut it to a 3/4-inch length; use the lathe to bore a 7/16-inch No. 30 hole through the center. Now drill a hole in each of the three sides of the armature stock where the poles of the armature will be fixed. A No. 21 drill is used and the holes tapped for 10-32 screws.

The shaft is a piece of .128 × 2 1/4-inch drill rod. It is press-fitted in the hole in the center core so that the end projects 9/32 inch beyond the core.

Three pieces of 1/16-inch-thick soft steel are next shaped for the pole pieces. Cut to size and dress the edges with a file. Give them a slight curvature by placing them on a V-block, laying a 3/4-inch pipe coupling on top, and striking the coupling with a hammer.

Drill a hole in the center of each pole piece for a 10-32 flathead machine screw, one of which is turned into each tapped hole drilled in each of the three sides of the center core. Countersink the holes in the curved pieces so the screws will fit flush.

Assembly of the armature core parts uses a pipe spacer between the curved pole pieces and the core (see Fig.1-30). Prior to the installation of commutator and winding, place pieces of thin fiber or armature paper at each end of the pole areas; press-fit Bakelite washers on the ends of the spacer; and wrap insulating tape around the spacer. (See Figs. 1-27 through 1-29.)

The Commutator

A piece of Bakelite rod on which a sleeve of thin brass tubing is pressed and secured with six 2-56 machine screws serves as the commutator. Hacksaw three cuts through the tubing to create a three-

Fig. 1-27. Lathe setup is used to drill .128-in. hole through center of hexagonal center core of mild steel which serves as motor armature. A drill press can do this job if a lathe is not available—be sure to hit center.

Fig. 1-28. Drill, tap and countersink holes in three alternate sides of the armature to accept flush-fitting 10-32 flathead machine screws.

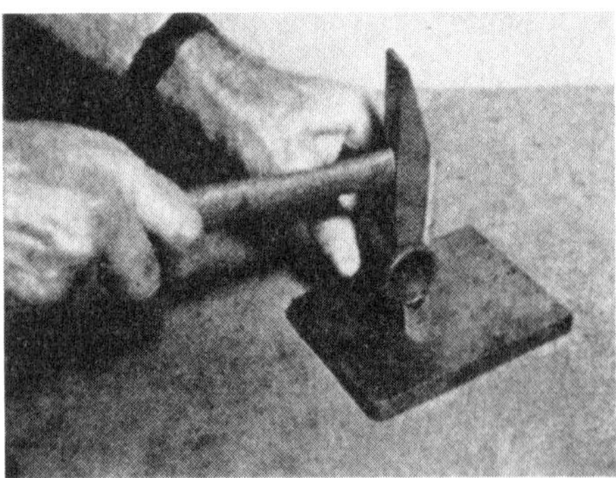

Fig. 1-29. Slight curvature is given to the pole end pieces by striking a pipe coupling on a V-block with end piece in between as shown.

section commutator. Now drill a No. 30 hole through the Bakelite commutator which is then pressed on the long end of the shaft. Leave a space of about 1/32 inch between the steel core and the commutator. Adjust the commutator so the slots line up between the poles.

The winding around each pole is done by hand, placing 100 turns of No. 24 Formex or enameled magnet wire around each pole. Put the turns on evenly and tightly and bring the start and finish ends out close to the commutator. Connections are made by taking the start end of one coil and twisting it up with the finish end of the next one, removing the insulation, of course, before twisting the ends. These connections are carried out around the armature to prevent the three twisted leads coming between the three wound poles. Wind the coils in the same direction. (See Fig. 1-30.)

Now connect the leads to the commutator segments, carrying each to the nearest segment to the right where it is soldered to the appropriate screw heads (see drawing of armature detail).

Apply lacquer to the windings to keep the turns tight, but keep it off the commutator and shaft; polish these parts with crocus cloth.

Field Section Assembly

A piece of 1/8 × 3/4-inch soft steel is bent around a pipe coupling to begin forming the two side pieces. Drill and tap the holes in these pieces as shown, then join them in position by means of the 5/16-1 3/32-inch pipe sleeve bolted between their bases. The field winding consists of 300 turns of No. 24 Formex or enamel magnet wire wound on the insulated pipe spacer before placing it in position between the two side members.

The start and finish ends of the wire are carried through small holes drilled in one of the spacer's ends. Wind the wire in neat layers with the turns tight and close together. (See Figs. 1-31 through 1-37 and Table 1-3.)

Final Assembly

The armature supports are two brass pieces attached to the field side members with screws at the center of the curved point on the side members. The actual shaft bearings are drilled holes in two end brass pieces which are secured to the armature supports with screws. Careful lining up of all parts is required in order to get the armature to turn freely. The holes in the end pieces or shaft supports are slotted to allow some adjustment as required. The air gap between the armature and the field poles should be about 1/16 inch and approximately uniform all around.

The two brush-support blocks must now be cut, drilled and tapped as shown in the top left detail of the drawing. These are then attached to the side supports and serve as bases for the brushes.

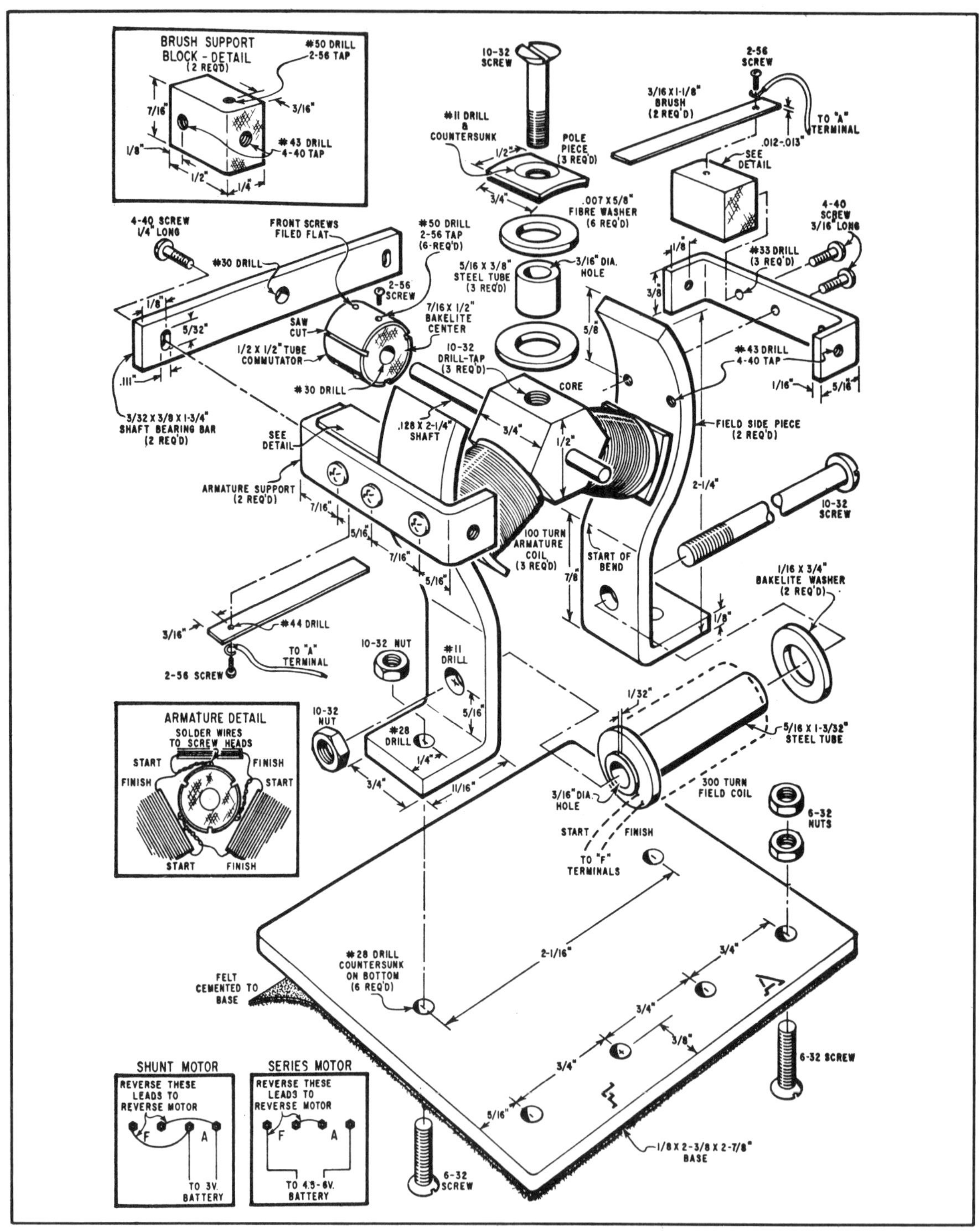

Fig. 1-30. The exact construction details for the author's unit are shown in the above detail drawing. Minor variations can be made to suit available materials.

Fig. 1-31. Each of three pole end pieces is drilled with a countersunk hole and tapped to take 10-32 flathead machine screws filed flush.

Fig. 1-32. Completed armature less the commutator and winding. Note thin fiber washers on each of the poles for end insulation of the coil.

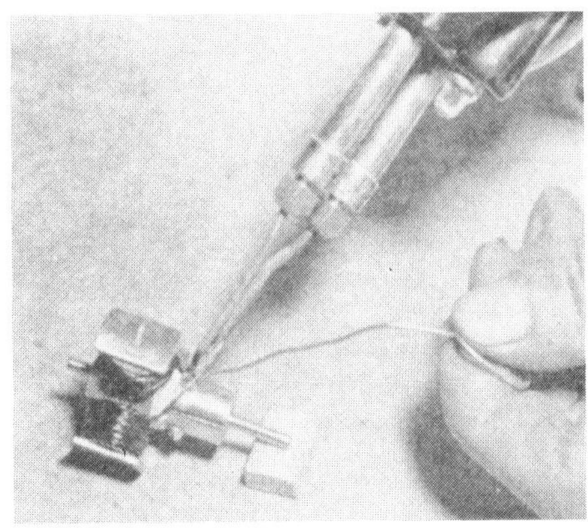

Fig. 1-33. With the armature wound, cleaned and twisted leads from start of one pole to finish of next are soldered to commutator segment.

Fig. 1-34. Field side pieces are made of soft, flat steel stock. Their curved portions are bent around the pipe coupling held in a vise as shown.

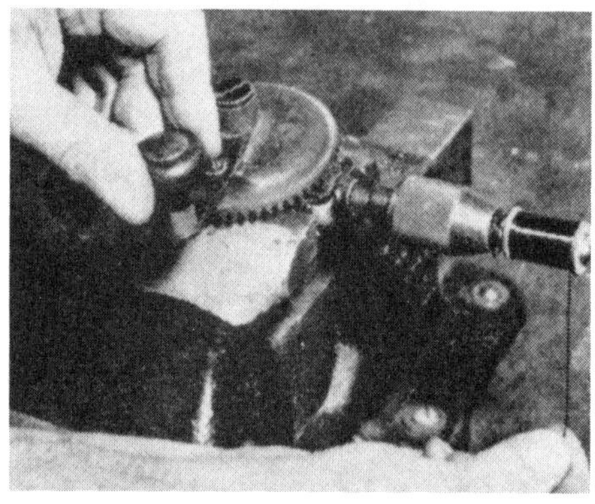

Fig. 1-35. Hand drill used as shown helps speed the winding of 300 turns of wire on the field coil—a spool that measures 5/16 × 1-3/32 in.

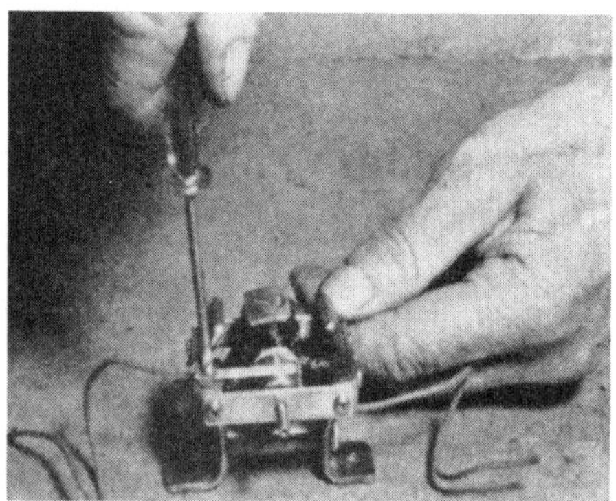

Fig. 1-36. An insulated wire is connected under each brush screw; the other ends are connected to the terminals marked A on base of the motor.

Fig. 1-37. Close-up view of motor reveals simplicity of construction. Of an extremely compact design, the motor only 2 3/8 in. high.

Table 1-3. Materials List—Midget Motor.

Amt. Req'd	Size & Description	Use
1 pc.	1/8 × 2 3/8 × 2 7/8" Bakelite	base
2 pcs.	1/8 × 3/4 × 3" mild steel	field side pcs
3 pcs.	1/16× 1/2 × 3/4" mild steel	armature pole ends
1 pc.	1/2 × 3/4" hexagonal mild steel	armature core pc.
3 pcs.	5/16" O.D., 3/16" I.D. & 3/8" long pipe or steel tubing	armature pole spacers
1 pc.	5/16" O.D., 3/16" I.D. & 1 3/32" long pipe or steel tubing	field coil spacer tube
1 pc.	.128" dia. × 2 1/4" long drill rod	shaft
2 pcs.	3/32 × 3/8 × 1 3/4" brass	shaft bearing bars
2 pcs.	1/16 × 3/8 × 2" brass	armature supports
1 pc.	1/2" O.D., 7/16" I.D. & 1/2" long brass tubing	commutator
2 pcs.	.012" or .013 " × 3/16 × 1 1/8" phosphor bronze	brushes
2 pcs.	1/4 × 7/16 × 1/2" Bakelite	brush support blocks
1 pc.	7/16" O.D. × 1/2" long Bakelite rod	commutator
2 pcs.	1 × 1" Bakelite or fiber	cut to make washers on field coil
1 pc.	.007 × 2 1/2 × 3" hard fiber	cut to make 6 washers for armature poles
4 ozs.	No. 24 Formex or enameled approx. magnet wire	windings
4	6-32 1/2"-long flathead brass machine screws	binding posts
2	6-32 3/8" long flathead brass machine screws	motor-to-base
10	6-32 hexagonal brass nuts	
8	4-40 3/16"-long roundhead brass machine screws	armature support pieces
2	4-40 1/4"-long roundhead brass machine screws	bearing bar at commutator end
2	2-56 3/16"-long roundhead brass machine screws	brushes
6	2-56 1/8" to 5/32"-long roundhead machine screws	commutator
1 pc.	thin felt (2 3/8 × 2 7/8")	pad for base
3	10-32 5/8"-long flathead iron machine screws	armature poles

Brushes

Two phosphor bronze strips about .012 to .013 inch thick are cut 3/16 inch wide and 1 1/8 inch long. An insulated lead wire is attached under each screw turned into the No. 43 holes tapped into the brush support blocks, these serve as leads to the terminal posts on the base.

The balance of the project consists of making up a suitable base from either Bakelite or hardwood. Finally, cement a piece of felt to the underside of the base.

ELECTRO-SNOOP

HERE'S AN IDEAL SCIENCE FAIR PROJECT. ELECTRO-SNOOP IS A static electricity detector that instantly discloses whether a static charge is positive or negative. What's more, it also gives a relative indication of the charge's strength. Operation of the unit is simplicity itself. The meter reads to the left for negative charges and to the right for positive charges; the extent of deflection is dependent on the magnitude of the charge. Electro-Snoop will tell you what kind of charge you acquire walking across a wool rug, what the polarity of the charge on your car becomes as you drive down the street on a dry day, or what the polarity and magnitude of atmospheric electricity your ham antenna is picking up from the surrounding air.

The author found the instrument extremely useful around a physics laboratory. On one occasion it was desired to know the polarity of the dome of a newly constructed Van de Graaff generator. The Electro-Snoop was placed about eight feet from the generator. The generator and Electro-Snoop were both turned on and the meter went off-scale to the right, indicating a strong positive charge. This proved that electrons were being removed from the dome, as had been desired.

Electro-Snoop's Advantages

The old gold leaf electroscope has its problems. The gold leaves are hard to maintain and the instrument can't distinguish directly between a plus and minus charge. The Braun electroscope represents a considerable improvement over this, but still requires an external neon lamp to determine polarity. Vacuum-tube electroscopes work nicely for negative charges, but a positive charge placed on the grid is quickly neutralized by electrons from the filament. This problem is completely circumvented by the use of a field-effect transistor (FET). The absence of a filament coupled with its extremely high input impedance allows a charge of either polarity to remain undisturbed on the gate (g) while the meter is being read.

The unit forms a neat self-contained package—no external connections or power source are needed, and it can be used anywhere, indoors or out. Battery drain is quite low, less than 1 mA when the bridge is balanced. It increases to something better than 1 mA with a positive charge and drops to 1/2 mA or even less with a negative charge.

How Electro-Snoop Works

We've redrawn the heart of Electro-Snoop's circuit into a

conventional Wheatstone Bridge configuration, as shown in Fig. 1-38. From this it can be seen that current flows in two separate paths. Using the negative input at the bottom of Fig. 1-38 as a starting point, it can be seen that electrons may travel up the left side through resistors R3, R6, and R5 to the positive, or up the right side through the FET and R4, and meet at the positive pole at the top of the diagram.

The purpose of R2 is to limit the voltage on the FET to approximately 2V. By adjusting R6 a balance position can be found at which points A and B in the diagram are both at the same potential, approximately 6.5V. Therefore, since there is no potential difference across the meter, it will read zero. In this balanced state, whenever a charge is placed on the gate of the FET, the bridge will respond, with the meter swinging either to the right or left depending on the polarity of the charge.

Whenever a negative charge is placed on the gate of the FET, electrons will be inhibited from passing through the FET. This in effect is equivalent to raising the resistance in this arm of the bridge, which, in turn, increases the voltage drop across the FET proportionally. Point B now assumes a higher potential than point A, and since there now is a difference in potential across the meter, current flows through the meter, deflecting the pointer to the left.

When a positive charge is placed on the gate, electrons will flow more easily through the FET, thus in effect lowering its resistance. The voltage now divides between R4 and the FET in such a manner that the voltage of point B is lowered with respect to point A. Again, because there is a difference in potential, current will flow through the meter, this time deflecting the pointer to the right. By using a value for R2 specified in the Parts List there will be latitude for good deflection in both directions.

Referring to Electro-Snoops's complete schematic (Fig. 1-39) it

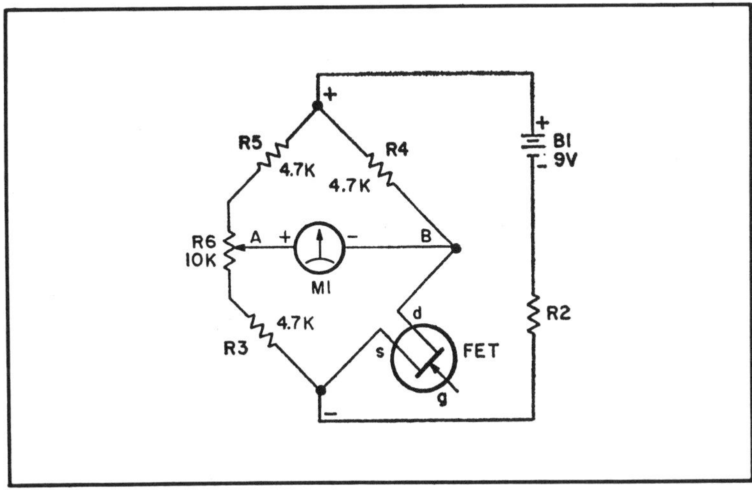

Fig. 1-38. Redrawn Electro-Snoop shows Wheatstone Bridge formed by resistors R3-R5, pot R6, and FET.

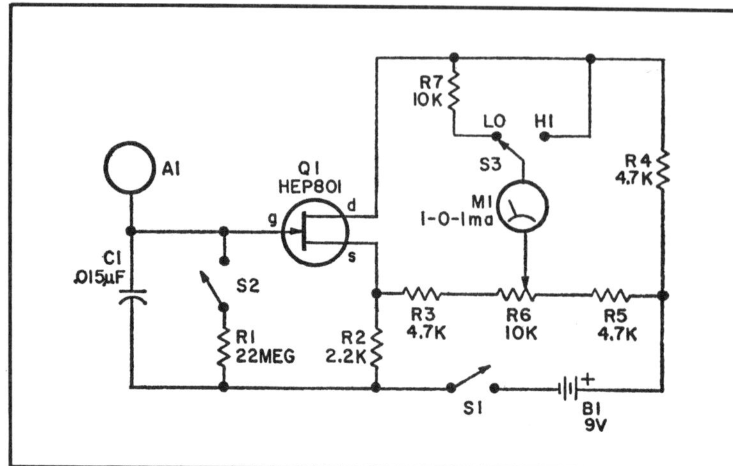

Fig. 1-39. Electro-snoop schematic.

will be noted that a capacitor (C1) and a resistor (R1) are in the input circuit. When S2 is closed (Discharge position) these form a dc RC circuit having a time constant of about 1/3 second. This provides sufficient time for the meter to be read when a charge is placed on the antenna of Electro-Snoop. The circuit then quickly returns to normal as C1 discharges through it.

Capacitor C1 also prevents the meter from oscillating unduly as a charged object is being withdrawn from the antenna loop. With S2 open (Charge position), C2 merely stores cumulatively whatever charges are placed on the antenna until switch S2 is again closed to discharge the capacitor through R1.

Switch S3 is a meter sensitivity switch. With S3 in the high sensitivity position the meter is connected directly to the bridge. When S3 is placed in the low sensitivity position the meter is connected in series with R7 to limit current through it.

Construction

Our model Electro-Snoop, shown in Figs. 1-40 through 1-43, was housed in a 7 × 4 × 4 1/4-in. sloping panel utility cabinet. You'll have to punch out a big hole (size dependent on the meter you use) to mount the meter in the sloping front panel. If you don't want to work so hard punching out this hole, buy a standard sloping panel meter case. It comes with a hole ready punched for a 2-in. meter and a knockout to enlarge it to 3-in., if need be. (See Table 1-4.) However, it doesn't come in the 7-in. width so you'll have to use a smaller piece of perf board to mount the FET, resistors, and capacitors used in the circuit. Even so, this should present no hardship since they are small and don't require as much space as was actually used in the model.

If you don't want to go to the expense of a special sloping panel cabinet the unit will work just as well in any case you have available

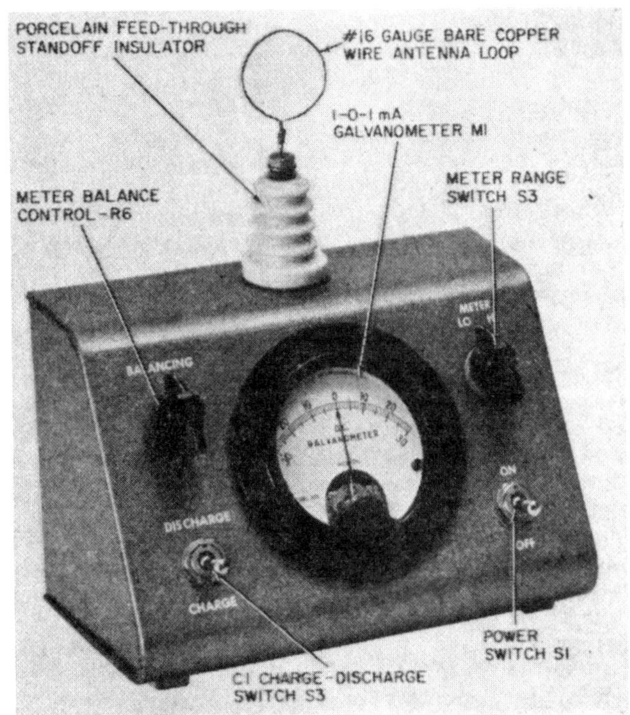

Fig. 1-40. Don't like antenna loop topside? Metal foil square also works.

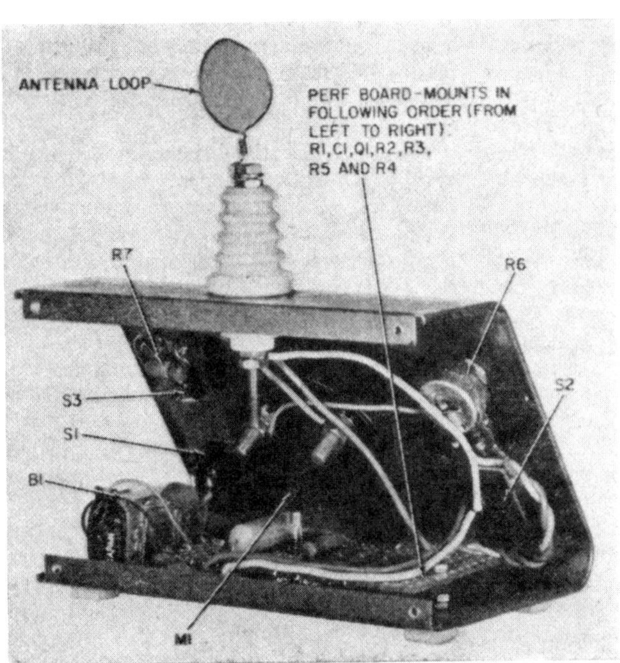

Fig. 1-41. Electro-Snoop's neat innards show parts placement.

Fig. 1-42. Bringing positively charged lucite rod near 'tenna loop, you'll see meter swing to right.

since the circuit isn't critical to parts placement beyond the normal good wiring practices.

In addition to the meter hole, two 1/2-in. holes for the toggle switches are drilled near the bottom of the sloping panel, one on either side of the meter. Another 1/2-in. hole is drilled in the top of the case for the feed through insulator for the antenna. Two 3/8-in. holes are drilled near the top of the front panel spaced to line up with the two bottom holes, one to the right of the meter for the meter-range switch and one to the left of the meter for the balance-potentiometer. When these holes have been drilled and de-burred you are ready to mount the various components in their respective mounting holes.

The antenna is a length of #16 bare copper wire formed into a closed loop with a continuing lead-in long enough to attach it by the

Fig. 1-43. Find out what state of charge your horoscope is in. Leo's positive while Aries's negative.

Table 1-4. Parts List for Electro-Snoop.

A1—Wire loop antenna, made from #16 bare copper wire, loop 1 1/2-in. diam.
B1—9 volt transistor radio battery (Burgess 2U6 or Eveready 216, or equiv.)
C1—0.015μF, 600 volt tubular capacitor (Lafayette 34E82536 or equiv.)
M1—1-0-1dc galvanometer (Weston model 375 or equiv.)
Q1—Field effect transistor, Motorola HEP801
R1—22-megohm, 1/2-w resistor
R2—2200-ohm, 1/2-w resistor
R3, R4, R5—4700-ohm, 1/2-w resistor
R6—10,000-ohm, linear-taper potentiometer, (Lafayette 33E11255 or equiv.)
R7—10,000-ohm, 1/2-w resistor
S1, S2—Spst toggle switch (Lafayette 34E33026 or equiv.)
S3—Single pole, two position rotary switch (Lafayette 30E49202 or equiv.)
1—Battery connector (Lafayette 99E62879 or equiv.)
1—Battery holder (Keystone 203P or equiv.)
1—Porcelain stand-off feedthrough insulator (Lafayette 33E32012 or equiv.)
1—7 × 4 × 4 1/4-in. utility cabinet (Bud AC1613 or equiv.)
OPTIONAL (see text)
1—Transistor socket and mounting ring (Lafayette 32E42195 & 32E42260 ring or equiv.)
1—4 3/16 × 4 1/2 × 4 1/4-in. universal meter case (Lafayette 12E83175 or equiv.)
MISC.—Perf board, push-in pins (Lafayette 19E83022 or equiv.), rubber feet knobs, wire solder, spacers, bolts, nuts, etc.

top nut of the feed-through insulator.

For the model in the photos we mounted the balance of the components on a 4 1/2 × 2 1/4-in. piece of perf board. If by chance you use the smaller meter case, the perf board will, of necessity, be smaller. We used a socket to plug-in the FET. This isn't an absolute necessity, and you may want to mount all of the parts, including the FET on push-in pins (they make good supports and also make it easier to replace soldered in parts). Should you decide to eliminate the socket for the FET, be sure to protect the FET with a heat sink, made from a small alligator clip temporarily slipped on the lead being soldered.

The perf board is fastened to the cabinet by two 6-32 machine screws and nuts. Raise the board away from the base of the case either by using 1/4-in. spacers or extra nuts on the mounting bolts to avoid possibility of shorts between the board and the case. The interconnecting leads are now wired to the proper points. Leave the leads long enough for the circuit board to be lifted out of the cabinet if the need should arise. Resistor R7 is connected directly to S3. The lead from the lower end of the feed-through insulator should be connected directly to S2 rather than to the circuit board. The battery holder is mounted near one end of the circuit board. Trim the leads from the battery connector to fit the location.

If the high cost of the galvanometer specified in the Parts List deters you from building Electro-Snoop we've found an inexpensive alternative instrument. Lafayette Radio offers an edgewise balance and tuning meter in which the pointer rests center scale when no current is flowing. It will swing either right or left of center, depending on the polarity of the current flow.

The sensitivity of this meter is $\pm$ 100 μA, which is considerably more sensitive than the meter we used in the model. You should use this meter with the meter sensitivity switch in the Low sensitivity position at all times.

One point to consider: if you build Electro-Snoop for classroom or other large group demonstrations this alternate meter is harder to read from a distance a few feet away from the meter. Also, if you do use the alternate meter, remember not to punch the large round hole in the front panel. It mounts in a slot 1 5/16-in. long by 1/2-in. high.

Calibrating and Operating

The only calibration necessary is to balance the bridge before using the instrument. With S3 in High sensitivity position, and S2 in the Discharge position, turn S1 to on and proceed to operate Balance control R6 until the meter is centered on zero. This completes the balance calibration and you're ready to experiment with Electro-Snoop.

A negatively charged object held near the antenna will deflect the meter pointer to the left while a positively charged object will deflect it to the right. You may hear a slight sparking sound as the charge jumps across the gap between the object and the antenna.

A negative charge can be generated by rubbing a hard rubber (ebonite) rod with wool; the minus charge appears on the rod. This is the classical method and is hard to beat. It is best to stroke the rod repeatedly in the same direction rather than rubbing back and forth. The rod is then touched to the antenna, or better still, pulled along the antenna in order to build up the charge.

Another way of developing a negative charge is by combing the hair with a nylon comb; the nylon will acquire a fairly respectable negative charge. Still another method is walking across a thick carpet, then, when holding a finger near the antenna a spark will jump from the finger to the antenna sending the meter pointer strongly to the left.

The old textbook method of rubbing glass with silk to produce a positive charge isn't recommended. Too often only a very feeble charge will be the result. A good healthy positive charge can be generated by rubbing a lucite rod with wool or cotton. Thus the same piece of cloth can be used to develop both positive and negative charges by alternating a lucite rod (which will produce positive charges) with an ebonite rod (which will produce negative charges).

With S2 placed in the Discharge (closed) position, charges placed on the antenna are merely sampled and the bridge quickly returns to normal. However, with S2 in the Charge (open) position, charges will be accumulated on C1 and the meter reading will hold constant until the next charge is applied. Several consecutive charges of the same polarity will increase the meter reading up to a maximum high value. Then, closing S2 returns the reading to zero even though the battery is left turned on.

Editor's note: The author wishes to express his thanks to Bill Greaves, Chief Engineer of station WMUU, who suggested the basic idea for this project.

THE BOTDC MOTOR

NOW HERE IS AN ELECTRONIC PROJECT THAT WILL BAFFLE your non-scientific friends. Sans commutator, brushes, and/or mechanical contacting points, this motor gets its *modus operandi* from a unique application of the switching capabilities of transistors. Our BOTDC (Battery Operated Transistor Direct Current) motor will be a traffic stopper at any science fair and should put you in the running as a winner.

What Makes TM Run

In a static condition (rotor stationary), no current will flow through the circuit even though the battery is connected. Reason is that the transistors are biased to cut off (non-conducting). Thing is, though we've said no current will flow, actually a small leakage current (inherent in nearly all transistors) does flow. But this isn't sufficient to create a strong enough magnetic field in the driving coils to sustain rotation.

After the rotor has been given a push to start rotation with the transistors energized by battery B1, a voltage is induced in the coil as one of the magnets approaches pickup coil L1. This voltage, coupled through diode D1 produces a negative pulse on the base of Q1. This pulse turns on Q1, which delivers a positive current pulse to the base of Q2, turning it on. This, in turn, produces a negative pulse at the base of Q3, turning it on. As conduction of Q3 increases it's driven to saturation, thus placing full supply voltage across driving coil L2, creating a maximum magnetic field in it. This magnetic increase and decrease drives the rotor on its axis.

Since all of the magnets on the rotor have been oriented (see Figs. 1-44 through 1-50 and Table 1-5) so that the magnetic field in L2 attracts them, the motor magnet is magnetically pulled towards L2, thus sustaining the motion of the rotor.

Because of the positioning of the magnets, one approaches L2 while another is passing L1. This creates a new pulse, which again turns on the transistors. The pulsing on of the transistors develops magnetic saturation pulses in L2 that keep the motor in motion. Its speed is limited by the voltage of battery B1, which, in our motor, can be any dc voltage from 6 to 24 volts.

We've included a small speaker together with switch it on or off, merely to attract attention if you are exhibiting your motor. Each time a pulse is developed a click can be heard in the speaker.

Current consumption is quite low (our model, using coils of 30 and 1000 ohms respectively for L1 and L2, draws 55 mA at 6 V).

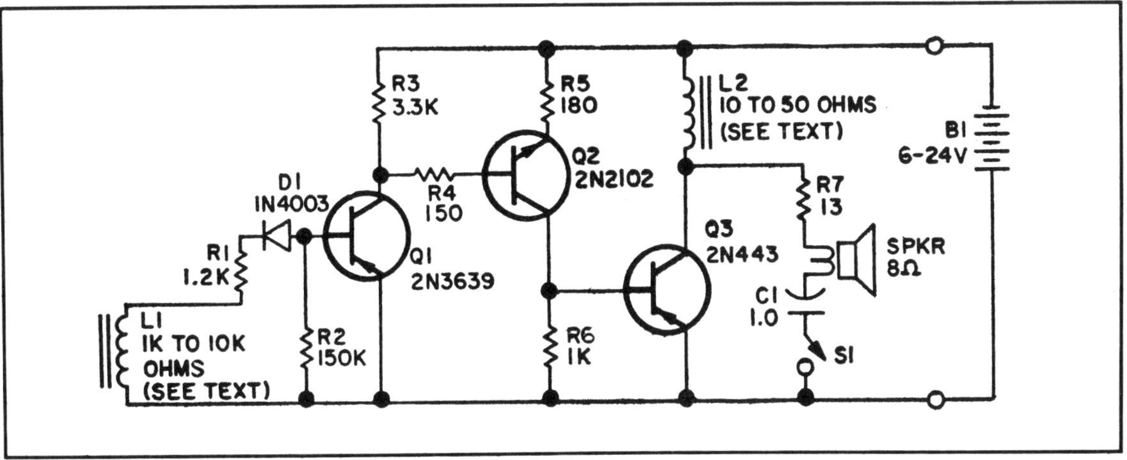

Fig. 1-44. Schematic diagram for the electronics circuitry of the BOTDC Motor. Battery is disconnected by removing the leads from the binding posts on this board.

Therefore, you can expect relatively long battery life. If a small friction load is placed on the rotor shaft the total current drain will increase slightly. As this load is increased, slowing the rotor and eventually stopping it, current consumption will drop proportionately. When the rotor is stopped, current consumption will drop to the same level as the unit drew before rotation started (all transistors turned off).

This decrease in current drain with an increase in load is just the opposite condition of that for a conventional motor in which current drain increases as the load does. If a dc motor is stalled and the current isn't shut off, the excess heat generated by the current flowing through its windings will eventually destroy the motor completely.

Let's Make It!

We built our Transistor Motor on a 7 1/4 × 8 × 3/4-in plywood

Fig. 1-45. Rear view showing speaker, electronics board L2, and general positioning of the various parts of the motor. Switch S1 turns off speaker which monitors the pulses as they are generated. The clicks attract attention.

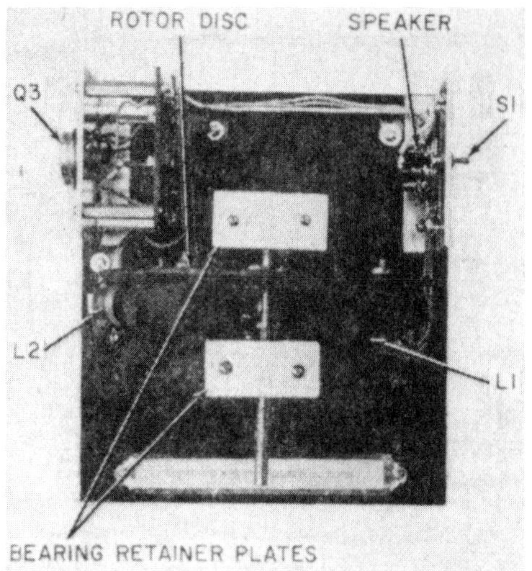

Fig. 1-46. Top view of motor board showing position of rotor bearings that must be aligned to ensure minimum friction for rotor shaft. Retaining plates hold rotor bearings firmly in supports.

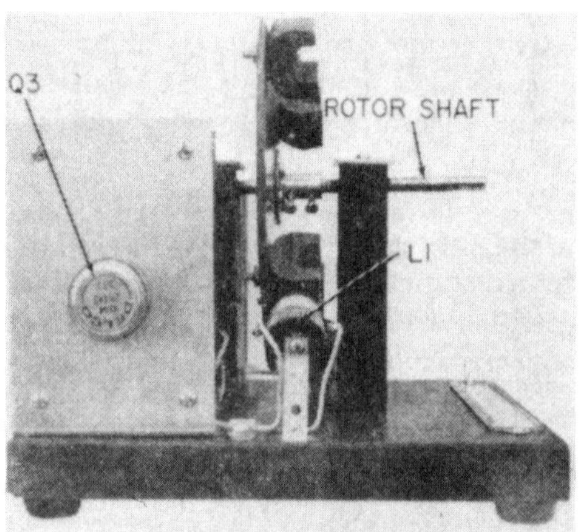

Fig. 1-47. Just as there are two sides for every story out BOTDC Motor has another side, too. One viewed here shows positioning of Q3 on its heat sink as well as location of coil L1.

Fig. 1-48. Right side of motor assembly detailing location of speaker and its mounting plate, coil L2, one bearing support block, and the rotor disc. Note shaft coupler referred to in text.

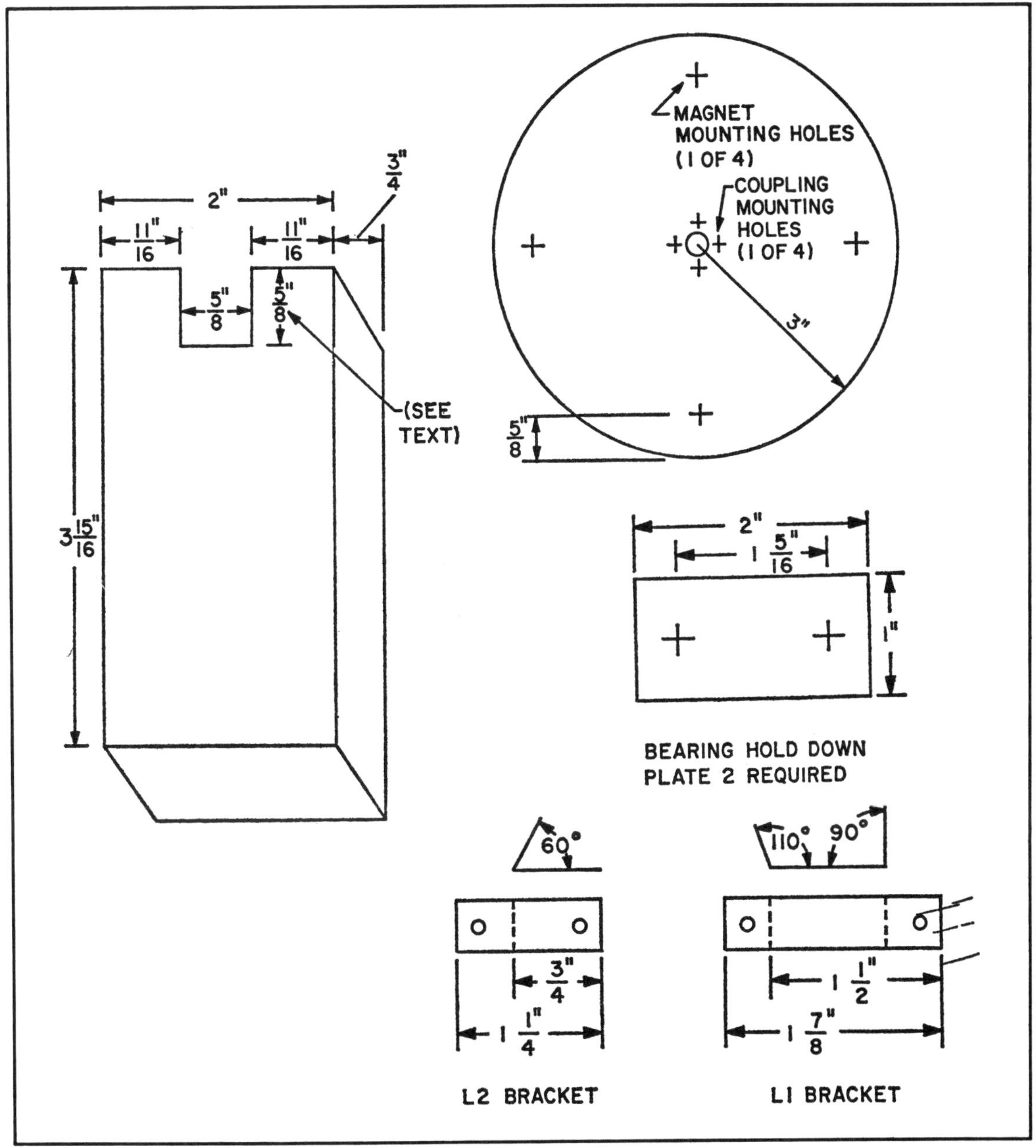

Fig. 1-49. Construction details on parts you must fabricate. It should be noted that angles for coil brackets may have to be adjusted to match the coils you purchase locally.

baseboard. We made two wooden blocks (3 15/16 × 2 × 3/4 in.) to support the rotor. Any nonmetallic material such as plywood, hardboard, phenolic sheet, epoxy glass sheet, etc., can be used for the rotor disc (we used hardboard). The rotor shaft is made from a

Fig. 1-50. Rear view showing general placement of various parts of motor. Electronics board is held a way from mounting plate with spacers.

length of 1/4-in. dia. steel rod, running in anti-friction bearings. We used small ball bearings which can be purchased from your hardware dealer, mill supply house, or surplus machinery dealer.

Coils L1 and L2 are standard relay coils. If you can't get the ones we list in the Parts List, perhaps you can find surplus relays using coils having specifications similar to those we used.

With the exception of transistor Q3, coils L1 and L2, and the speaker and its on/off switch, all electronics components are mounted on a 2 7/8 × 4 1/4-in. piece of perf board using push-in pins to hold the various parts and also to serve as points for electrical connections.

Transistor Q3 and the speaker are each mounted on separate and identical 3 × 4 1/2 × 1/16-in. aluminum brackets. The mounting bracket for Q3 also serves as its heat sink. The speaker grille can be a series of holes drilled in the bracket in a suitable pattern within a 1 1/2-in. circle. Alternatively, you can cut a circular hole 1 1/2-in. diam. and back it up with a piece of perf board, perforated metal, or screening

Table 1-5. Parts List for Transistor Motor.

C1—1-μF, 200-V capacitor
D1—General purpose silicon diode (type 1N4003 or equiv.)
L1—1000 to 5000-ohm relay coil, similar to coil used in Potter & Brumfield KA11AY relay
L2—10 to 50 ohm DC relay coil, similar to coil used in Potter & Brumfield MR11D relay
Q1—2N3639 silicon epoxy pnp transistor (Raytheon)
Q2—2N2102 silicon npn power transistor (Motorola or Delco)
R1—1200-ohm, 1/2-watt resistor
R2—150,000-ohm, 1/2-watt resistor
R3—3300-ohm, 1/2-watt resistor
R4—150-ohm, 1/2-watt resistor
R5—180-ohm, 1/2-watt resistor
R6—1000-ohm, 1/2-watt resistor
R7—12-ohm, 1-watt resistor
S1—Spst miniature toggle switch (Lafayette 99T6162 or equiv.)
1—Speaker, 2-in., 8 ohm (Lafayette 99T6036 or equiv.)
4—Magnets, horseshoe 1 × 1 1/8 × 5/16 in. (Lafayette 14T3303 or equiv.)
2—Binding posts (Lafayette 99T6233 or equiv.)
Misc.—3/4-in. plywood, 1/8-in. plywood (or phenolic, epoxy glass, hardboard sheet), 1/8-inch aluminum sheet, aluminum or steel strapping for mounting brackets, ball bearing assemblies, 1/4-in. steel rod, perf board, push-in pins, rubber feet, name plate, shaft coupler (Hammarlund FNC465 or equiv.), solder, hookup wire, hardware, etc.

to protect the speaker cone.

The perf board containing the circuit components is fastened to the rear of the Q3 heat sink with 1 1/8-in. to 1 1/4-in. long spacers to hold it away from the heat sink and Q3's terminals in order to prevent short circuits in the wiring on the perf board.

The only other structural parts that have to be made are the mounting brackets for coils L1 and L2 and the bearing retainer plates. Details of dimensions and bending angles are shown in the drawings (those for the coil mountings are only approximate). You'll have to establish final size and angles, depending on the type of coils you actually buy. Coil L1 should be mounted on the baseboard and the bracket angled so that there is a 1/4-in. clearance between its pole piece and the face of any magnet on the rotor as it passes the coil. Similarly, L2 should be mounted on the baseboard as shown so that there is 1/8-in. clearance between its pole piece and a magnet face.

When cutting the notch that holds the bearing in the wooden blocks, keep its depth slightly less than the diameter of the bearing you're using. This will help clamp the bearing in position when the hold-down plate is fastened to the block.

If you can't find a flange plate with a bushing to hold the shaft to the rotor disc, a simple way to make one is to start with a flexible coupling designed for mounting between a variable capacitor and dial of a radio. Carefully remove the bushings from the center supporting the washer bushings leaving the flexible arms attached to the bushings. Drill a hole in the center of the motor's rotor disc so that it will sit snugly around the shaft.

This done, slip the bushings removed from the coupler, one over each end of the shaft, and fasten the arms to the disc. What you have done, really, is to substitute the motor disc for the smaller diameter washer originally holding the two bushings together in the flexible coupling. Be sure the set screws in the bushings are tightened against the shaft to ensure proper alignment and rotation capability of the rotor assembly.

Assemble the electronics and wire the motor in accord with the schematic. Be sure to doublecheck your wiring to make certain there are no errors and that D1 is correctly polarized. Now that you've completed the hardest work of the project, you're ready to finish putting together your motor and having some fun.

Fitting the Pieces Together

First mount the bearing mounting blocks and coil brackets to the baseboard. Slip the bearing assemblies over the ends of the rotor shaft and mount this assembly in the bearing support blocks. Before tightening the bearing hold down plates, be sure the bearings are aligned so that the shaft will turn freely with a minimum of friction.

Now mount the magnets to the disc, arranged as shown in Fig. 1-48. After mounting and wiring the electronics assembly, the speaker, and coils L1 and L2, you're ready to orient the magnets. To do this, connect the battery to the motor and connect a temporary jumper from the collector to the emitter of Q3. Slowly rotate the rotor disc by hand so that each magnet is brought past L2. If the magnet is attracted towards L2, it's correctly positioned and should be tightened in this position. If, on the other hand, the magnet is repelled, loosen its mounting screw and turn the magnet 180 degrees on its axis; it then should be magnetically attracted by L2 and can be tightened in this corrected position.

Final Adjustment

Remove the temporary jumper from Q3, leaving the battery connected, and give the rotor a turn in either direction. If all is well the rotor will continue its rotation, slowly picking up speed to a maximum (dependent on battery voltage) and will continue running at full speed until the battery is disconnected.

If the rotor doesn't continue to turn and pick up speed after you've given it its initial start, disconnect the battery and transpose the connections to L1. This reverses the phasing of this coil. Reconnect the battery and your motor should run merrily along. If it doesn't, you must have made an error in wiring that was not revealed when you double-checked it. It's easy to make a mistake in connecting the transistors or diode, so check them once more.

When the motor is running properly and the speaker switch is turned on, you'll hear a clicking in the speaker every time a magnet passes L1 and generates a pulse. The repetition rate of the clicks will increase as the speed of the motor increases.

Whenever the motor isn't operating be sure to place the magnet keepers on the magnets and also be sure to remove them whenever you want to run the motor.

To make an attractive unit for a display, why not paint the baseboard and the rotor disc and magnets in contrasting or complementary colors? Perhaps the addition of an old commutator and brushes removed from a discarded conventional motor and some old worn-out ignition points that have been removed from your car can be worked into your display. These would show the difference between the older methods of switching current to make a motor run and the use of transistor switching to accomplish this function and how your Transistor Motor has done away with parts that wear out.

This project will provide you with mechanical, electrical, and electronic experience and could, at the same time, also win a prize for you at your next science fair. So go ahead and get started now and be ready in time for the competition.

ROTO-STAT

FROM THE EARLIEST DAYS OF EXPERIMENTING WITH ELECTROstatic electricity—say in the 4th Century B.C., when Plato mentioned the wonderful attracting power of amber—electrostatic electricity was produced by laboriously rubbing glass rods or other electrostatic producing objects with dry fur or cloth. In 1663, in Germany, Otto von Guericke used a large ball of sulphur to generate electrostatic electricity by rotating the sulphur ball and rubbing it with his fingers. In 1706, in England, Francis Hauksbee employed rotating glass globes and cylinders to generate static electricity, and he used a metallic conductor to collect the generated static electricity from the generator.

In 1744, in Germany, J.H. Winkler invented a mechanical rubbing device to use in place of rubbing the glass cylinder with the fingers. His rubber used a leather-covered cushion pressed against the rotating globe. In America, in 1747, Ben Franklin used an electrostatic generator in some of his electrical experiments; it contained a rotating glass cylinder with a mechanical rubber.

Even in this day and age, electrostatic experiments still fascinate the avid experimenter. You can perform electrostatic electricity experiments by building and using our Roto-Stat electrostatic generator, instead of generating the electrostatic charges by hand-rubbed glass or plastic rods. Our Roto-Stat, designed for easy construction, uses a plastic cosmetic or similar jar in place of a glass ball or cylinder. The generator is built on a 3/4-in. white pine base and uses a wool cloth rubber and a copper wire electrostatic collector that's formed round the jar. (See Figs. 1-51, 1-52, and Table 1-6.)

How It Works

Turning the generator handle rapidly in a clockwise direction causes the wool cloth to rub against the plastic jar's surface. The friction of this rubbing releases electrons which electrostatically charge the jar's surface. As the jar is rotated, the pickup wire mounted on the ceramic standoff collects electrostatic charges from its surface and conducts them to the metal ball output electrode. A Leyden jar can be charged by contacting its terminals to the metal ball output electrode and ground. (See Figs. 1-53 and 1-54.)

Plastic Power

We used a plastic jar 2 3/4-in. high × 2 3/4 in. diameter with plastic screw top for the rotating element of our Roto-Stat. If another size plastic jar is used, scale the dimensions of your unit proportionately.

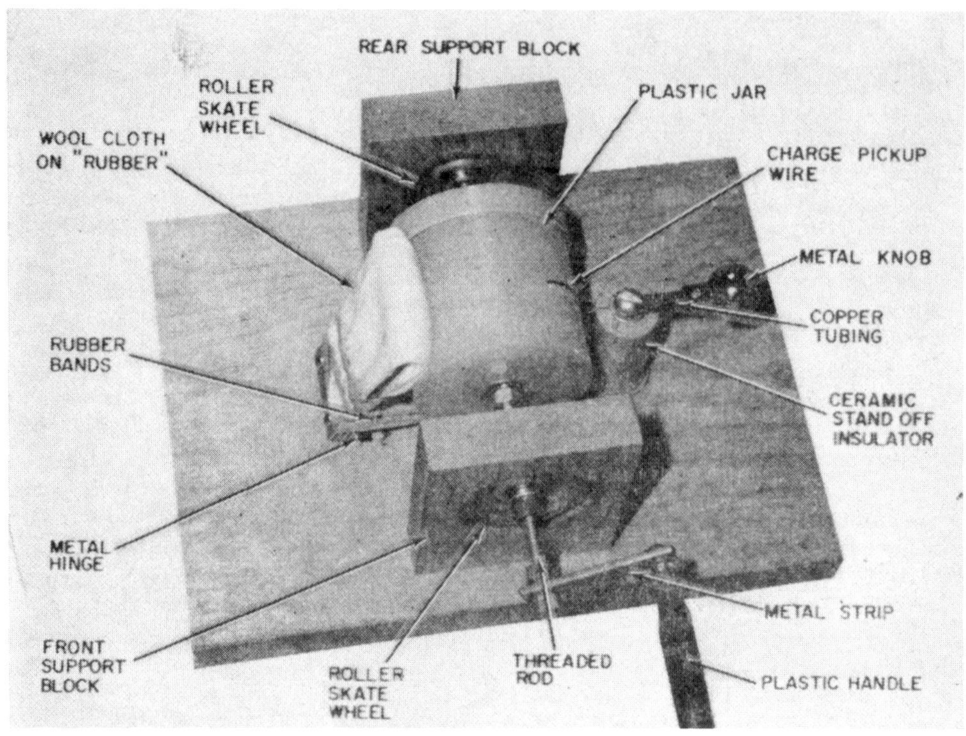

Fig. 1-51. Our Roto-Stat electrostatic generator, though not as huge as original ones built in early 18th Century, is quite efficient. From details in photo and drawing you can build it.

Since different types of plastic vary in their ability to generate electrostatic electricity, test the jar you've selected by rubbing it with a wool cloth and noting whether the jar attracts small pieces of paper when the jar is moved over them. If it doesn't, try a jar made of different plastic material.

Any type of soft wood can be used for the base. Just make sure that the wood is clean and dry. The dimensions given in our drawing are approximate, to serve as a guide. Any size generator unit can be built, but for best results it's suggested you follow the general layout of our unit.

Begin construction by cutting a 7 1/2 × 10-in. base of 3/4-in. thick pine or other soft wood, then cut two 3 5/8 × 3 × 3/4-in. wood blocks. Roller skate wheels, available as replacements at most hardware or bicycle shops, are used as driveshaft bearings. Cut a hole in each wood block to fit roller skate wheel used for this purpose. The hole in each block of our unit is made just large enough to force-fit the wheel into the hole in the block. Duco cement or Elmer's Glue is used to hold the wheel securely in place. You may prefer to use long sheet metal screws through the sides of the mounting blocks to hold the wheel.

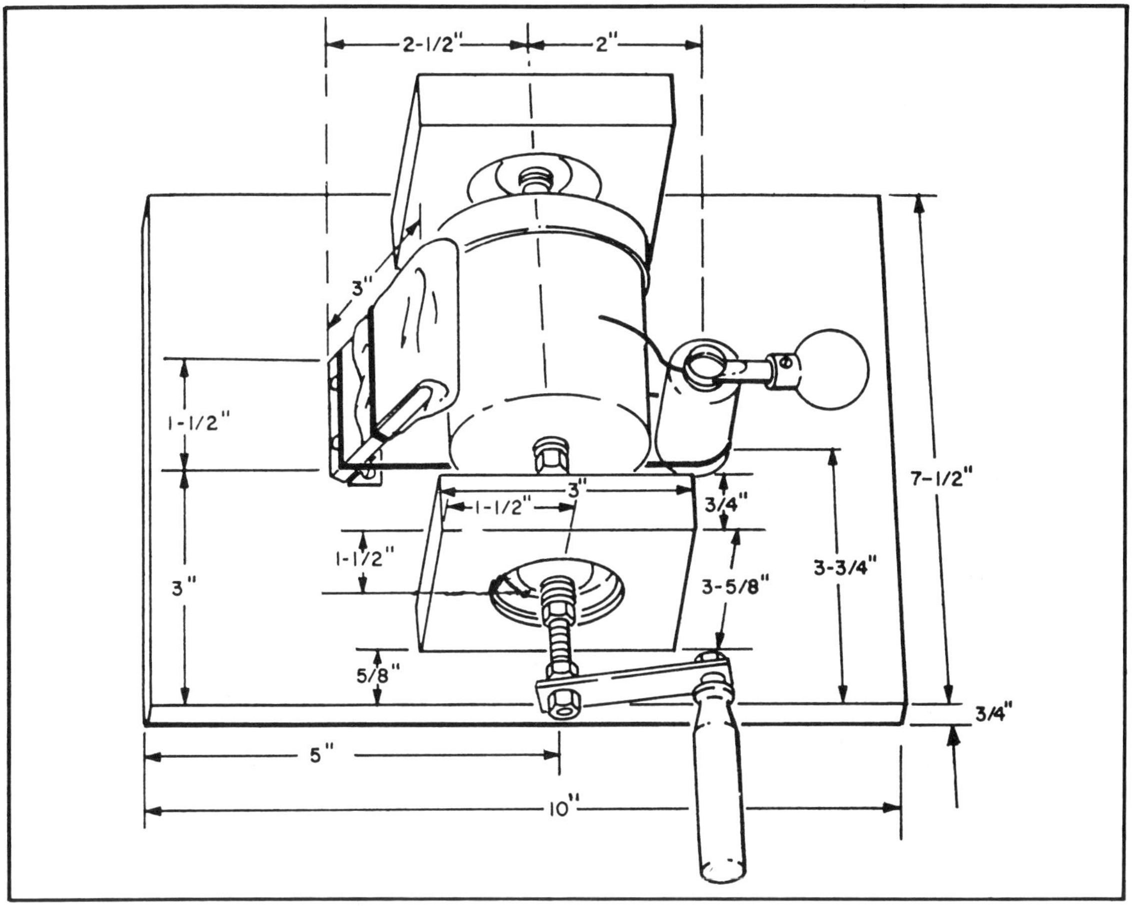

Fig. 1-52. Layout of the Roto-Stat.

Table 1-6. Parts List for Roto-Stat.

1—Ceramic (L5 glazed) standoff insulator, threaded at both ends, 2-in. high × 1-in. dia. (JAN type NS5WO416, E.F. Johnson 135-503, or equiv.)
1—Hard rubber of plastic handle, 2-in. long × 1/2-in. dia. (we used handle from radio aligning tool)
1—1 1/2 × 1/2-in. metal hinge
1—Plastic jar with screw-on or snap-on plastic lid, 2 3/4-in. high × 2 3/4-in. dia. (you may also want to use this size for Leyden jar and electroscope—see text)
2—Metal knobs, approx. 7/8-in. dia. (available as automobile dash control or seat control knobs at auto parts stores)
1—2 1/4 × 1/2 × 1/8-in. metal strip for mounting handle
1—NE2 neon lamp
2—Roller skate wheels, ball bearing (available as replacement wheels at toy stores and toy counters in department stores)
1—Threaded metal rod, 8-in. long × 1/4-in. dia.
Misc.—1 1/2 × 4-in. wool cloth strips, wood screws, nuts and washers for threaded rod, screws to fit ceramic insulator, cement, rubber bands, #18 to #22 bare copper wire, 3/4-in. thick pine for base, etc.

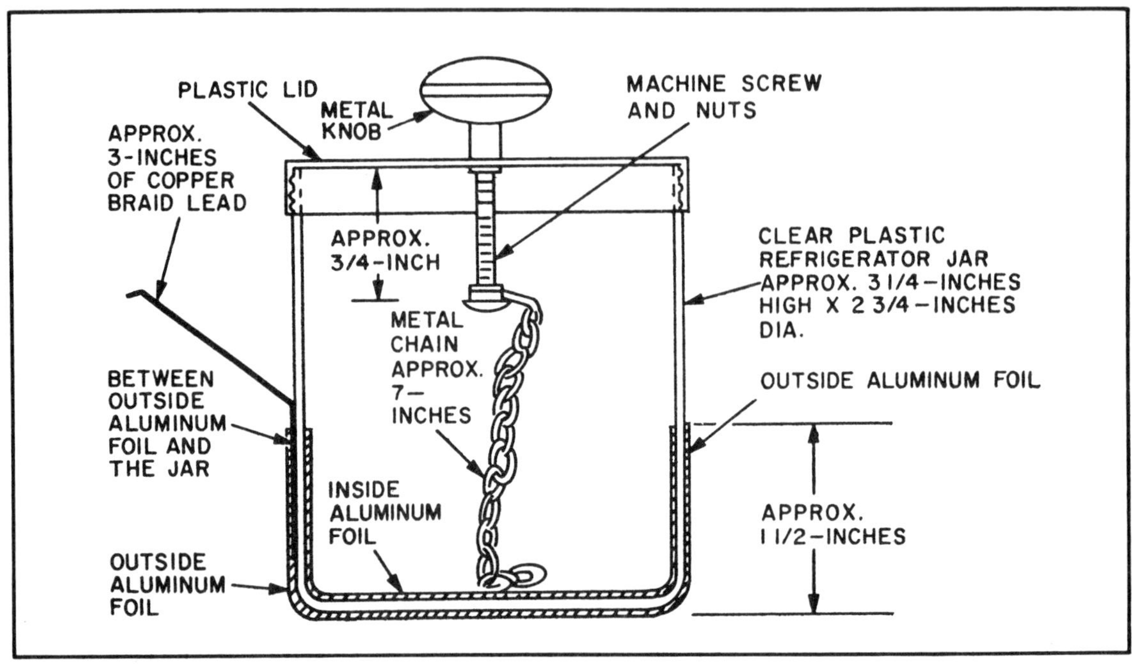

Fig. 1-53. Even though we used materials found either in kitchen or bathroom this Leyden jar can store electrostatic charge generated by our Roto-Stat, so be sure it's discharged when stored.

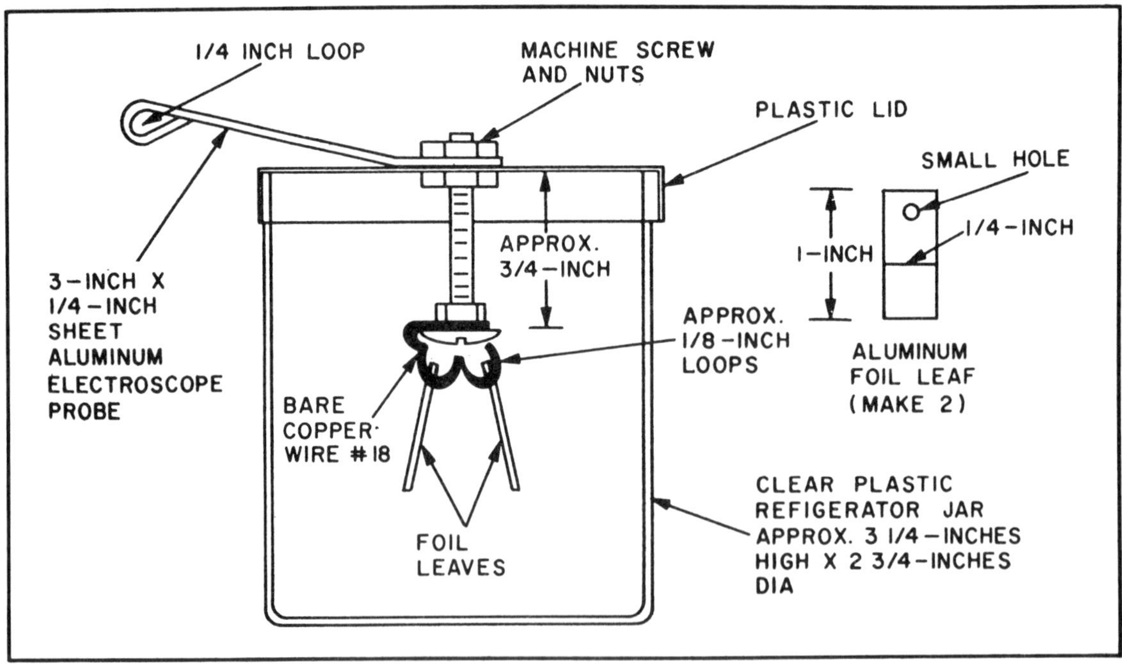

Fig. 1-54. You'll want an electroscope to reassure you that your Roto-Stat is actually generating current before you start each experiment. It's easy to build and well worth the effort.

Cone Or Cylinder

Drill holes in the center of the bottom of the plastic jar, and also its lid, to fit the 3/8-in. threaded metal rod. Cut and drill a conical wood section to fit inside the plastic jar if the jar isn't straightsided (if it is, then you'll need a wooden cylinder), extending from the jar bottom to the jar lid for internal support. A clearance hole for the metal rod, which serves as the axle for the jar, is drilled through the center of this wooden block.

Mount front supporting block on the base as shown in our drawing. We used two wood screws through the base to hold the block to the base. Insert threaded metal rod through jar and skate wheel bearing and hold them in position on the rod with a nut and washer top and bottom of the jar and on either side of the bearing mounted in the wood block. Don't tighten the nuts now; you'll probably reposition the jar.

Position the rear block-mounted bearing on threaded metal rod with a nut and washer on both sides of the bearing. Adjust spacing of nuts on the metal rod so that the jar is in the center of the base as shown in photos and drawing. Position the rear wood block so that metal rod and jar can turn freely without binding, and fasten this block in position to the base with wood screws. Make sure that about 1 3/4 in. of metal rod projects out from the front bearing for attaching the metal strip that holds the handle, then tighten nuts against the jar and bearings.

Plastic Handle

We made the plastic handle from an alignment tool and bolted it to a 2 1/4 × 1/2 × 1/8-in. metal strip with washers to allow the handle to rotate freely. Fasten a 3 × 1 1/2 × 1/4-in. piece of plywood to a hinge, and mount the hinged plywood section to the wood base adjacent to one side of the jar. Mount a 2-in. high × 1-in. diameter ceramic standoff to the base on the opposite side of the jar as shown in Figs. 1-55 and 1-56.

Mount a small unpainted metal knob onto a piece of copper tubing, flatten the free end of the copper tubing, and mount it on the ceramic standoff. Also fasten a length of #22 or larger copper wire to the ceramic standoff and bend it so that it curves around the jar for a length of about 1 1/2 in. but doesn't touch it. Position the wire approximately 1/16 in. away from the jar's surface and cut off the excess length of wire. Small rubber bumpers are fastened to each of the corners on the bottom of the base.

Fold a piece of clean, dry wool cloth over the top end of the hinged plywood piece, holding the cloth in place by means of a rubber band. Clean the surface of the jar carefully. Place several rubber bands around the base of the ceramic standoff and stretch them 'round the bottom of the hinged plywood section so that the wool cloth that is

Fig. 1-55. Here's how to hold your Leyden jar when you charge it from your Roto-Stat. Keep two metal balls in constant contact while turning handle to generate charge.

folded over its free end will be seated firmly against the side of the jar.

Rotate the jar by turning the handle, making sure that the jar turns freely, but with a slight resistance from the wool cloth rubber, and that the pickup wire does not touch the surface of the jar. Do not touch the surface of the jar or the wool cloth after the jar has been cleaned, because of the possibility of transferring moisture on your hands to either or both.

Experiment 1

Before performing any experiment, make sure that both the cloth on the rubber and the jar's surface are clean and dry. If necessary, expose both cloth and jar to the rays of a heat lamp to dry up any moisture. These experiments may not work as well, or may not work at all in a humid area, since a dry environment is necessary for best results. We suggest you perform them in an air-conditioned room if at all possible for driest atmosphere.

Rotate generator handle rapidly in a clockwise direction, and hold the electroscope so that its electrode makes contact with generator's metal ball. Observe that the electroscope leaves deflect away from each other. This indicates that the electrostatic generator is operating and producing an electrostatic output voltage.

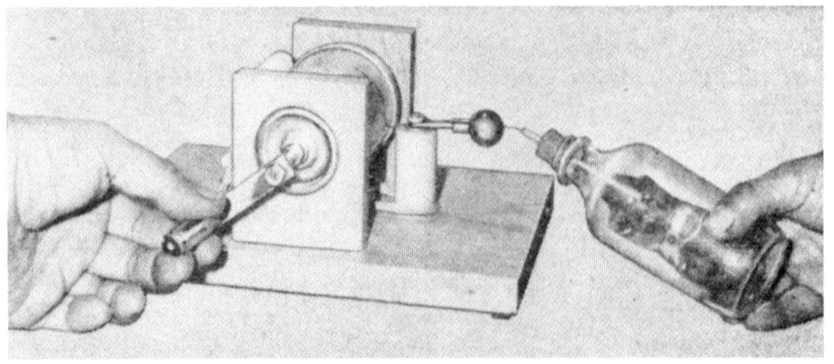

Fig. 1-56. If there's a doubting Thomas amongst those you're showing your Roto-Stat, prove it's generating by placing Electrostat's collector against Roto-Stat's output ball.

Experiment 2

Connect the outer foil of a Leyden jar to ground or a large metal object, and bring the Leyden jar top electrode in contact with the generator metal ball. Rotate generator handle rapidly in a clockwise direction for a few minutes, then move the Leyden jar away from the generator. Make sure you do not touch Leyden jar top electrode with your fingers. Carefully disconnect the Leyden jar outer foil lead from the ground. Then move the outer foil lead very close to the top electrode. Note that a small spark will jump between the top electrode and the outer foil lead of the Leyden jar. This indicates that the Leyden jar was charged with the electrostatic output voltage from the generator.

Repeat the experiment, except connect a VTVM (preferably with a high voltage probe) between the Leyden jar outside foil and its top electrode, after Leyden jar has been charged. Fasten one lead to ground strap and touch top electrode with the other lead of the VTVM. Observe that the VTVM momentarily indicates a large negative voltage. This shows that the generator has a negative electrostatic output voltage.

Experiment 3

This experiment requires a dimly lit area in order to best see the neon lamp. Rotate generator handle rapidly in a clockwise direction, and momentarily bring one lead of an NE-2 neon lamp in contact with the generator metal ball while you hold the other lamp lead. The neon lamp should flash momentarily, indicating that the generator is operating.

Move one of the neon lamp leads around the surface of the rotating plastic jar. Note that the neon lamp flashes, indicating the electrostatically charged areas.

Remove the neon lamp lead from the jar, rotate generator handle rapidly for a minute, and then stop. Now move neon lamp lead around on the surface, noting that the neon lamp still flashes, indicating that the electrostatically charged areas on the plastic jar will remain active for a period of time after the surface of the jar is excited by rubbing.

Try different types of cloths for the rubber in place of the wool cloth and compare their operation with that of a wool cloth. Note rotation speed affects size of charge. You can also try different configurations of the wire collector.

EXPERIMENTER'S ELECTROSCOPE

WHEN BEN FRANKLIN CONDUCTED HIS FAMOUS KITE-FLYING experiment in the midst of a thunderstorm, he wasn't just showing his cool while the lightning flashed. His was a genuine scientific experiment to demonstrate the similarity between lightning and ordinary static electricity. Of course, this was like going into a tiger's cage to see the similarity to a pet pussycat.

Static electricity is normally produced by friction. In cold, dry weather, walking across a rug and then touching a grounded metal object can give you quite a shock. Even sliding out of a car that has a plastic seat cover can end in a jolt.

Static electricity is either an accumulation or deficiency of electrons on an insulating material such as plastic or glass. Even though materials that are electrical insulators cannot freely conduct electricity, electrons can still be dislodged from their atoms by the application of an external force. This force is usually the friction of one electrically insulating material rubbing against another.

When a glass rod is rubbed with a cloth, for instance, some of the electrons that are loosely bound to the atoms of the glass are transferred to the cloth. When the cloth is removed from the rod's surface, the glass has a deficiency of electrons and is considered to be positively charged. If a plastic rod is rubbed with a cloth, electrons are transferred from the cloth to the plastic rod. This gives the plastic rod a negative charge.

You can experiment with static electricity by assembling an *electroscope*. The electroscope will indicate the presence of a static electric charge by the mutual repulsion of identically charged, metal foil leaves.

Our electroscope is built into a glass bottle that has an insulated wire suspending two aluminum foil leaves. When an electrically charged object touches the wire-loop electrode at the top of the electroscope, the static charge will be conducted down the wire to the foil leaves, causing them to separate. The degree of separation depends upon the strength of the electric charge.

Construction Caper

We used a 7-oz. Listerine bottle for our electroscope. The bottle is approximately 5 1/4 in. high and 2 1/4 in. in diameter. However, most any clear glass bottle can be used, since the exact size is not important. You'll need two more or less identical bottles, though, as we are using two electroscopes in our experiments. Make sure that both bottles are perfectly clean and dry.

Start construction by stripping the outer covering and braided shield from a 6-in. length of RG-59/U coax cable. Cut about 3/4 in. of the plastic insulation away from one end of the cable and bend the inner-conductor wire to form a right angle about 1/4 in. from the insulation edge. Solder a length of the inner-conductor wire taken from another length of RG-59/U cable to the wire you've already prepared (see Fig. 1-57). Bend both wires into a 1/8 in. "D" shape and cut off any excess.

Now strip off the insulation of the wire about 3/4 in. away from the bent wires. Ream a hole through a cork that fits the bottle and insert the prepared cable as shown. Bend the free wire at the other end into a 1/2 in. loop, and either crimp or solder the free end.

Use a single-edge razor blade or a sharp knife to cut out two 1/4 × 3/4 in. aluminum foil leaves. You might (as we do) use Reynolds wrap aluminum foil; don't use heavy-gauge or embossed types of foil. Carefully center a small hole as close to the top of the leaf as possible. Install the leaves on the "D" rings as shown. If necessary, bend the

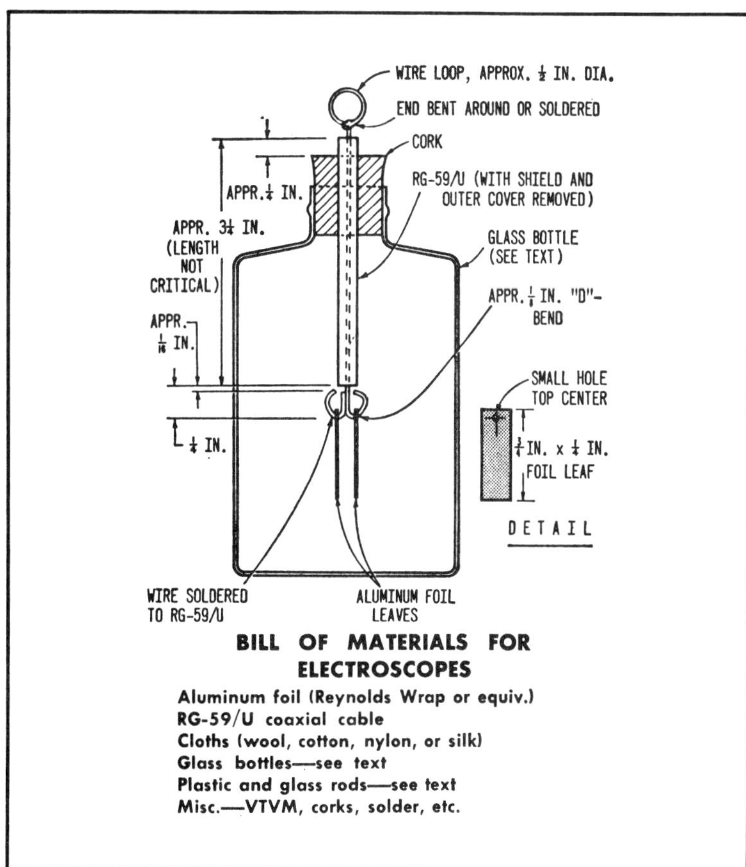

Fig. 1-57. Cutaway view of the electroscope.

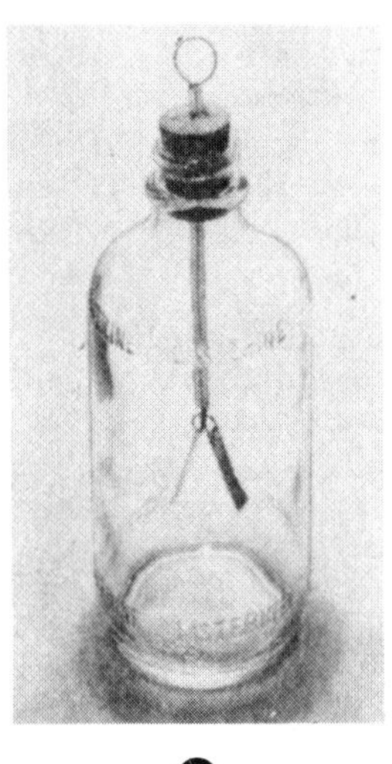

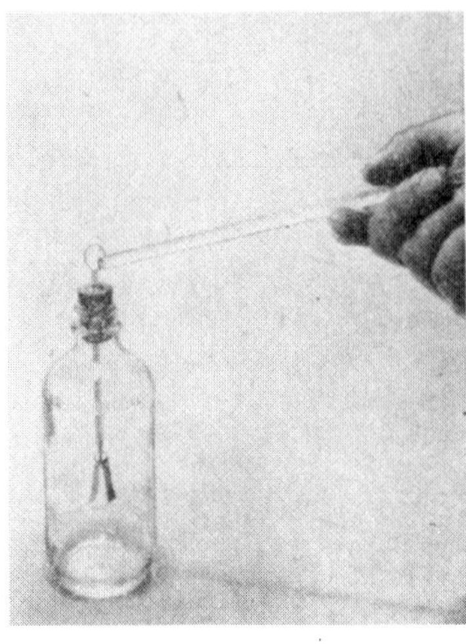

A B C

Fig. 1-58. Basic setup for electroscope is shown in A. Size of glass bottle is optional, but it should be free from moisture. Metal-foil leaves are suspended freely on D rings and should not touch sides.

B shows how to apply static charge to electroscope after rod has been rubbed vigorously at one end. By moving this activated end along ring electrode at top, you can gradually increase charge potential.

C reveals touch method of applying charge from one electroscope to other unit. White paper placed under both bottles should enhance observation of metal-foil leaves when you compare charges existing at each separate electrode.

"D" wires out for easier installation and bend them back into shape when the leaves are properly hung. Close the wire ends to prevent the leaves from accidentally falling off.

Carefully insert the assembly into the bottle and make sure that the leaves don't touch the inside walls. Reposition the wire or trim the leaves if necessary.

Now repeat the preceding instructions to make a second electroscope. Try to make both units as identical as possible.

Building a Charge

To perform the following experiments you will need glass and plastic rods, as well as some cotton, wool, and nylon (or silk) cloths. We used a 10 in. by 1/4 in. dia glass rod that you can obtain at any hobby shop selling chemistry supplies. For the plastic rod, we used a length of plastic insulation from a section of the RG-59/U coax, with both the shield and inner conductor removed. You can also use a toothbrush handle or a plastic alignment tool.

A cool, dry environment is best for these experiments; they may not work in a hot, humid area. The cloths must be perfectly dry. If necessary, you can heat them to drive off any moisture. Change them frequently to avoid any moisture from your hands. (See Fig. 1-58.)

Experiment No. 1

Rub the plastic rod with a cotton cloth folded around one end. Use long strokes and moderate pressure. Three or four strokes should be enough to charge the rod, depending on the dryness of your work area. Be sure not to touch the activated end.

Place this activated end (the end that was rubbed) against the wire-loop electrode; the foil leaves will move apart. Try running the side of the rod along the loop electrode. This may increase the charge on the electroscope. The foil leaves will stay apart after you remove the rod from the electrode.

Rub the rod some more and touch the electrode again. The foil leaves should now extend even further, indicating that the charge has increased. Keep this up until the leaves remain motionless. (Placing the electroscope on a sheet of white paper will make the leaves easier to see.) Discharge the electroscope by touching the electrode with your finger. The foil leaves should close together, indicating discharge. And feel safe—there is no shock hazard.

If you have a VTVM with a large input resistance, set it to its lowest negative dc range and connect the common lead (ground) to a foil section placed under the electroscope. Charge the electroscope with a plastic rod until the leaves separate and show full charge. Touch the VTVM probe to the electrode and observe that the VTVM momentarily indicates a negative voltage. This shows that the charge from the plastic rod has negative polarity.

Rub a glass rod with a woolen or silk cloth (or nylon), and charge the electroscope with the activated rod. The glass rod may be harder to activate than the plastic one. Try to rub the rod briskly. Now set the VTVM for the lowest positive dc range and placc thc probe against the electroscope electrode. The VTVM will momentarily indicate a positive voltage, showing that the glass rod has a positive charge.

Finally, charge the electroscope with a plastic rod, and then touch the electrode with a small neon lamp (NE-2 or equiv.). One lead from the neon lamp should be held in your fingers, while the other lead goes to the electroscope. The lamp will flash and the foil leaves drop. This indicates there was sufficient electrical energy stored up in the electroscope to activate the neon lamp.

Experiment No. 2

Bend a 1/2-in. loop in a 2-in. length of #22 bus wire, and connect the free end to an alligator clip. Attach the clip to the electrode of one of the two electroscopes. Charge up the other electroscope with a plastic rod.

Carefully move the other electroscope so that it makes contact against the charged electrode by way of the clipped-on wire loop. Note that the previously uncharged electroscope now has a charge, and that the charged electroscope's leaves have moved inward a bit, indicating that its charge has diminished. This experiment shows that one electroscope can transfer its electrical charge to another, just as a charged capacitor can charge another capacitor.

Experiment No. 3

Discharge both electroscopes by touching them with your finger, move them apart, and charge them again with a plastic rod. Do this until the foil leaves in both electroscopes are at the same angle (i.e., showing the same potential).

Move the electroscopes together until the electrode on one is touching the clipped-on loop of the other electroscope. Note that the foil leaves do not move. This means that the electroscopes still have the same initial electrical charge. This experiment shows that no conduction of static electricity takes place when there is no difference in the amount of charge (potential difference). Both of the electroscopes had the same electrical charge, so there was no conduction.

Experiment No. 4

After discharging the electroscopes, charge one with a plastic rod (negative charge), and charge the other with a glass rod (positive charge). Make sure that the charges are equal (so the leaves in both electroscopes are at the same angle).

Move the electroscopes together until the electrode on one is touching the wire ring on the other. The foil leaves in both electroscopes will drop, indicating that they are fully discharged. This shows that opposite electric charges will cancel each other out.

Try experimenting with different types of plastic rods and different types of cloth material. You can check charge polarity by first charging the electroscope with a known polarity (glass rod is positive; plastic rod is negative), then placing the unknown rod against the electroscopes electrode. If it discharges the electroscope, the unknown charge is of opposite polarity.

Chapter 2

Science Projects

"WINDY" THE WIND GAUGE

UNTIL NOW, IF YOU'D HAD A NEED FOR AN ANEMOMETER (WIND gauge) or wanted one just because you were interested in keeping tabs on the prevailing winds, you'd have had but two choices. Toy ones, though the price may be right, leave much to be desired in performance, reliability, and accuracy. On the other hand, the better-quality instruments, available from specialty stores, start at about $125.00 and increase in cost very fast.

With our Windy you bridge the gap. Its accuracy is 5% or better, and its cost is reasonable, being in the $30.00 range. Dual meter ranges cover 0-30 mph and 0-90 mph. Readout is indicated on a large, clear, easy-to-read meter scale. And its remote pickup head can be located up to 150 feet from the readout indicator.

Windy's low cost and high accuracy are achieved through use of two integrated circuits (ICs), which together replace 12 transistors and 24 resistors. A novel optical sensor in the remote pickup head speeds construction by replacing a more complicated mechanical design.

How Windy Works

Whenever the wind blows, it revolves the windcups. The remote pickup head, built into the housing that supports the windcups, is a photoelectric pulse generator whose pulse rate is directly proportional to the speed of the wind. A disc, having holes punched uniformly around its edge, is fastened to the end of the shaft opposite the windcups. Mounted above this disc is a light source that shines through the perforations into a variable-resistance photocell positioned below the disc directly under the light source (the disc is sandwiched between the light source and the photocell).

When the wind blows, the cups rotate the shaft, which, in turn, rotates the perforated disc. This allows light to alternately shine through to, and to be cut off from, the photocell. Each time light strikes the cell, its resistance drops sharply. The photocell and resistor R3 form a voltage divider across the power source. When the resistance of the photocell is momentarily reduced by excitation from the light source, the voltage in that part of the divider is reduced. A pulse results from the sharp increase in current and resultant voltage drop.

This pulse triggers the hex inverter (IC1) which shapes and amplifies the pulse signals appearing across the voltage divider. The first inverter of IC1, biased by resistor R4, operates as a class-A amplifier. Succeeding stages are connected in cascade and operate with no bias. This considerably improves the input pulse rise and fall time that is necessary for accurate performance. A small amount of positive feedback in stages 4 and 5 further improves the rise and fall time of the pulses. Capacitor C3 on the input acts as a high-frequency filter, eliminating false triggering that could be created by spurious signals picked up in the long lead line.

Stages 3, 4, and 5 of the IC are wired as a one-shot multivibrator that is triggered by the shaped and amplified pulses from the previous stages.

The sharp input pulses from IC1 are differentiated by capacitor C6 and resistor R5. The leading edge of the pulse triggers a constant-width, monostable multivibrator, formed by three of the inverters in IC2. Each time the one-shot multi is triggered, it flips from its stable state to an unstable state. The amount of time that it remains in this unstable state is determined by the values of resistance and capacitance in the coupling network. The on time is set by range selection capacitors C7 and C8, calibration control R6, and resistor R7. The output pulse from the one-shot multi is buffered and inverted by the remaining three inverters in IC2, which are connected in cascade (see schematic for ICs).

Protected Meter

When the one-shot is triggered, the output at pin 7 from IC2 drops from 3.6 V, the supply voltage, to a mere few tenths of a volt. This effectively grounds the end of resistor R8 connected to the IC, and a pulse of current flows through meter M1. As the wind picks up speed, the one-shot is triggered more often, directly in proportion to the wind speed. The pulse rate increases, and meter M1 and capacitor C9 integrate the output pulses into a wind speed reading. Should the voltage across the meter exceed 0.6 volt, diode D6 conducts, shunting current around the meter and protecting it from overload.

A Zener-diode regulated power supply provides + 3.6 Vdc power for the instrument. Output from the secondary of transformer T1 is rectified by a fullwave bridge rectifier comprised of diodes D1 through D4. Capacitor C1 brute-force filters the rectified output; Zener diode D6 holds the voltage on the base of transistor Q1 at 4.2 V. Since transistor Q1 is connected as an emitter follower, the filtered dc output appears on Q1's emitter. Low-voltage ac power to operate exciter lamp I2 is provided by the 6.3-V secondary winding of the power transformer.

Construction Tips

Prior to starting the actual fabrication of the various units comprising Windy, we suggest you study Figs. 2-1 through 2-13 and Tables 2-1 and 2-2 to familiarize yourself with the basic units, how they were constructed, and their relationship to one another. Take into account the dimensions shown in relation to materials you have readily available. It may be necessary for you to compromise somewhat in order to use available sources.

Epoxy cement contributes a great deal to the building of Windy.

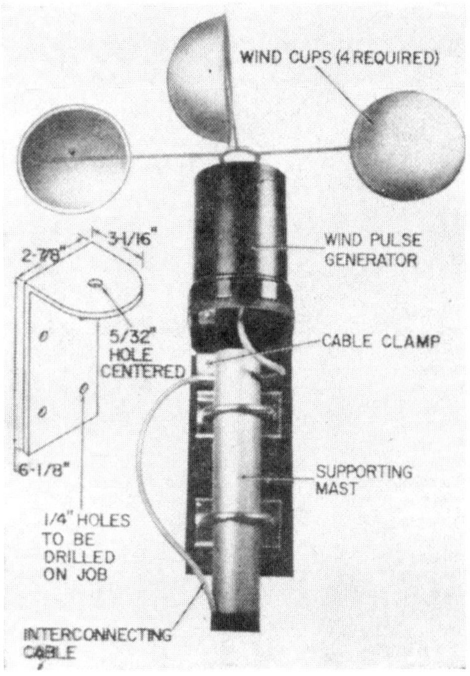

Fig. 2-1. Wind Cup generator is fastened to its mounting mast. Details on making the mounting bracket are shown.

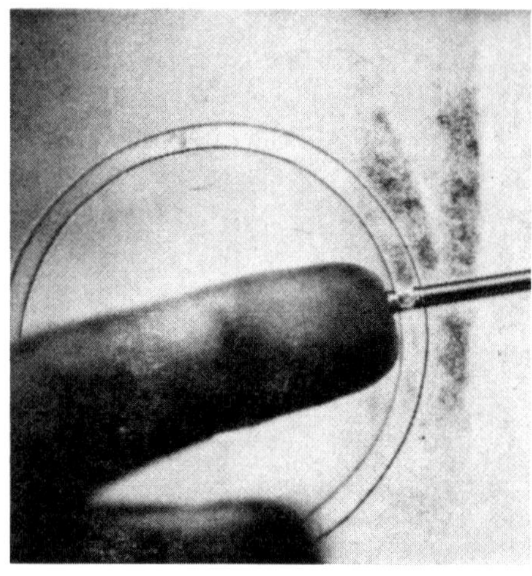

Fig. 2-2. A finger is used as a mandrel when punching holes in the polystyrene Wind Cups with a tool made by sharpening a piece of 1/8-in brass tubing.

In order to receive the most benefits from epoxy cements, the resin and the hardener must be thoroughly mixed as quickly as possible. Try to use the 5-minute curing epoxies; they'll speed up the waiting time.

The remote pickup head, which actually is a windcup pulse generator, is housed in a small plastic jar, preferably one with a screw-type cover. To ensure that no extraneous light reaches the photocell, we recommend that you spray the jar and its cover with several coats of flat black paint to completely opaque it. (We purposely did our painting after completion of construction in order that details in construction would show-up better in our photos.)

Drill a 5/32-in. hole in the lid of the jar to permit the lead cable to exit from the jar. Also drill the same size hole in the exact center of the bottom of the jar.

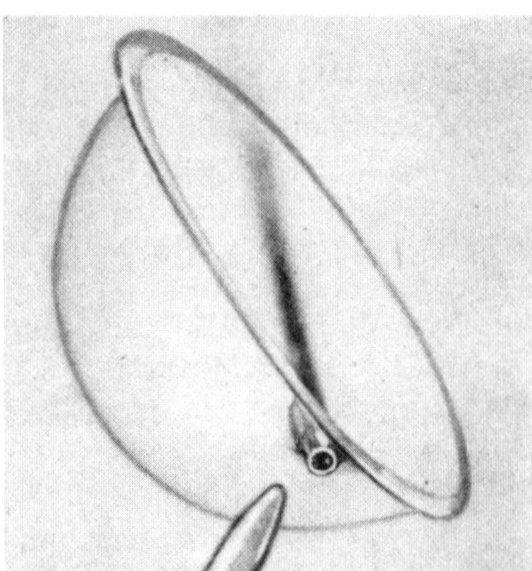

Fig. 2-3. The pointer shows where epoxy is placed to fasten Wind Cups to brass mounting rods.

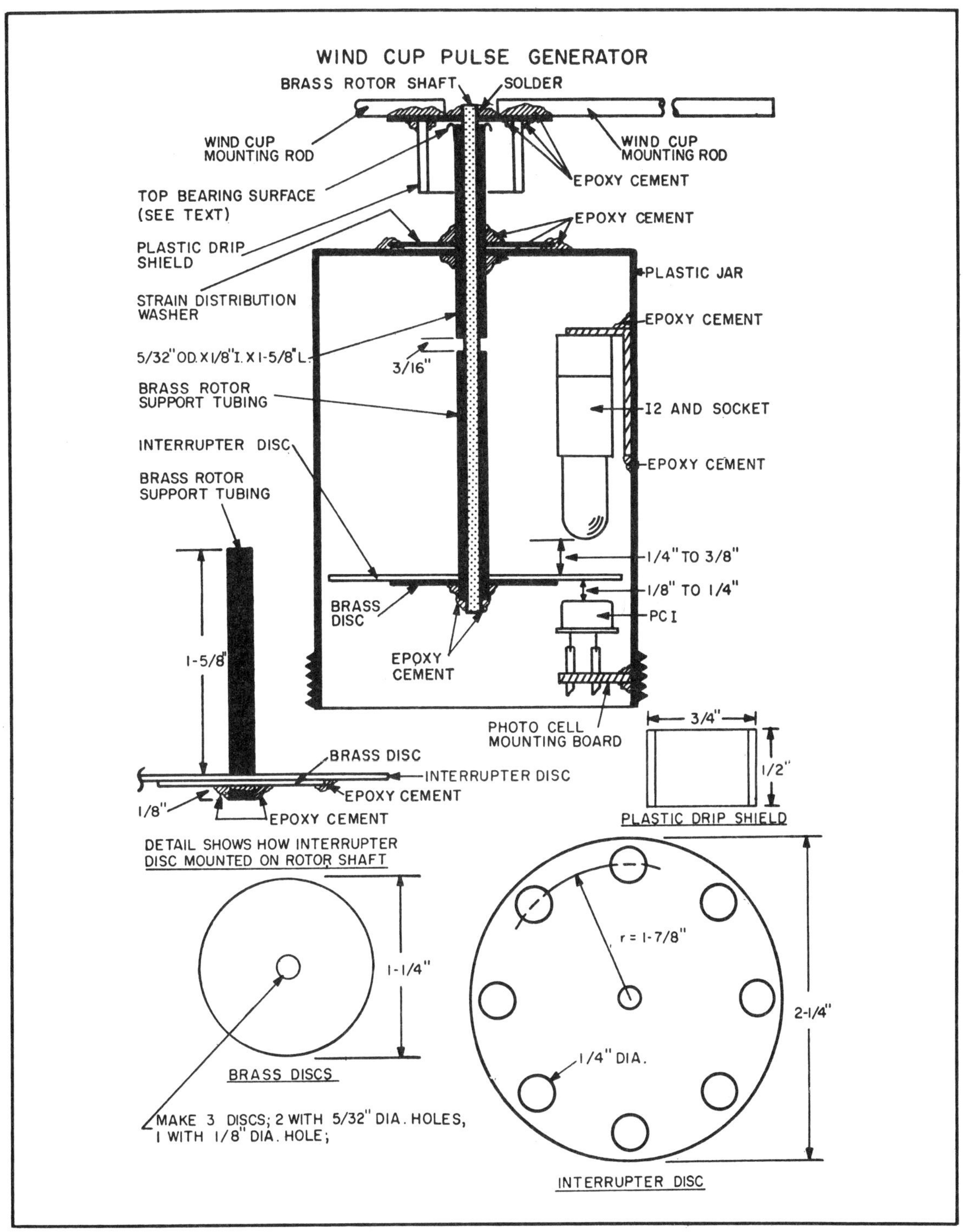

Fig. 2-4. The wind cup generator. Leads from lamp I2 must be tacked to side wall of jar to keep them away from the rotor disc.

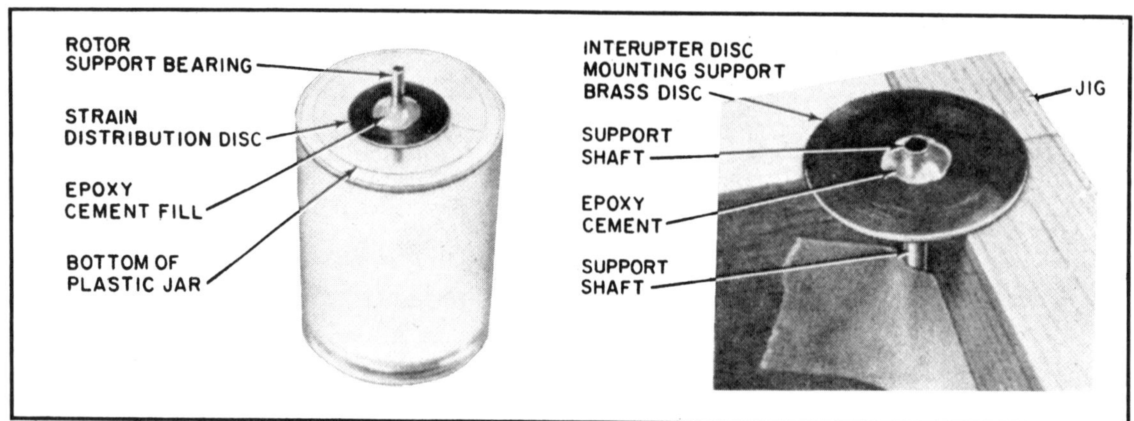

Fig. 2-5. Details of the rotor support and interrupter disc support.

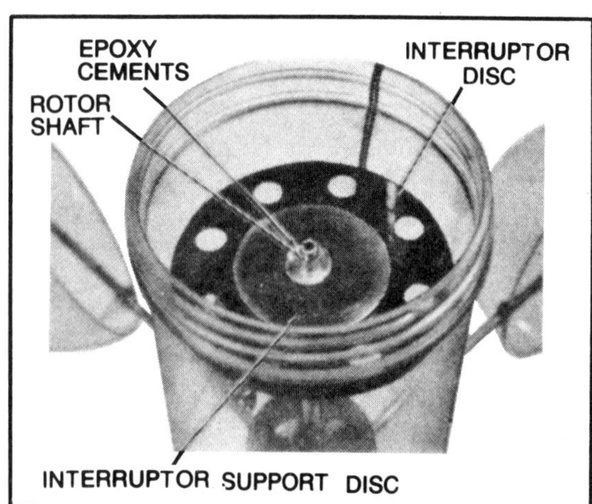

Fig. 2-6. After installing I2, interrupter disc is held 1/8-in. from bottom of rotor shaft and cemented with epoxy to the rotor shaft.

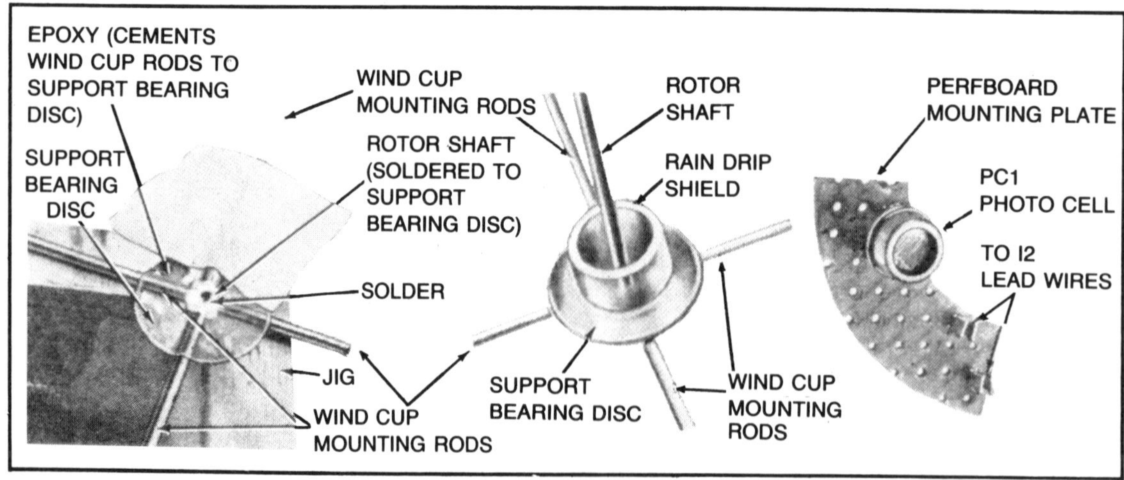

Fig. 2-7. Photocell mounting board and rain shield.

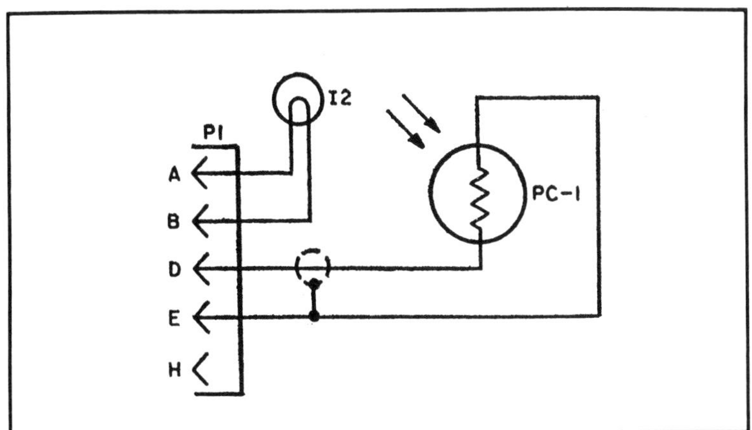

Fig. 2-8. Schematic for Wind Cup generator. Cable may be extended to 150 ft.

You'll need three discs made from 1/32-in. thick half-hard brass. The outside diameter of the discs is 1 1/4-in. Two should have a 5/32-in. hole drilled at the exact center; the remaining one should have a 1/8-in. diameter hole drilled in its center. One of the discs with a 5/32-in. hole serves as a strain distribution washer. The center holes in the strain washer and the bottom of the cup must be aligned to permit bearing support tubing to pass through both easily for free shaft rotation.

Prepare the bearing support tubing, made from a 1 5/8-in. length of 5/32-in. OD, 1/8-in. ID brass tubing for mounting in the base of the cup. It's important that the inner and outer surface of one end of this piece of tubing be as smooth as possible, since these surfaces are top bearing surfaces. The tubing should be chucked in a slow-speed drill (400-600 rpm) and smoothed both on inner and outer surfaces with a fine needle file. Bring the file against the rotating tubing to create a smoothed radius on one end.

We cannot emphasize too strongly the importance of a smooth surface for the bearing support tubing. Rough spots at this point can create future trouble either by slowing down the rotor because whatever produced the rough spot gouged the surface of the support bearing disc or, perhaps, when the atmosphere is quite humid and the temperature drops suddenly, the moisture trapped between the gouge in the disc and the bearing support tubing freezes and stops the rotor completely.

Cement this bearing support tubing in position to the bottom of the plastic jar with a blob of epoxy spread uniformly around the tubing both inside and outside the plastic jar to give added support to the bearing. The end of the tubing with the smoothed radius should protrude 5/8-in. beyond the strain distribution washer.

The Interrupter Disc

This disc is made from thin, rigid plastic sheet. If not opague, spray

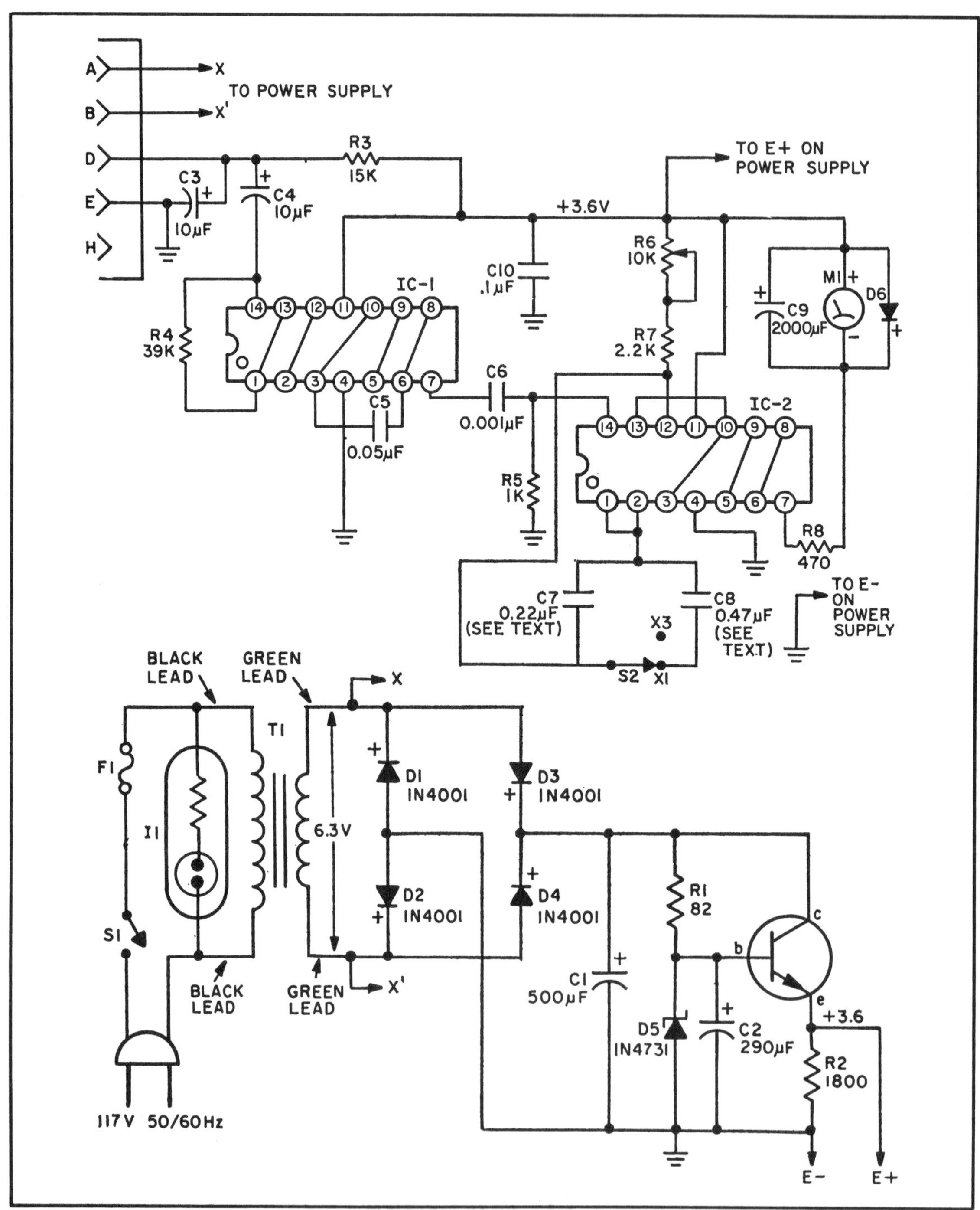

Fig. 2-9. The schematic at the top details the circuit for the indicator unit of Windy, except for its power supply. The diagram shows proper orientation for the IC's, looking down on them. The lower diagram details the power supply, which employs a 4.2 V Zener diode to regulate the output voltage that energizes the indicator unit electronics circuit.

Fig. 2-10. Right side of Indicator unit shows location of J1, exit hole for power cord and mounting screws for T1 and fuse mounting board.

it with flat black paint after cutting to size and punching holes in it. Punch eight 1/4-in. diameter holes, in the disc, spaced uniformly around the circumference on a radius of 1 7/8-in. Also drill a 5/32-in. hole in the exact center of the disc.

At this point make a jig from two pieces of wood, at least 3/4-in. thick by 3 1/2-in. wide, fastened at right angles. This jig is used to assure proper alignment of the interrupter disc on its bearing disc to the rotor shaft.

Insert a 1 3/4-in. long × 5/32-in. OD, 1/8-in. ID piece of brass

Fig. 2-11. Photo shows the neat layout for the electronic components making up the indicator unit. The power supply is located on the right (except for diodes and capacitors), the electronics card is on the left side and meter and controls on front.

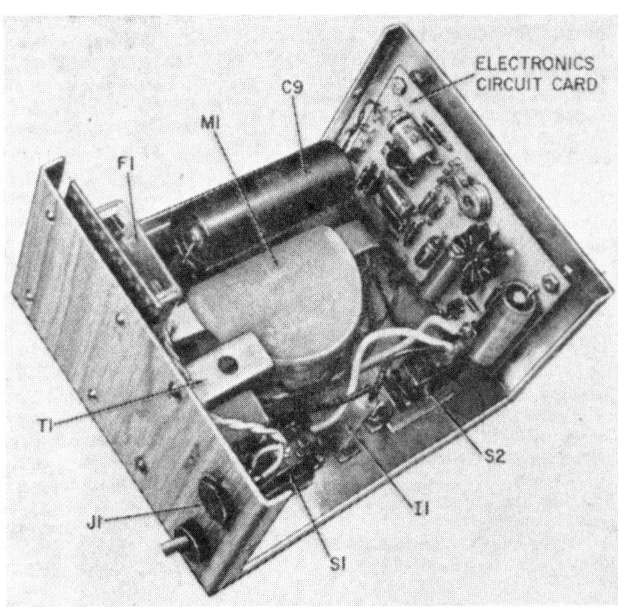

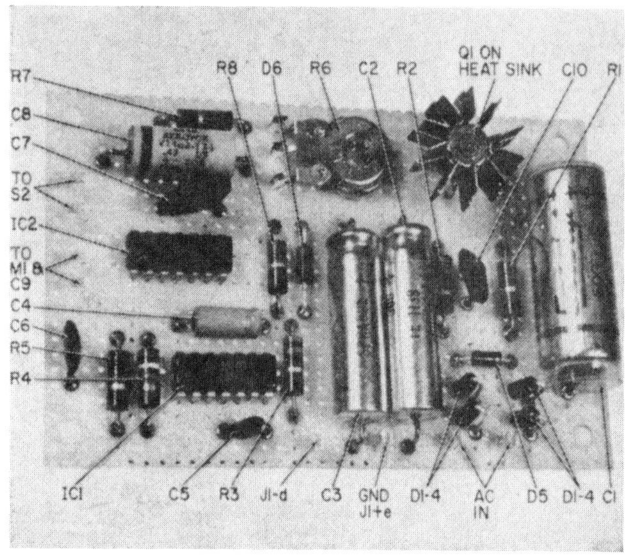

Fig. 2-12. The electronics circuit card is detailed here. Although the photo shows both C2 and C3 the same size, the author recommands C3 a 10 μF, 15 V electrolytic.

tubing into the center hole of the plastic disc so that it protrudes 1/8-in. beyond the outer surface of the interrupter disc. Temporarily fasten the tubing with masking tape to the jig as shown in Fig. 2-5. Next, epoxy one of the brass discs to the interrupter disc and cement both the perforated plastic interrupter and brass discs to the brass support tubing, spreading the epoxy uniformly around the tubing.

Rotor Shaft

A good time to prepare the rotor shaft is while the epoxy cement

Fig. 2-13. Note the clean long scale of the meter used to make it easy to read calibrations. Also note rubber feet on bottom (not mentioned in Parts List). Rocker type switches used for ranging and on/off control are easy to operate.

Table 2-1. Parts List for Windy's Pulse Generator.

12 #755 single contact, miniature bayonet base, 6.3 V-0.15 A lamp bulb (Lafayette 32E69032 or equiv.)
P1 5-pin plug with hood and cable clamp (Amphenol 126-217 or equiv.)
PC1 Photocell, Clairex C L-703L
1 Miniature bayonet base, pilot lamp holder (Lafayette 37E28079 or equiv.)
1 2 5/8 × 3 1/2-in. plastic jar with screw-on cover
1 2 7/8 × 9 3/16 × 1/4-in. plexiglas for mounting bracket (see text)
1 3/4-in. OD, 5/8-in. ID × 1/2-in. long plastic tubing for rain drip shield
4 3-in. dia. light plastic half-hemispheres
4 Pieces 1/8-in. OD × 6-in. long brass tubing
1 Piece 5/32-in. OD, 1/8-in. ID × 1 1/2-in. long brass tubing
1 Piece 5/32-in. OD, 1/8-in. ID × 1 3/4-in. long brass tubing
3 1/32-in. thick, half-hard brass discs, 1 1/4-in. OD (if discs not available cut from sheet brass)
1 Bakelite disc 1/32-in. thick × 2 1/4-in. dia.
1 2 × 1-in. piece perfboard
Misc. Length as required (not to exceed 150 ft.) Belden #8734 3-conductor cable with vinyl insulation and overall vinyl jacket (one conductor shielded), black spray paint, antenna mast mounting hardware (Lafayette 18EO1950 or equiv.)

Table 2-2. Parts List for Windy's Indicator.

C1 500-μF, 15-Vdc electrolytic capacitor (Sprague TVA1162 or equiv.)
C2 290-μF, 12-Vdc electrolytic capacitor (Sprague TE1139 or equiv.)
C3, C4 10-μF, 15-Vdc electrolytic capacitor (Sprague TE1155 or equiv.)
C5 0.05-μF, 12-Vdc ceramic (Erie 5635-000 Y5FD-503M or equiv.)
C6 0.001-μF, 100-Vdc ceramic capacitor (Erie 801-000X5FD102K or equiv.)
C7 0.22-μF, 12-Vdc ceramic capacitor (Erie 5615-000Y5FD224M or equiv.)
C8 0.47-μF, 200-Vdc capacitor (Aerovox V1462-134 or equiv.)
C9 2000-μF, 25-Vdc electrolytic capacitor (Cornell Dubilier BR2000-25 or equiv.)
C10 0.1 μF, 12Vdc ceramic capacitor (Erie 5655-000-Y5F0-104M)
D1, D2, D3, D4 1N40001 silicon diode, 50 PIV, 1 A
D5 1N4731 Zener diode, 4.2 volt, ? watt, 10% tolerance
F1 Fuse, type 3AG, 1/4 A
I1 Neon pilot lamp assembly, amber lens caps (Lafayette 34E52174 or equiv.)
IC1, IC2 Integrated circuit, hex inverter (Motorola MC789P)
J1 5-pin chassis socket (Amphenol 126-218 or equiv.)
M1 0-1 mA meter (3 × 4 1/2-in.) 100 ohms or less coil resistance (see text)
Q1 Npn silicon transistor, type 2N697
R1 82-ohm, 1/2-watt resistor
R2 1800-ohm, 1/2-watt resistor
R3 15,000-ohm, 1/2-watt resistor
R4 39,000-ohm, 1/2-watt resistor
R5 1000-ohm, 1/2-watt resistor
R6 10,000-ohm, PC board mounted miniature potentiometer (Mallory MTC1L41 or equiv.)
R7 2200-ohm, 1/2-watt resistor
R8 470-ohm, 1/2-watt resistor
S1, S2 Spst rocker type switch (Cutler Hammer 8144K21A1M52or equiv.)
T1 Low voltage power transformer; primary 117 V, 50/60 Hz, secondary 6.3 Vac at 0.6 A (Stancor D6465 or equiv.)
1 Aluminum minibox 4 × 5 × 6-in. (Lafayette 12E83746 or equiv.—see text)
1 Dual fuse holder, 1 active, 1 spare (Lafayette 99E63372)
1 Piece perfboard (0.2 holes on 0.1-in. grid pattern) (Lafayette 19E83584 or equiv.)
1 Heat sink for Q1 (Wakefield NF-209)
2 sockets for ICs (Lafayette 47A2152 or equiv.—optional, see text)
Misc. Transfer letters (Datak or equiv.), bolts, nuts, hardware, push-in terminals and eyelets, pressure sensitive vinyl finishing material (Contac or equiv.), 5-minute curing epoxy, RTV Silicone Seal, rubber feet, ac line cord, wire, solder, etc.

for the interrupter disc assembly is curing. It is made from a 3 9/16-in. length of brass tubing 1/8-in. OD. Check it for trueness and fit in the bearing support tubing previously epoxied in the plastic jar. The rotor must fit inside the bearing tubing snugly, but must still rotate freely in it.

Four lengths of brass tubing 1/8-in. OD by 6-in. long serve as support arms for the four wind cups. These arms are epoxy cemented to the top of the bearing support disc at right angles to one another. One end of each of the rods should be 5/16-in. from the center line of the rotor shaft to leave a clear area so that rotor shaft can be soldered to the disc. For balance it's important that the arms are each separated by 90°. You should use a protractor to double-check this placement.

As soon as epoxy on the interrupter disc assembly has cured, the jig can be freed for proper alignment of the rotor when fastening the rotor shaft to the brass support bearing disc. Solder the brass rotor shaft to the brass disc, employing the jig to ensure accurate alignment. Be careful not to bend wind cup mounting rods.

The rotor-shaft assembly and the interrupter-disc assembly are now ready to be mounted in the plastic jar. But first, a lamp holder, to which a pair of leads has been soldered, must be epoxied inside the plastic jar as shown in our illustration. At this stage you should also prepare a mounting board on which the photocell and terminals for the cable between the wind generator and the indicator are installed. The lead wires from the photocell and to the exciter lamp are contained in this cable.

Make the photocell terminal mounting board from a piece of perfboard cut into a truncated pie section having an outside radius of 1 1/4-in. and an inside radius of 3/4-in. Overall length of the board should be 1 1/2-in. and it should be 1/2-in. wide. The photocell is mounted on push-in terminals. Terminal points between the lamp and photocell leads and the lead cable to the indicator are also push-in terminals.

Cement a rain shield, which is a 1/2-in. length of plastic tubing having a 3/8-in. OD × 5/8-in. ID, to the bottom of the brass-support bearing disc. It should be positioned concentric to the disc, as shown in Fig. 2-7.

Assembly of Pulse Generator

Before final assembly it's best to insert the lamp in its socket and test it to be sure it's working. Once the assembly has been completed it will be difficult to reach the bulb. For this reason we've specified the 50,000-hour long life bulb instead of an electrically interchangeable #47 pilot lamp, which doesn't claim anywhere near that length of life before burnout.

At this stage opaque the housing with dark spray paint if your plastic jar requires it.

Silicone grease, the type used in heatsinking power transistors, will prevent freeze-up when the temperature drops and will also provide lubrication to allow the rotor to turn with little resistance. Place a pea-sized dab on the bearing surface of the support bearing disc. This lubricant should be applied each year before the start of cold weather.

Final Assembly

Insert the rotor assembly into the support bearing tube in generator housing. Now invert the housing and slip the interrupter disc assembly, with its support tubing, over the rotor so that the end of the support tube rides 1/8-in. below the end of the rotor shaft. Use a single drop of epoxy to cement the support tube to the rotor shaft. If you located the lamp socket correctly within the generator housing, the lamp bulb should clear the interrupter disc by 1/4- to 3/8-in. when the housing is positioned so that the interrupter disc faces down. In this position you should note about 3/16-in. up-and-down play in the rotor shaft.

With the photocell mounted in position on its circuit board, cement this assembly inside the generator housing directly below the lamp so that the space between the bottom of the housing and the circuit board is 3/16-in. The lead cable will be connected and the cover of the jar fastened in position after the wind cups have been epoxied in position. The reason for this is that the jar can rest on the bench during this assembly if the wire is not in position at this time.

Wind Cups

We made our wind cups from thin, styrene plastic, half spheres, 3 in. in diameter. You may use smaller ones, but no smaller than 2 1/2-in. in diameter. Regardless of the diameter of the wind cups, the center-to-center spacing should not be changed, since this would affect overall calibration of the instrument.

Make a punch by sharpening one end of a scrap of 1/8-in. diameter brass tubing, for punching the holes in the plastic hemispheres. The cups should be epoxied to their respective lengths of 1/8-in. OD tubing, positioned as shown in Fig. 2-1.

Mounting Bracket

The mounting bracket for the completed wind cup pulse generator unit can be made from plastic (which we used), or from metal (iron or aluminum), or from wood.

If you use plastic, make the 90° bend by gently heating the plastic with a small butane torch, being careful not to touch it with the flame. When the plastic softens and becomes pliable, form it over a right-angled block. Keep the material in position over the block until it has cooled down, at which time it will be rigid. If wood is used the bracket is formed by nailing two pieces of wood together at right angles in the shape of the bracket shown in Fig. 2-1. Metal is formed either in a brake or a bench vise.

Epoxy cement the plastic jar cap to the bracket so that the jar containing the pulse generator and wind cups can be screwed into the jar cap, thus holding it in position. Drill a hole in the bracket to permit the lead wires from the generator assembly to feed out of the jar.

Now The Indicator

The major mechanical construction is complete now and the only remaining assembly work is the indicator unit, which contains the electronics.

We started by trimming a standard 6 × 5 × 4-in. minibox to a 6 × 5 × 3-in. dimension. Since we used aluminum it was easy to pare 1 in. off the depth.

First step is to cut out the large round hole for the meter, and the rectangular holes for the rocker switches, and drill the hole for the pilot lamp, all on the front panel of the major half of the minibox. Also drill mounting holes for the power transformer, fuse holder, input jack, and ac cord on the right-hand side of the box and mounting holes for the circuit board on the left side.

To cut the meter hole and the rectangular switch holes, use a hand nibbler, or, if one isn't available, drill a series of small holes very close together around the periphera of the main holes. Then knock out the large pieces of metal and file the edges smooth to the exact sizes and shapes required. Deburr all holes before assembly. We used a rectangular 0-1 mA meter we happened to have in the spare-parts box. However, any 0-1 mA having a coil resistance of 100 ohms or less will work. Be sure you have enough room in the cabinet for the size meter you use.

Mount the fuse holder on a 2 × 2 1/2-in. piece of perfboard. The mounting screws for this board should be 4-40s at least 1/2-in. long so that the board can be held away from the metal box with extra locking nuts. The circuit board is mounted in the same way.

When all holes have been drilled cover the outer surface of the minibox with wood grained pressure-sensitive adhesive vinyl (Contact or equiv.) to make an attractive-looking instrument. A word of caution: when tightening mounting screws be sure to hold the heads of the screws rigid with a screwdriver and tighten mountings by using a socket wrench on the nuts; otherwise, the vinyl sheeting will be pulled and stretched by the bolt heads. Trim vinyl around the holes with a razor blade before mounting components.

To make your project really professional-looking, letter the controls with press-on letters (Datak or equiv.). Spray lettering with several coats of clear acrylic for protection.

Electrical Assembly

Most of the electronic circuit parts are mounted on the circuit board. We suggest you use G or P pattern perfboard as the hole spacing matches the pin spacing of the ICs we used. The components are mounted flat on the board and push-in clips and/or eyelets are used to facilitate mounting and connecting. The leads of the ICs are pushed through the perfboard and bent outward against the board. This holds the IC in place and provides a tab to which leads are soldered. Inter-component wiring is made with #26 bare copper wire. Where wires cross over they are insulated with plastic tubing.

Wire the circuit card in accord with the schematic. Be sure electrolytic capacitors and diodes are properly polarized before soldering to them. Also make certain that the ICs are correctly positioned before you solder them in.

Alternate IC Mounting

You may want to use a socket for the IC. As a matter of fact, the investment of less than a dollar for a socket is well worth it. You solder to the socket, rather than to the IC, thus reducing the possibility of damaging the IC with excess heating. You also have the advantage of being able to plug in the IC for proper orientation and/or replacement should this be necessary.

Use an alligator clip temporarily clipped to a lead when soldering Q1 and the diodes. If you elect to solder in the ICs, you should use the heatsink on each of their leads, too.

The circuit card is mounted on the left side of the indicator housing with four 4-40 bolts and nuts so that the card is supported away from the metal of the housing, as mentioned earlier. Inter-connect the various components not part of the card except for the meter.

Meter Modification

Any 0-1 mA meter having a coil resistance of under 100 ohms can be used for M1; the one we used measures approximately 14 ohms. However, the meter scale will have to be changed from 0-1 mA calibrations to 0-30 mph. You can just turn it over, spray it with flat white, and then follow the steps outlined in referenced article. To mark the scale, use press-on letters.

Checking It Out

Plug in the remote pulse generator, turn on the ac power, and give the rotor a spin. If all has gone well you should get an indication on the meter. Check both ranges (X1 and X3).

If nothing happens, start out by checking all wiring for possible glitches, cold soldered joints, shorts between pins of ICs and transistor

Q1, etc. See if + 3.6 V is present on pin 11 of both ICs. Also check to see if the exciter lamp in the pulse generator is lit. Doublecheck the polarity of all electrolytics and diodes and also check to be sure the ICs are oriented correctly.

Calibration

When you get an indication on the meter by rotating the wind cups, the meter reading in the ×1 position should be three times the reading in the ×3 position for a given speed of the rotor. While maintaining rotor speed by hand, switch back and forth to determine if meter readings are correct.

Tracking between these two ranges is dependent on the capacitances of C7 and C8. The capacitance of C7 should be exactly half that of C8. Since capacitors can vary as much as ± 20% or more from the nominal value indicated on them and still are considered commercially acceptable, you should check their capacitance on a bridge if at all possible. If not, you can trim them by adding small capacitors until the desired meter range is reached.

To do this turn the rotor by hand to produce a reading of 15 mph in the ×1 range. If the reading drops below 5 mph in the ×3 range add capacitance in small increments until it reads 5 mph. If it indicates more than 5 mph add capacitance to C8. Add capacitance in steps of 0.01 μF or 0.02 μF to align the two ranges.

Adjusting Meter Reading

Once the proper range tracking has been established, probably the easiest way to complete the calibration is to do it in your car where you have a reasonably accurate speedometer to serve as a calibration standard. Unless you happen to have a car with a 6-V battery (very rare these days—most use 12-V batteries) you will need 6 Vdc, either from 4-D cells in series, or a 6-V lantern battery. Disconnect one side of T1 and bring out a pair of leads, one of which is connected to the indicator's ground and the other to the collector of Q1. The ground lead is connected to the negative and the collector lead to the positive of the 6-Vdc source.

Also remove the leads connected to X and X^1 on the secondary of T1. Connect a pair of leads between pins A and B of J1 and the external battery. This provides current to light exciter lamp when operating Windy from an external dc power source while calibrating in a car ride. Once the calibration has been completed remember to restore this modified wiring to its original condition as well as the modification to the battery wiring.

You'll need a friend, either to drive the car while you make adjustments or to make the adjustments for you while you drive. Calibration should be done on a calm, windless day if at all possible.

Should there be a light breeze you'll have to average the calibration by checking readings obtained by driving in both directions.

With the car traveling at 30 mph (according to its speedometer) and Windy's indicator set on ×1 range, adjust R6 until the meter reads 30 mph. This is the only calibration necessary as you have already corrected the ranging, as previously mentioned. (Of course you've temporarily mounted the wind cup pulse generator outside the car so as to be in the wind's stream.)

Installation

Now that Windy has been built and calibrated, where is the best location for the remote wind cup pulse generator to give a true indication of wind speed?

The pulse generator unit should be mounted 5 to 10 ft. above the building on which it's being used. It should not be mounted in the lee of a taller building and the arms of the rotor should remain level as they rotate.

We recommend that easily-available TV antenna mounting hardware (e.g., mast clamps, mast mounting base, etc.) be used to mount the remote unit above the roof of the building.

The lubrication recommended won't be affected by temperatures below 0 F.

GIVE YOUR PLANTS A VOICE

CAN PLANTS REALLY TALK? OF COURSE, NO ONE KNOWS FOR sure; but this author's experience with this project indicates some basis for such research. This easy experimenter's project can help you make up your own mind while providing a multitude of interesting experiments related to plant response. (See fig. 2-14.)

A Type Of Lie Detector

Proponents of the idea that plants have feelings—that plants can respond to human thought and may even have the ability to remember and think—have found that by measuring plant skin resistance, in much the same manner as the polygraph measures human skin resistance, changes are detected that can be interpreted as logical responses to psychic and physical stimuli. The instrument in this project is a high sensitivity ohmmeter which, when connected across a resistance of from 100,000-ohms to 1-megohm, will detect resistance changes in the order of 0.5 percent.

Checking the schematic (Fig. 2-15) we see the circuit is simply a battery-operated "709" operational amplifier in a differential configuration across an adjustable bridge. Bridge imbalance is amplified by the op-amp and displayed on a sensitive meter or, if you're lucky enough to have or borrow one, a chart recorder.

One half of the bridge consists of the specimen resistance connected to terminals J1 and J2, an adjustable coarse zero control, and R1 and R2. The second arm of the bridge consists of R4, R6, and the fine zero control, R5. Since the resistance across J1 and J2 can range from 100,000-ohms to 1-megohm, R1 (in combination with R2) is adjusted to equal the resistance of the speciman. Control R5 permits final zero adjustment of the bridge. Once balanced, any change in specimen resistance will apply a voltage change to the amplifier, which is amplified and displayed by the meter or other indicating device.

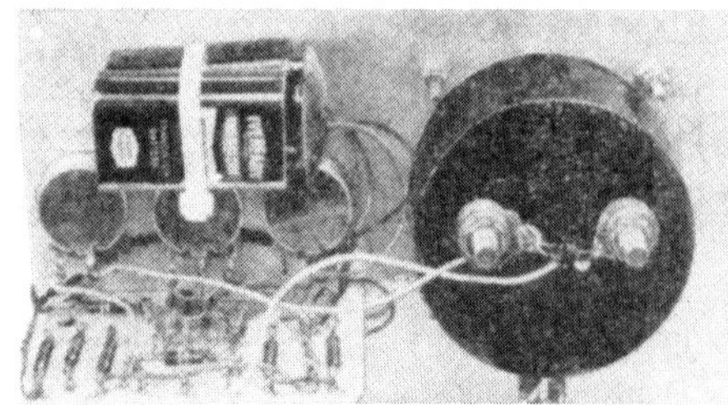

Fig. 2-14. All electronic wiring and components can be easily assembled on a single perfboard. Bipolar battery supply simplifies project.

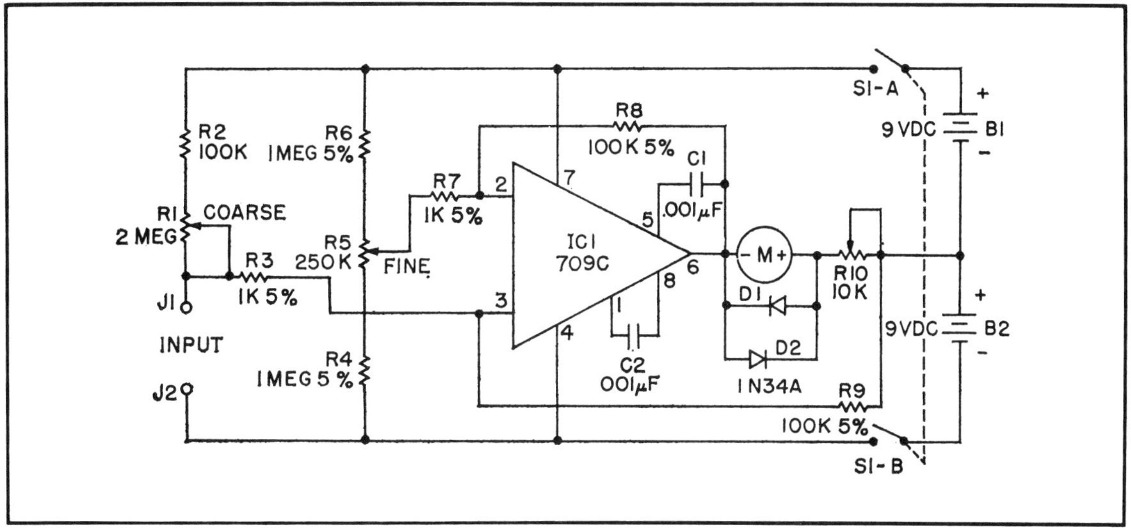

Fig. 2-15. Give your plants a voice schematic diagram.

Selecting A Meter

R10, in series with the meter movement, permits adjustment of the meter sensitivity. Diodes D1 and D2 protect the movement during zero adjust and provide a nonlinear meter function which makes the meter more sensitive near zero than at full scale.

Since the most expensive component in this project is the meter movement, two meter options are given. You may want to use a 50-0-50 millivolt movement in your model, or a re-scaled 0-50 millivolt movement as used by the author. The latter is more easily obtained, and has the advantage of providing a 0-25 millivolt indication when re-scaled to put zero in the middle of the scale. Since the bridge can be balanced at any point on the meter scale, it is a simple matter to carefully re-scale a 0-50 millivolt movement. If you are not inclined to make this modification, which entails removing the meter face and relabeling the scale, a 50-0-50 millivolt movement can be used.

Construction For Good Looks

The polygraph is compactly constructed in a readily available 7 3/4-in. × 4 3/4 in. × 2 3/8-in. experimenters Mini Utility Box (Radio Shack 270-232) with all components mounted to the aluminum front panel. Batteries B1 and B2 are secured to the top of the front panel with a plastic cable tie and adhesive pad to permit easy removal of the entire unit from the back enclosure.

The amplifier circuit, for simplicity of construction, is built on a 2 × 3 1/2-in. perfboard chassis and mounted to the front panel with a small aluminum bracket. Construction is simple and straightforward and can be accomplished with simple hand tools.

A test stand is suggested and can be constructed of plywood, a piece of lucite, and two banana jacks. Connections to the plant are made by fine phono wire and two gold or silver plated "earring findings" obtained from a local hobby supply house. Figure 2-16 illustrates the connection made to the specimen used by the author. A good steady connection to the specimen is important since the response and sensitivity of the instrument can render readings useless if there is the slightest movement of the specimen probe. Adjust the earring finding so that it holds the leaf tightly and firmly between its jaws. Conventional banana leads can be used to connect the instrument to the jacks of the test stand.

Operational Set-Up

With a specimen in place and connected, set the meter sensitivity control to full counter-clockwise and turn the plant polygraph to the on position. Set the fine control knob at center position, and slowly adjust the coarse zero adjustment until the meter is near center scale. Make the final adjustment to zero with the fine control. The full scale sensitivity of the meter can now be adjusted by rotating the meter sensitivity control clockwise and readjusting to zero with the fine zero control.

Some experimentation may be necessary in adjusting the meter sensitivity and fine zero adjust control, depending upon the specimen and the resistance across the two test points. The author found that plants in poor health make very bad subjects, while the responses of healthy plants is much more pronounced and rapid.

A good indication that meter sensitivity is properly adjusted is

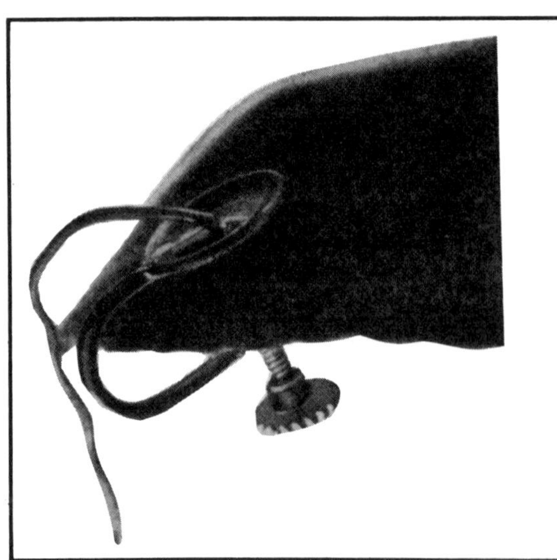

Fig. 2-16. Solder fine phono wire to a pair of stripped earrings—gold or silver work the best. Then bug your favorite flora!

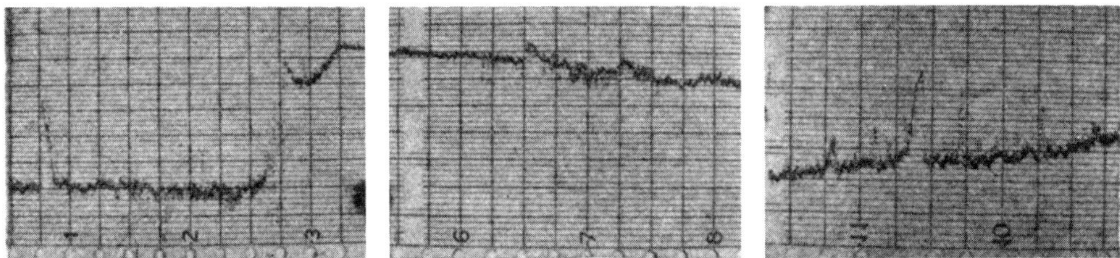

Fig. 2-17. These graphs were made with an automatic chart recorder. On left, major change at 2:45 AM was unexplained by author. However, center graph at 6:30 AM peaks when author's family had breakfast. Plant showed major change when watered at about 10:30. Plan subject was an African Violet.

when a slight bouncing of the meter movement is noted either side of zero. If the meter movement continually goes off scale during your experimentation, reduce the meter sensitivity and re-zero the bridge.

What You See

Interpretation of meter fluctuations is largely a matter of experience and repeated experimentation. Figure 2-17 gives some indication of the types of responses you will see. Most of the characteristic resistance changes can be observed by recording me-

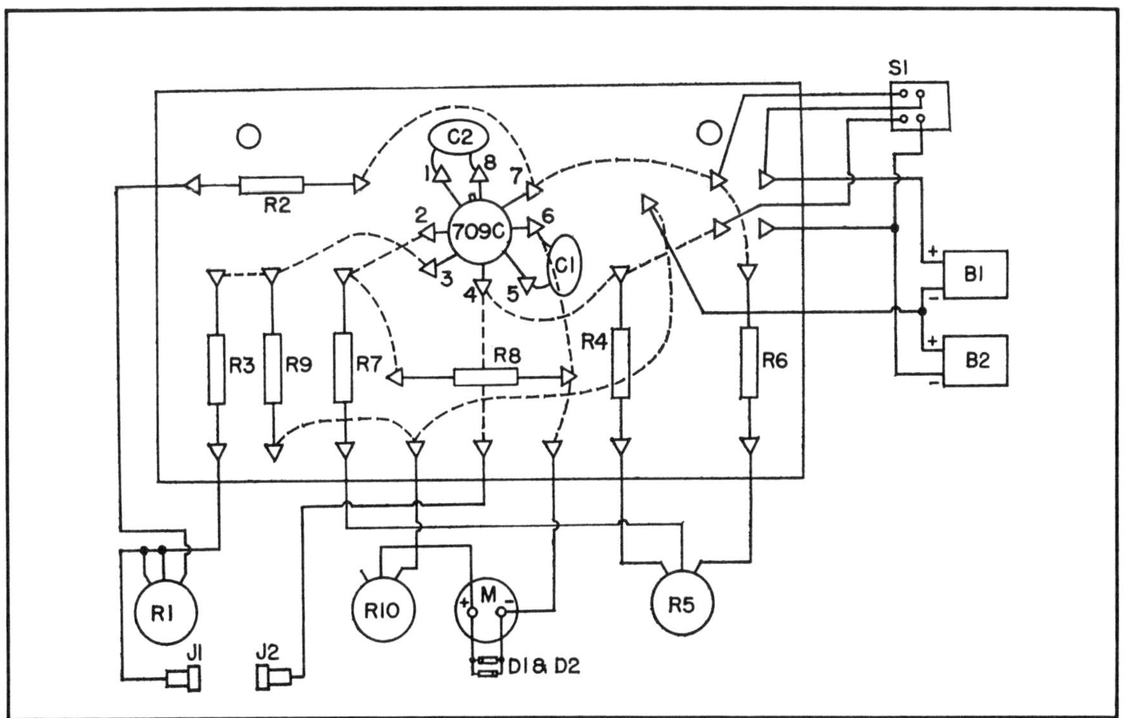

Fig. 2-18. The Plant Polygraph (sensitive resistance measuring circuit) is very simple to wire. Wire under circuit board is shown in dashed lines. Parts placement is not critical.

Table 2-3. Parts List for Give Your Plants A Voice.

B1, B2—9-volt battery (Radio Shack 23-464 or equiv.)
C1, C2—0.001 μF (10,000 pF) disc capacitor, 50, VDC or better (Radio Shack 272-131 or equiv.)
D1, D2—1N34A diode (Radio Shack 276-821 or equiv.)
IC1—Type 709 integrated circuit (Radio Shack 276-017 or equiv.)
J1, J2—5-way binding posts (Radio Shack 274-661 or equiv.)
M1—Meter, 0-50 millivolts DC, Triplett 320G or equiv. (see text)
R1—2-megohm potentiometer, linear taper (Radio Shack 271-093 or equiv.)
R2, R8, R9—100,000-ohm, 1/2-watt resistor (Radio Shack 271-000 or equiv.)
R3, R7—1,000-ohm, 1/2-watt resistor (Radio Shack 271-000 or equiv.)
R4, R6—1-megohm, 1/2-watt resistor (Radio Shack 271-000 or equiv.)
R5—250,000-ohm potentiometer, linear taper
R10—10,000-ohm potentiometer, linear taper (Radio Shack 271-1715 or equiv.)
S1—Switch, DPST or DPDT (Radio Shack 275-666 or equiv.)
Misc.—Perfboard, push-in clips, battery connectors, wire, solder, Minicase (Radio Shack 270-232), etc.

ter fluctuations of fixed time intervals, or through a graphic recording instrument such as the one used by the author (borrowed from a friendly high school teacher). The latter is invaluable in making long term observations. See Fig. 2-18 and Table 2-3.

Many short term experiments, however, are possible without the aid of a recorder. You may water the plant, for instance, and observe the same type of resistance change shown. A gradual rate of change will be noted with temperature and light intensity changes as well as rapid changes from abrupt stimuli. As to whether plants can read thoughts, like some people and dislike others, react to people miles away, or remember an experience, you'll have to devise your own experiments and make your own deductions. But be careful, you may be pleasantly surprised at what you come to see and to believe!

SOUNDS FROM THE GROUND

No matter how long you've been a radio listener, no matter how sophisticated your receiver may be, chances are you're missing out on an entire spectrum of communications and broadcasting stations. Where are the signals from these unheard stations? They circulate in the earth beneath your feet!

It all started more than two-hundred years ago when Ben Franklin and others found that electrical impulses could be sent from one place to another by using the earth itself as the conductor. Later, Samuel Morse succeeded in sending code through the ground. Early in the 1900's, Nathan Stubblefield devised a method of sending audio many miles through the earth's water table. This sparked the interest of many and was the principle behind the first wireless field phones.

The use of underground radio dates back to World War II. Our Army, Navy, and Air Force used it in situations where conventional radio was useless (because of enemy jamming, etc.). Ham operators, forced off the air because of the war, tried underground radio as a secondary system of communications. While the system was found to be less efficient than above-ground radio, some surprising contacts were made.

Backyard Propagation

To get a basic idea of how an underground communications systems works, look at Fig. 2-19. As you can see, the signal to be transmitted (be it radio or otherwise) is fed directly into the earth by

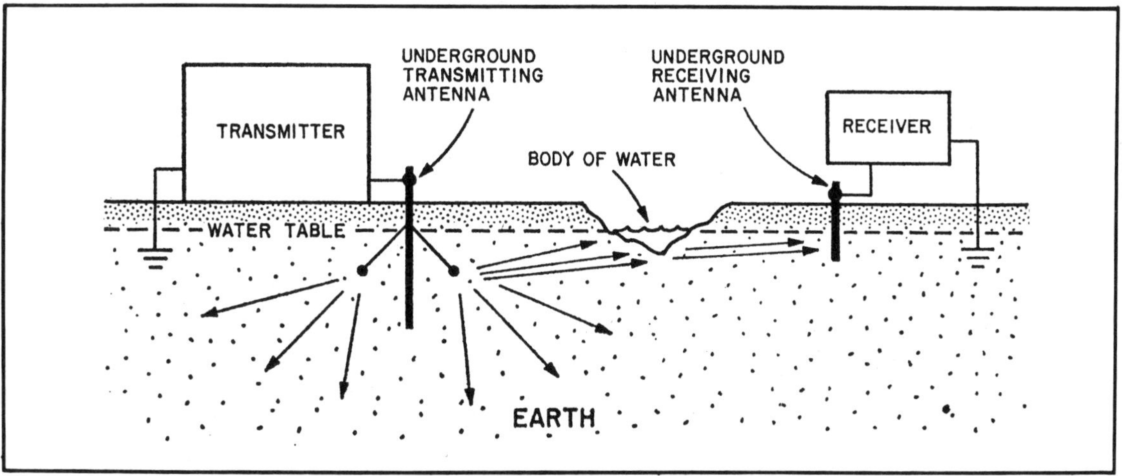

Fig. 2-19. Transmitter is either radio or audio type. Practical receiver is shown right.

way of an underground antenna. Since the earth is a mixture of water and minerals, the soil is a highly conductive medium known as a chemical electrolyte. The signal propagates through the ground just as it would travel in a large, low value resistor. But, unlike a resistor, the resistance of the earth is not the same in all places. This is due to variations in chemical make-up, water content, and temperature. Because of this, the signal is distributed unevenly, with maximum signal in the areas of lowest resistance. Fig. 2-19 shows the high concentration of signal in the wet earth surrounding a body of water. Also shown in Fig. 2-19 is the all-important water table. This is the upper extreme of the earth's zone of saturation, where the space between each grain of soil is completely filled with water. At this point, usually eight feet below the surface, the resistance of the soil is at its lowest, making signal conditions excellent. In fact, the water table is just as important to underground communications as the ionosphere is to above-ground radio. The major requirement for the underground transmitting antenna is that it be buried deep enough to make good contact with the water table.

Putting Your Ear to Ground

It's just as easy to receive underground radio signals as it is to hear the normal variety. In fact, all you need to do is bury your present above-ground antenna! This is absurd, but in theory it would work fine. A more practical approach is to use an "antenna" like the one illustrated in Fig. 2-20. Here, a metal pipe (or rod) is driven into the ground as deep as possible. While the pipe should be long enough to reach the water table, I have had satisfactory results using pipes as short as three feet. The pipe can be of copper, bronze, galvanized steel, or any relatively non-corrosive metal. The surface of the pipe should be bare metal—free from paint or grease. The diameter is not of great importance. On top of the pipe, some type of wire clamp should be mounted. This may be a regular ground clamp or a large self-tapping metal screw.

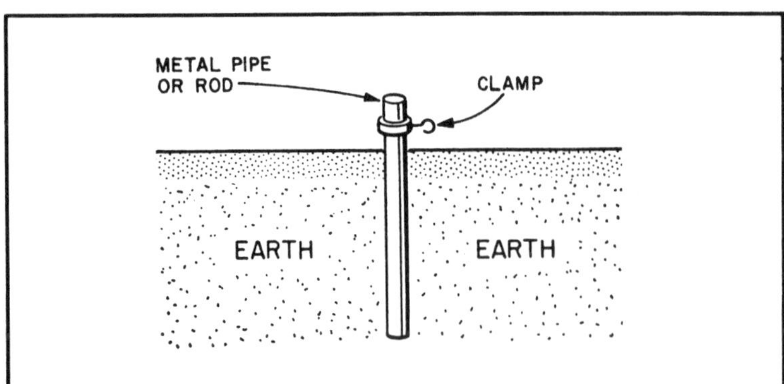

Fig. 2-20. Underground antenna extends into water table for best results.

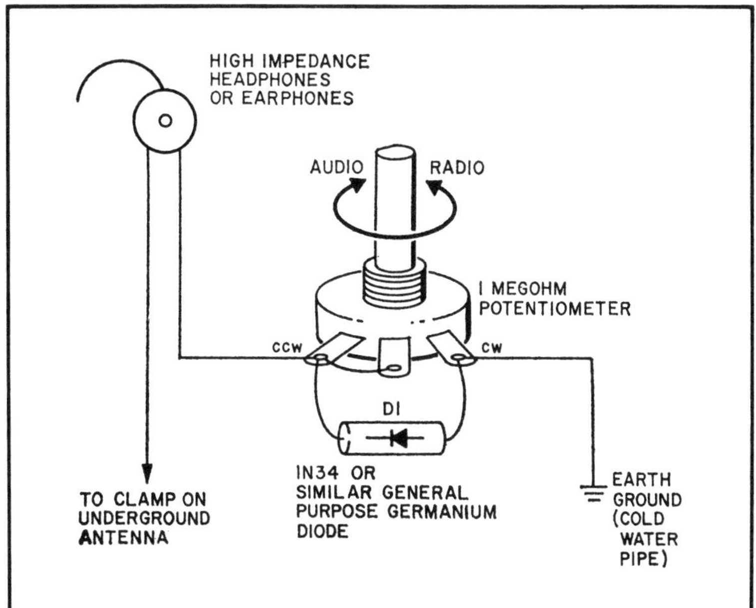

Fig. 2-21. Circuit uses 3 parts. Use this simple circuit to pick up both AF and RF signals from the ground.

The success of your underground reception depends a great deal on the location of your underground antenna. To be effective, the antenna should be driven into an area of high signal concentration. As you know, the mud around a pond or other moist area is an excellent antenna site. But even if there is no such condition around your yard, there are other factors to consider. For example, it has been found that certain types of soil make better electrolytes than others. Soil containing large amounts of refuse material (ashes, cinders, etc.) is the most conductive type. Next best is soil containing adobe, clay, shale, or loam. The least conductive soils are composed mainly of sand and gravel. One final note about the location of your antenna; do not drive your underground antenna into an area which is closer than ten feet from any other ground rod or water pipe. Read on and you'll see why.

Dirt Cheap Receivers

Well, now that you have your underground antenna set up, it's time to start thinking about the receiver. The first thing that comes to mind is to use a standard shortwave radio. But unless your receiver tunes down to around ten or twelve kHz (that's kilohertz), you will be missing out on most of the underground action. Also, the input impedance of most receivers can't be varied enough to stay matched to widely changing ground conditions.

For the past few years, I have been using the simple "receiver" shown in Fig. 2-21 with very good results. When connected to the underground antenna and a good earth ground, the circuit is capable of receiving signals on any frequency, including audio. As shown pictorially, the entire receiver can be built around the connecting lugs on the potentiometer. The sensitivity of the circuit is surprisingly good. Best results have been obtained using a high impedance crystal earphone, although a headset with an impedance of 20,000 ohms or more may be used.

Double-Ground Hookup

For proper operation, the circuit must be connected to a good earth ground (cold water pipe, ground rod, etc.) as well as the clamp on the underground antenna. Any signal which is received has developed a voltage between the receiving antenna and the electrode used as earth ground. This explains why the underground antenna must be separated by at least ten feet from the grounding electrode—otherwise, the incoming signal would be short-circuited by the low resistance of a small patch of earth between them.

If it is desired to have the receiver located far from the underground antenna or grounding electrode, you may run long interconnecting wires. However, if the wires are made longer than fifty feet or so, they will begin to act as above-ground antennas, causing you to pick up local broadcast station interference.

What You Will Hear

With everything connected properly, while listening to the earphone, "tune" R1 through its range until you hear something. Figure 2-21 shows which direction to rotate the shaft on the potentiometer to select either radio or audio signals. If you hear two stations at once, the potentiometer may be adjusted to bring in one over the other to some degree.

Most of the stations you hear will be operating on the Very Low Frequency range and below. All modes of operation are used ranging from CW (code) to AM (voice), including many types of "radiolocation" beacons. Some of what you hear, including most of the beacons, are not intentionally transmitted underground. The extensive antenna grounding methods employed at these low frequencies set up a strong underground signal that travels many miles. One such station to listen for is the Navy's two-million watter operating from Cutler, Maine. The station sends CW on 14.8 kHz. The CW is received as a loud low-pitched hum.

Through the years, I have heard everything from CW and beacons to hard rock on my underground receiver. You must understand that some of what is transmitted underground was sent this way to obtain some degree of privacy. I found this out one hot summer day (when conditions are best) as I casually tuned across a weak signal that seemed to be a three-way telephone call! Well, you'll just have to listen for yourself . . .

Audio? Why Audio?

You may be wondering why the underground receiver was designed to receive audio signals. It seems that there's a new fad among electronics minded Hippies. Recently, they have been feeding their high-power guitar amplifiers into the earth! They tell their local friends to drive a pole into the ground, connect it to the input of their own guitar amplifier (along with a good earth ground), and listen to the speaker!

THERMISTOR THERMOMETER

TRANSDUCERS ARE DEVICES THAT SENSE ENERGY IN ONE FORM and convert it to another form. The thermistor senses changes in temperature and responds with changes in resistance. The changes in resistance can be converted to changes in electrical current in a circuit.

The unit described in this project demonstrates the operation of a thermistor; change in temperature is indicated by a change in electrical meter reading. It was originally designed as a demonstration unit and a conversation piece, but some simple experiments are described here, as well as a method of calibration, which will suit it for use as a laboratory thermometer.

The circuit is shown in Fig. 2-22. R3, the thermistor, is one of the arms of a Wheatstone bridge; R1 in parallel with R2 is another arm, and R4 and R5 are the other arms. The 50-microamp meter M is the bridge null and small temperature change indicator.

The thermistor's resistance is a function of temperature. When temperature increases, the thermistor resistance decreases, and vice versa. A bridge circuit with a sensitive meter will detect smaller temperature changes than a less sensitive one, as the change in resistance for each degree of change in temperature is small.

Construction

Drill the metal case as shown in the layout (Fig. 2-23). Saw the

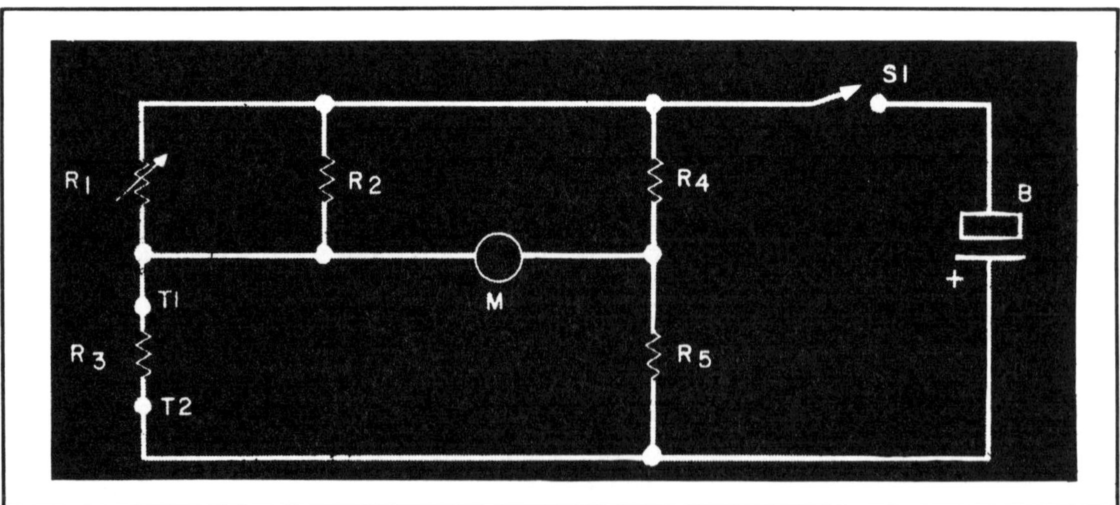

Fig. 2-22. Thermistor thermometer schematic.

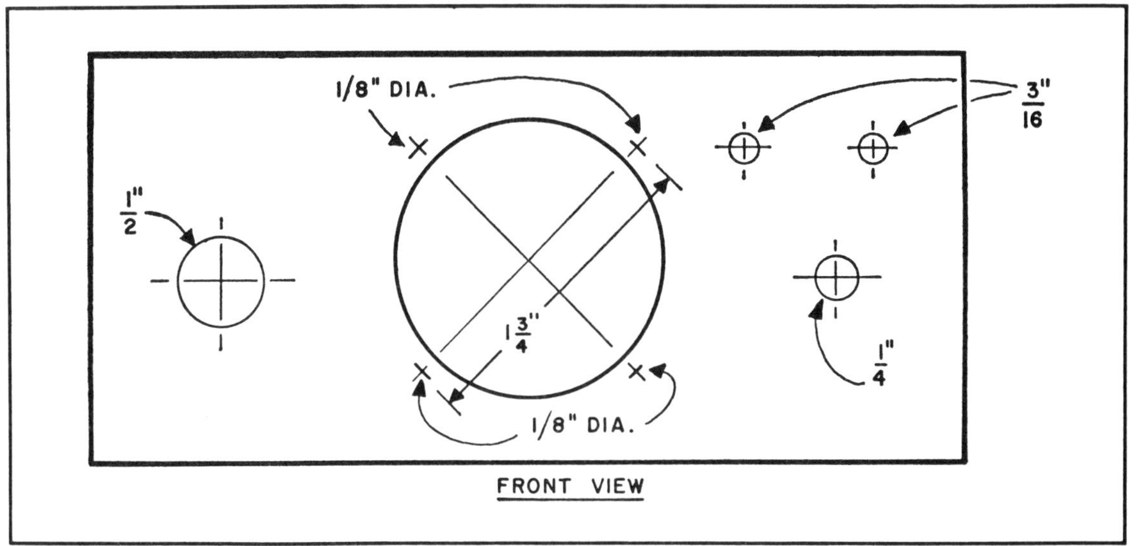

Fig. 2-23. Design layout.

shaft of R1 to a length of 3/8 in. Mount the switch S1, the potentiometer R1, the terminals T1 and T2, and the meter M on the front panel of the case (see Fig. 2-24). T1 and T2 must be insulated from the panel.

Mount the battery holder on the back panel (see Fig. 2-25). Wire the instrument with the help of Figs. 2-22, 2-24 and 2-25.

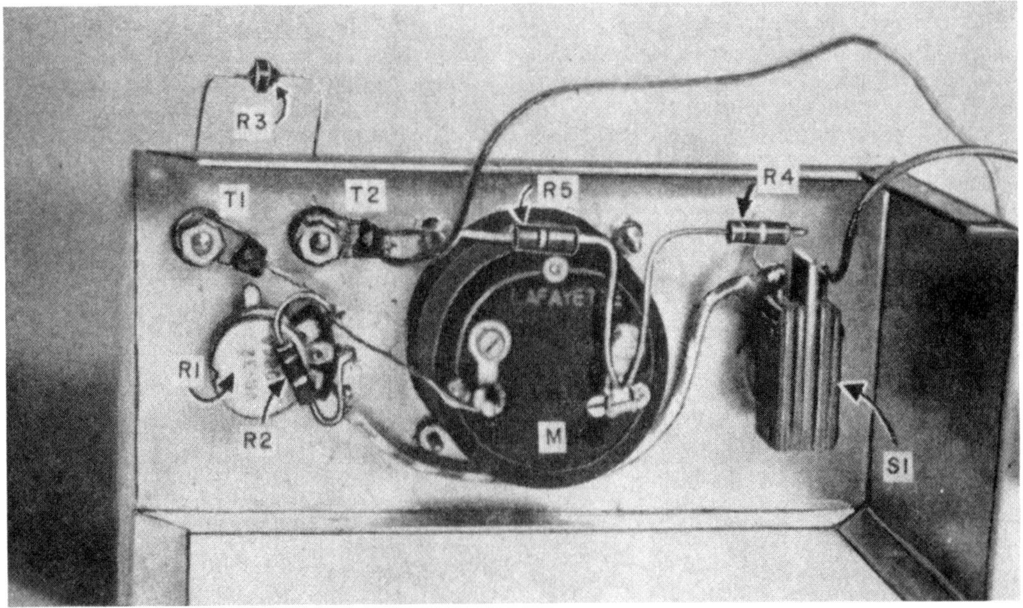

Fig. 2-24. Interior view showing components and wiring.

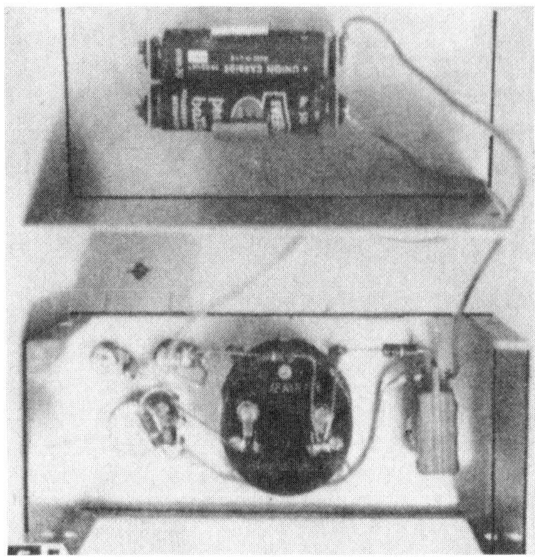

Fig. 2-25. Mount batteries on the back of the case.

Uses

Fasten the thermistor R3 in the terminals T1 and T2. Turn the instrument on and adjust R1 for mid-scale meter deflection.

Now, touch the thermistor: the meter reading should increase. If the meter reading decreases, reverse the meter connections. In other words, the meter deflection should be in the direction of temperature change.

The terminals T1 and T2 have been provided so the thermistor can be used for remote temperature reading. Attach wire leads of the required lengths for the desired application.

One experimental demonstration is to show the change in meter reading when the thermometer is touched with the hand or an ice cube; another is to place a drop of cigarette lighter fluid on the thermistor, and note the cooling effect as the fluid evaporates. If the thermistor is placed at the focus of a parabolic reflector, the instrument may be used as an infrared detector. The sensitivity is limited, however.

If you care to calibrate the thermometer, you can use it as an experimental quantitative instrument.

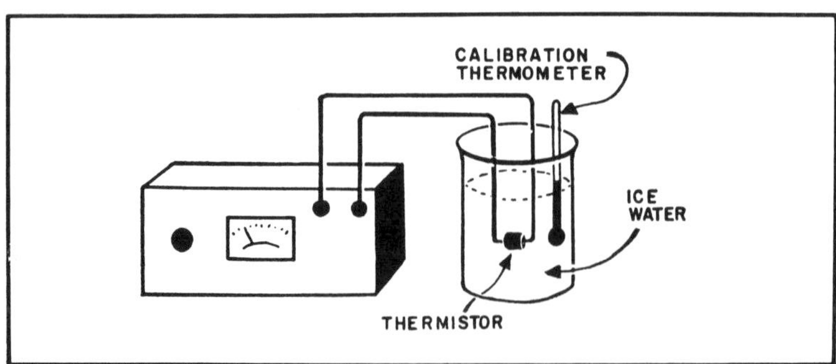

Fig. 2-26. Thermistor thermometer bridge.

Fig. 2-27. Energy changes are clearly indicated on the meter.

Calibration

This requires calibration of R1. With a triangular file, make a groove in the edge of the knob. Fill the groove with contrasting India ink to provide an index. Prepare a paper scale with a 1-in. diameter circle marked on it, and fasten it to the case with Carter's rubber cement.

Place the thermistor (equipped with extension leads connected to T1 and T2) in ice water (Fig. 2-26). Adjust R1 for zero meter reading, and place a calibration mark on the paper scale and mark it 0 (for zero degrees Centigrade).

Heat the water gradually, stirring constantly, until the meter deflects full scale. Adjust R1 for zero meter reading, note the calibration thermometer reading, and enter it beside the calibration mark for the new R1 setting. Repeat this process up to boiling point of the water, and R1 will be calibrated in steps.

Reading the R1 setting plus the interpolated value of the meter reading to the next higher R1 calibration will give you the temperature. The precision of the instrument will approach that of the calibration thermometer used (See Fig. 2-27 and Table 2-4).

Table 2-4. Materials List—Thermistor Thermometer.

Desig.	Description
R1	1K miniature potentiometer (Lafayette VC-32)
R2	2.7K, 1/2-w. carbon resistor, 10%
R3	400 ohm thermistor (VECO 23E3) or 500 ohm thermistor (Glennite 25TD2)
R4, R5	100 ohm, 1/2-w. carbon resistor, 10%
M	0-50 microamp. square meter (Lafayette TM-200)
S1	SPST toggle switch (Lafayette SW-21)
T1, T2	5-way binding posts (Lafayette MS-566, kit of 10)
B1	2 1.5-v. penlite cells connected in series (Eveready 915)
Misc.	2-cell battery holder (Lafayette MS-181) 2 1/4 × 2 1/4 × 5″ aluminum minibox (Premier MC-379) miniature knob (Lafayette MS-185)
	Parts for this project are available from Lafayette Radio, 111 Jericho Turnpike, Syosset, L. I., N.Y.

HOUNDOG: THE ELECTRONIC METAL DETECTOR

One of the problems with the hobby of treasure-hunting is that much more money has been spent looking for treasure than the value actually found. One of the best ways to balance the books is to start out as inexpensively as possible, and that opportunity is provided by Houndog, a relatively simple and inexpensive metal detection device. Houndog can sniff out metal objects as small as a penny buried as deep as 3 to 5-inches, and will operate reliably for up to a year on one 9-volt transistor battery.

Operational Principle

Houndog's "nose" consists of three large inductance coils which, when placed in proximity with a conductive metal will exhibit a change in their total inductance value, the change being read by the circuitry and translated into an audible signal. In short, when Houndog "barks," it's time to start digging.

The Circuit

The heart of the circuit is U1, an audio amplifier, whose differential inputs are fed by a bridge circuit consisting of L1, L2, and R7, fed through R6A and R6B. U1's output is coupled to L3 by either C1 or C1 and C2, depending upon the setting of sensitivity switch S1. The placement of L1, L2 and L3 is such that the total field set up in L1 and L2 by current flowing in L3 is effectively zero. Therefore, the inputs to the amplifier are equal and opposite (zero), and its output will be zero. See Figs. 2-28 through 2-32 and Table 2-5.

When a conductive metal enters the field, it changes the distribution to the effect that the field across L1 and L2 is no longer zero, and a voltage appears across the amplifier's inputs. The coil

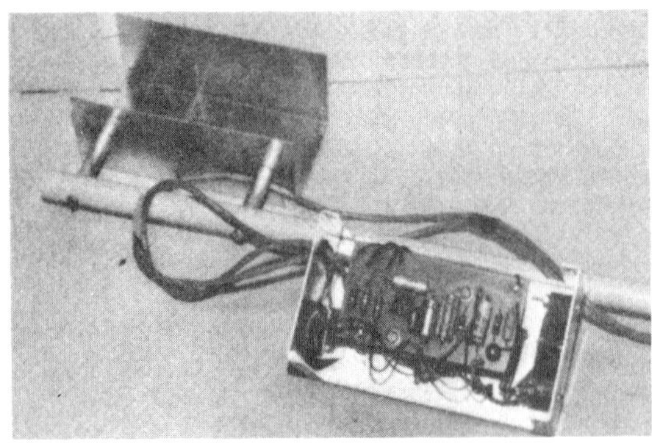

Fig. 2-28. This photo shows the circuit board mounted in the cabinet, and the method used for attaching the cabinet cover to the handle.

Fig. 2-29. Closeup of the search head shows the position of coils L1/L2 and L3, and their respective overlaps as described in the text.

connections are such that when this condition exists, the positive input voltage is in phase with that of the output, and the circuit oscillates. The signal is fed to Q1, causing it to turn on, allowing current to flow to buzzer BZ1, creating Houndog's "bark."

Because the coils used in Houndog are designed to be hand-wound, and also due to the effects of stray capacitance and noise generated internally in the circuit itself, a feedback loop has been included

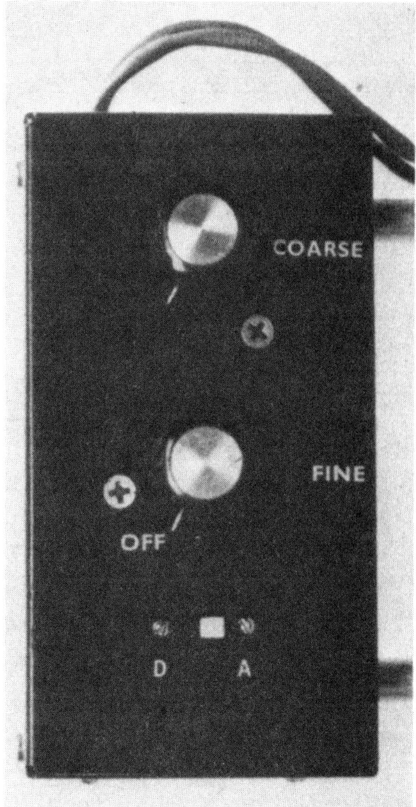

Fig. 2-30. Houndog's control head is laid out simply—there's an SPDT switch and two adjustments.

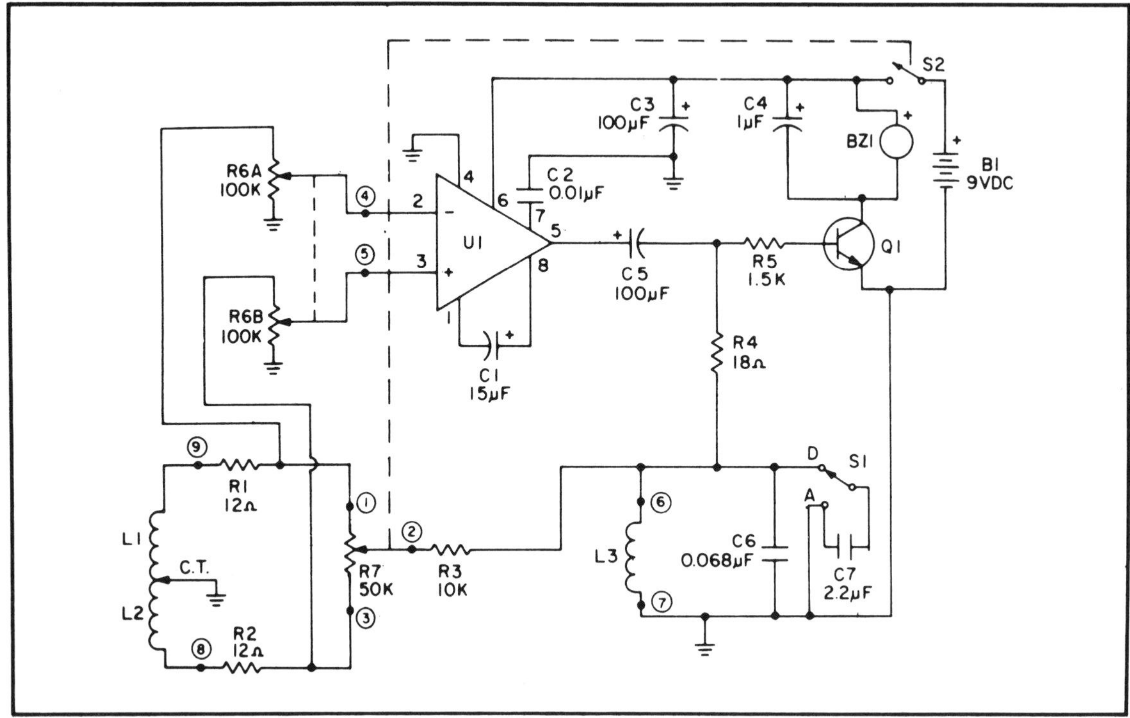

Fig. 2-31. Houndog schematic.

(through R7) which will allow the user to keep Houndog from sounding off due to false signals caused by variations from the theoretically perfect zero field.

Construction

There are actually two steps involved in the assembly of the Houndog; wiring the PC board for the control circuitry, and the construction of the coils for the search head (which we'll discuss later). With the exception of C7, the potentiometers, the switches and BZ1, all components mount directly on the PC board, as indicated in Fig. 2-33. C7 is soldered directly to the terminals of S1, and the potentiometers and switches and the buzzer are mounted to the aluminum or plastic chassis. As always, pay careful attention to the polarities of the electrolytic capacitors during installation. Although not completely necessary, use of an IC socket for U1 is recommended.

The circled numbers appearing on the schematic (Fig. 2-31) and parts layout guide (Fig. 2-33) are for keying up the connections to the off-board components. It is not necessary for you to etch the numbers onto the PC board, so long as you refer to them during the final wiring stages.

To assist you in construction of the coils (L1, L2 and L3), we have

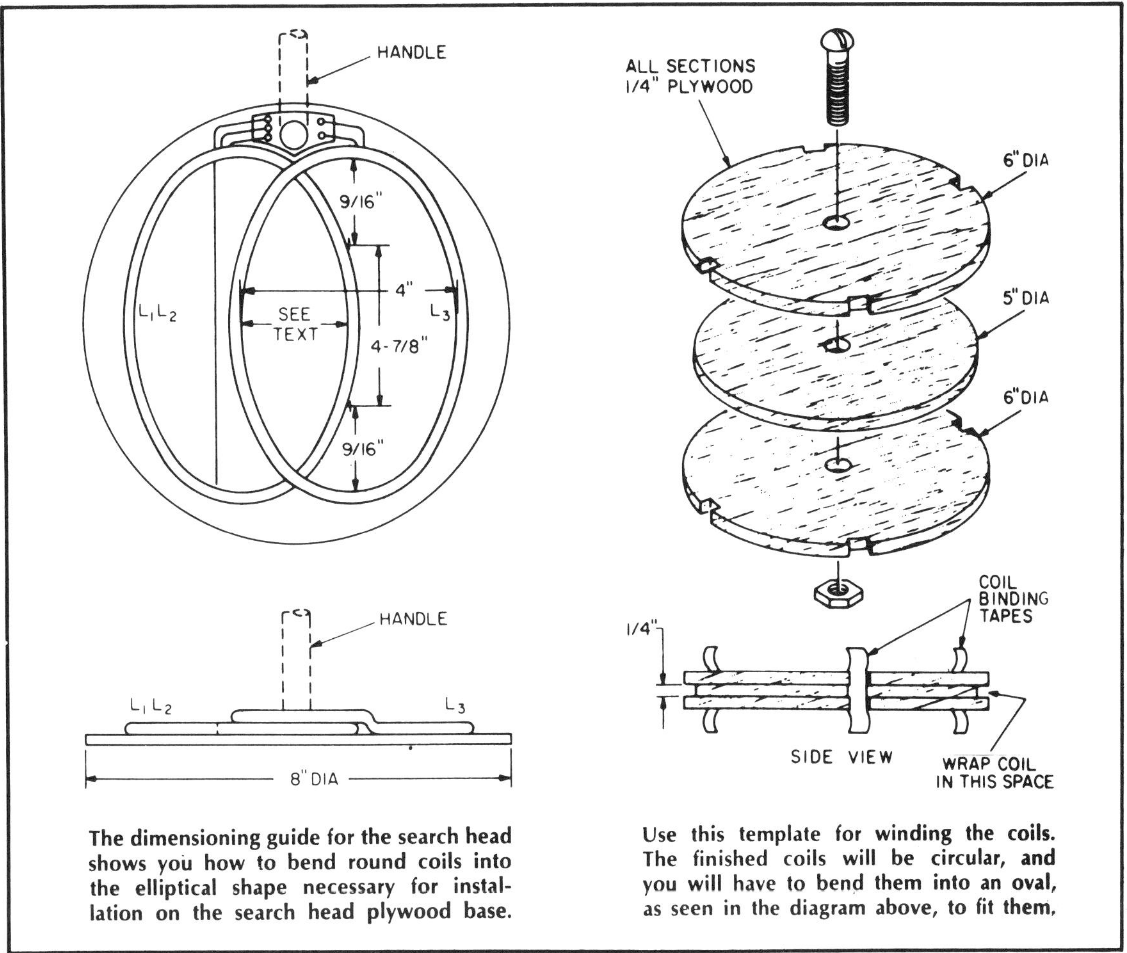
HANDLE
ALL SECTIONS
1/4" PLYWOOD
6" DIA
9/16"
4"
L1 L2
SEE
TEXT
L3
4-7/8"
5" DIA
6" DIA
9/16"
COIL
BINDING
TAPES
HANDLE
1/4"
L1 L2
L3
8" DIA
SIDE VIEW
WRAP COIL
IN THIS SPACE
The dimensioning guide for the search head shows you how to bend round coils into the elliptical shape necessary for installation on the search head plywood base.
Use this template for winding the coils. The finished coils will be circular, and you will have to bend them into an oval, as seen in the diagram above, to fit them.

Fig. 2-32. Search head assembly.

provided a diagram of a coil form which may be cut from plywood. This, at the very least, will allow you to wind L1/L2 and L3 to the same basic dimension, which is about the only critical factor (outside of getting the number of turns of wire correct) in the construction of the search head.

When winding L1/L2, rather than winding two sets of 30 turns each, we suggest that at turn 30 of L1, you scrape away a bit of the insulation and solder the ground tap in, wrap the solder junction with a small bit of tape, and then begin the next 30 turns for L2. This provides a stronger final assembly, and less of an alignment problem (you now need deal only with aligning two coils instead of three).

When the coils are completely wound, bind them with tape before removing them from the form. This will help to hold their shape until they are installed on the search head.

Table 2-5. Parts List for Houndog.

B1—9-VDC transistor battery
BZ1-piezoelectric buzzer (Radio Shack #273-060)
C1—15-μF, 15-VDC electrolytic capacitor
C2—0.01-μF, 50-VDC ceramic capacitor
C3, C5-100-μF, 35-VDC electrolytic capacitor
C4—1-μF, 35-VDC electrolytic capacitor
C6—0.068-μF, 25-VDC mylar capacitor
C7—2.2-μF, 35-VDC non-polarized electrolytic capacitor
L1, L2—30 turns of #20 enameled copper wire—see text
L3—60 turns of #20 enameled copper wire
Q1—2N5210 NPN low-level transistor
R1, R2-12-ohm, 1/2-watt resistor, 10%
R3—10,000-ohm, 1/2-watt resistor, 10%
R4—18-ohm, 1/2-watt resistor, 10%
R5—1,500-ohm, 1/2-watt resistor, 10%
R6A/R6B—dual-section 100,000-ohm linear-taper potentiometer
R7—50,000-ohm linear-taper potentiometer with SPST switch (S2)
S1—SPDT slide switch
S2—SPST rotary switch (part of R7)
U1—LM386 audio amp integrated circuit
Misc.—battery clip, aluminum chassis, hookup wire, solder, spacers, knobs, 100-foot roll of #20 enameled copper wire, weatherproofing finisher (varnish, shellac, polyurethane, etc.), nonmetallic support rod, 10-feet of 2-conductor shielded wire, 10 feet of 1-conductor shielded wire, 1/4-inch plywood stock, etc.

A complete parts kit for Houndog including pre-etched PC board and all components (but less case) is available from Niccum Electronics, Rte. 3, Box 271B, Stroud, OK 74079. Price for the complete kit is $24.50; a pre-etched and labeled PC board is only $5.50. No CODs, please.

Final Assembly/Calibration

Before permanently attaching the coils to the plywood head, it is best to tack them down temporarily with either tape or rubber cement (for obvious reasons, no metal fasteners can be used now or during the final attachment).

Connect L1/L2 to the PC board with 2-conductor shielded wire, attaching the inner conductors to the outside ends of L1 and L2 (points 8 and 9), and using the braided shield for the center tap ground connection. The shield should be grounded to circuit ground on the PC board. Single conductor shielded wire is used for the connection of L3 to the circuit, with the braided shield used for the grounded side of the coil. Solder the braid to circuit ground on the PC board as you did for L1/L2.

Set R6A/R6B to a two-thirds clockwise position, and set R7 to its midpoint. When you throw power switch S2 on, the buzzer should not sound. If it does, reverse the L3 connections at the coil end and try again. Slowly reduce the amount of overlap between the two coils until the buzzer sounds. At this point, backing off counter-clockwise on R6A/R6B should cause the buzzer to silence. If this is the case, carefully mark the position of the two coils, and prepare to attach them permanently to the search head.

As a final test, return R6A/R6B to the two-thirds position, set R7 just below the point where the buzzer sounds, and S1 to the "discriminate" position. Bring a penny directly above the coils' overlap, and lower it to a height of about 3-inches above the coils. If the buzzer does not sound, try re-peaking R6A/R6B and R7 for a lower

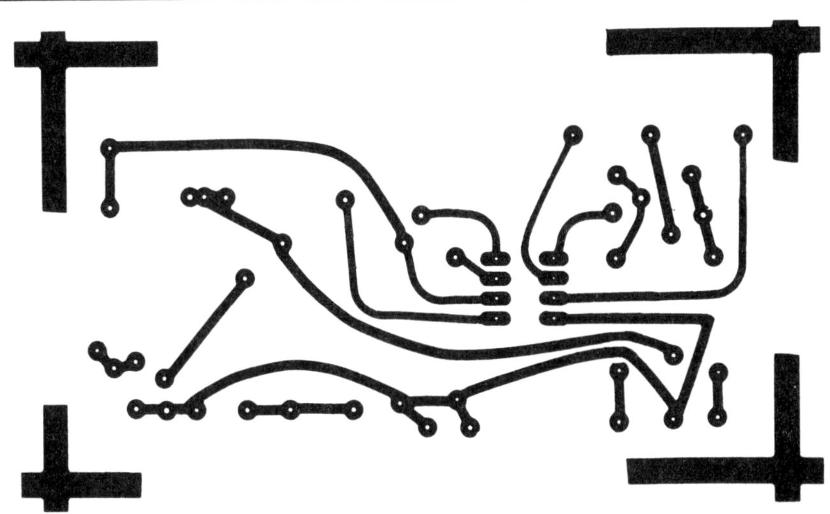

Here is the full scale etching guide for Houndog's PC board. If you purchase a Niccum PC board, the layout may differ slightly. Follow their assembly instructions for it.

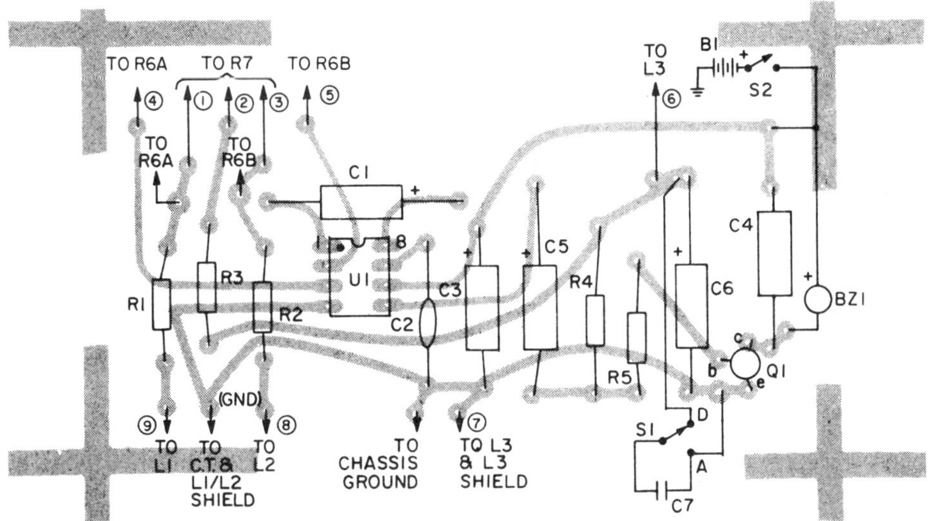

The component layout guide gives you the connections for the off-board components. If you use another method of assembly, rest assured that parts layout isn't critical.

Fig. 2-33. PC board layout.

threshold (increase R6A/R6B more clockwise, while backing off more on R7 to stop oscillation) and repeat the procedure. Three inches should be the minimum distance at which Houndog detects the presence of the penny.

Remember that when conducting these tests, you should be in an area free from the presence of large metallic objects, such as radiators, pipes and ducts, etc. Their presence may cause you to set the sensitivity of R6A/R6B too low, making actual measurements against coins ineffective to the point of believing that the unit is not working.

You may now attach the coils to the head in a permanent manner with epoxy or several coats of polyurethane or shellac, in order to affix the coils firmly and make the assembly weatherproof.

Conclusion

Once you get out of doors with Houndog, it might be wise to bury some treasure of your own, and adjust the controls for maximum sensitivity depending upon the type of soil found in your locality. These adjustments will vary from area to area, depending upon soil composition, which is why we haven't used a calibrated dial for the potentiometers. Don't be discouraged if your first few hours of searching with S1 set to the "discriminate" (coins) position don't unearth Captain Kidd's treasure chest. With S1 set in the "all" position, you'll get a lot more "barks," but you might find a lot of tin cans and beer can pull-tops for your efforts. Patience is a virtue in this hobby.

GRANDPA'S WHISKER

IN THE BEGINNING OF THIS CENTURY, WHEN RADIO WAS STILL called "wireless," the crystal set was used by most of the early radio pioneers. The simple "catwhisker" touching a piece of galena or silicon crystal, and a coil wound on an oatmeal box, formed a primitive yet effective radio receiver that stayed popular for many years. Even the later development of the vacuum tube could not entirely bury the crystal set; it still remained popular as a first set for many radio experimenters who later went on to more complicated electronic developments. Even today, the simple crystal set is still being built using modern germanium or silicon diodes in place of the moveable catwhisker and crystal.

Back in the old days, the popular galena and silicon crystals had a rival for the more specialized ship-to-shore communication work. It was the carborundum crystal detector. The carborundum crystal detector did not require a light touch with the catwhisker, but instead required a heavy contact pressure. This heavy catwhisker pressure was more suitable for the early radio stations on ships. The lesser sensitivity of the carborundum detector was compensated by the crystal's ability to take stronger radio signal energy (such as leakage from nearby spark transmitters) without burning out, than the galena and silicon crystals could. What is really different about the carborundum detector, is the requirement for a bias battery. This bias battery is normally not used with galena and silicon crystals.

You can experiment with the carborundum detector by building our Grandpa's Whisker, which is patterned after the early crystal sets. The receiver uses a tapped coil and two variable capacitors (one capacitor tunes the antenna) to allow coverage of the entire broadcast band and for maximum signal coupling to the detector. A separate assembly is provided for the carborundum detector and a control is mounted for convenient adjustment of bias battery voltage for maximum detector sensitivity. The receiver is built "breadboard style" on a 8 1/2-inch by 7 1/4-inch by 3/4-inch wood base which is similar to the style of construction used by early radio experimenters.

The Receiver Circuit

Signals from the antenna are fed through J1 and coupled through C1A-C1B to the parallel tuned circuit of L1-C2. C1A-C1B is in a series tuned circuit with L1, and serves to tune the antenna for maximum rf current flow. The resultant tuned signals are detected by D1 and the audio is fed through the R1 bypass C3 to J5-J6 and external headphones. R1 adjusts the D1 bias voltage from B1 and C4 is the rf bypass for the headphones.

Carborundum

Not a natural mineral like galena or silicon, carborundum is the name given to a compound of silicon carbide by its American inventor Edward Goodrich Acheson (a former assistant of Thomas Edison), Acheson was experimenting with a primitive electric furnace in 1891, when he fused a mixture of clay and powdered carbon. He found that the resultant crystals would cut glass similarly to a diamond (silicon carbide is next to a diamond in hardness), and he called his discovery Carborundum; thinking it was a substance composed of carbon and corundum (a crystalized form of alumina). Scientific analysis later showed it to be silicon carbide, but the designation Carborundum was kept as a trade name. Industrial usage of carborundum is primarily grinding compounds and grinding wheels.

Its use as a detector was discovered by experimenters around the beginning of this century who tried various minerals and substances in their search for better types of radio wave detectors; much as Edison tested many materials in his search for the proper material for his incandescent lamp filament.

A crystal diode has a high current flow with voltage applied so that it conducts in the forward direction (catwhisker to crystal), and a very low current flow in the reverse direction. The amount of current flow in the forward direction depends upon the characteristics of the crystal material and the applied forward voltage. As shown in Fig. 2-34, Germanium minimum voltage is approximately 0.3 V, Silicon is 0.6 V, and Carborundum is 3 V. (The high Carborundum voltage is the reason why a bias battery is necessary to move the threshold down so that the weak rf signal voltages can be detected.)

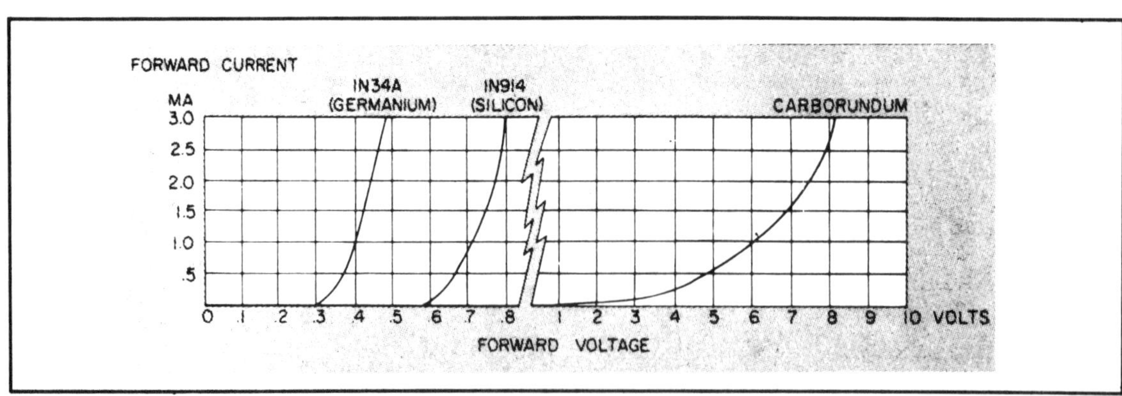

Fig. 2-34. As you can see, the minimum forward voltage for carborundum to forward conduct is very nearly ten times that for germanium. This is the reason that our Grandpa's Whisker requires a bias battery. Moving the threshold down allows weak RF signals to be detected.

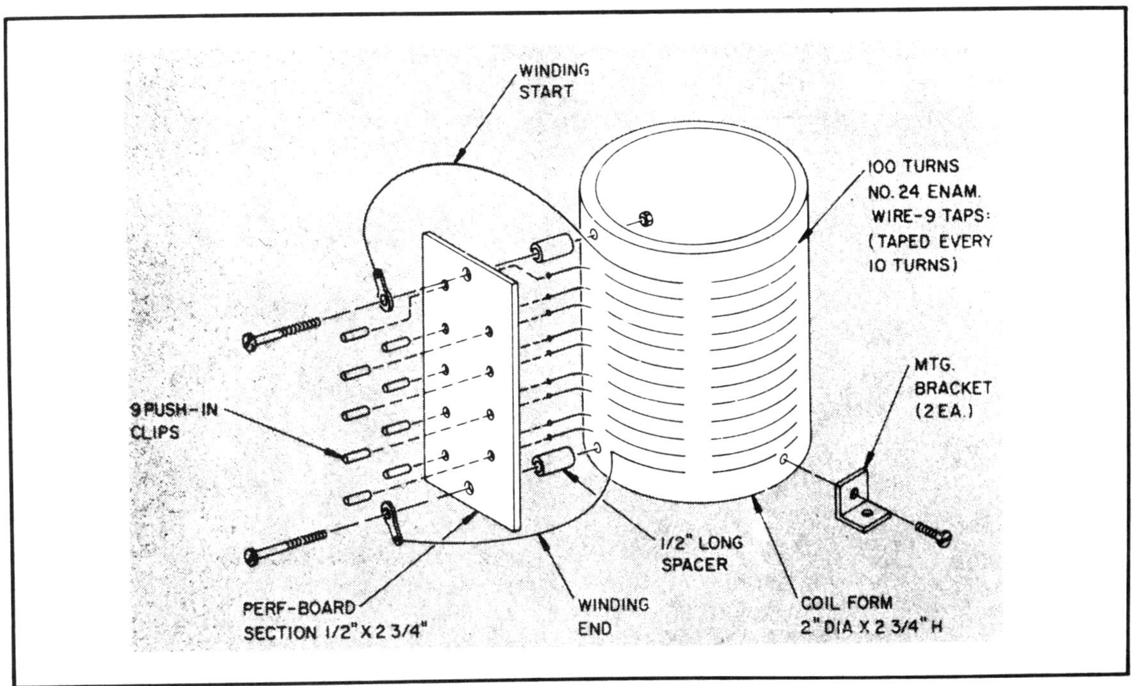

Fig. 2-35. The tuning coil is wound on a cardboard mailing tube section for 100 turns of #24 enameled wire, tapped every ten turns. The taps should be stripped bare with sandpaper before soldering to the clips which are mounted on a section of perfboard. See the text.

Tuning Coil (L1) Construction

Look at Fig. 2-35 (L1 construction details). The tuning coil is wound on a cardboard mailing tube section 2-inches in diameter and 2 3/4-inches long. Start winding approximately 1/4-inch from the form edge with #24 enameled copper wire. Punch a small hole to feed the wire into the cardboard before you start winding, then wrap the wire around the edge of the form to hold it in place while winding; or, a section of plastic tape can be used to keep the wire from moving.

As shown in Fig. 2-35, the tuning coil is wound with 100 turns and is tapped every 10 turns. An easy way to make the taps is to twist the wire together for a half-inch and position the free end out. Then, when all of the taps have been made, use sandpaper to take the enamel off the tap-wire ends. At the end of the winding, punch another hole in the coil form and after cutting a three-inch lead, thread the free end of the coil wire through the hole and wrap it one turn around the coil form edge (or tape it in place).

Mount 9 push-in clips in a 1/2-inch by 2 1/4-inch perfboard section and mount it on the coil form with machine screws and nuts and two 1/2-inch long spacers (as shown in Fig. 2-35). Then solder the coil taps to the push-in clubs. Connect the coil start and end wire leads to solder lugs mounted on the perfboard screws. Punch two holes on opposite sides of the base of the coil form, mount two brackets, and the tuning coil is completed.

Detector Assembly Construction

Most of the crystal detector assemblies available nowadays are of a horizontal type; designed for fine adjustment of a galena crystal. The carborundum crystal requires a heavier catwhisker pressure than the galena crystal, so the detector assembly (as shown in Fig. 2-36) is constructed in a vertical configuration.

Begin construction by cutting a 2-inch × 3/4-inch × 1/4-inch wood section, and then gluing or using wood screws to fasten it to a 2 1/2-inch diameter × 1/4-inch high wood base. This wood base is readily available from art, or hobby, supply stores that stock wood plaques. Or, a suitable base can be cut out of a section of plywood. The dimensions of the detector assembly are not critical and should be modified as necessary to fit your particular crystal mount and catwhisker configuration. If necessary, the rivets holding the catwhisker mount to a metal strip can be drilled or ground out, and then reassembled with a solder lug as shown in Fig. 2-36.

Mount the crystal holder on the base of the detector as shown in Fig. 2-36 and then mount the catwhisker assembly on the vertical section with small wood screws, or machine screws and nuts. Make sure that the crystal holder screws do not protrude below the base bottom. Connect a lead between a solder lug on the catwhisker assembly and a terminal clip mounted on the base. If the crystal cup does not have an attached metal strip and terminal clip as in our model, it will be necessary to mount a solder lug with the cup and connect a lead to a terminal clip mounted on the base. See Fig. 2-37 and Table 2-6.

Receiver Construction

Most of the receiver components are mounted on a 8 1/2-in. × 7 1/4-in. × 3/4-in. wood base. The base dimensions are not critical and any size wood base can be used that will be large enough to mount the components. The model wood base shown was obtained from an art supply store and was originally intended for use as a wood plaque. Small wood screws were used to hold most of the components on the base, except the variable capacitors C1A-C1B and C2 are mounted with machine screws in countersunk holes drilled through the base bottom. If the particular capacitors in your model do not have tapped bottom holes, metal brackets must be fabricated to fit either front or back capacitor mounting holes. The Bias Adjustment Control R1 is also mounted on the wood base with a metal bracket.

Begin construction by locating the component mounting holes on the wood base, and then mounting the parts as shown in Fig. 2-38.

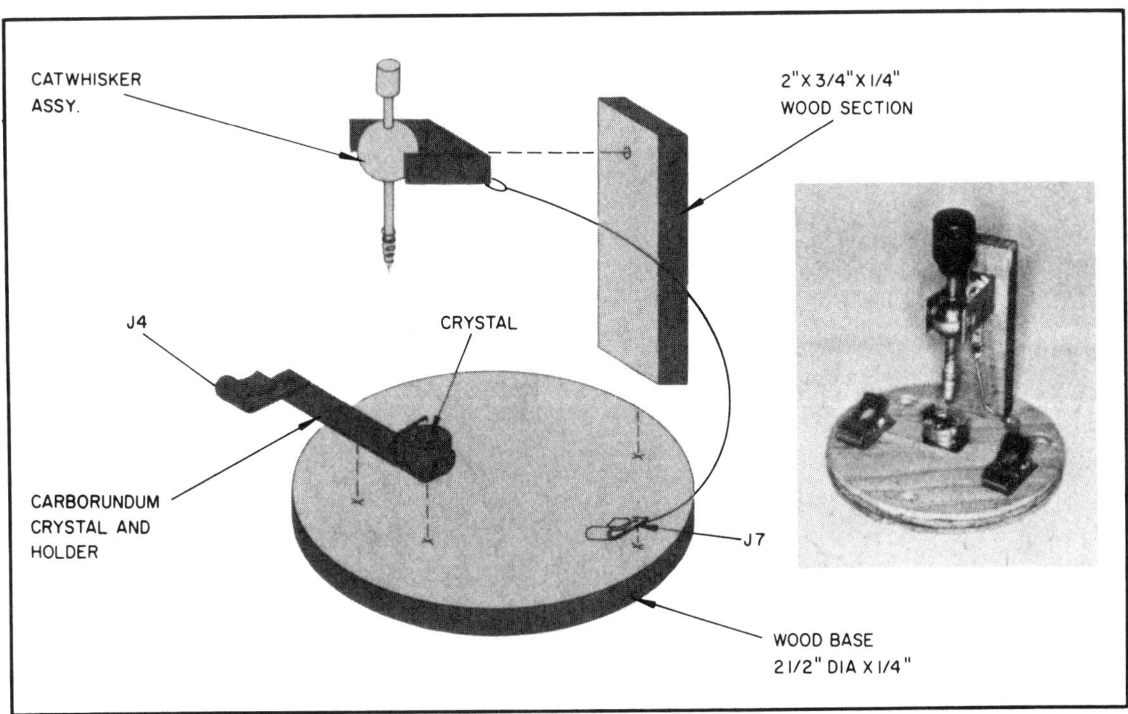

Fig. 2-36. Most of the crystal detector assemblies you can turn up will be of the horizontal type. You will need a heavier pressure for the carborundum crystal, so convert the assemblage to a vertical format. None of the dimensions shown are all that critical.

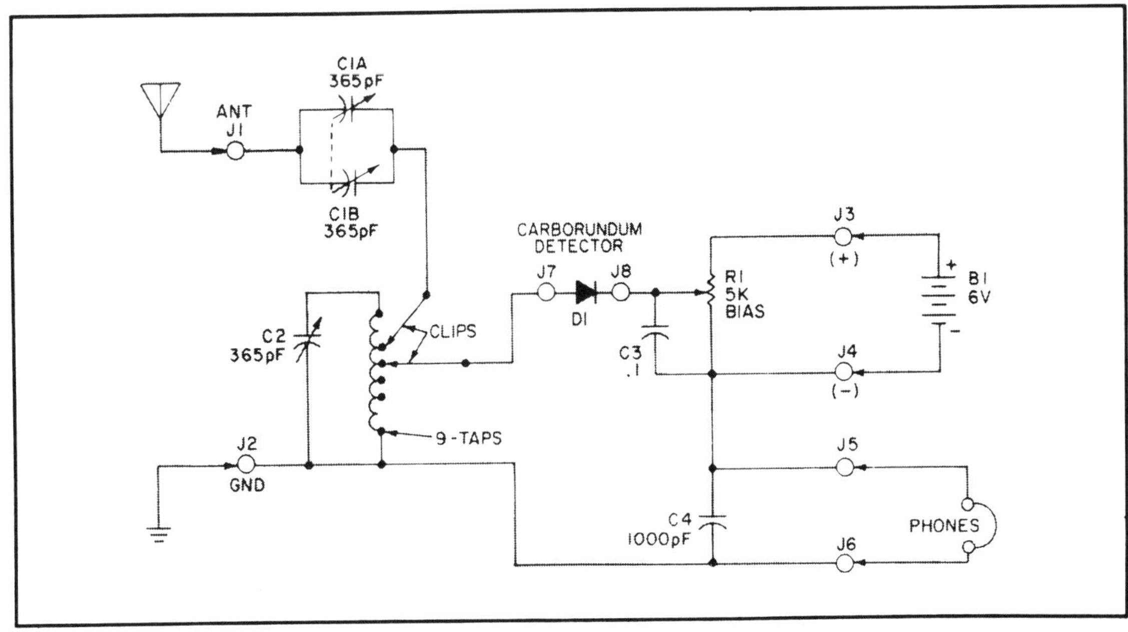

Fig. 2-37. Grandpa's Whisker schematic.

Table 2-6. Parts List for Grandpa's Whisker.

B1—6 V battery
C1A-C1B—Dual 365-pF tuning capacitor (dual gang)
C2—365 pF tuning capacitor (single gang)
C3—0.1-μF capacitor
C4-1000-pF capacitor
D1—Carborundum Crystal (Modern Radio Labs, P.O. Box 1477, Garden Grove, CA 92642), and Crystal Detector Assembly (Philmore #7003 open type detector, or equiv.)
J1-J8—Fahnestock Clips
L1—See drawing and text
R1—5,000-ohm potentiometer. (linear taper)
MISC: 2000-ohm earphones, 2 3/4-in. × 2-in. dia. coil form, clips, #24 enam. wire, 1/2-in. long spacers, perfboard strip, push-in clips, solder lugs, mtg. brackets, wood sections for detector assembly, knobs, 8 1/2-in. × 7 1/4-in. × 3/4-in. wood base, hook-up wire, wood screws, headphones (2000-ohms), and a 1N34A germanium diode (or equiv.) for initial adjustment of the receiver.

Install solder lugs on all of the terminals J1 to J6 and also on the metal frames (rotors) of the variable capacitors C1A-C1B and C2. Install the detector assembly with three wood screws to the wood base and then install L1 positioned as shown in Fig. 2-38 (with the taps facing the detector assembly).

Wire the components as shown in Fig. 2-37 and position the wiring for short, direct connections. Install a clip on the lead to C1A-C1B and also on a lead to J7 of the Detector Assembly (the connection to the catwhisker). These clips will be connected to the coil taps during operation of the receiver. Install knobs on the variable capacitors and also on the Bias Adjustment Control, then mark the terminals with rub-on lettering or with small slips of typed, paper designations cemented on to the board.

Operation

All types of crystal set receivers require a good, outside antenna and a good ground for best results. If you are located near a high-power radio station, an inside antenna and a waterpipe ground will probably work. For distant stations, an outside antenna, 50 to 100 feet long will be necessary. Check the mail order houses for supplies and antenna kits.

The taps on L1 are provided to compensate for antenna loading as well as for the loading effect of the carborundum detector. The position of the clip leads on the coil taps must be determined by experiment as they will vary according to the length (loading) of your antenna and the frequency of the radio station being received. Inasmuch as the carborundum detector also requires adjustment (both in determining a sensitive crystal point and in the proper bias voltage adjustment), a saving in initial L1 tap set-up time can be achieved with the use of a fixed crystal diode (1N34A, or equivalent germanium type).

CAUTION. *Make sure that the battery is disconnected for this initial adjustment.*

Fig. 2-38. Grandpa's Whisker is a nostalgic look back at the days when a ship's radio lifeline to shore was dependent on no more than a coil, a battery, a catwhisker, and carborundum.

Connect an antenna to J1, a ground to J2, and a pair of high-impedance headphones to J5 and J6. A pair of 2000-ohm phones was used with our model; do not use low impedance headphones (8, or 16 ohm stereo types). Do not connect the 6-volt battery at this time.

Make sure that the catwhisker is not touching the crystal or the crystal cup (open circuit to the carborundum crystal), and then connect the crystal diode across J7 and J8 (the polarity is not important; it will work either way). Connect both of the clip leads (lead to J8 and lead to C1A-C1B) to L1 coil taps; any of the mid-coil taps will do for an initial start. Set C1A-C1B to mid-capacity range and then tune C2 until you hear a radio station in the headphones. Readjust the setting of C1A-C1B for best headphone volume. Then readjust each one of the clip leads for best headphone volume of the received radio station. All of the adjustments and coil tap settings will interact, and will require careful retuning of both C1A-C1B and C2 for best results.

When a radio station is tuned in for best headphone volume, carefully disconnect the germanium crystal diode from J7 and J8 without disturbing the tuning capacitor settings or the positions of the L1 tap connections. Then place a carborundum crystal in the detector assembly and connect the 6-volt battery to J4 (negative lead) and J3 (positive lead). Adjust the catwhisker until it touches the carborundum surface and then set the bias control R1 to mid-range.

Carefully adjust the catwhisker for a sensitive spot on the crystal surface at the same time adjusting R1 for best volume of received signal. If this seems like a lot of trouble to hear a radio station, remember the radio pioneers around the turn of the century would spend considerable time with equipment even cruder than Grandpa's Whisker in order to capture the elusive wireless signals. After a station is found with the carborundum detector, it may be possible to achieve a bit more received volume by readjusting the coil taps and tuning capacitors.

You can experiment with different types of silicon and germanium crystals as well as other materials with this circuit; but remember, do not use the battery unless it is with a carborundum crystal. The battery will burn out the more conventional germanium and silicon crystals. You can also try chips of carborundum broken off of sharpening stones, etc. and held with melted solder or lead. Or you can also try packing the crystals with sections of crumpled aluminum or lead foil in place of the melted lead bodies. The received crystal set volume will vary according to the type of crystal used; generally germanium will be loudest, and silicon a bit less, and the carborundum crystal will usually be lower in volume.

SOLAR SWINGER

HAVE YOU EVER SEEN A MODEL SHIP INSIDE A BOTTLE? THE next logical step is to build a small radio inside of a radio or TV vacuum tube! We call it the Solar Swinger and it has no on/off switch, batteries or power supply. If you want to turn the Solar Swinger off, just place a cap or hood over the tube. You may want to let it play all the time—it doesn't hurt a thing. No need to worry about batteries running down, for the little radio is solar powered. It will operate in the sun, shaded daylight or under a desk lamp in the evening. Of course, the radio won't blast your ear drums with music, but you can listen to local AM broadcast stations with ease.

Tube Preparation

Select a defective radio or TV tube with a bakelite base. The larger the glass tube, the greater building area for the small radio components. An antique radio tube is ideal, but not necessary. If you can't find one in the junk box, check with your local Radio-TV shop—they may throw out several hundred of these old tubes every year.

There are many old power output tubes available, such as 6L6G, 6C6G and 5U4G. Don't select a 6BK4 type as you cannot remove the top metal anode from inside the glass envelope. You may use a large tube (6LQ6) with a glass base and then mount it on top of a black tube base. Pickup five or six old tubes to practice on.

Before attempting to remove the bakelite base from the tube, let air into the bottom of it. All radio and TV tubes operate with an internal vacuum—the air having been pumped out. A small glass seal is located at the bottom of the tube. See Figs. 2-39 through 2-43.

Always wear a pair of gloves when working around glass or warm components.

Now you want to let air back inside the tube. Break off the black bakelite center key locator between the tube side the tube. Then break off the black bakelite center key located between the tube prongs.

Fig. 2-39. Break off the black tube-locator pin and the glass tip with some long nose pliers.

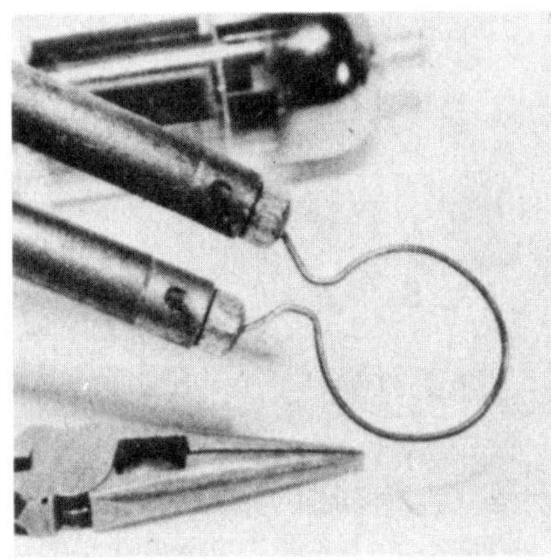

Fig. 2-40. Form a loop of copper wire that fits snug around the tube and into a soldering gun.

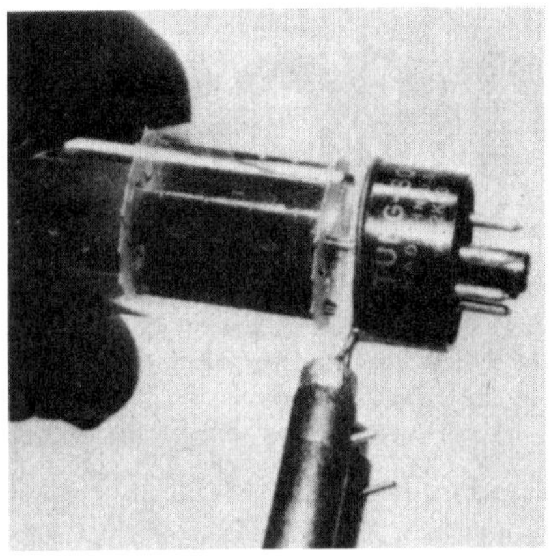

Fig. 2-41. Put the loop over the part of the tube you wish to cut and hold the tube firmly. Wear gloves to keep from burning yourself on the hot glass. Next apply heat to the loop and rotate the tube until the grass cracks.

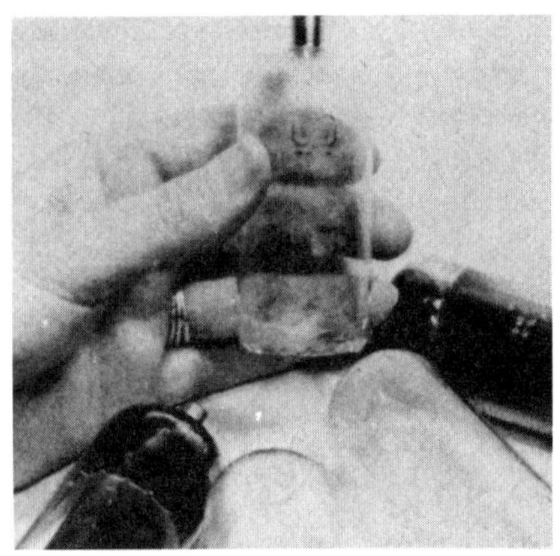

Fig. 2-42. Note the clean easy cuts this technique produces. Make sure you have a back-up tube.

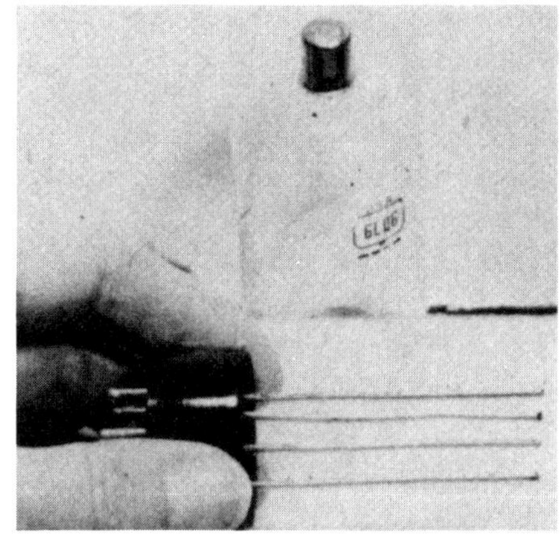

Fig. 2-43. The four copper support wires are soldered into the pin bases. The components are soldered and glued to these supports.

You should see the pointed glass seal. Take a pair of long nose pliers and break off the glass tip. You may hear a rush of air, or see a couple of white areas form near the bottom of the tube envelope.

To prevent glass pieces or excess solder from falling on the floor or work bench, do all of the glass preparation inside a large pasteboard box.

Next remove the soldering iron tip from a 150- or 250-watt soldering gun. Take a six-inch piece of number 14 copper wire, (you can remove the insulation from a piece of number 14 romex or a single conductor electrical wire for this purpose) and form a loop shaped soldering element. Wrap the bare wire around the base of the tube next to the bakelite base area and insert about one inch into the gun tip and bend over. Tighten down the soldering iron nuts—real tight. After cutting a couple of glass bases you may want to snug up the soldering iron nuts for a greater transfer of heat. Keep the copper loop close to the gun tips so the loop will heat up faster. Pinch it close together, and snug, clear around the tube with a pair of long nose pliers. You have now constructed a copper wire loop to replace the soldering iron tip.

Slip the wire loop over the end of the tube base and press the loop together at the ends—but not so close as to touch. Now hold the tube in the left hand and soldering gun in the right. Very slowly turn the vacuum tube inside the heated loop. Within a few minutes you will hear the glass crack and break in a perfect cut at the base of the tube. Some glass tubes take longer to break than others. In the meantime you may smell a hot bakelite odor from the wire loop, which is normal. Often the glass will crack clear around and just a tap on the end of the bakelite base separates the two pieces.

If you have selected a tube with a metal cap on top, turn the inside components until the connecting wire breaks off. Be careful not to break the remaining glass envelope, which is very brittle. It's best to cut off the wires connecting the tube elements to the base with a small pair of side cutters. In case the tube elements and mica insulators will not pull through the small opening, use a pocket knife to cut out sections of the insulators. You may have to crush or remove the tube elements in sections. Again, proceed slowly to prevent breaking the glass envelope. If you break or crack the tube envelope, start on another on—one out of three is not a bad average.

If you choose a TV tube with a glass base (6LQ6), press the copper loop around the prongs and against the glass bottom of the tube. Break off the small glass seal between the prongs and let air into the tube. Heat up the soldering gun and rotate the tube until the glass cracks in a round circle. Now break and crush the glass base with the wire tube prongs into little pieces. Be very careful in removing the tube elements, they must be reduced in size until all parts fit through the small opening. You may want to cut and remove each element piece individually until all parts are removed from the tube envelope. Later on, you can glue this glass envelope over a separate bakelite tube base.

It's best to cut out three or four tube envelopes. After removing the tube elements, choose the best one. If the glass edge is a little irregular, don't worry; when placed upon the black base the area will be covered with rubber silicone cement and will look like it belonged there all along. Now wash out the white and dark areas inside the glass envelope.

Tube Base Preparation

To remove the remaining glass and connecting wires from the tube base, each tube prong must be unsoldered. Hold the tube base upright and over a pasteboard box. Apply heat from the soldering iron against each prong. Let the excess solder begin to boil and then fling the tube base downward and the excess solder will fall into the bottom of the pasteboard box. Use this method on each tube prong a couple of times to remove all of the solder. After the excess solder has been removed, pull the connecting wires out of the tube base area. You may have to break the glass in several pieces to remove some stubborn connections. Clean out the excess glass cement with a pocket knife and place the tube base with the glass envelope for safe keeping.

Tube Base Construction

Cut four pieces three inches long, of number 14 or smaller copper wire. These four support wires will become tie-in circuit and mounting supports for the small components. You may use any stiff wire for these supports as long as the wire itself can be soldered. Number 14 copper wire will just fit inside the tube pins and solder should be fed up from the bottom terminal. Also, you may solder the wire supports from the top side, down inside the tube base. Place support wires in terminals 1, 2, 6 and 8. Look at the bottom of the bakelite socket and start with Pin #1, to the left of the center pin. (Although the tube locator pin is broken off you still can see where it was located.)

After all support wires are soldered into position, clean excess solder from each wire with a pocket knife. Scrape off rosin and excess solder down inside the base, next to the support wires.

Place a 6-32 3/4 inch machine screw and washer in the center hole of the tube socket. Slip a nut on the outside of the screw to hold it in position until the socket can be bolted to the wooden base. Temporarily, slip the glass envelope over the support wires to see if they will clear the top area. You may use longer support wires if the glass envelope is a lot longer in length. This may help string out the parts and keep them from shorting against each other. A cut glass envelope from a 5U4GT tube runs about three inches long.

A tube's pin terminal connections (bottom view) are shown in Fig. 2-44. Remember the tie-wire supports are reversed when the tube socket is upright. Scratch a line straight up from the tube locator pin, along the side of the socket, with a pocket knife. Now place a piece of masking tape around it and mark the support wires. You can now solder to your heart's desire. The four supports will be used for component tie points and they are marked on the schematic (Fig. 2-45). Wire support number 8 is used only as a wiring tie-point for the small components. All other support terminals will be tied into the circuit after the tube socket is bolted to the wooden base. See Table 2-7.

Wiring in the Parts

Mount the antenna coil (L1) in the center of the support wires since it is the largest component. Solder the top wire to pin 2 and the bottom

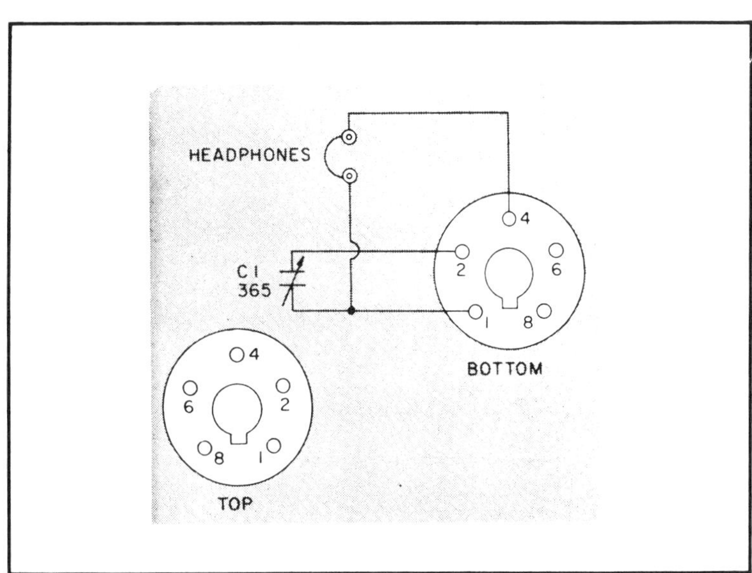

Fig. 2-44. Tube pin terminal connections.

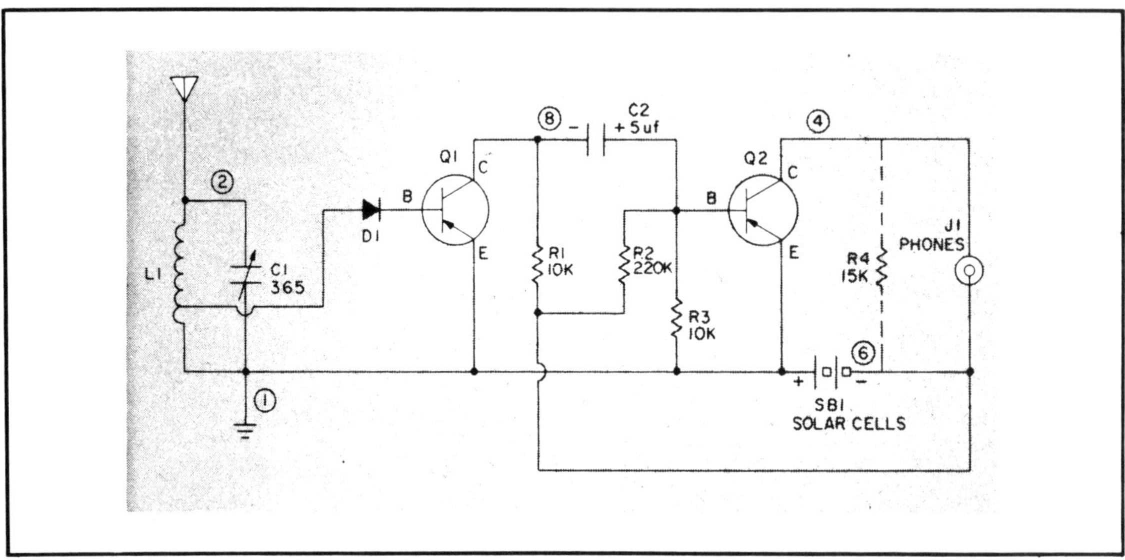

Fig. 2-45. Solar Swinger schematic.

terminal to pin 1. Leave it loose until all parts are soldered and then use a dab of silicone cement to hold it in place. Solder the collector terminal of Q1 and negative terminal of C2 to support wire number 2. Keep the leads fairly short and place a pair of long nose pliers next to the transistor body as a heat sink. The emitter terminals from each transistor will tie to terminal support number 1.

Now solder in all small components to their correct support wire terminals. Place a piece of spaghetti over the collector wire of Q2 and solder into pin terminal 4, if it is long enough. If not, lengthen the terminal wire with a piece of hookup wire. Connect the small diode between the coil tap (L1) and the base terminal of Q1. Slip a piece of spaghetti over the wiring to prevent touching of other components.

Mount the solar cells last—inside the tube area. Be careful to observe correct wire polarity. The positive terminal will solder to

Table 2-7. Parts List for Solar Swinger.

C1—365-μF variable capacitor
C2—5-μF electrolytic capacitor, 15-volts
D1—1N34A germanium diode
J1—any jack to fit headphones
L1—ferrite antenna coil (Radio Shack 270-1430 or equiv.)
Q1, Q2—2SA52 transistor (RCA SK-3003, GE-2, Radio Shack 276-2004)
R1, R3—10,000-ohm resistor, 1/4-watt
R2—220,000-ohm resistor, 1/4-watt
R4—15,000-ohm resistor, 1/4-watt
SB1—two solar cells (Radio Shack 276-120 or equiv.)
Misc.—headphones of 1000-200-ohms; 3/4 bolt and nut; tube base; old tubes; wooden plate; etc.

terminal 1 and the negative wire to 6. After all wiring has been completed inside the tube socket, double check each component and tie wire before bolting to the wooden base. Now tack the antenna coil (L1) and solar cell into position with a dab of silicone cement. See Fig. 2-46.

Base Layout

You may pick up a wooden base mounting plate at any novelty or hobby store. Ours was 6 3/4 by 4 1/2 and cost .99 cents. They may come in many sizes and shapes with a higher or lower price tag. Mark the parts layout on the bottom side of the wooden base. The tube socket may be mounted 1 1/2″ from the rear and in the center of the base plate. Place a work cloth under the wooden base to protect the soft wood from scratches and dents.

Cut a 1 1/2″ hole about 1/4″ deep for the tube base. The 1/4″ indentation will take a large pasteboard washer to bolt the tube socket into position. Finish drilling out the 1-inch hole for the tube prongs to fit comfortably inside. Depending upon the size of the tuning capacitor, lay it upon the bottom area and drill a large hole to enclose the whole body. Do not drill clear through the board but leave about 1/4″ at the top side for the mounting area of the tuning capacitor.

The tuning capacitor and the headphones are the only components mounted outside of the tube envelope. A small 1/4″ hole is drilled in the center and at the rear of the base towards the tube socket. The

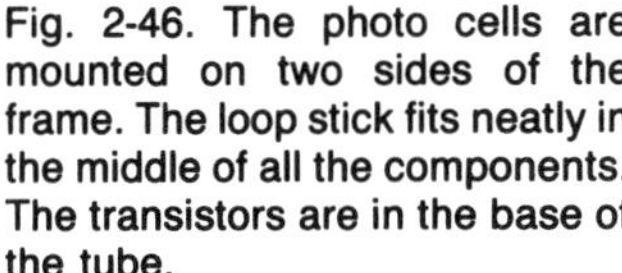

Fig. 2-46. The photo cells are mounted on two sides of the frame. The loop stick fits neatly in the middle of all the components. The transistors are in the base of the tube.

headphone and antenna wires will feed through this area to the tube socket pins. Cut a groove into the wood area between the capacitor and the tube socket hole. The capacitor's two small connecting wires will lay flat in this groove.

If needed, sand down the top of the wooden base area with fine sandpaper. Stain, varnish or spray paint the top side. Choose a light color spray paint, such as white or yellow, to give the base and component parts a contrasting appearance. Spray on at least three coats of paint and let it dry between each coat to produce a slick, enamel appearance. Let the wood base dry overnight before mounting any parts. See Fig. 2-47.

Final Touchup

After the base appears dry mount the variable capacitor and connect two pieces of hookup wire from it to tie into the tube socket. Next, mount the small tube socket. Temporarily, place a piece of masking tape over the socket and wooden base plate. Lay the base upside down (over a shoebox) to wire up the remaining components. Feed the earphone cable through the rear hole and connect to terminals 4 and 6 of the tube socket. Feed a short piece of hookup wire through the same hole to serve as an external antenna connection. Solder this wire to terminal 2. Now solder the capacitor's two wires to terminals 2 and 1. Once again, check over the entire wiring procedure. Solar Swinger should be ready to roll (and rock).

Connect the antenna wire to the outside antenna—or you can try to pick up local stations with a 12-ft. piece of wire laying around the baseboard of a wall. You should be able to pick up local stations at each end of the broadcast band. If a ferrite, adjustable antenna coil is used, adjust the core until the stations are loudest at each end of the band. Turn solar Swinger's solar cell toward the sunlight or operate under a table lamp.

After all adjustments are made, spread silicone cement over the

Fig. 2-47. The only wood work needed is to make two large holes in the base. One for the tube and one for the tuning capacitor. A bolt through the base holds the tube in place.

tuning capacitor wires. Cut out a large pasteboard or plastic washer and place it over the tube pins. Use the 3/4-inch machine screw and bolt the tube socket into position. To keep the earphone wires from pulling out, apply silicone cement in the small hole. Place four rubber grommets or metal spacers on each corner for feet, and cement in place. Let the radio lay upside down until the silicone cement sets up.

The glass envelope should be mounted last and glued to the tube base with black silicone cement. Place a thin layer of rubber cement around the top, just inside the tube base. Hold the envelope in a straight upright position and set it down in the fresh cement. Now apply rubber silicone cement to the outside of the glass and base area. Wipe off all surplus with a paper towel and make a neat joint with your fingers. Let the envelope and the base dry overnight.

Many of our Solar Swinger's parts may be found in the junk box. In fact, low priced transistors are used in the directly coupled audio circuit. If you are starting out cold and purchasing all new parts, you may pick up a 2 transistor AM radio kit from Radio Shack. Most all the parts needed for the Solar Swinger can be robbed from this kit.

Solar Swinger—a great conversation piece and a sunny savings over the high cost of batteries!

Chapter 3
Digital Projects

CHIP-CLIP

THE DUAL-INLINE-PACKAGE (DIP) INTEGRATED CIRCUIT (IC) IS not a new electronics device. While it was the microprocessor and mini-computer revolution that focused attention on this device, even those of us not involved in computers use ICs. For example, tape decks, radios, and television receivers use them. Unfortunately, ICs are not infallible, and do on occasion breakdown. Due to the compact size of the IC, working space between devices is scant, to say the least. The need for an IC tester becomes apparent when one tries to follow a schematic diagram, manhandle two snake-like probes, and keep one eye on a meter and the other on an IC pin at the same time. That's where our deluxe Chip-Clip becomes a necessity.

Most frequently, repairmen come across digital ICs. In digital logic circuits there are only two input and output values (called states), low or high, corresponding to off or on. Most digital logic ICs use a voltage of +5 volts dc for the high state and 0 volts for the low state. We use the low or high voltage to turn off or on a light-emitting diode (LED) and let a number of LEDs tell us what the present state is at every IC pin simultaneously. Chip-Clip will close on the small, tightly spaced pins. Imagine how difficult it would be to keep your meter probe in the right spot without wandering and shorting between pins!

We have also diagrammed the 7404 hex inverter logic IC. Here we have not two logic devices but six independent inverting circuits. In operation, if a high voltage appears on the input pin, the output drops to a low voltage. Should the input go low, the output goes high. By taking advantage of the high and low voltage states, we can observe the on or off condition of the LEDs and see the status of all six inverters simultaneously. Here, too, theChip - Clipwill prove an invaluable aid.

Building the Chip-Clip

The foundation of the Chip Clip is the standard 14 pin or 16 pin IC test clip available at any Radio Shack store or from any number of electronic mail order firms. See Fig. 3-1. To the IC test clip we add subminiature LEDs and a current limiting resistor between each logic test-clip pin and the IC ground pin. When low voltage is present on the IC pin, the LED does not light. When +5 volts appears on the logic input pin, the LED turns on. In addition, Chip-Clip has a different color LED on the Vcc connection (pin 14 or 16) to confirm the presence of Vcc IC pins without shorting adjacent pins. Equally important, it can be attached to an IC when there is only a quarter of an inch of space between circuit components.

To further illustrate the utility of our Chip-Clip, lets take a look at two types of logic ICs (See Fig. 3-2). We have illustrated a 7420, quad input, positive, NAND gate. It actually contains two separate four-input NAND gates, one on each side of the DIP. In either circuit, the output voltage will be high if a low voltage appears on any of the four input pins. When all four input voltages are high, the output voltage goes low. The contrasting LED color prevents confusing Vcc indication with a logic indication.

The assembly drawing illustrates (Fig. 3-3) the necessary connections for the 14-pin Chip-Clip. If you are building a 16-pin unit, two additional LEDs and resistors are needed for the two extra test points. The IC ground changes to pin 8 and Vcc input changes to pin

Fig. 3-1. Shown is a nearly completed, 16-pin Chip-Clip. The green LED is connected to the Vcc pin, number 16. The contrasting size and color serve as pointers to the correct positioning.

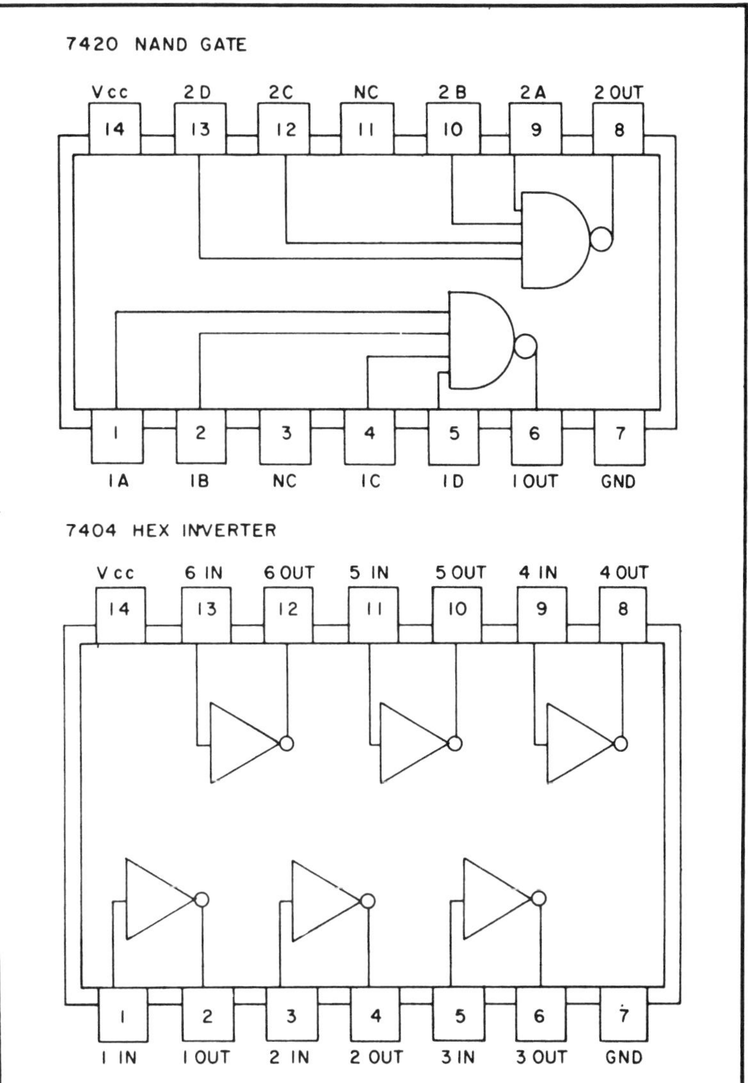

Fig. 3-2. A NAND unit's output is low only if all inputs are high. If any inputs are low, the output must be high. The 7420 is actually two separate NAND logic units housed in the same package and powered from the same source. An inverter's function is to convert a high signal into a low signal, or vice-versa. The 7404 Hex inverter contains six independent units. Like the 7420, the only interfaces are common packages and V_{CC} inputs.

16. The additional LEDs are connected to pins 7 and 15. No other changes are necessary.

The ground pin is connected to a common ground wire loop. It consists of two rectangular loops fashioned from 20 gauge solid wire. One of these loops is placed around each edge of the test clip one-half inch down from the top of the plastic. Four 0.028 holes are drilled to anchor the ground bus to the test clip. Since there is one ground bus loop on each half of the test clip, they must be connected together with a short piece of #20 flexible stranded wire to allow free movement of the test clip's sections and enable the test clip to clamp onto the IC DIP pins.

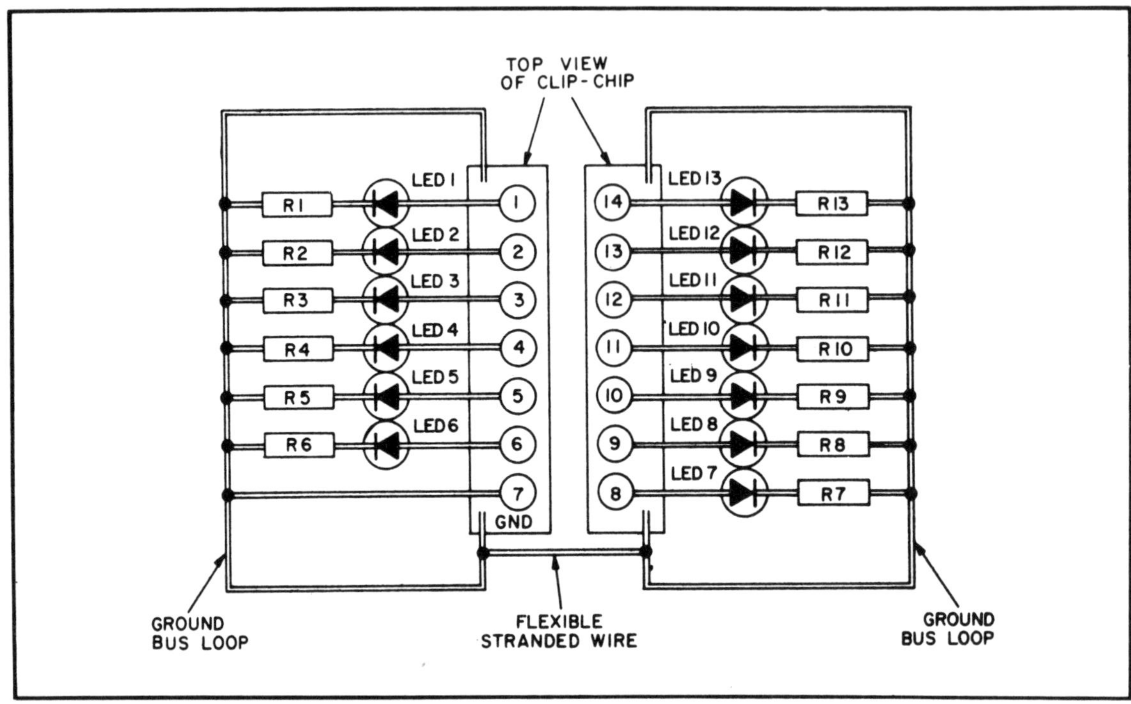

Fig. 3-3. Composite wiring-component placement drawing for 14 pin Chip-Clip. The LEDs are shown connected to the test clip's metering pins. They are attached to the current limiting resistors which are in turn all fastened to the ground bus loops. The ground bus loops must be firmly anchored to the test clip. Flexible wire connects both loops electrically making them into a common ground wire loop which is wired to pin 7.

On the 14 pin test clips, six 150 ohm, quarter-watt resistors are soldered to the ground bus loop on each side of the test clip and are positioned vertically. The body of the resistors should not stand above the top of Chip-Clip's frame and the resistor leads should be trimmed to the level of the metering pins. The resistor for the Vcc pin is positioned at the same level as the rest of the resistors but instead of being positioned on the side of the test clip, it is placed at the end of the clip next to the Vcc pin.

Finishing Touches

Installing the LEDs is only a matter of soldering the cathode LED lead to a resistor and the anode lead to one of the test clip's metering pins. The cathode lead can be identified by its notch or flat side. Remember, no LED goes to the test clip's pin 7 on a 14 pin Chip-Clip, or pin 8 on a 16 pin one. All other test clip metering pins have a LED and resistor attached. It should be noted that the specified LEDs have a forward voltage rating of 1.6 volts dc and a maximum current rating of 20 mA. For voltages greater than 5 volts at Vcc, a new value of current limiting resistance must be used. (See following page.)

Determing Limiting Resistance

$$R = \frac{Vcc - 1.6}{.020}$$

Vcc = voltage greater than +5 volts.
1.6 = forward voltage of LED
.020 = maximum LED current
R = the new resistance

While almost any size LED can be used, the subminiature LED is recommended because of the limited space across the side of the IC test clip. In the author's model, a great emitting LED, jumbo size, was used to indicate the presence of Vcc voltages. The contrasting color prevents mistaking the lit LED as a logic function and serves as a pointer to the correct positioning of the test clip on the IC under test since the Vcc indicator is on pin 14 or 16.

Final Checkout

There are two things to be sure of. Be certain that the LEDs polarities are observed. Also, identify pins 1 and 14 on the 14 pin test clip or 1 and 16 on the 16 pin test clip and always be sure that these numbers always point towards the IC identifying notch, dot, or indenture on the top of the IC case. Final note: while these logic status test clips have been designed only for logic type ICs, it may be possible to employ them for other 14 or 16 pin ICs providing your schematic diagram confirms pins 7 or 8 as ground and pins 14 or 16 as Vcc. If in doubt, don't use the Chip-Clip.

ELECTRONIC PENDULUM

EVERYONE LIKES THE GRACEFUL SWING OF A GRANDFATHER clock's pendulum. The motion and tick-tock sound are pleasing to the senses and reinforce the idea that the clock is working. Here is a quick and easy project that duplicates the motion of a pendulum electronically and if desired, the sound as well. Parts cost should run around $10 and if you use the PC layout in this article construction time will be a couple of hours.

The Circuit

The pendulum operates by having an LSTTL oscillator drive a CMOS 4017 decade counter with decoded outputs. The CMOS chip has ten output lines 0 through 9, each in turn going "high" after a clock pulse appears on pin 14. Now if you took those outputs and used them directly to light LEDs the result would be a series of bulbs illuminating in sequence 0 to 9 and then going back to 0. But a pendulum doesn't work like that, it swings to the right then to the left. Its electronic counterpart would retrace its path something like 0, 1, 2 3, 4, 5, then 5, 4, 3, 2, 1, 0, 1, . . . One could use an up-down counter, changing its direction at each end of the count to achieve the above pattern, but there is a simpler way to approximate a pendulum's motion for the hobbyist.

Let's use six bulbs, labelling them A to F. Remember, the counter chip has ten output lines. If we allow some of the lamps to be lit by two outputs instead of just one, we can get oscillatory motion for free, so to speak. Let's see how. Look at Fig. 3-4. If we let bulb A be turned by output line 0, bulb B by output 1 or 9, C by 2 or 8, D by 3 or 7, E by 4 or 6, and F by output line 5, the desired result is produced. You can see this easily if you count from 0 to 9 and repeat this modulo ten (base ten) sequence over and over using Fig. 3-4 for your guide.

Be use to notice that L1 is inserted properly into the PC board holes because the LEDs are activated by a "low" or ground signal. Also note that pins 15 and 13 of the 4017 must be at 0 volts for the CMOS chip to count.

Construction

The two boards shown in Figs. 3-5 and 3-6 show the respective orientation of the parts. C2, C3 and S are optional, depending on an audible click with the pendulum swing. This circuit can also easily be wire-wrapped, beginners may wish to do this since the PC layout is somewhat tight and could be difficult to reproduce easily.

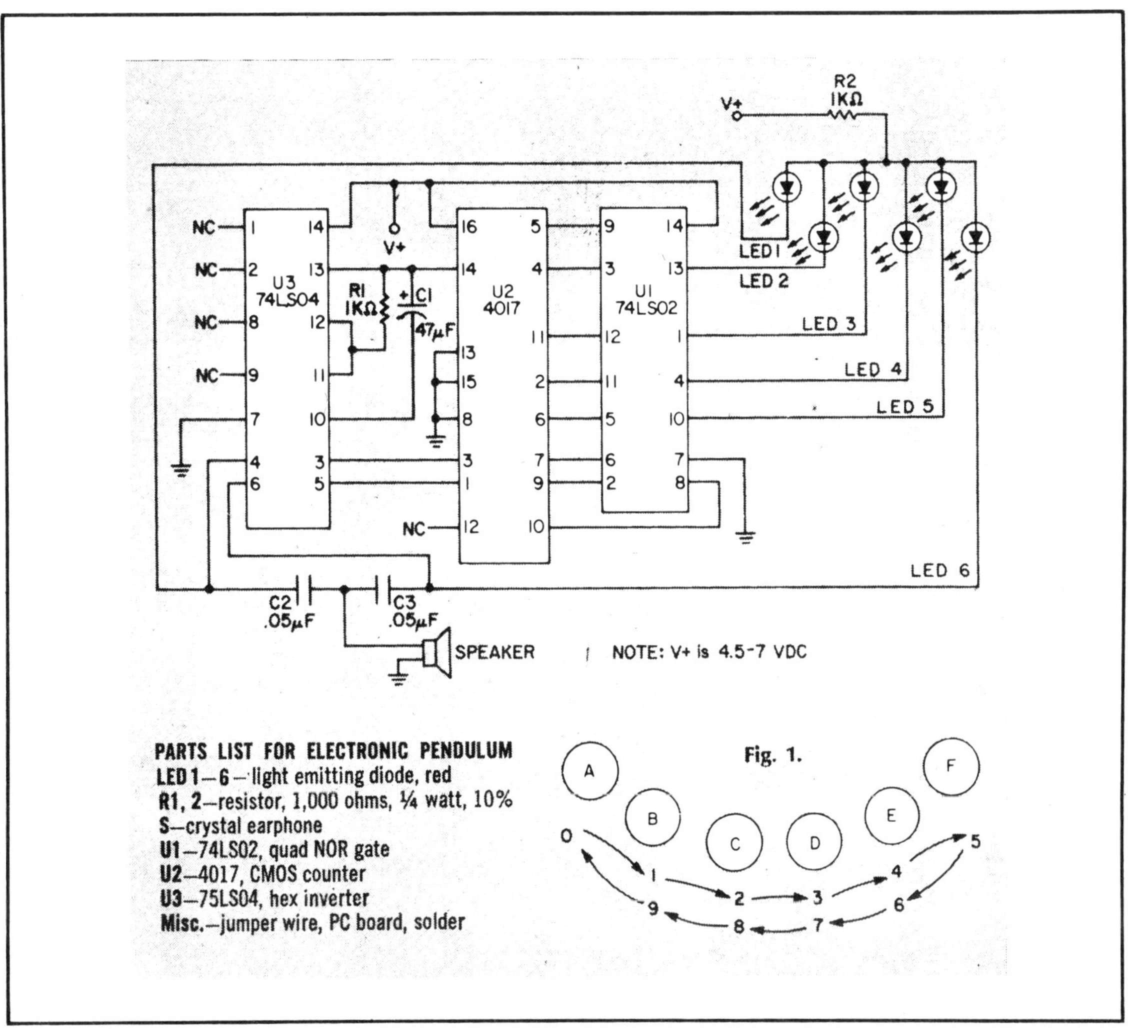

Fig. 3-4. As you see, Electronic Pendulum's circuit is simple and straightforward. Just beware of solder bridges. Note the sequence of firing for the six light-emitting diodes.

Sound output for the unit is provided by a crystal earphone fed by LED 1 and LED 6. This arrangement gives plenty of noise in a quiet room, but if desired, more volume can be obtained using an audio amp like the LM386. You will have to experiment with the circuit components to get the proper loudness.

Operation

Simply connect power and ground and Electronic Pendulum should start up. It should be easy to add this project to an existing clock or incorporate it into a new design. Voltage to the board should not exceed 7 V, as the 74LS chips will fail, but V+ can dip to about

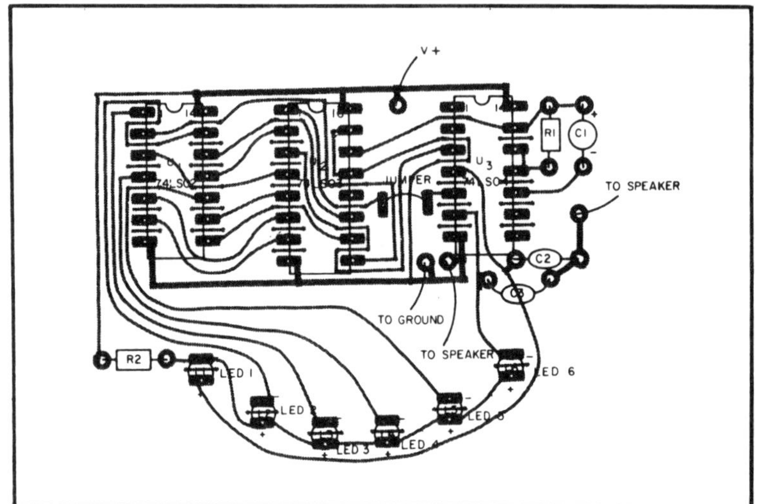

Fig. 3-5. Six LEDs are the center of the Electronic Pendulum. Watch polarity when you install them otherwise you could ruin hours of hard work.

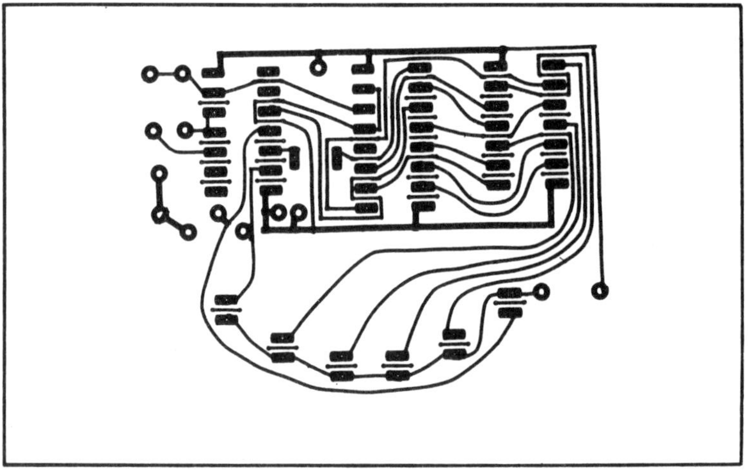

Fig. 3-6. A small printed circuit board, such as the one given for Electronic Pendulum requires good soldering skills. Try to be careful.

4.5 V if you don't mind dim lamps. The circuit draws less than 10 mA so drain from existing supplies will be minimal. Adding a red plastic filter in front of the lamps will improve the illusion of oscillatory pendulum motion.

DASHBOARD DIGITAL VOLTMETER

YOU'RE MAKING TIME DOWN THE INTERSTATE AT THREE IN THE morning, and all of a sudden you become aware that the lights on the dash seem kind of dim, and that the headlights don't seem to be reaching out as far ahead to warn you of darkened semis parked on the shoulder. Are your eyes just playing tricks on you, or is there something the matter with your car's electrical system? A quick glance down at the three glowing LED numerals on the dash gives you the instant answer. Either you pull into a rest area and grab a few hours of shuteye, or you pull into a service area and have the battery, alternator and voltage regulator given a good scrutinizing by the mechanic.

In either case, your car's digital voltmeter has given you the information sought about the state of the electrical system, and maybe saved you either a headache, a smashup, or a king-sized repair and towing bill. Maybe all three.

Recent advances in the design and availability of industrial integrated circuits have opened up many doors to the electronics hobbyists. Analog-to-digital devices have become more complex internally, thus making the portions of the circuitry that have to be assembled by the hobbyist that much more simple. The Dashboard Digital Voltmeter takes advantage of these advances, utilizing three ICs and a small handful of discrete components to give you an instrument capable of better than $\pm$ 1% accuracy in reading the voltage level delivered by your car's (or boat's) electrical system.

The ICs

The system is built around three ICs: the LM340T-5 (a 5 volt regulator now available for several years); a CA3162E; a CA3161E; and a support combination of diodes, resistors, and capacitors. It is the CA3161E and CA3162E that now open the door to new horizons in possible applications not only because of their unique capabilities, but also because they reduce substantially the numbers and types of formerly required support components. The heart of this system is the CA3162E, a dual-slope, dual-speed, A/D converter industrial chip. Its almost equally important companion, the CA3161E, is a BCD, 7-segment, decoder/driver chip. It is also unique in that it has a current-limiting feature. This eliminates the necessity of resistors in series with the 7-segment displays that were required in earlier designs.

The above feature not only reduces circuit board space requirements, but reduces the probability of component failure. Power required to operate this voltmeter is minimal (160 mA or less), a re-

Fig. 3-7. This view of the assembled PC board shows the voltage regulator, (U1) mounted on the underside of the PC board. This was done in order to accommodate a flushmount installation in a smaller car. Let your space needs dictate placement of this component.

sult of the multiplexing feature of the CA3162E. With that as a background, let's consider some of the more important operations of this simple, but very accurate digital instrument. See Fig. 3-7.

Circuit Function

Analog voltage from 000 mV to 999 mV can be applied between pins 11 (+) and 10 (−) of the CA3162E (U2). That IC converts the voltage into a Binary Coded Decimal (BCD) equivalent. The BCD leaves pins 2, 1, 15, and 16 (the group represents the 1's, 2's, 4's, and 8's) and enters pins 7, 1, 2, and 6 respectively of the CA3161E (U3). The latter IC takes the BCD code, converts the output, then uses it (in conjunction with the 7-segment display) to generate (form) the number that correlates to the BCD input of the CA3161E. The multiplexing driver pins 5, 3, and 4 (5 being the least significant and 4 the most significant) turn on that display by means of the PNP switching transistors. Concurrently, the CA3162E is providing the BCD information to the CA3161E driver/decoder.

As indicated earlier, the system includes a combination of diodes and capacitors. These are required to control or minimize the voltage spikes (positive and negative) that result from turning inductive devices on and off; e.g. windshield wiper, air conditioner, and electric windows, etc.

The maximum input differential between pins 11 and 10 of CA3162E is 999 mV. A resistor network (R1, R2) is used to attenuate the applied 13.8 volts to 138 mV. An Ohm's Law calculation would give a result of 136.6 mV. The gain-adjust potentiometer compensates for the slight drop. The FND 507s display this as 13.8-volts.

Note the point marked OPTION on the schematic (See Fig. 3-8). With Pin 6 of the CA3162E grounded or disconnected, there are four conversions or comparisons made each second. Tying pin 6 to the 5-volt line will result in 96 conversions or comparisons per second. The 96/second rate moves with excessive rapidity, is not appealing to the eye, and usually results in the least significant digit appearing

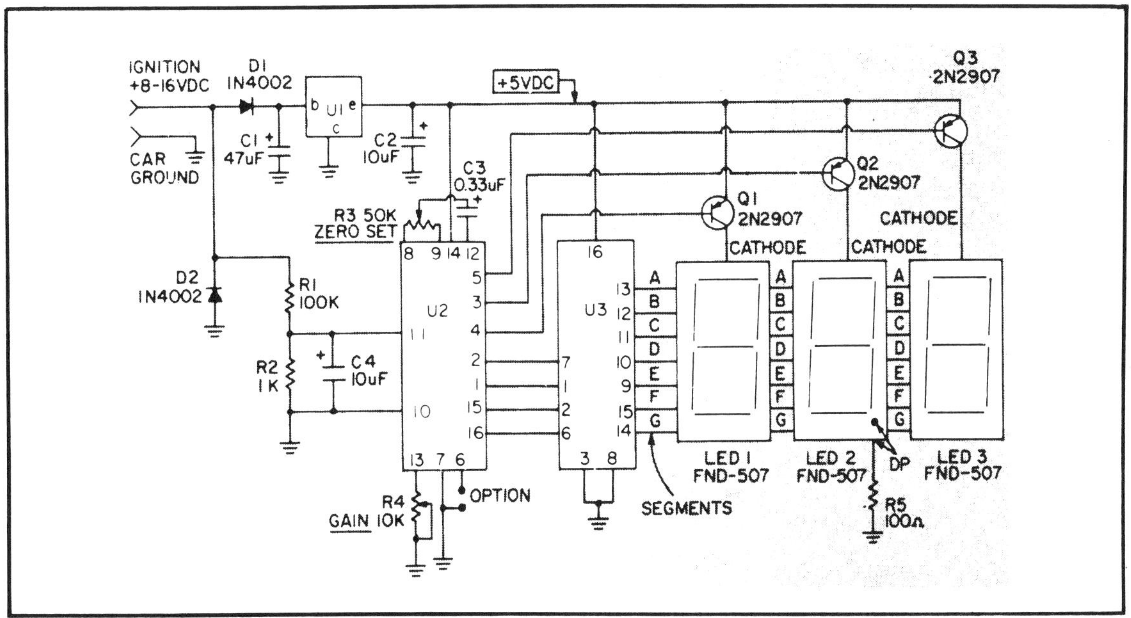

Fig. 3-8. Dashboard Digital Voltmeter schematic.

to be blurred. Of the two rates, the 4/second conversion (4 Hz) is by far the more pleasing to the eye, is easier for the eye to focus on quickly, and is the recommended rate. These rates could vary slightly because of capacitor difference and manufacturer variance from stated values.

Table 3-1. Parts List for Digital Voltmeter.

C1—47-μF electrolytic capacitors, 25 Vdc
C2, C4—10 μF tantalum electrolytic capacitor, 16 Vdc
C3—0.33-μF tantalum capacitor, 35 Vdc
D1, D2—1N4002 diode
F1—1-amp fuse
LED1, 2, 3—FND-507 7-segment LED display
Q1, 2, 3—2N2907 PNP transistor
R1—100,000-ohm, 1/4-watt resistor, 5%
R2—1,000-ohm, 1/4-watt resistor, 5%
R3—50,000-ohm PC trimmer potentiometer
R4—10,000-ohm PC trimmer potentiometer
R5—100-ohm, 1/4-watt resistor, 5%
U1—LM340T-5 5-volt voltage regulator
U2—CA3162E Analog-to-Digital converter
U3—CA3161E BCD display driver

MISC—solder, hookup wire, red plexiglass (for display filter), IC sockets, transistor sockets, suitable enclosure, etc.

Note: An etched and drilled circuit board for the Digital Voltmeter is available for $6.60 (postpaid in U.S. and Canada), and a complete parts kit, including PC board but not including plexiglass, is available for $27.50 from: Digital World, P.O. Box 5508, Augusta, GA 30906. Please allow 4 to 6 weeks for delivery. No C.O.D.s or foreign orders, please.

Assembling the Voltmeter

The unit may be assembled quickly and relatively easily using a predrilled and etched circuit board. If a Digital World circuit board is being used, the four corner holes will have been drilled. If a blank board is being used, drill the corner holes before starting to "stuff" the board. It is easy at this point to scribe the plexiglass panel and mark the corner holes on it for later drilling and perfect alignment. Additionally, examine the recess or place where the completed unit will be mounted. Determine how it will be secured (bolted, clamped, or glued), doing any additional drilling that may be required. See Figs. 3-9 and 3-10.

Get the workbench ready for soldering. Use a low wattage, electrically isolated, fine-tipped soldering tool and fine solder. A blunt-nosed tool could damage or destroy the ICs and create foil bridges between pins. This is both expensive and frustrating. If you have had limited experience in soldering in small areas, it may be wise to practice on something else before you start.

Now, locate all resistors and potentiometers on the circuit board placement diagram and install them in their respective holes. Next, do the same for all capacitors, observing polarity. Install the CA3161E and CA3162E. Caution! When inserting the ICs, be careful not to fold the pins under or bend them in any way.

IC orientation is critical. Be sure these chips (CA3162E and CA3161E) are aligned as shown in Fig. 3-10. Note the notch marks on the chips and the corresponding notch marks in Fig. 3-10, or the "1" on pin 1 on top of the plastic case. All manufacturers use one or both of these base reference directional indicators.

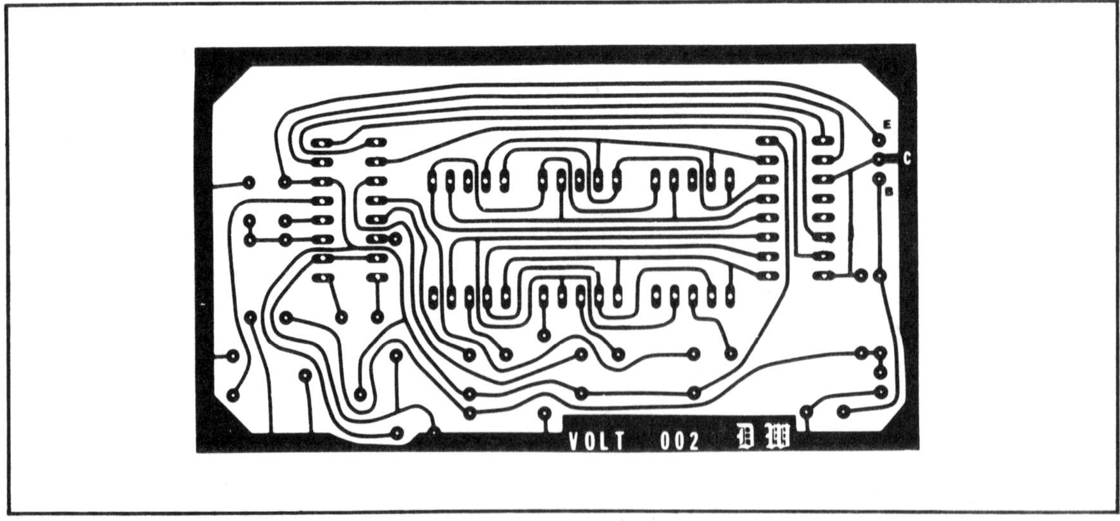

Fig. 3-9. This full-scale etching guide for the voltmeter's PC board is one of the trickiest we've offered. Unless you know your stuff, we suggest you use a Digital World board.

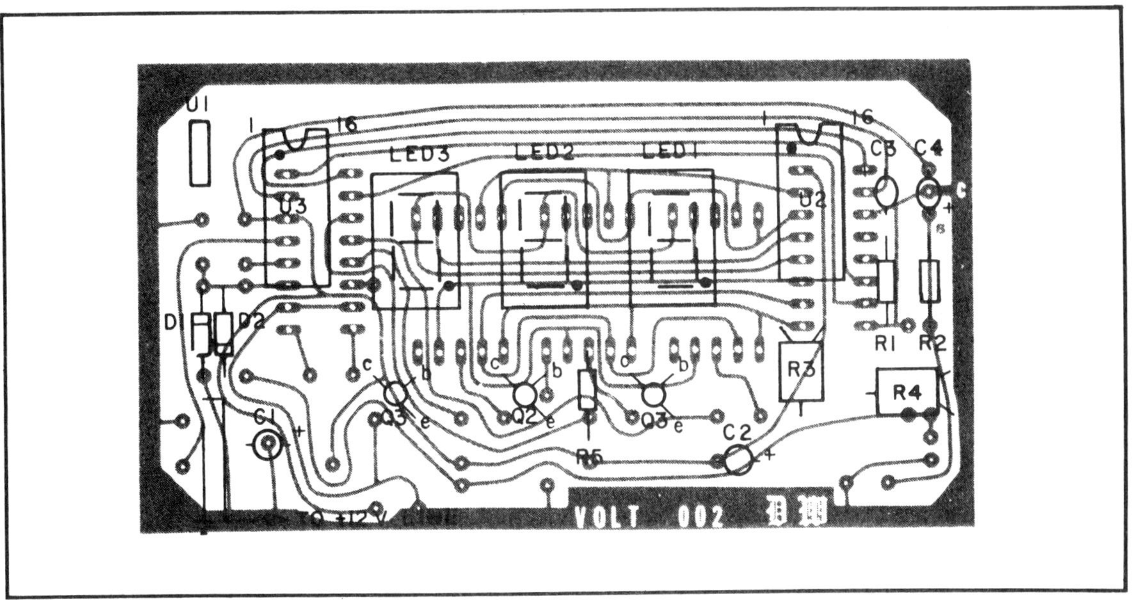

Fig. 3-10. The component placement diagram for the PC board shows all IC and capacitor polarities. Take special care to observe them during assembly phases of project.

If you have doubts about your soldering ability or the type of solder tool you have (grounded or not grounded), place two 16-pin sockets in the chip holes. The ICs may then be placed (not soldered) in the sockets. Next, insert the three LEDs, noting the notch marks on the LEDs and the notch marks indicated on the diagram. For the final action on this side of the board, insert both diodes in their respective holes (observing cathode markings).

Reverse the circuit board and install the LM340T-5 regulator. Caution! This must be correctly placed or it will destroy your unit when power is applied. The metal side of the regulator must be facing the FND 507 pins. Recheck it to make sure.

Now, turn the board over again. Use a red wire for the ignition line and a black wire for the chassis ground. Determine the lengths required (usually three-feet is sufficient). Solder the red wire to the point marked IGNITION in Fig. 3-8 and the black wire to the GROUND.

Calibration Procedure

Correct calibration determines the accuracy of your voltmeter. Follow these steps carefully and sequentially. Apply a known voltage source (above 10 and below 16 volts) to the IGNITION point. We recommend a 13.8-volt source. Next, for zero adjustment, ground pins 11 and 10 to the circuit board ground momentarily. Using a small screwdriver, slowly rotate the wiper arm on R3 until there is a reading of 000. Remove the ground from pins 10 and 11. Set the gain control (R4) by rotating the wiper arm until the displays are displaying the same voltage as is being applied.

Installation

One final action is necessary before your unit is ready to be mounted in the dash location of your choice. Secure the black wire to the metal chassis ground and the red wire to any accessory line that is active only when the motor is running. Secure and mount the voltmeter in the location of your choice.

A colored plexiglass facing (cover) is required and we recommend red for most display contrast. A location which is not usually exposed to the sunlight will make the displays easier to read during the brighter periods of the day. If the unit is going into an existing recess, the present glass cover may be used as a template for the plexiglass cover dimensions. One-eighth or 1/16 inch thickness plexiglass works well and is relatively easy to cut using a roofer's shingle cutter knife. Place two clamps on a straight line along the template edge, then cut one side at a time. Scribe it deeply with a dozen or more strokes, then break off the excess with a pliers. When drilling screw holes, use a small starter bit first, then the larger bit. This should prevent the larger bit from wandering across the plexiglass.

The plexiglass must be "spaced" away from the board by approximately 5/8-inch, using either spacers to the bolt/nut method. The latter method is to insert a bolt through the plexiglass corner hole and put a nut on the reverse side. Put a second nut on the bolt, allowing a 1/2-inch inside space between the two nuts. Do this on all corners. Next, insert the bolts into the board corner holes and put on the final nuts. We recommend securing all four corners, rather than just two.

Troubleshooting

If the unit does not light up for the calibration procedure, first check that the wiper of R3 is centered. If it still does not light up, recheck your work. Carefully inspect for possible solder bridges and loose connections. If a solder bridge is discovered, remove it carefully. It is easy to destroy a chip during the removal process. If it still fails to light up, start a systematic test check to isolate possible faulty component(s).

If the unit does not function after installation, recheck for a good electrical connection on the line that supplies power from the car. Did you break or loosen the solder connections of the source wires during installation? If so, this will require removal and resoldering, plus a bit more care during installation the second time.

One Final Note

Some ICs, and quite possibly the ones used in this project, generate high frequency harmonics which might find their way into your car's radio. Try holding your LED readout pocket calculator next to the radio antenna with the radio tuned to a blank spot on the AM dial to see what we mean. If you experience any interference from the voltmeter circuit, try rerouting the antenna coax away from the voltmeter itself. A metal case around the voltmeter's PC board will also aid in the reduction of RFI. We suggest that you avoid using the radio's power lead as the voltage source for your voltmeter. The power lead to the horn (or horn relay) or the hot lead of the windshield wiper switch (find it at the fuse box) is probably the best place to attach the voltmeter.

MAXICLOCK

TIME FREEZE! WHAT'S TIME FREEZE? TO TELL YOU THE TRUTH, nothing that great . . . we think it's everything else about this digital clock that's so great!

Today the best feature is one that is uppermost in everybody's mind—the major parts cost. It's the least expensive electronic digital clock we could find—kit, project, or assembled—that has just about feature you can think of in a line-powered digital clock.

It is a 6-digit clock. It is a calendar. It is a 24-hour alarm clock. It has a 10-minute snooze alarm. It has provision for internal battery power operation. It can be operated in either the 12-or 24-hour mode. It knows the days of the month (you update just once every four years at leap year). It is simple to build without a printed circuit board because there are no driver transistors for the display. It uses a standard low-cost "calculator" type display, and the display is internally wired—only 13 connections operate all 42 segments of the six-digit display. And all the display connections are made to an IC connector for ease of assembly.

It all adds up to one thing: You should be able to build this clock for a price considerably lower than digital clocks with fewer features. And, oh yes, about time freeze: It's the simple "seconds hold" feature you get with this clock. With it you set the time ahead a minute or two, wait for your time standard (WWV, local radio, Ma Bell, etc.) to count down to zero, flick the function switch, and watch your clock starting counting from "00" seconds every time. A small feature, perhaps, but something everyone appreciates.

Other features of the clock are as follows: You can select between time, date, alarm "set" time, or time/date display (a time display for 8 seconds followed by a date display for 2 seconds). A 50 or 60 Hz switch and the time freeze feature let you set time with ease (in the 50 Hz position, the clock will run 20 percent faster on a 60 Hz line). You also have a "snooze" button to recycle the alarm by ten minutes. *There is only one switch for setting hours, minutes, days, and months!* Additional features are an "alarm is set" red LED indicator, leading zero blanking, and a green LED to indicate p.m. The clock also provides an optional 24-hour display, stand-by battery power, and display brightness control. See Figs. 3-11 and 3-12.

How Does It Work?

The brain of the clock is the Cal-Tex CT7001 integrated circuit consisting of thousands of transistors; it counts down the line frequency to seconds, minutes, days, and months. Internal memories record the

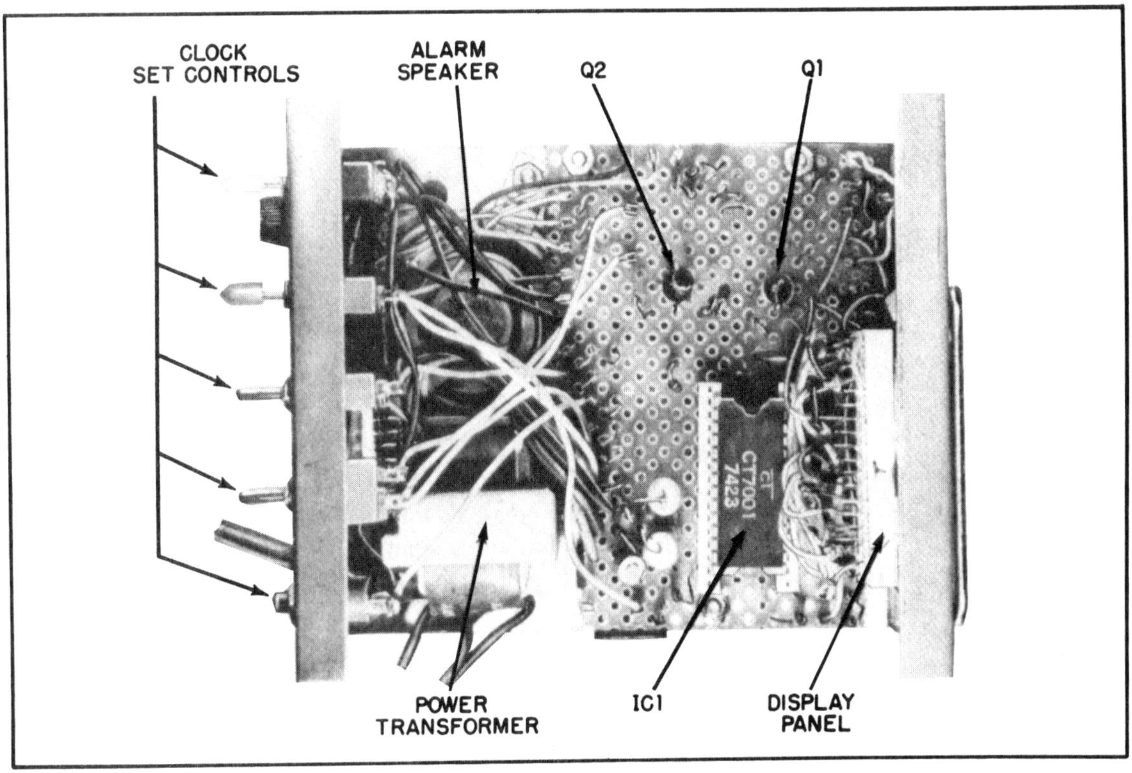

CLOCK SET CONTROLS
ALARM SPEAKER
Q2
Q1
POWER TRANSFORMER
IC1
DISPLAY PANEL

Fig. 3-11. Birds-eye view of major parts location in a compact and very tight design. Consider building your clock in a more original setting for wall (or even built-in) display with hidden power cord.

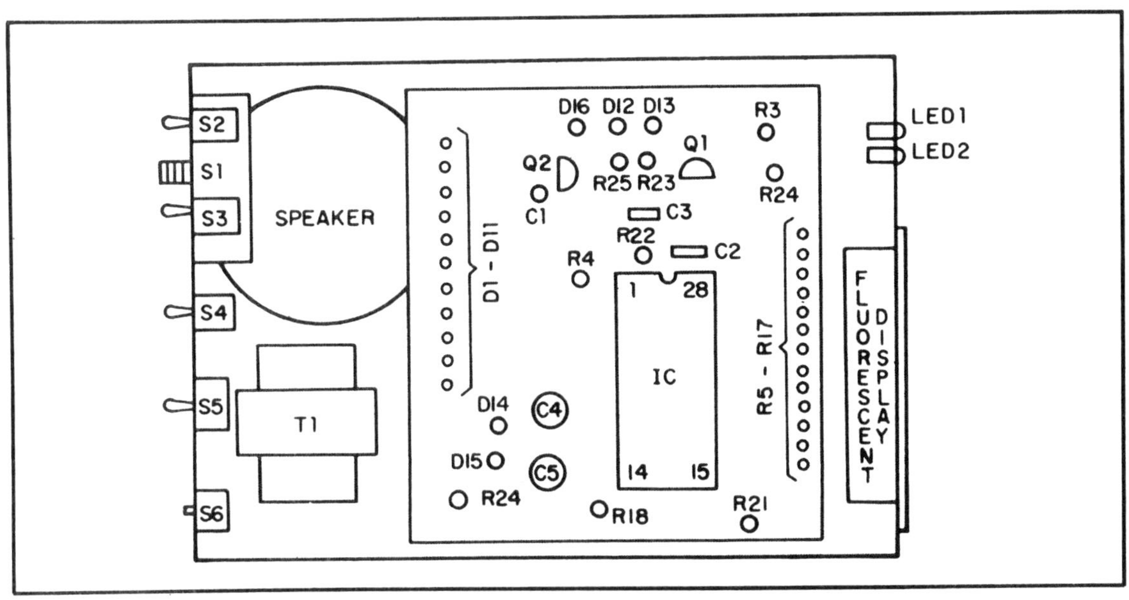

Fig. 3-12. Parts layout diagram.

number of days in each month and the alarm settings. To avoid large numbers of wire leads, the display digits are multiplexed, which means that "gating" signals (digit turn-on signals) are applied in sequence to the "control" grid of each digit. But it happens so fast you "see" a continuous 6-digit display. The display segments of all digits are connected in parallel right inside the display case. It comes pre-wired that way in its compact enclosure.

The first transistor, Q1 turns the leading zero off when the "SF" segment (See Fig. 3-13 and Table 3-2) appears—this is the only segment not required to form digits 1 and 2. The second transistor, Q2, is a programmed unijunction transistor which drives the speaker to sound the alarm. You can change the sound of the alarm by making C1 smaller or larger as you desire. See Figs. 3-14 through 3-18.

Construction

To build the clock we used point-to-point wiring on a 3 × 4 in. perfboard. The clock fits into a 3 × 4 × 5-in. cabinet, but you may want to build it in a slightly larger cabinet with different styling. If your soldering skills are limited, we would recommend a 4 × 5 × 6-in. cabinet. All external connectors are brought out to push-in terminals at the edge of the perfboard.

Be careful handling the integrated circuit. A socket for the IC is a must. Install the IC in the socket only when you are finished with all the wiring to prevent a static charge from damaging it.

The display is quite sturdy, though dropping it on its edge on the concrete basement floor (as we did during construction) will definitely wipe it out! Cut a hole in the front of the cabinet for the display and attach it with a bracket, glue or masking tape. All display connections are brought out on pins similar to a 14-pin dual in-line IC. The pins have to be bent slightly to fit into the IC socket. To improve visibility, we recommend putting a sheet of smoked or green-blue plastic or glass in front of the display.

Optional Features

You may want to drop some of the features provided in the basic clock to simplify its construction. You may also want to add a few extra features if you feel strongly about them. Mix and match; it's up to you.

☐ Leading or blanking zero in the 24-hour mode. If you prefer a leading 0 (05 15 45 instead of 5 15 45) leave out Q1 and R19 to R21.

☐ Display brightness. If you would like to control the intensity of the display, replace R24 with a 500-ohm potentiometer connected as a rheostat.

☐ Twenty-four-hour display. You can choose the 24-hour mode

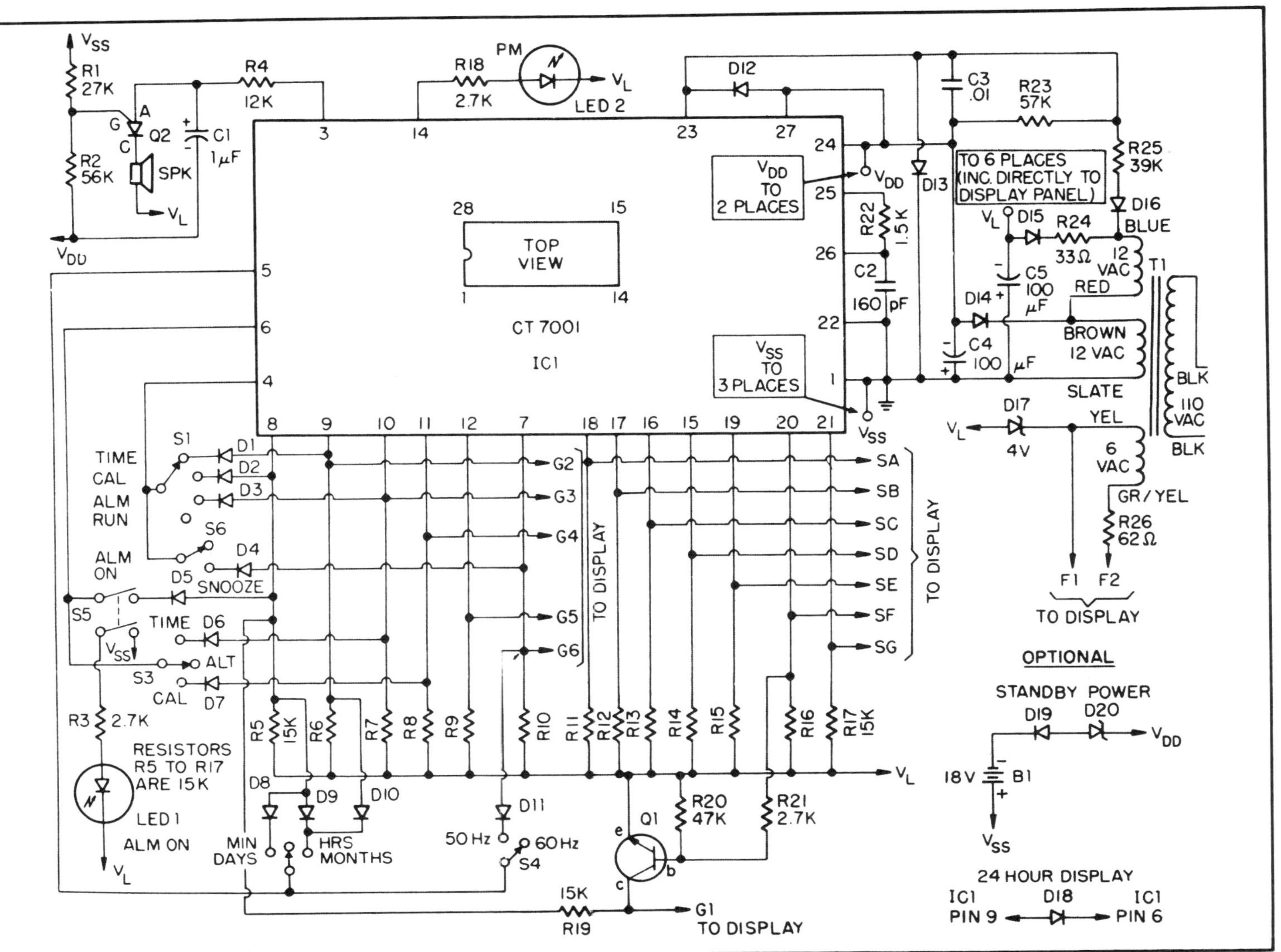

Fig. 3-13. Maxiclock schematic.

Table 3-2. Maxiclock Parts List.

B1—pair of 9-volt transistor radio batteries.
Note: required only when standby battery power option is included.

C1—1 μF capacitor, any type, 50 Vdc or better (Radio Shack 272-1055 or equiv.)

C2—150 or 160 pF disc capacitor, 50 Vdc or better
Note: You can parallel-connect a 100 pF and 47 pF to obtain an approximate value.

C3—0.01 μF disc or tubular capacitor, 50 Vdc or better (Radio Shack 272-1065 or equiv.)

C4, C5—100 μF electrolytic capacitor (Radio Shack 272-1044 or equiv.)

D1 to D11, D16, D18—General purpose silicon diodes such as 1N914

D12, D13—General purpose germanium diodes such as 1N34 (Radio Shack 276-821 or equiv.)

D14, D15, D19—1-amp, 200-volt silicon diodes, 1N4003 (Radio Shack 276-1102 or equiv.)

D17—4-volt, 1/2-watt zener diode (Radio Shack 276-620 or equiv.)

D20—6-volt, 1/2-watt zener diode (Radio Shack 276-621 or equiv.)

IC1—time/date/alarm clock-on-a-chip (Cal-Tex CT7001, do not substitute.)

LED 1—red light emitting diode, alarm-on indicator (Radio Shack 276-042 or equiv.)

LED 2—green light emitting diode, p.m. indicator (Radio Shack 276-044 or equiv.)

Q1—npn silicon transistor, HEP 50007 (Radio Shack 276-2016 or equiv.)

Q2—Programmable unijunction transistor, HEP S9001 (Radio Shack 276-119 or equiv.)

R1—27,000-ohm, 1/2-watt resistor (Radio Shack 271-000 or equiv.)

R2, R23—56,000-ohm, 1/2-watt resistor (Radio Shack 271-000 or equiv.)

R3, R18, R21—2700-ohm, 1/2-watt resistor (Radio Shack 271-000 or equiv.)

R4—12,000-ohm, 1/2-watt resistor (Radio Shack 271-000 or equiv.)

R5 to R17, R19—15,000-ohm, 1/2-watt resistor (Radio Shack 271-000 or equiv.)

R20—47,000-ohm, 1/2-watt resistor (Radio Shack 271-000 or equiv.)

R22-1500-ohm, 1/2-watt resistor, see text (Radio Shack 271-000 or equiv.)

R24—33-ohm, 1/2-watt resistor, (Radio Shack 271-000 or equiv.)

R25—39,000-ohm, 1/2-watt resistor (Radio Shack 271-000 or equiv.)

R26—62-ohm, 1/2-watt resistor (Radio Shack 271-000 or equiv.)
Note: You can use 1/4-watt resistors which are smaller (but more expensive) if space is limited in the case you use.

S1—4-position, single-pole rotary or slide switch
Note: You can use one of the 4-position, 3-pole rotary switches available such as Calectro E2-166, Malory 3134J, or Allied 851-1534, simply leave extra poles blank.

S2—spdt center-off toggle switch
Note: This switch can be selected with spring return-to-center (International Rectifier TS 105C or equiv.) or with manual return (Radio Shack 275-325 or equiv.)

S3—spdt center-off toggle switch (Radio Shack 275-325 or equiv.)

S4—spst toggle switch (Radio Shack 275-324 or equiv.)

S5—dpst toggle switch
Note: You can use another dpdt here; simply leave unused contacts blank.

S6—normally open pushbutton switch (Radio Shack 275-1547 or equiv.)

T1—power transformer, P8361 (Stancor)

Z1—7-segment, 8-digit fluorescent display with internally strapped segments for multiplex display system, ISE DP89A used by author.

Misc.—Small 3.2- or 8-ohm speaker used only if alarm option is included (Radio Shack 40-262 or equiv.); cabinet (author used 3 × 4 × 4 1/2-in. unit but suggests larger size for novice builders such as Radio Shack 270-253 which is 5 1/4 × 3 × 5 7/8-in.); wire, solder, hardware, 14-pin DIP IC sockets for display (2 required), etc.

A partial kit of parts consisting of a Col-Tex CT7001 (IC1), the 15E DP89A display panel (Z1), and a 28-pin socket for IC1 is available from Photolume Corp., 118 E. 28th Street, New York, NY 10016.

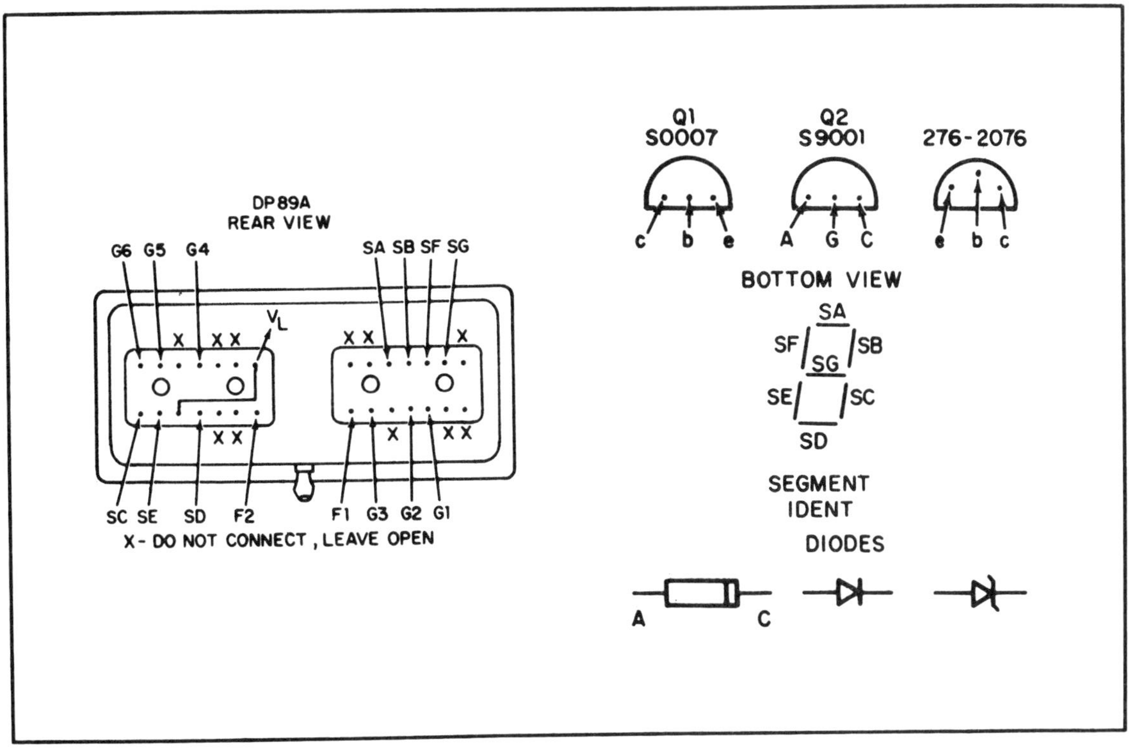

DP89A
REAR VIEW
G6 G5 G4
SA SB SF SG
X X X
V_L
X X
X
X X
X
X X
SC SE SD F2
F1 G3 G2 G1
X - DO NOT CONNECT, LEAVE OPEN
Q1
S0007
Q2
S9001
276-2076
c b e
A G C
e b c
BOTTOM VIEW
SA
SF
SB
SG
SE
SC
SD
SEGMENT
IDENT
DIODES
A
C

Fig. 3-14. Component connections.

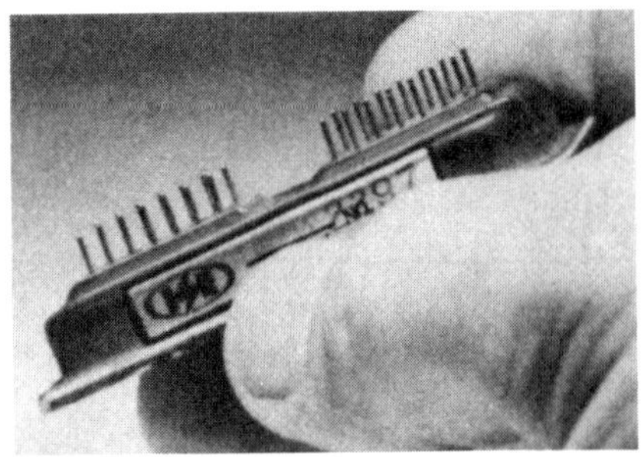

Fig. 3-15. Just a pair of 14-pin dual-in-line IC sockets are needed to connect this compact display with the circuit board. Display is actually an 8-digit device originally for calculator use. Here we blank the third and fifth digits to separate hours, minutes, and seconds.

HRS/MO
CAL
50
ALM ON
ALT
MIN/DAY
TIME
60 Hz
SNOOZ
RUN
ALARM
DATE
TIME
SET

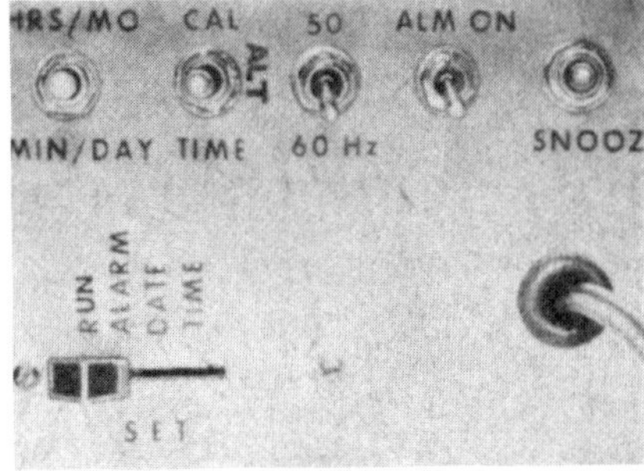

Fig. 3-16. "Set" switch S1 (see the schematic) tells the clock which of its three functions you want to adjust with the left hand switch (S2). Just hold S2 in the up position to set hours or months; hold it down to adjust minutes or day of the month.

Fig. 3-17. This hi-fi setting is strictly digital with your home-brew digital clock and Heath's AJ-1510 "digital" FM tuner. Hi-fi fans can even add Infinity Systems' Class D Switching Power Amp.

instead of the 12-hour mode simply by connecting D18 as shown on the schematic (Fig. 3-13). The clock must be reset when switched from 12- to 24-hour display.

☐ Stand-by battery power. A couple of 9-volt batteries as shown on the schematic will provide stand-by power. When the ac is on they do not supply any current to the circuit. When the ac is off the drain on the batteries is only about 3 mA. Though the display will be off, an internal oscillator will keep the counters running so that the correct time and date will be displayed when the power returns. For this option, replace R22 with a 5000-ohm potentiometer connected as a rheostat. Adjust it by unplugging the clock for one minute at a time (with a stand-by battery installed). Then, check whether it is fast or slow when the ac power is again applied and adjust R22 in the direction which will reduce error.

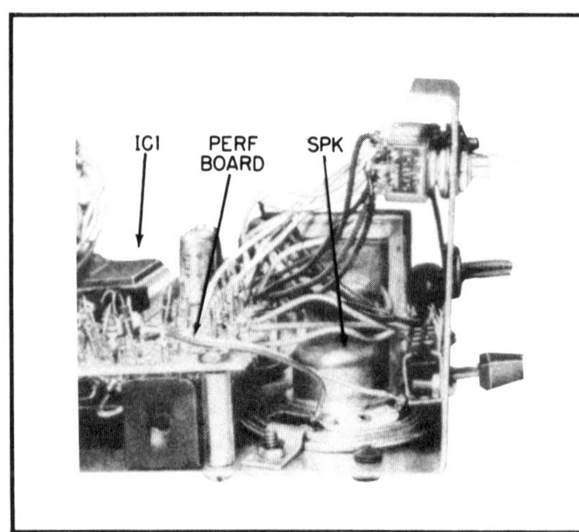

Fig. 3-18. Perf board mounting is simple enough if you use spacers, screws, and nuts as shown. You can mount the display panel (Z1) with anything from double-sided tape to epoxy glue. If you select the alarm option, you must use a small speaker; it can face downward (as shown) or forward for more sound. The kit of basic parts includes the 28-pin IC socket—see parts list (Table 3-2) for details.

Operation

Set the time, date, and alarm by turning S1 to the proper position (either time, date, or alarm). Then flip and hold S2 in the hour/months or minute/day position—whichever you wish to set. You will notice that the function you have elected to set will increment at one digit per second for as long as S2 is in the off-center position. You will also notice that setting one function will not affect any other function. This feature allows you to set February 29 in a leap year without upsetting any other function. You will also note that moving S1 to time stops the clock. When S2 is then actuated, seconds will reset to 00. These two imaginative features make for precise and easy time setting. After making all your settings, return S1 to its normal run setting.

The display mode, time-only, date-only or alternate (time and date), is selected with S3.

The alarm on switch S5 also turns on a red LED to make you aware that the alarm is set. The warning light may save you from being awakened at 7 a.m. on a weekend.

The alarm can be set up to 23 hours, 59 minutes in advance (let the alarm ring for a minute, or better still, just turn it off for a minute before flipping S5 back on for tomorrow morning's greeting). Switch S6 is the snooze button and will give you another ten minutes sleep in the morning if you can manage to give it a nudge.

When you set time or alarm, the p.m. light will indicate whether your setting corresponds to a.m. (light off) or p.m. (light on).

SONOPULSE TIMER

WOULDN'T YOU RATHER LISTEN TO A DULCET TONE WHEN timing a science project, or in the darkroom timing exposures and/or development, or when timing sports events, or any timing you may require, rather than to have to use a stop-watch? You can, you know, by building an electronic timer.

Why bother, you say. Well, for one thing, think of the pleasure and experience you will have building this intriguing solid state device; for another, particularly when in the darkroom, you are not forced to strain your eyes concentrating on the face of a dimly illuminated (safe light) clock. And, if you use a foot switch to trigger the SonoPulse, both hands will be free to perform other necessary functions during the timing process.

The SonoPulse employs one unijunction transistor (UJT) and one pnp general purpose transistor, plus five resistors, two electrolytics, a 9-V transistor radio battery, and an interesting solid-state miniature audible-signal device that emits a pleasant beep tone, develops a husky signal (approx. 50-80 dB). Although the audible signal unit draws just a couple of mA, it's all housed in a neat 6 × 3 1/2 × 2-in. plastic instrument case. The timing pulses can be varied from one every 3/4 of a second to 3.5 pulses per second.

How It Works

The UJT (Q1) is connected as a conventional relaxation oscillator wherein C1 and C2 charge—but wait a minute—how can these capacitors be charged when the ends of the series connection are both returned to the positive side of the battery? And if, as stated above, this is a series string of two electrolytic capacitors, each having definite plus and minus connections, how do you account for the two negative leads being connected together and floating, with each positive lead connected through resistors to the positive side of the battery?

The prime reason this manuscript was published by the Editors was the open challenge the schematic diagram presented to those who wish to find out how the circuit works. Take a good look at the schematic diagram (Fig. 3-19) and tell us honestly that you know how the circuit operates (See Table 3-3). If your answer is affirmative, then dollars to doughnuts you are either a genius or you're just fooling yourself. Before you read on any further, the Editors suggest that you copy the diagram onto a piece of paper and sit down with others who understand schematic diagrams and see if you can dope out exactly how this circuit works. You'll be surprised to discover how complicated a simple circuit can be.

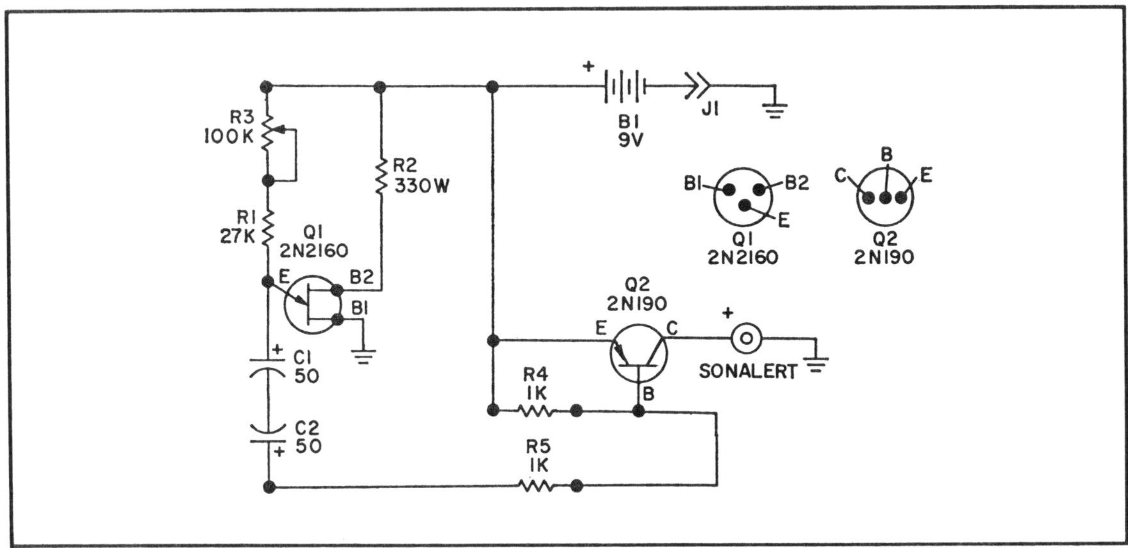

Fig. 3-19. SonoPulse schematic.

Here is a simple explanation of how the capacitors are charged. Since the collector-to-base-junction of Q2 is the equivalent of a diode and has diode leakage, the mystery should be solved. What is required to charge these capacitors is a negative reference point, which in this circuit is the collector-to-base junction. When the firing point of the emitter of the UJT (Q1) is reached, C1 and C2 discharge through the UJT and produce a negative pulse at the base of Q2, causing it to conduct. Capacitors C1 and C2 are connected "back-to-back" to produce, in effect, a bipolar capacitor since both open ends of that series connection are positive with respect to ground while idling between charges.

Table 3-3. Parts List for SonoPulse.

B1—9-V transistor radio battery (Eveready 216 or equiv.)
C1, C2—50-μF, 16-V electrolytic capacitor (Lafayette 34E85521 or equiv.)
J1—Open circuit phone jack (Lafayette 99E62135 or equiv.)
Q1—GE unijunction transistor type 2N2160
Q2—GE transistor type 2N190
R1—27,000-ohm, 1/2-watt resistor
R2—330-ohm, 1/2-watt resistor
R3—100,000-Ohm linear potentiometer (Lafayette 33E1104 or equiv.)
R4, R5—1000-ohm, 1/2-watt resistor
S1—Switch, single-pole momentary, normally open, pushbutton (Lafayette 99E62184 or equiv.)
1—6 3/8 × 3 3/16 × 1 7/8-in. bakelite box with aluminum panel (Lafayette 99E62721 or equiv.)
1—Keystone #203P battery holder
1—Battery connector (Lafayette 99E62879 or equiv.)
1—Mallory "Sonalert" electronic audible signal device (Lafayette 12E74018)
Misc.—Bolts, nuts, 1/2-in. spacer, perf board, flea clips, knob, etc.

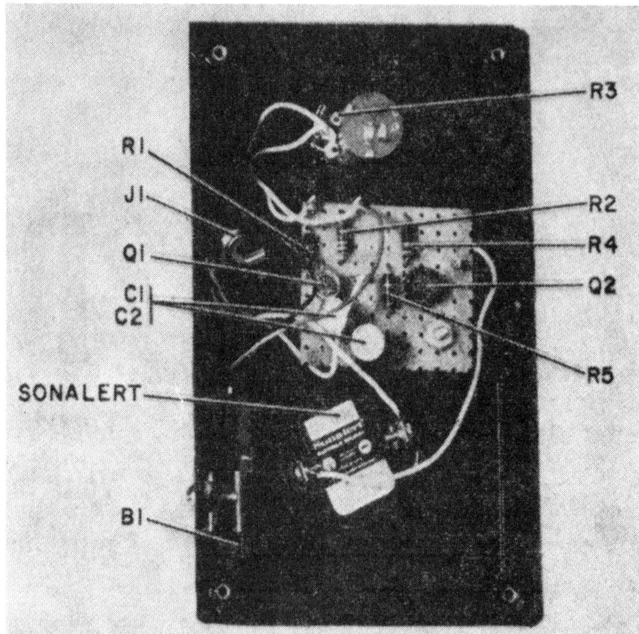

Fig. 3-20. The works of our SonoPulse timer. Though layout isn't critical this parts arrangement assists in hooking up the unit. The UJT and the unique audible alarm device help make this compact package a reality.

How to Build It.

A review of the photos (Figs. 3-20 and 3-21) reveals the simplicity of construction. The layout is not critical. We mounted all of the components, with the exception of the audible signal unit, the jack to which switch S1 is connected, and the battery, on a 2 × 2-in. piece

Fig. 3-21. Operating side of the SonoPulse timer. Note the simplicity of controls that make it easy to use.

of perfboard which, in turn, was mounted within the housing by one bolt and 1/2-in. spacer. The audible unit is mounted in the base of the plastic case, centered in the upper half, by drilling a single 1 3/16-in. hole in the base of the case. You may use a chassis punch, circle cutter or nibbling tool to cut this hole.

The timing control is mounted centered in the lower half of the base and the jack to which the starting switch is plugged for connection to the circuit is mounted on the case wherever it will be most convenient. (Our unit has it mounted in the base near the timing control.) A blank piece of aluminum covers the plastic case and serves as a bottom plate.

We used flea clips in the perfboard as intake-off points for the potentiometer, battery and jack connections. You may want, also, to use flea clips to mount and connect the transistors and other parts, which makes it easier to replace the parts that may become defective. Although we held the battery in place with a simple clip bolted to the side of the plastic case, you may prefer using a battery holder.

As you can see in in Fig. 3-21, we used a miniature pushbutton switch which we mounted in a discarded container from solder for S1. It serves the purpose well. However, should you prefer a foot-operated switch you may improvise one or buy a commercially built foot switch. You can easily make one by mounting the miniature pushbutton switch in a rubber, hollow door wedge (available from hardware or variety stores). We purposely have not specified the length of the pair of wires between the switch and SonoPulse. Make it a convenient-to-use length. You may use zip cord, 2-conductor jacketed cable, or twisted hook-up wire. If you use a double-pole switch in place of the single pole, the extra contacts can be used to turn on or off the enlarger or device being timed. You can best see this technical point by referring to the schematic diagram (Fig. 3-19).

Using SonoPulse

When completed you will hear a pleasant beep tone burst, repeated continuously as long as switch S1 is closed. The repetition rate is controlled by potentiometer R3. The fastest pulse rate is attained at full counter-clockwise (minimum resistance) rotation of R3; the slowest is full clockwise (maximum resistance) rotation.

We did not take the time to locate calibration points on our model. You will find the SonoPulse timer more useful if you do calibrate the control. This can be done easily by using a stop-watch. Just start the watch at the beginning of a count of 10 (or 20 if you prefer) beeps and stop it at the end of the count. Divide the total elapsed time registered on the stopwatch by the number of beeps counted (10 or 20) to arrive at the time duration between beeps. These various settings of R3 at the time the count is made will become your calibration marks.

BASIC CMOS NAND OSCILLATOR

CLOSING S1 CAUSES THIS CMOS NAND OSCILLATOR TO FLASH the LED. The "ON" time is controlled by R1 and the "OFF" time is controlled by R2. This oscillator can sit for months with S1 open because, being CMOS, it draws very little power. It is a basic oscillator useful for driving buzzers, computer clocks, counters, various alarm circuits, windshield wipers and uncountable other applications. The output from pin 4 can drive small loads, even small relays, directly, or you can drive a transistor or SCR to handle bigger loads. See Fig. 3-22 and Table 3-4.

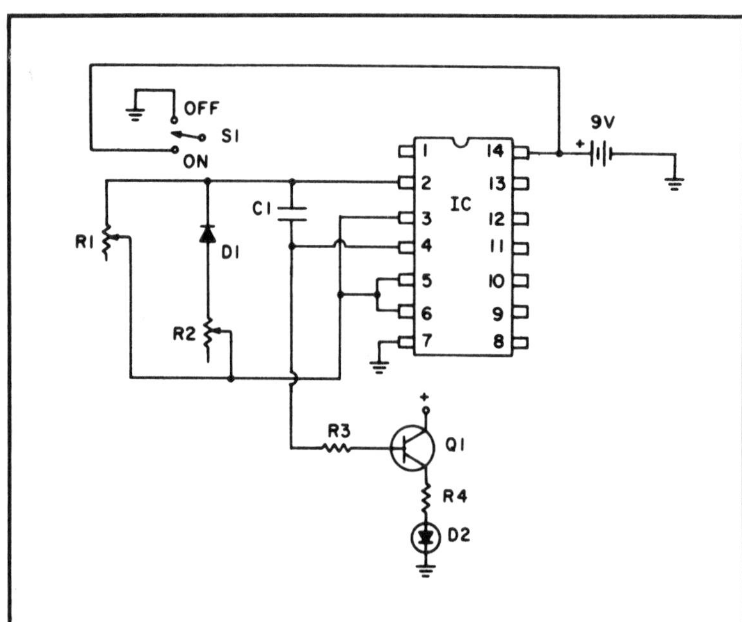

Fig. 3-22. Basic CMOS NAND oscillator schematic.

Table 3-4. Parts List for Basic CMOS NAND Oscillator.

C1—0.1-μF ceramic capacitor, 15 Vdc	R2—100,000-ohm linear-taper potentiometer
D1—1N4001 diode	R3—1,000-ohm, 1/2-watt resistor
D2—small LED	R4—10,000-ohm 1/2-watt resistor
IC1—4011 quad NAND gate	R5—570-ohm, 1/2-watt resistor
Q1—2N4401 transistor	S1—SPDT slide switch
R1—10,000,000-ohm linear-taper potentiometer	

TTL LOGIC PROBE

THIS CIRCUIT CAN BE USED AS AN INDICATOR OF THE LOGIC conditions at any point in a TTL digital circuit. It will indicate the presence of a continuous logic 1 or logic 0, an illegal voltage level, or the presence of pulses at any frequency or duty cycle. The presence of a continuous logic level is detected by IC1A and IC1B, which are voltage comparators set to detect levels of 2.0 and 0.8 volts respectively. The presence of pulses is detected by a 555 timer connected as a one-shot multivibrator, which illuminates an LED for about 0.5 second if pulses are present. A second 555 timer is used to disable IC2 for about 0.5 second each time it fires. This provides a flashing LED regardless of the frequency of the detected pulses. The circuit is powered by the 5 volt supply feeding the digital circuit under test. To calibrate the circuit, apply a voltage of 2.0 volts dc to

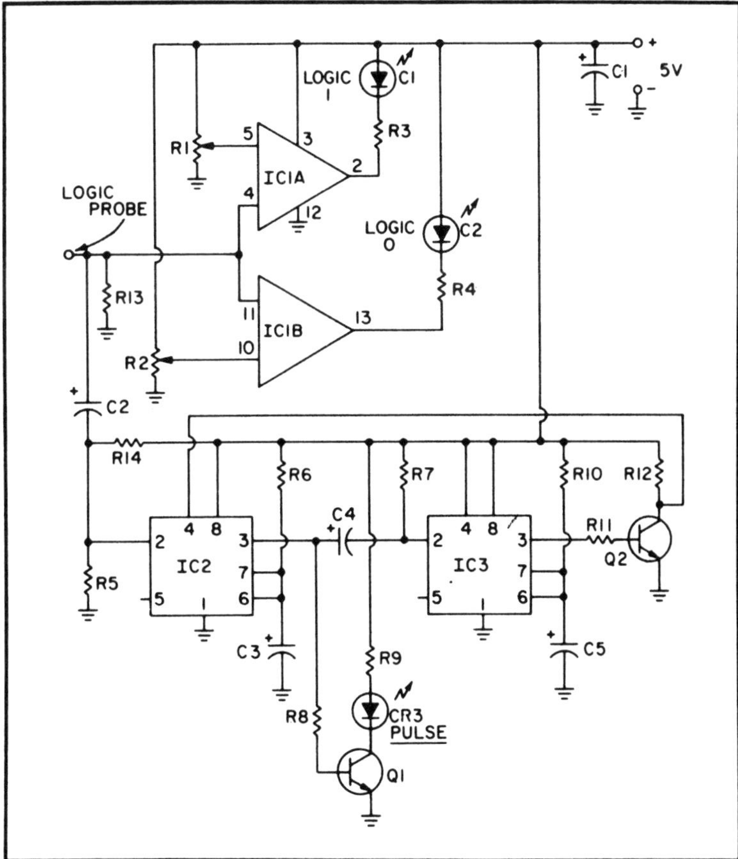

Fig. 3-23. TTL logic probe schematic.

Table 3-5. Parts List for TTL Logic Probe.

C1—10-μF electrolytic capacitor, 25 Vdc	Q1, Q2—2N4401
C2—0.01-μF ceramic capacitor, 15 Vdc	R1, R2—50,000-ohm linear-taper potentiometer
C3—1-μF electrolytic capacitor, 15 Vdc	R3, R4—220-ohm, 1/2-watt resistor
C4—0.01-μF ceramic capacitor, 15 Vdc	R5, R7, R14—100,000-ohm, 1/2-watt resistor
C5—1-μF electrolytic capacitor, 15 Vdc	R6, R10—470,000-ohm, 1/2-watt resistor
D1, D2, D3—large LED	R8, R11, R12—4,700-ohm, 1/2-watt resistor
IC1—339 quad comparator	R9—180-ohm, 1/2-watt resistor
IC2, IC3—555 timer	R13—10,000-ohm, 1/2-watt resistor

the logic input terminal. Adjust R1 so that D1 is on the borderline between off and on. Apply 0.8 volts to the logic input terminal and adjust R2 so that D2 is on the borderline between off and on. When using the circuit either D1 or D2 or both must be lit to indicate a correct logic level. If both are out, the detected voltage is between 0.8 and 2.0 volts and is an illegal voltage level. D3 will flash only if there are pulses present on the line under test. See Fig.3-23 and Table 3-5.

LOGICAL PROBE

THIS SIMPLE BUT USEFUL CMOS PROBE GOES BEYOND LEDS TO tell the status of a logic circuit. It shows, via a numerical readout, whether the condition is literally 0 or 1. In addition, if the switching action is high enough to cause 0 and 1 to merge into an ambiguous blur, the center (G) segment comes into play, causing the display to show a distinct 8. In operation, when the probe is at a logic-high, the 1 is illuminated, as it is when the probe is open-circuited, to show that the circuit is operative. When a logic-low is touched, segments C, D, E, and F are illuminated, producing the 0 indication. Every time a transition is made between high and low, this action is gated by the capacitor to the inverter driving the G segment. Thus, all states are covered. See Fig. 3-24 and Table 3-6.

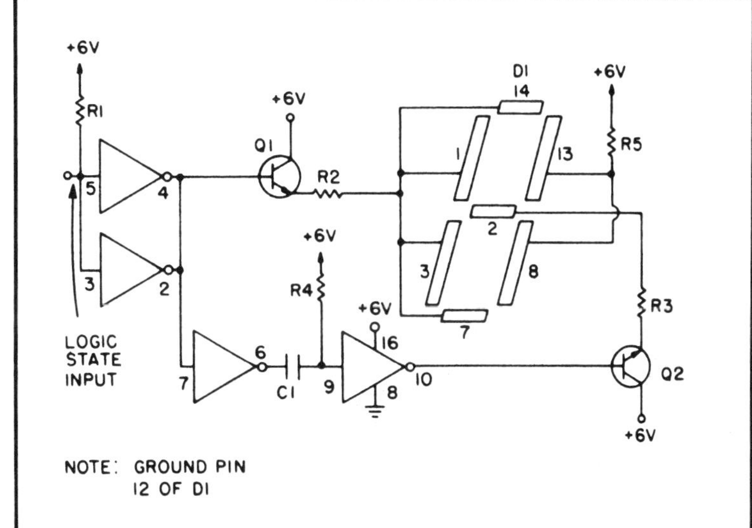

Fig. 3-24. Logical probe schematic.

Table 3-6. Parts List for Logical Probe.

C1—0.1-μF ceramic capacitor, 15 Vdc
D1—DL-702 LED display
IC1—4009A hex buffer
Q1, Q2—2N4401
R1, R4—100,000-ohm, 1/2-watt resistor
R2, R3—1,000-ohm, 1/2-watt resistor
R5—330-ohm, 1/2-watt resistor

CRYSTAL-CONTROLLED TTL

This inexpensive color-TV crystal of approximately 3.58 MHz can readily be persuaded to oscillate in the following 7404 circuit. The resultant waveform can be divided down, via other popular IC chips, such as the 4017 CMOS type. See Fig. 3-25 and Table 3-7.

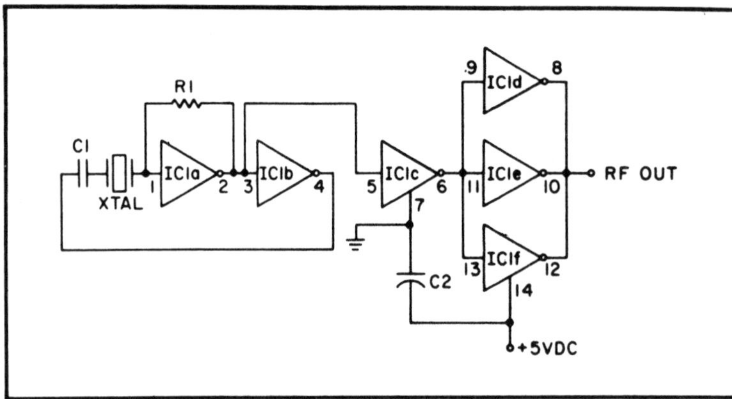

Fig. 3-25. Crystal-controlled TTL schematic.

C1—75-pF mica capacitor, 15 Vdc
C2—0.01-μF ceramic capacitor, 15 Vdc
IC1—7404 hex inverter
R1—1,000-ohm, 1/2-watt resistor
XTAL—3.58 MHz crystal (color TV carrier type)

Table 3-7. Parts List for Crystal-Controlled TTL.

BASIC PULSE MAKER

NEED A BASIC SQUARE-WAVE GENERATOR FOR ALL THOSE DIGital projects? This quad NOR gate 4001A CMOS chip, which can be easily obtained, stands ready to do the job with great simplicity. Note the two pots, R1 and R2. These govern both frequency and duty-cycle (symmetry), via diodes D1 and D2. C1 determines the overall frequency range. A C1 value of 0.1 μF, produces a range of about 11 to 2500 Hz. Using a 0.2 μF value, the range is about 4 to 700 Hz. The remaining two gates (pins 8-13) act as buffers, to isolate the oscillator from the effects of circuit loading. Duty cycles of almost 10 to 1 can be obtained. See Fig. 3-26 and Table 3-8.

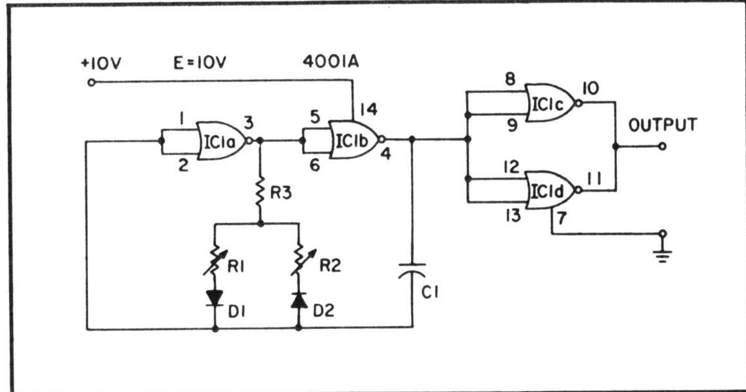

Fig. 3-26. Basic Pulse Maker schematic.

Table 3-8. Parts List for Basic Pulse Maker.

C1—0.1-μF capacitor for 11-to-2500 Hz range, 0.2 μF capacitor for 4-to-700 Hz range
D1, D2—1N4148 diode
IC1—4001 A quad NOR gate
R1, R2—500,000-ohm, linear-taper potentiometer

DO-IT-YOURSELF LOGIC

SOMETIMES THE INTEGRATED CIRCUITS TAKEN FOR GRANTED are not always available, and one must fall back on more basic components. We do not go quite as far as discrete transistors here, but show how a frequency divider flip-flop can be improvised from simple gates. The following divide-by-two circuit was used for dividing a 60 Hz square wave, but should work well at other frequencies. A 7400 or 74LS00 quad NAND gate was selected, with the two extra gates employed as buffers to keep the input toggle clock from appearing when the flip-flop was biased off. If the cut-off resistor R3 is the same value as R1 and R2, a lock-out will be obtained. If it is about doubled, then the circuit will function, but will hold one output high (or low) when the clock signal drops out. See Fig. 3-27 and Table 3-9.

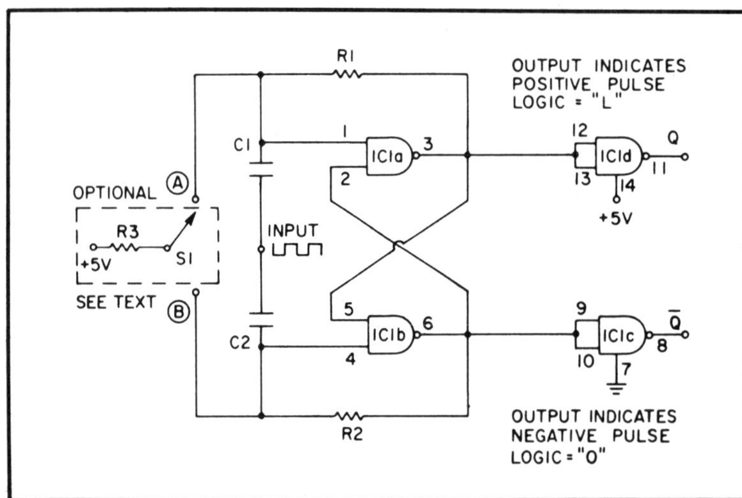

Fig. 3-27. Do-it-yourself logic schematic.

C1, C2—0.01 to 0.1-μF ceramic capacitor, 15 Vdc
IC1—7400 quad NAND gate
R1, R2—50,000 to 100,000-ohm, 1/2-watt resistor (see text)
R3—50,000 to 200,000-ohm, 1/2-watt resistor (see text)
S1—SPDT toggle switch

Table 3-9. Parts List for Do-It-Yourself Logic.

AND LOGIC DEMONSTRATOR

IN DIGITAL LOGIC, AN AND STATEMENT IS TRUE ONLY IF ALL parts of the logic leading to it (its inputs) are all true. If we take "true" to mean "on," a logic state we define as "1" (and not true = off = 0), we can see that a series switch configuration is a good way to illustrate the AND logical statement.

In integrated circuit logic, instead of actual mechanical switches, transistors are used as switches. Specifically, this circuit demonstrates the action on a "two-input AND gate." Only if both switches are on will the LED turn on. Similarly, you can expand the demonstrator to demonstrate as many inputs to an AND gate as you have switches to connect in series.

Once again, we present the "truth table" of this particular circuit, which will tell you exactly what's happening and when. Truth tables are often used in digital design, and can be indispensible. Depending on the device they can be quite long. See Fig. 3-28 and Table 3-10.

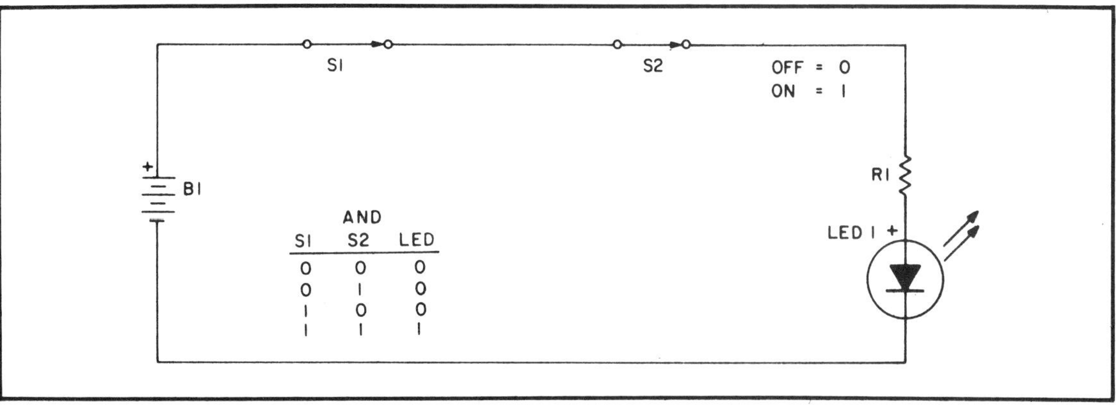

Fig. 3-28. AND logic demonstrator schematic.

Table 3-10. Parts List for Logical "AND" Demonstrator.

B1—9Vdc battery
LED1—Light emitting diode
R1—470-ohm resistor, 1/2-watt
S1, S2—SPST switch

NAND LOGIC DEMONSTRATOR

NAND IS LOGIC SHORTHAND FOR "NOT AND." SO A NAND GATE has an output of 1 only when an AND gate would not. Compare the right column (results, or output) of an AND gate truth table to that for the NAND gate and you will see that they are exactly opposite.

Here, the LED will turn on only if the two switches are not both turned on. Be careful that the series combination of S1 and S2 can short out only the LED and not R1 as well or your battery will not last more than a few seconds. R1 limits the current drain on the battery to about 20 milliamps. See Fig. 3-29 and Table 3-11.

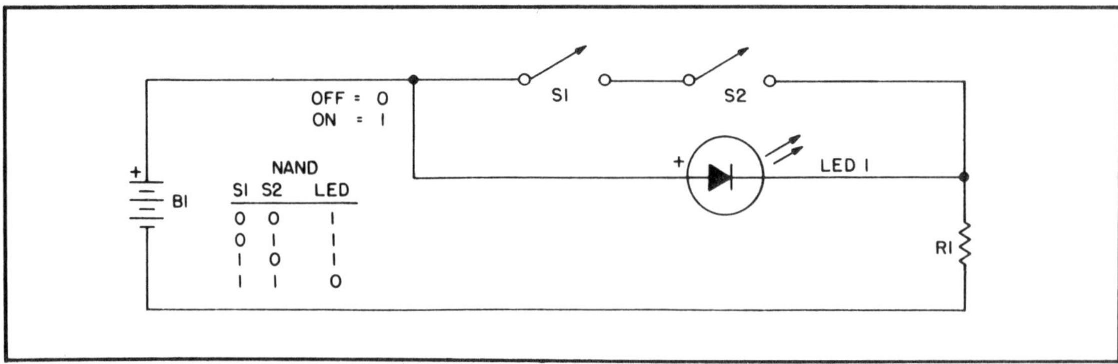

Fig. 3-29. NAND logic demonstrator schematic.

R1—470-ohm resistor, 1/2-watt
S1, S2—SPST switch
B1—9 Vdc battery
LED1—Light emitting diode

Table 3-11. Parts List for Logical "NAND" Demonstrator.

OR LOGIC DEMONSTRATOR

IN DIGITAL LOGIC, AN OR STATEMENT IS TRUE IF ANY ONE OF the statements leading to it is true. Parallel switches are a good analogy for the OR logic function. If any of the parallel switches are on (= true = "1"), the LED turns on. While this circuit demonstrates the operation of a "two-input OR gate," you may add as many parallel switches as you like to demonstrate the action of "wider" OR gates.

OR gates are very widely used in alarm circuits, for example, where an alarm should be sounded whenever anything occurs at any one of the several inputs. The chart of numbers is known as a "Truth Table." The columns at the left identify the states of the various inputs, the column at the right the state of the output. Compare the results (right column) of this Truth Table with the results of other types of logic and you will see why digital logic systems can be so versatile.

The nice thing about this circuit is that it's so visual. You'll find that it's so much easier to understand digital logic when you can watch what's happening rather than reading about it. See Fig. 3-30 and Table 3-12.

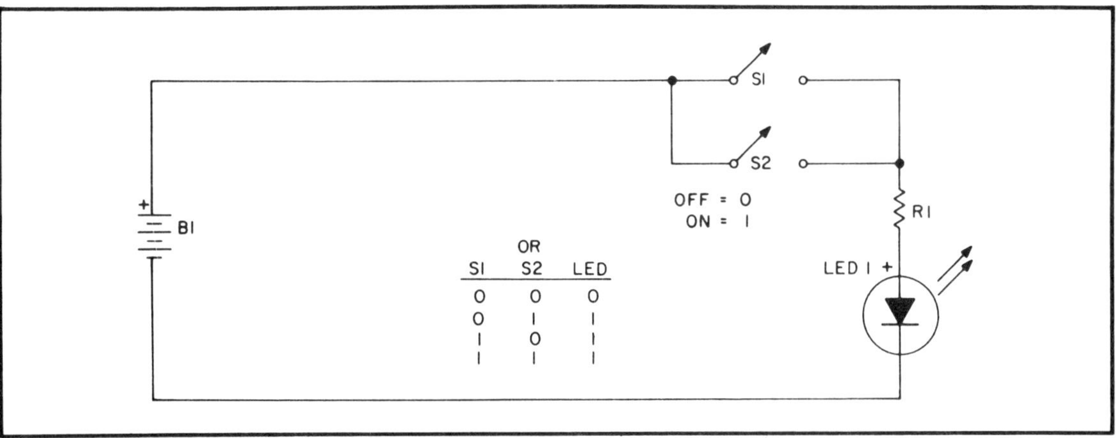

Fig. 3-30. OR logic demonstrator schematic.

Table 3-12. Parts List for Logical "OR" Demonstrator.

B1—9 Vdc battery
LED1—Light emitting diode
R1—470-ohm resistor, 1/2-watt
S1, S2—SPST switch

NOR LOGIC DEMONSTRATOR

JUST AS THE OUTPUT OF A NAND GATE IS THE OPPOSITE OF THAT for an AND gate, this NOR gate produces results opposite those of an OR gate. LED1 will turn on when neither S1 nor S2 are on.

A NOR gate is a good way to handle a failsafe system in which a circuit cannot operate unless all systems are "go"; in other words, if any of the inputs are on, the system cannot be.

This truth table compares the operation of different types of logic gates:

Think of 0 = off = not true,
1 = on = true

Digital logic is certainly in the forefront of modern electronics. Circuits such as this NOR Demonstrator can help to prepare you in understanding complex circuitry. The principles you learn remain the same as in actual digital circuitry—only the method of achieving demonstrable results changes. See Fig. 3-31 and Table 3-13.

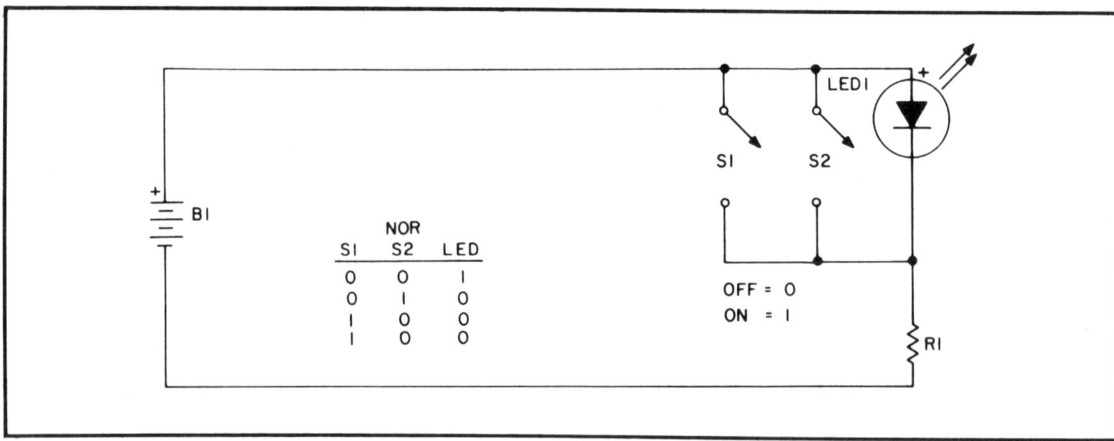

Fig. 3-31. NOR logic demonstrator schematic.

B1—9 Vdc battery
LED1—Light emitting diode
R1—470-ohm resistor, 1/2-watt
S1, S2—SPST switch

Table 3-13. Parts List for Logical "NOR" Demonstrator.

Chapter 4

Fun 'N Game Projects

BLINKEY

BLINKEY IS AN ELECTRONIC "FRIEND" FROM ANOTHER GALAXY. He is asleep as long as nobody disturbs him. However, press your finger to his lips and Blinkey becomes agitated. His eyes blink on and off. If you press your fingers more firmly, he becomes even more furious, blinking more rapidly. When you remove your fingers, Blinkey goes back to sleep again and his eyes stop blinking. See Fig. 4-1.

The simple circuit uses one integrated circuit and a few components. If you like, Blinkey can be built inside a doll or constructed on a PC board as the author has done. The remaining copper foil on the PC board resembles a mouth, ears and eye brows. The IC resembles a nose, and the two LEDs are Blinkey's eyes.

How He Blinks

Blinkey's circuit is show in Fig. 4-2. Consider U1A and U1B alone (without R1 or U1C and D connected). If we replaced the Touch Place (lips) with a resistor, we would have an ordinary oscillator. The frequency of oscillation would be determined by the value of C1 and the resistor. Instead of using a resistor, you place your finger or hand across the touchplate, the resistance of your hand determines the frequency of oscillation. As you press harder, the resistance decreases

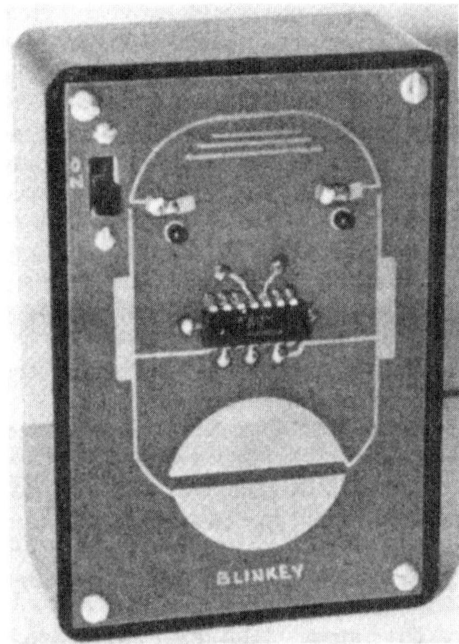

Fig. 4-1. This is Blinkey.

and the frequency of oscillation increases. Now, if we connect U1C and D to the oscillator, LED (left) and LED (right) will simultaneously blink. U1C and D are buffers that provide enough current for the two LEDs to turn on.

If you removed your hand when the LEDs were on, they would remain on indefinitely. This would drain the battery. Since we often forget to turn off a toy, we provide an automatic shutoff of the LEDs. This automatic shutoff is R1. When your hand is removed from the Touchplates, R1 allows the voltage at pins 1 and 2 of U1A to rise to-

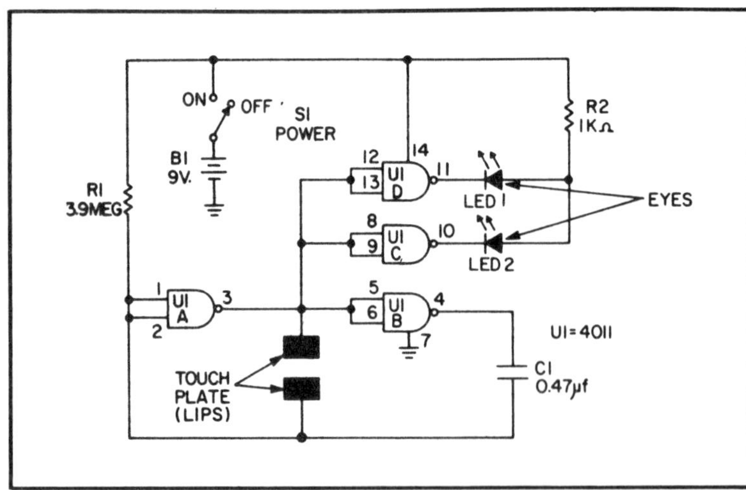

Fig. 4-2. The Blinkey schematic.

Table 4-1. Parts List for Blinkey.

B1—9-Vdc transistor battery
C1—0.47-μF, non-polarized electrolytic capacitor
LED1, 2—light emitting diode, 1/8-inch
R1—10,000,000-ohm, 1/4 watt resistor, 10%
R2—1,000-ohm, 1/4-watt resistor, 10%
S1—slide switch, SPST
U1—CD 4011 quad, 2 input NAND gate integrated circuit
Misc—PC board, 9-volt battery clip, suitable case, wire, solder, etc.

wards 9 volts. Eventually (after a second or two) this will cause the output of U1A to go low, turning off the LEDs. In this state, the current draw by the circuit is very low, ensuring a long battery life. R2 limits the current drawn by the LEDs and S1 provides the voltage from the battery for operation. See Table 4-1.

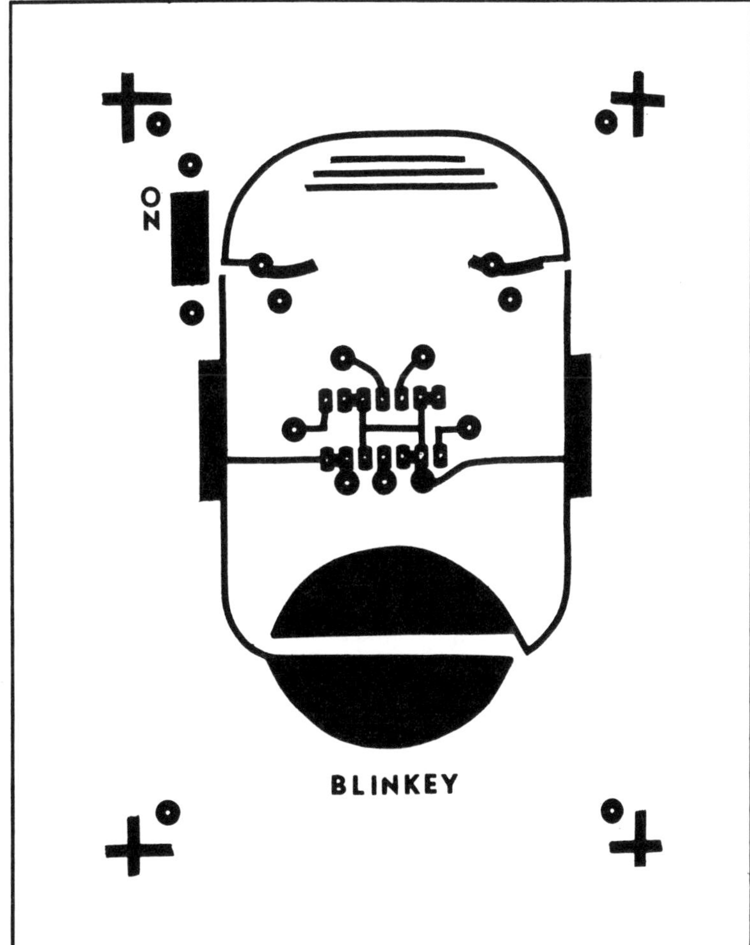

Fig. 4-3. This is the Printed Circuit board template for Blinkey. As you see, the switch is actually etched on the board. It uses a bit more copper than usual. Schematic, above, is simple and straightforward. The whole thing should take less than an hour.

Construction

Any means of construction is suitable. An easy way of reproducing the circuit is to use the PC Board layout shown in Fig. 4-3. The overall size of the PC Board should be adjusted to allow it to substitute for the top plate of the box you are using. U1C is mounted on the FOIL side of the PC Board, while all other components are mounted on the reverse side. Mount the two LEDs through the "eye" holes and secure with epoxy. After R1 is installed, solder a short length of wire between it and S1 as shown in Fig. 4-4. If a 0.47 μF non-polarized capacitor is not available, five 0.1 μF disk capacitors can be paralleled together and used instead. While R1 is stated as 10 megohms, any value greater than 3.9 megohms can be used.

How to Make Him Blink

Place S1 to the ON position. Press your finger(s) across the two semicircular portions of the "mouth" (or place one finger on each hand on each of the two "ears"). You will note that the LEDs blink at same rate. By applying less pressure, the LEDs will blink at a slower rate. By pressing harder, the LEDs blink faster until (if your skin resistance is low enough) the two LEDs appear to be on continuously.

Factors such as dryness of the skin affect the skin resistance and, therefore, the blinking rate that can be achieved by an individual. It is interesting to note the rates that can be achieved by different people. Considering this, the basic circuit could be changed slightly to create a "strength" tester similar to those seen in Penny Arcades. All that is needed is to replace the Touch Plates with a "strength tester." This

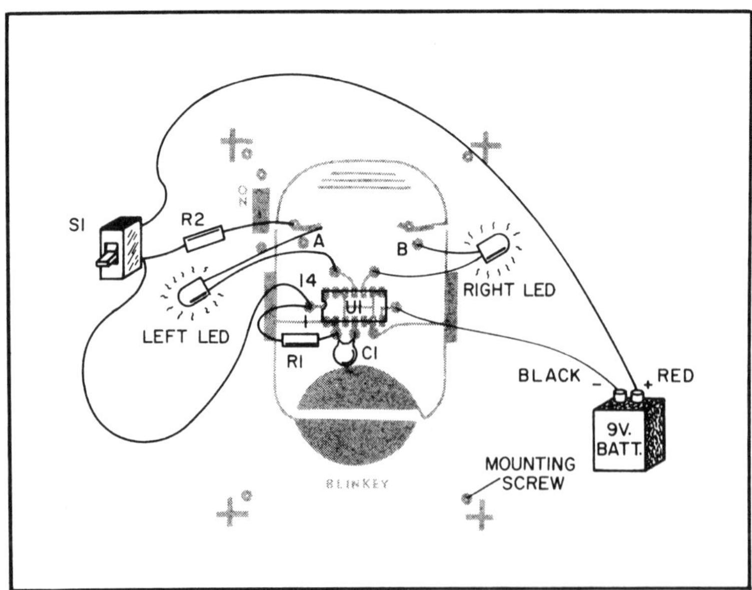

Fig. 4-4. This is the only tricky part of Blinkey. Follow the directions in the text carefully, and you will not have a single bit of trouble.

can be a short (6-inch or so) length of 1-inch dowel. Glue a 1/8-inch strip of aluminum foil down the length of the dowel. Glue an identical strip opposite the first. Connect the two strips to the Touch Plate of the circuit and you have your strength tester. Although not a true indication, this is very entertaining.

ELEC-TAC-TOE

ELECTRONIC GAMES SEEM TO POP UP AGAIN AND AGAIN AS construction projects, presumably because a game is not only fun to construct, but fun to use. But how many of the games you've seen (or built) are really worth the time and money put into their construction? Sure, electronic dice or roulette wheels are fascinating for the moment, but it's doubtful that anyone clever enough to build such a game could remain intrigued with it for very long. Then consider the other extreme; a cassette-programmed, microprocessor-based TV game. These devices are certainly more entertaining than a simple construction project, yet there are the undeniable disadvantages of high cost and the inability to play without a television receiver.

As a solution to the whole dilemma there is Elec-Tac-Toe, a game that is simple to construct, yet always fascinating because it is a game of deductive logic. The rules of play are so simple that even a child can catch on after a few minutes of instruction, but winning will require razor-sharp wits. If you're up to the challenge, read on.

As the name suggests, Elec-Tac-Toe is derived from Tic-Tac-Toe; both use the same 9-cell grid as a playing field. The similarity, however, ends there. In Elec-Tac-Toe there are nine LEDs, arranged so that each one occupies a single cell of the grid. In addition, there is a separate grid of nine pushbutton switches. The internal electronics randomly select three cells out of the grid, and if the pushbutton corresponding to a selected cell is pressed, the LED in that cell will light up. If a pushbutton corresponding to a cell not selected by the electronics is pressed, that cell's LED remains unlit. Two players compete, and the first person to correctly deduce which three cells out of the nine have been selected is the winner.

It is important to note that the three cells selected by the internal circuitry will form one of the scoring sets of traditional Tic-Tac-Toe. The sets are shown in Fig. 4-5 and you can see that these are the familiar three row-sets (r1, r2, and r3), three column-sets (c1, c2, and c3), and two diagonal-sets (d1 and d2). A simple-minded way of finding out which set has been selected by the internal circuitry would be to press each of the nine pushbuttons in succession and note which three LEDs lit up. However, we can be more clever than that.

Let's begin by noting that the cells of the grid may be divided up into three classes, as shown. There are four corner-cells (1, 3, 7, and 9), four side-cells (2, 4, 6, and 8), and one middle cell (5). Furthermore cells of a particular class each belong to a characteristic number of scoring sets. For example, each corner-cell belongs to one row-set,

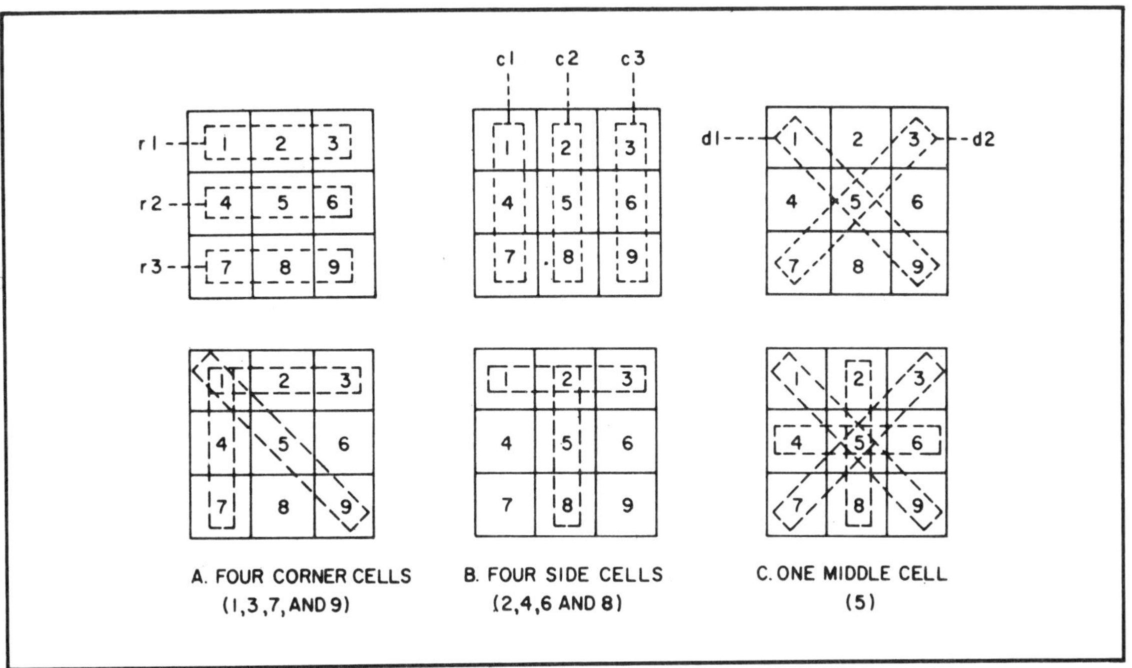

Fig. 4-5. Along the top are pictured Elec-Tac-Toe's rows, columns and diagonals. The fun begins when the two players try to outguess each other as to which three LEDs will light, as secretly selected by the game. As you can see on the bottom pictorial; if LED 1 is lit Row 1, Column 1 or Diagonal 1 may be the scorer. Deductive reasoning will win here!

one column-set, and one diagonal-set. Each side-cell belongs to one row-set and to one column-set. And the lone middle-cell belongs to the two diagonal-sets (d1 and d2), to one row-set (r2), and to one column-set (c2). Classifying the cells in the above way is a tremendous help to deducing the correct solution. You can try for yourself to see why this is so—and the examples at the end of this project will explain the reasoning in detail.

A rough outline of a game of Elec-Tac-Toe may be helpful at this point. To begin with, the SCRAMBLE button is pressed, thus causing a new set of cells to be selected by the internal circuitry. This scrambling operation simultaneously causes a random number (0 through 9) to be generated on a display. One player then commences by pressing the pushbutton of the cell (#1 through #9) whose number is called out on the display. If the display shows zero, the player may begin with the cell of his own choice. Next, the opponent presses the pushbutton of his choice. This pressing of buttons alternates until one player has enough information to correctly identify the unknown, electronically selected set. The first player to deduce the solution is the winner. Later on, we'll consider the rules of Elec-Tac-Toe more thoroughly, and examine examples of the logical elimination that is so important in this game. First let's consider the electronic circuit and its construction.

In the schematic (Fig. 4-6) you will see IC1, a 555 timer, hooked up as an astable multivibrator. At its output (pin 3) there is available a 14-kHz square wave. Momentarily pressing SCRAMBLE switch S11 causes the square wave to be applied simultaneously to two counters: IC2 and IC4. We will be interested in the resting state of each counter after S11 is released, and because the clocking signal is so rapid, and examine examples of the process of the resting states cannot be predicted by the person manipulating S11; therefore, the outputs of both counters at rest are random. Since the two counters have different count lengths (eight for IC2 vs. ten for IC4), they can both be randomized by the same clock signal without getting locked together. See Figs. 4-7 through 4-10 and Table 4-2.

Consider IC4 first. Inside this IC we have a decade counter plus a seven-segment decoder. The outputs of this IC are constant-current sinks that connect directly to the display, DIS1, without any intervening resistors. On the display we can read a random number (between 0 and 9), which denotes the cell at which play must begin in a game. This feature prevents players from starting at a particular cell and then working through the cells in a fixed pattern all the time. Such a procedure would make finding the solution somewhat easier because a fixed set of decisions would be made every time. Hence, fewer slip-ups would occur. IC4's inclusion means that players need to remember more facts, so more mistakes are made, and the game becomes more of a challenge. Furthermore, the fact that players alternate at choosing cells adds a little bit more confusion to the game.

Let's proceed to IC2 next. This IC is a 3-stage binary counter, at whose outputs (pins 8, 9, and 11) we may find the binary representation of any number from 0 to 7. The outputs drive decoder IC3, which converts each one of the eight unique input states into a specific output signal. These output signals are such that only one of IC3's eight outputs conducts current to ground in response to any given binary input. Suppose, for instance, that it is pin 1 of IC3 that happens to be capable of conducting. We then have three potential paths by which current might flow from the positive supply to ground: S1-LED1-R1-D1, S2-LED2-R2-D2, and S3-LED3-R3-D3. Thus, the set selected by the circuit consists of the three cells in which LED1, LED2, and LED3 reside. Pressing S1, S2, or S3 results in the lighting of LED1, LED2, or LED3, while pressing any other switch will not cause any LED to light. Similar results occur if any one of the seven other outputs of IC3 happens to be the one capable of conduction.

Power for the circuit comes from transformer T1, whose output is full-wave rectified by D25 and D26, then smoothed by electrolytic capacitor C1. Voltage regulator IC5 provides a regulated 5-volt potential between its output (pin 2) and ground. Capacitors C2, C3, and C4 bypass the supply and stabilize the circuit.

There is an optional part to the schematic; see Fig. 4-11 and Table

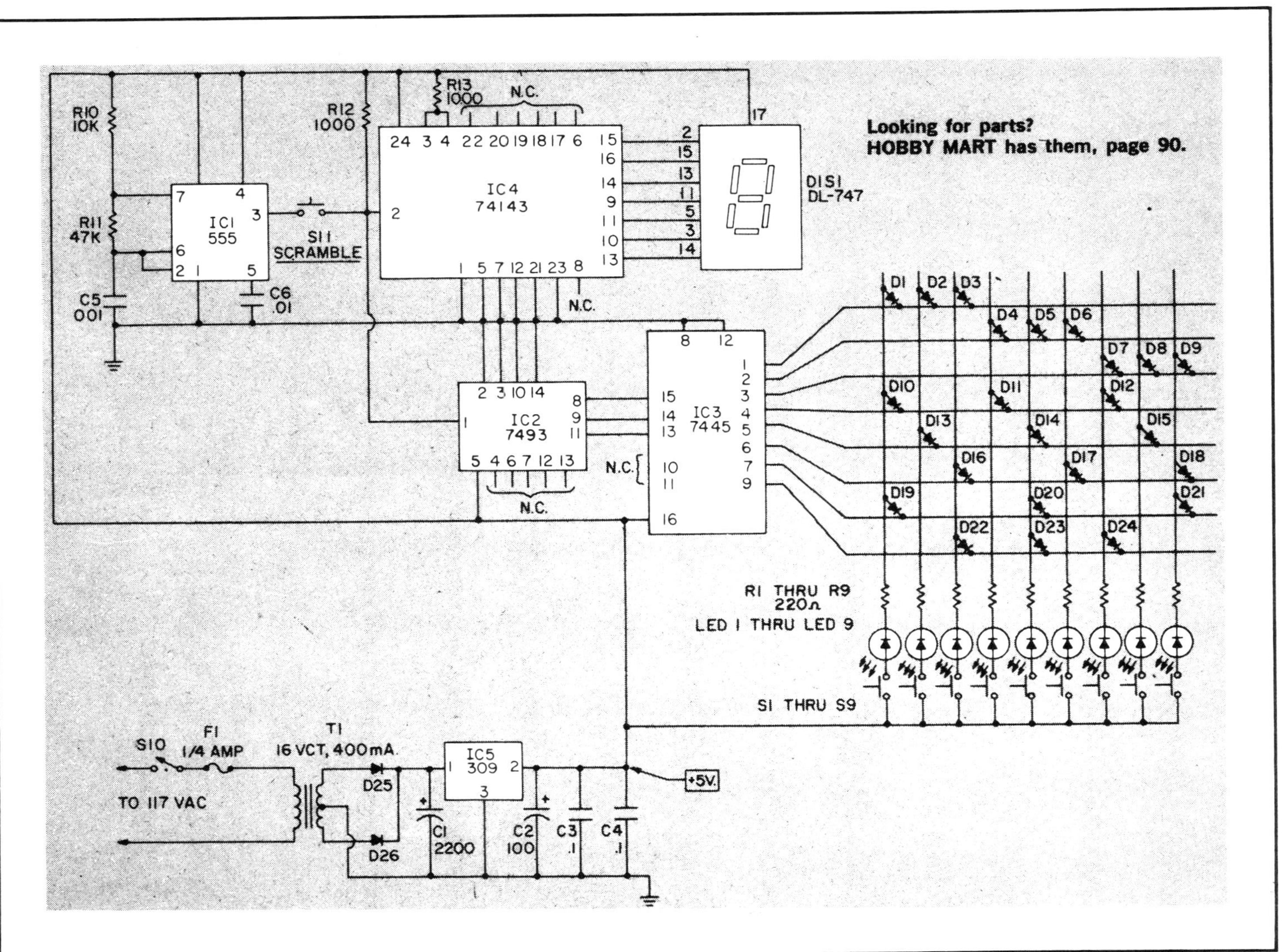

Fig. 4-6. Elec-Tac-Toe schematic.

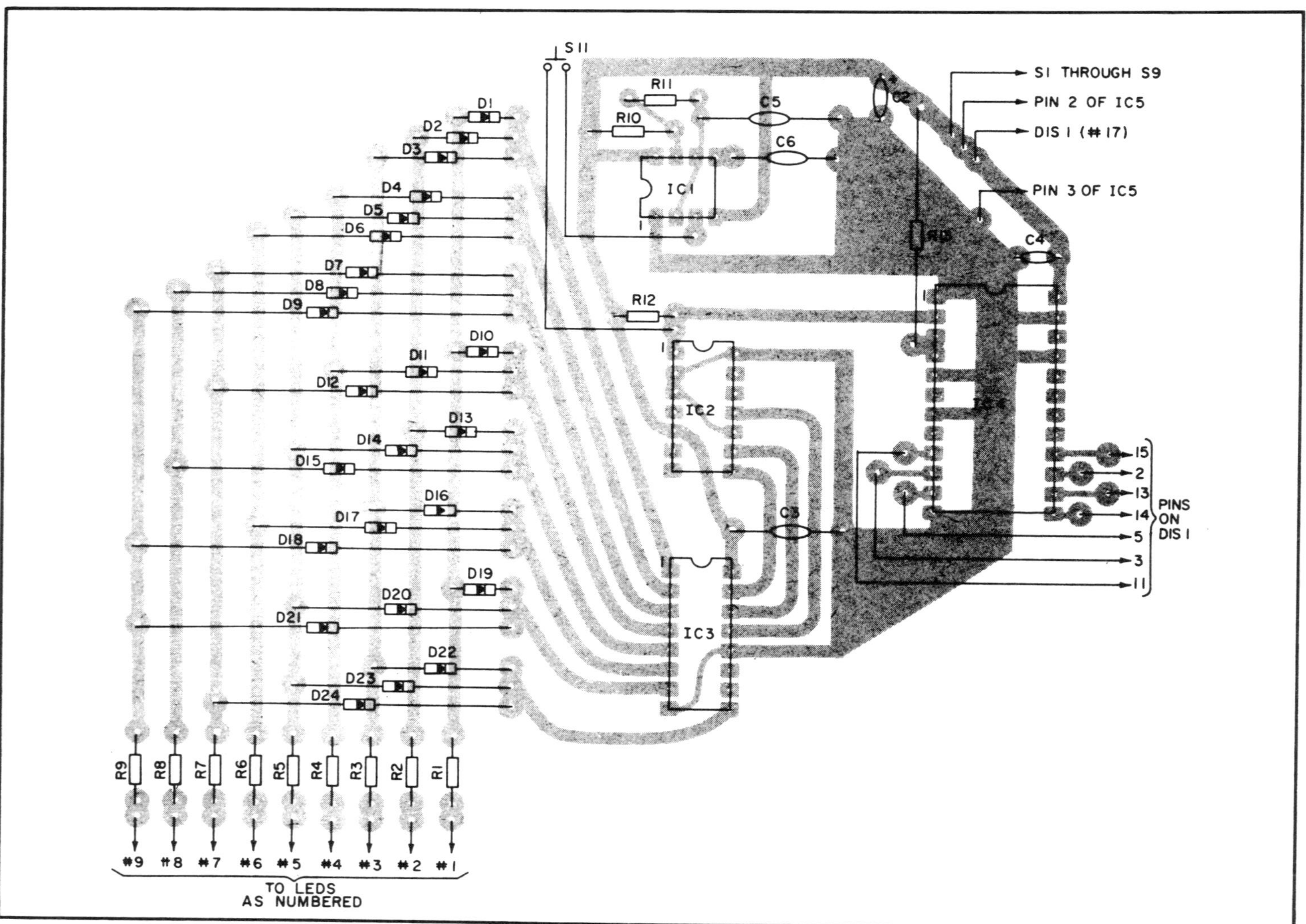

Fig. 4-7. When you assemble Elec-Tac-Toe, be certain to observe all device polarities such as C1, C2 and all the IC chips. Be very careful with the diodes, D1 through D24. They must all be arranged in the same direction. With so many it could be easy to make a mistake, so keep a watchful eye on that part of the assembly. You can use about any front-panel layout. The switches may be discrete, or a calculator keyboard.

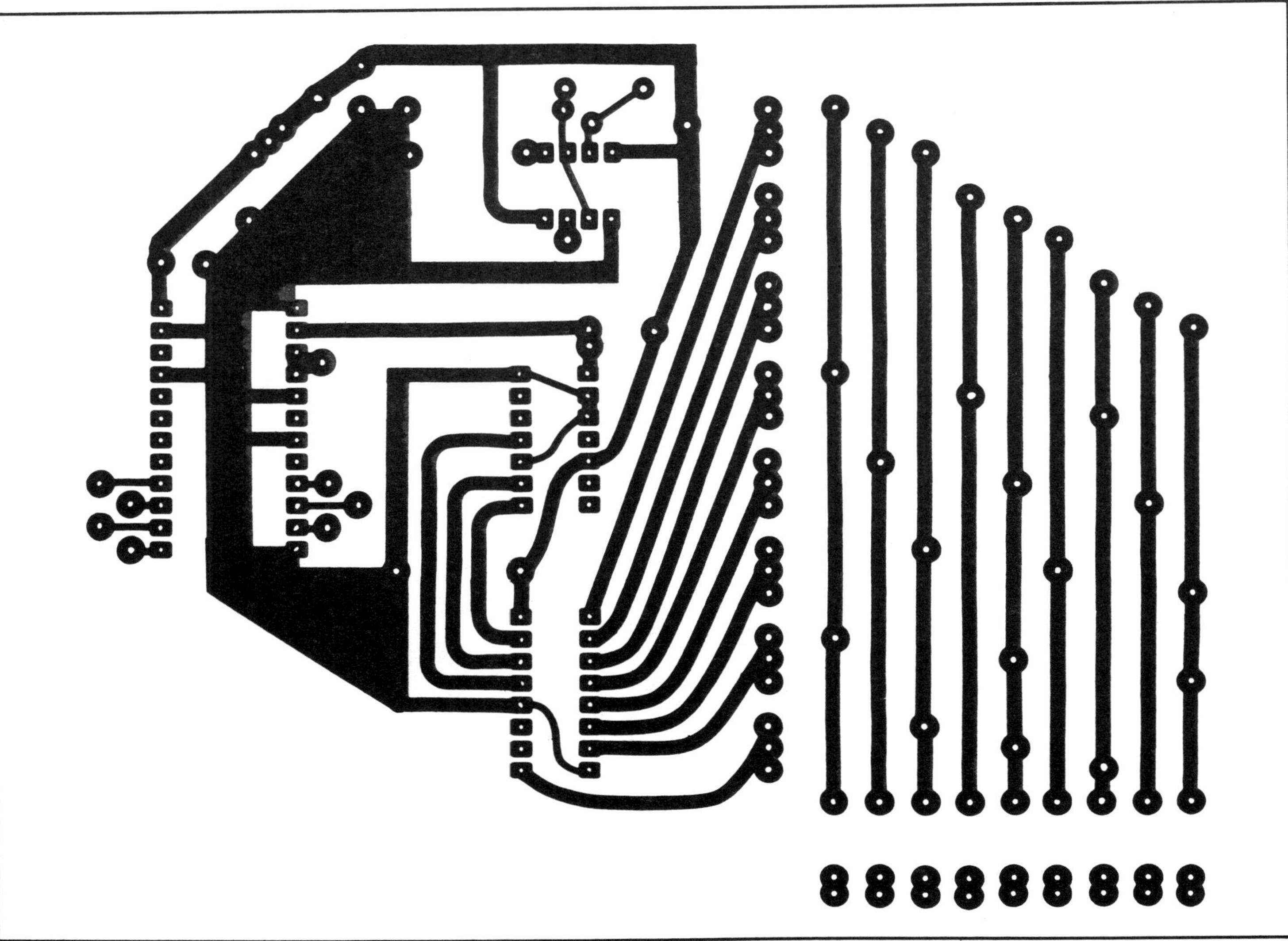

Fig. 4-8. As you can see, Elec-Tac-Toe uses a very neat PC board arrangement and the diodes are well-placed for easy construction. This is a full-size template so you can copy it exactly to make your own board. Use any of the many popular PC boards kits available.

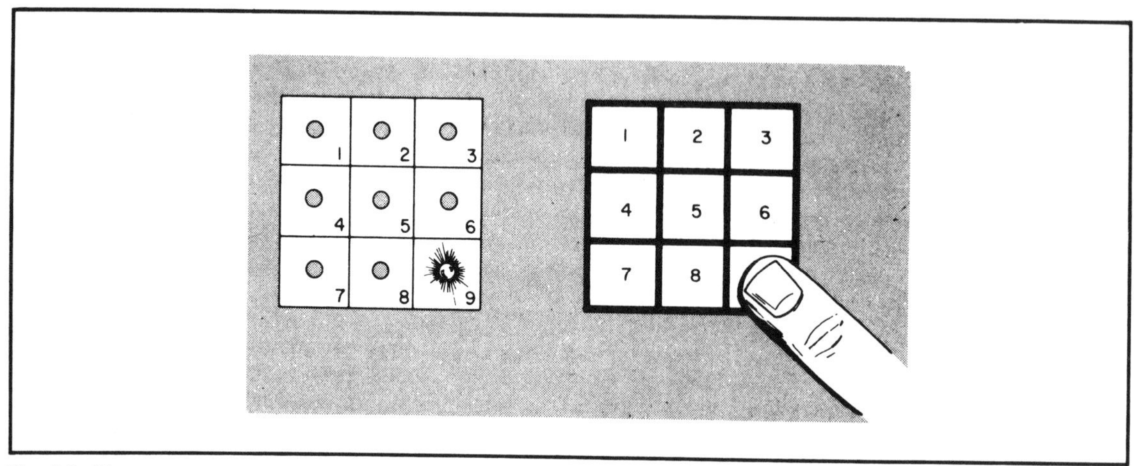

Fig. 4-9. Clues as to which LEDs are lit are simple to obtain. Just push the switch that controls the LED in question. If it lights, you're a step closer.

4-3. When players become experienced, they may find a solution nearly simultaneously. Because it is difficult to tell who shouted first when sounds are closely spaced, you may wish to build a priority latch. The latch's output consists of two LEDs, one for each contestant. The player who presses his pushbutton first causes his LED to light, and at the same time prevents the opponent's LED from lighting at a later time. Only one IC is necessary to build the latch: a 7474 dual D-type flip-flop. Pressing S11 sends the square wave from IC1 to the CLEAR inputs of the two flip-flops. The first time that this square wave goes low, it sends both 0 outputs high; consequently, neither LED is lit. When S11 is released, R12 holds the CLEAR inputs high, and they

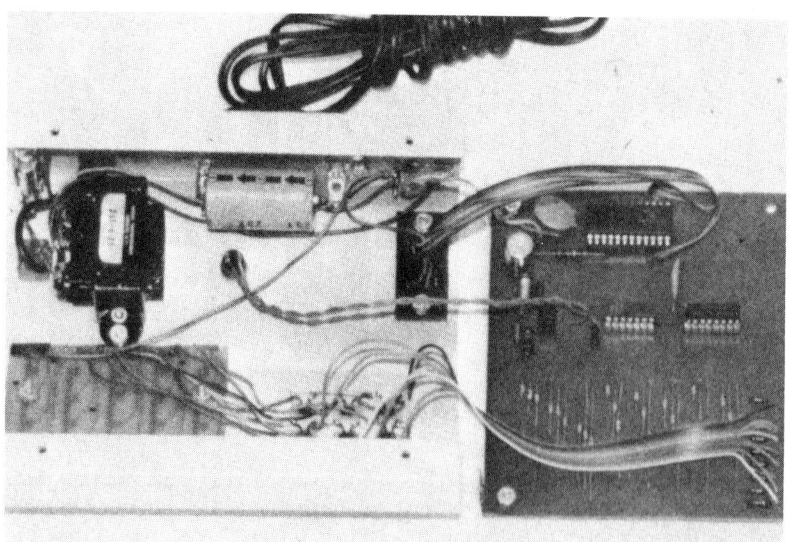

Fig. 4-10. Note the wires that go from the Elec-Tac-Toe keyboard to the PC board. Our unit made use of ribbon cable. You'll find that ribbon cable can be almost indispensable once you get used to it—no more messy wire tangles or having to use troublesome cable ties.

Table 4-2. Parts List for Elec-Tac-Toe.

C1—2200-μF electrolytic capacitor, 25-volt
C2—100-μF electrolytic capacitor, 16-volt
C3, C4—.1-μF capacitor
C5—.001-μF capacitor, mylar
C6—.01-μF capacitor
D1-D24—1N914 diode
D25, D26—1N4003 diode
DIS1—Litronix DL-747 7-segment display
F1—1/4-amp. fuse
IC1—555 timer
IC2—7493 counter
IC3—7445 decoder
IC4—74143 counter and decoder
IC5—LM309K 5-volt regulator
LED1—LED9—light emitting diode
ALL RESISTORS 1/2-WATT, 10% TOLERANCE
R1-R9—220-ohm resistor
R10—10,000-ohm resistor
R11—47,000-ohm resistor
R12, R13—1000-ohm resistor
S1-S9—pushbutton switches, normally open (or use discrete units or a converted calculator keyboard)
S10—SPST toggle switch
S11—SPST pushbutton switch, normally open
T1—Transformer, 16 VCT, 400 mA
Misc.—wire, PC board constructing equipment, cabinet, etc.
Note—Insta-Fab #MBK 2-7-6 cabinet is available from Circuit Specialists, Box 3047, Scottsdale, AZ, 85257 for $7.91 plus postage. Transformer T1 is a Signal #241-4-16 available from Signal Transformer Co., 500 Bayview Ave. Inwood, N.Y. 11696.
ICs are available from James Electronics, 1024 Howard Ave., San Carlos, Calif. 94070—write for current prices.

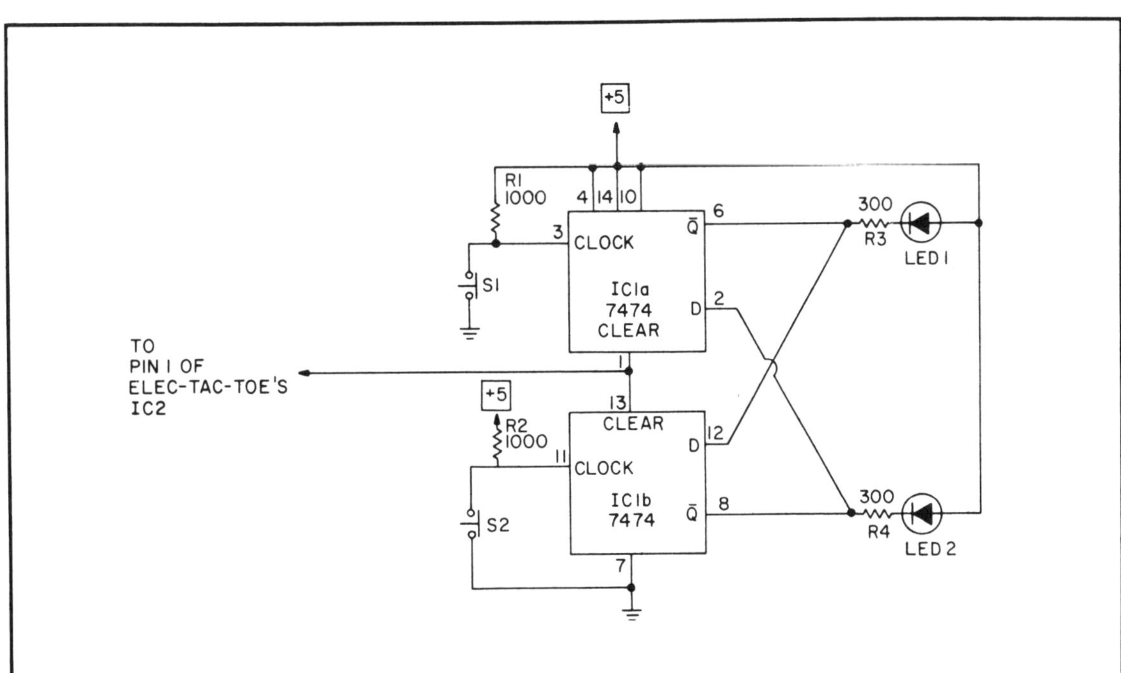

Fig. 4-11. You might like to build this option into your Elec-Tac-Toe game. It will help stop arguments as to who called out the right answer first!

IC1—7474 dual flip-flop
LED1, LED2—light emitting diode
R1, R2—1000-ohm resistor, 1/2-watt
R3, R4—300-ohm resistor, 1/2-watt
S1, S2—pushbutton switch, normally closed

Table 4-3. Parts List for Priority Latch Option.

no longer have any effect on their respective flip-flops. If the priority latch's S1 is the first switch to be pressed, the latch's IC1a gets clocked and its Q output drops low because its D input is connected to a high potential at the instant of clocking. Naturally, when the Q output drops low, LED1 goes on. Now, suppose at some later time the latch's S2 gets pushed, thus clocking the latch's IC1b. Because the latch's IC1b's D input connects to the latch's IC1a's Q output, which has already gone low, the latch's IC1b's Q output remains high after clocking, and LED2 cannot light. If latch S2 had been the first switch pressed, the situation would simply have been reversed. Pressing Elec-Tac-Toe's S11 again will reset the priority latch.

Since Elec-Tac-Toe's circuit is simple and stable, you can use any construction method you like. As always, however, a printed circuit will yield the neatest and most professional-looking results. The PC layout accompanying this project may be copied using any of the commercially available etched-circuit kits.

When building the circuit, you will find it wise to use sockets for all the ICs (except IC5). In this way, if an IC should prove to be defective, it can be easily replaced. IC5, the voltage regulator, needs to be heat-sinked. This is conveniently done by simply mounting it against your game's cabinet, provided that you've used a metal (preferably aluminum) cabinet. If this is not the case, you will need to bolt IC5 to a separate heat-sink. All in all, it is much easier to use an aluminum cabinet to begin with. A thin layer of silicone grease between IC5's mounting flange and the aluminum cabinet will improve the heat flow from the IC.

Transformer T1 is a 16-volt, center-tapped, 400 mA. unit. It may be ordered directly from the Signal Transformer Co. Be sure to specify the model number (241-4-16). Signal's address can be found in the parts list (Table 4-2).

While assembling the circuit, double-check all device polarities. This applies to all the semiconductors as well as capacitors C1 and C2. Be especially careful with diodes D1 through D24; they should all point in the same direction.

Solder connections must be made with rosin-core solder and a low-heat iron (25 watts or less). Too large an iron may char the circuit board and damage the components.

Finally, any suitable front-panel layout can be used. You may, however, wish to copy the prototype's front panel. That particular arrangement proved to be not only functional, but eye-catching as well. As noted in the parts list (Table 4-2), switches S1 through S9 may be discrete pushbuttons or a converted calculator keyboard. The LEDs must be mounted in the proper cells of the grid; put LED1 into cell 1, LED2 into cell 2, and so on. This wraps up construction, so let's return to our discussion of the game itself.

The complete rules of Elec-Tac-Toe are as follows: 1) Press SCRAMBLE at the start of each new game. 2) Decide which player goes first; in subsequent games players alternate at taking the first turn. 3) The player going first presses the pushbutton called out on DIS1. Zero denotes a free choice of the first button to be pressed. 4) The other player presses the button of his choice. Players now alternate at pressing buttons until someone has figured out the selected set. 5) The first person to declare knowledge of the solution tests his answer by pressing three pushbuttons simultaneously. If three LEDs light, he wins. 6) If he is wrong, the opponent gets one guess, which he tests as above. If he too is wrong, the game ends in a draw.

As noted previously, the priority latch can be used instead of shouting to determine who first finds a solution. From the rules you can see that this game possesses elements of chance and competition, which together make deduction more difficult. You should also note that a good visual memory is an absolute necessity for winning. In order to get some idea of the thinking necessary in Elec-Tac-Toe, consider the sample games which follow. Each game is a sequence of plays, with no indication who made a particular play or who eventually won.

GAME 1

Cell 2 lights/Set is r1 or c2.
Cell 1 won't light/Set is c2.

GAME 2

Cell 1 won't light/Eliminate r1, c1, and d1.
Cell 5 lights/Set is r2, c2, or d2.
Cell 3 won't light/Set is r2 or c2.
Cell 2 won't light/Set is r2.

GAME 3

Cell 2 won't light/Eliminate r1 and c2.
Cell 8 won't light/Eliminate r3.
Cell 1 won't light/Eliminate c1 and d1.
Cell 9 won't light/Eliminate c3. Set is r2 or d2.
Cell 5/lights/No new information.
Cell 3 won't light/Set is r2.

Note that in Game 3 the fifth step (testing cell 5) was useless. The players should have known beforehand that Cell 5 would light because it belongs to both r2 and d2, and one of those sets of LEDs had to be the one that would light. But it's easy to criticize when everything is on paper; in play you will often find it difficult to keep track of data. In fact, you may find yourself pushing buttons that have already been pushed. Clearly, a solution that becomes evident after only a few steps is easier to spot than one requiring more steps because there is less to remember (or forget).

In general, is there anything that can be said about the amount of information necessary to reach a decision? Well, each press of a button yields one bit of information to each player; all solutions require two or more bits. The maximum possible number of bits necessary for logical players (with perfect memory) reasoning with information from randomly chosen cells is six. If the cells are chosen in an intelligent sequence, the solution can always be reached with four or fewer bits of information (again assuming the players are logical and have perfect recall). Can you spot how this would be done? Real games are likely to be longer than the ideal.

THE NEW SHELL GAME

YOU WILL HAVE TO BE ALERT TO WIN AT THE NEW SHELL GAME. In this electronic version of the famous carnival shell game, the electronic "pea" is manipulated in full view, rather than hidden under one of three walnut shells. As the game starts, the three light-emitting diodes (LEDs) are dark. The operator presses the start button, a single LED lights and then moves back and forth in a straight or zig-zag pattern. After a time, the light goes out. The player's job is to follow the light's movement in an effort to determine which one was on last.

How fast the light moves, the total time of the manipulation, which light is on last, and for how long, are all controlled by the operator. The operator also selects either the straight or zig-zap sequencing pattern. The controls allow a full range of settings, from one that is fully obvious, to one that is totally misleading.

The skill of the player is pitted against that of the operator in this project that uses readily available CMOS devices, is powered by a single 9-volt battery, and can be built for about $20.00.

How It Works

As shown in the schematic diagram (Fig. 4-12), flip-flops IC1 and IC2 form a four stage shift register. When start switch S3 is depressed, a logic "1" is loaded into IC1a through the set input, while all other stages are set to zero. As the shift register is clocked, the "1" bit continually circulates like a standard ring counter. Outputs 2 (IC1b), and 4 (IC2b) are combined in the discrete OR gate made up of D1, D2, and R3. The 1, 2 (or 4) and 3 outputs drive LEDs 1, 2, and 3 respectively.

NAND gate IC3 and associated components form a one-shot (monostable) multivibrator. When S3 is depressed, C3 discharges rapidly through D4, and drives the IC3c gate output high. When S3 is released, C3 charges through R5 and R6 with a time constant proportional to [C3 × (R5 + R6)]. When the voltage across C3 reaches 4.5 V (the CMOS logic level), the output of IC3c returns to the low level. The positive portion of the IC3c output is differentiated by the C2, R7 combination, which provides a set pulse to IC1a and a reset pulse to the other flip-flops. The output of IC3c is also inverted in IC4f and provided to IC3d. The other input to IC3d is one of the three shift register outputs routed through select switch S2. Thus, when S3 is depressed, the output of IC3d goes high, enabling the clock. The clock is simply an oscillator (made up of IC3a and B, R1, R2, and C1) which is controlled by the output of IC3d. Aside from turning on the clock, the output of IC3d also charges C4 through D3. When the voltage

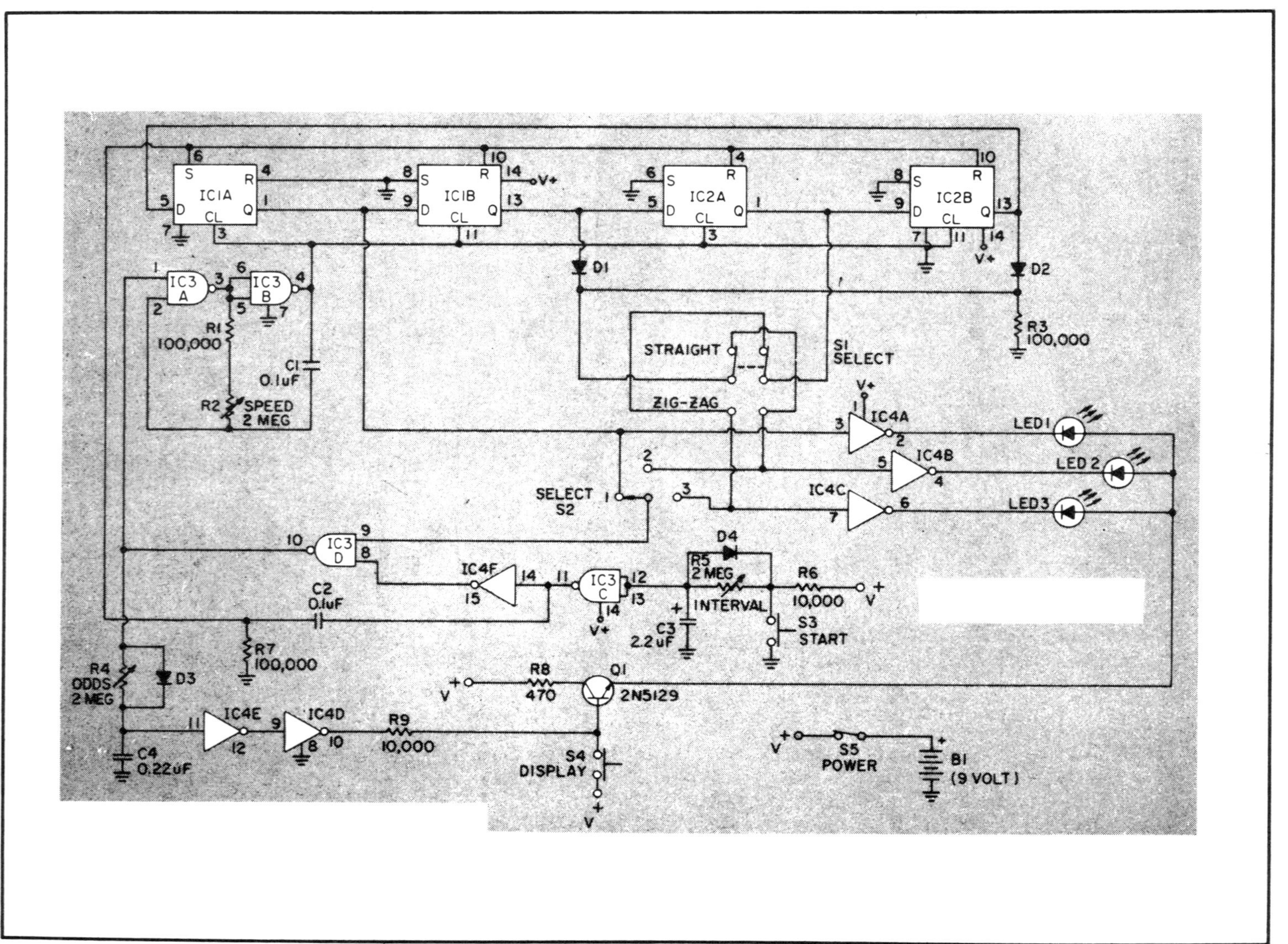

Fig. 4-12. Shell game schematic.

across C4 reaches 4.5V, the output of IC4d goes high, and turns on driver transistor Q1. This furnishes power to the LEDs, allowing them to light when driven be either IC4a, IC4b or IC4c.

At the end of the one-shot interval, the output of IC4f goes high. IC3d, however, will not go low and turn off the clock until both its inputs are high. When the output selected by S2 goes high, IC3d goes low and stops the clock. C4 discharges through R4 into the near ground potential of the IC3d output with a time constant set by the value of R4. When the voltage across C4 decays to 4.5 V, IC4d goes low, which turns off Q1 and removes power from the LEDs.

Switch S1 reverses the stage 2 and 3 connections to provide either a straight (1-2-3-2) or zig-zag (1-3-2-3) lighting sequence. Depressing S4 forward-biases Q1, allowing display of the static contents of the shift register.

With values as specified, the interval time can be as long as 3 seconds, the last LED on-time of up to 0.3 seconds, and the clock speed can be varied from 1 Hz to about 40 Hz. Power, which is applied through switch S5, is supplied by a single 9 volt battery.

Construction

While any standard means of construction, such as perfboard or wire wrap, may be used, a PC board is recommended. Solder all components onto the PC board, using as little heat as is required to make a good solder joint. Observe the indicated polarity for all diodes, C3, and the ICs. Be careful when handling the CMOS ICs to prevent static damage. IC sockets may be used if desired. You can use the excess component leads to form the fourteen jumpers identified in the component layout diagram (Fig. 4-13). After the PC board has been completed, interconnect the controls and switches to it as indicated. Any standard case may be used to house the project. The only restrictions are that the LEDs should be visible to both player and operator, display switch S4 accessible to the player, and all remaining controls visible only to the operator. See Figs. 4-14 and 4-15.

Use

A general description of the operation procedure is as follows:

1. Set select switch S2 to position 1, 2 or 3.
2. Set S1 to zig-zag or straight.
3. Adjust speed control R2, odds control R4, and interval control R5 as desired.
4. Press start switch S3. As soon as S3 is depressed, the LEDs will sequence, starting with LED1, in the pattern and at the speed selected. The sequence will continue for the interval chosen, whereupon the LED selected will remain on for the time chosen by the setting of the odds control.

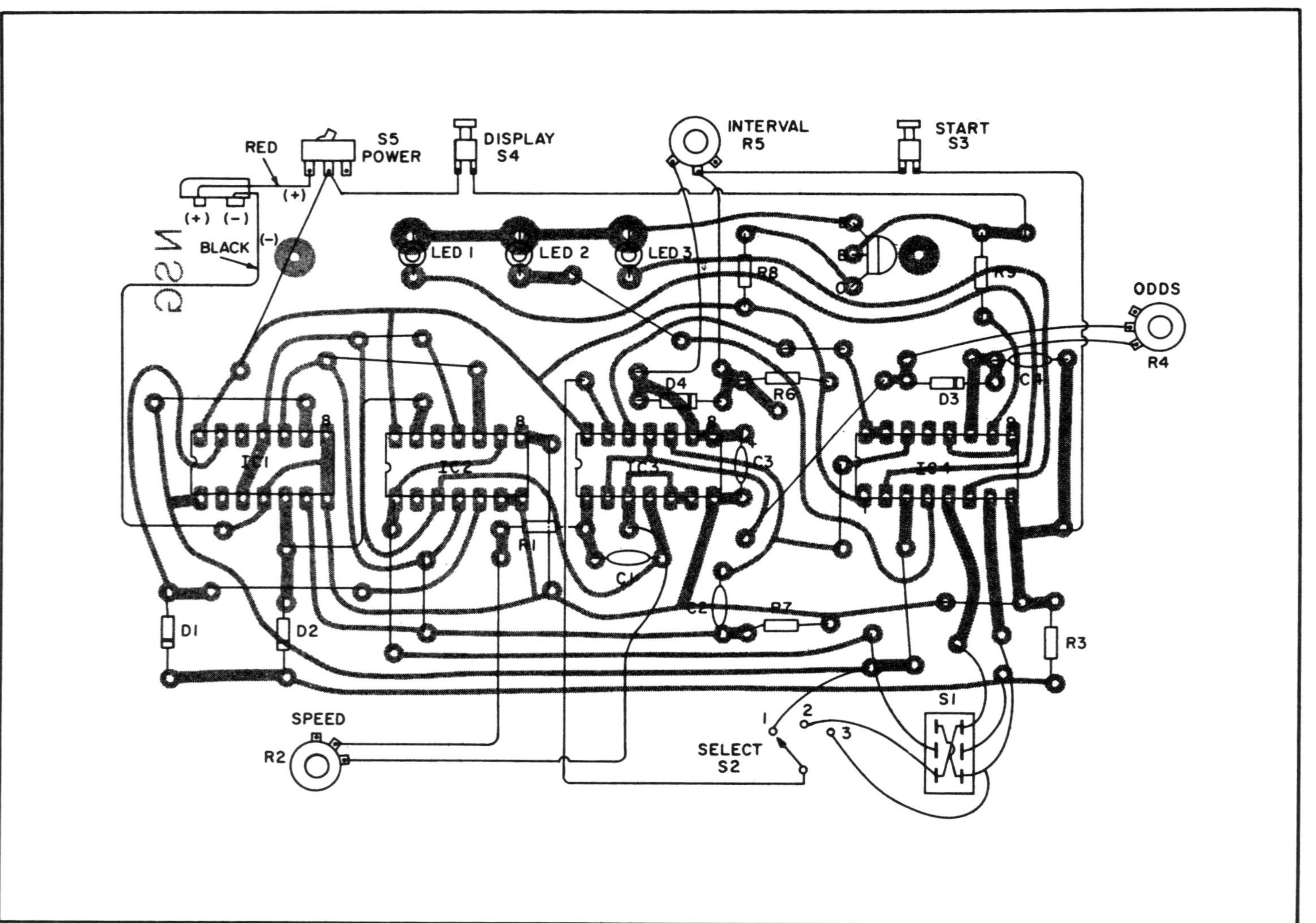

Fig. 4-13. Wiring the printed circuit board is a snap if you follow this parts location diagram carefully. The two, large nonelectrically connected holes in the upper left and right corners of the P.C. board are for the mounting bolts. Make sure you use the correct polarity on the 9-volt battery connector. Red positive, black negative.

Table 4-4. Parts List for the New Shell Game.

C1, C2—0.1μF ceramic disc capacitor, 10 Vdc
C3—2.2-μF electrolytic capacitor, 10 Vdc
C4—0.22-μF ceramic capacitor, 10 Vdc
D1, D2, D3, D4—1N4148 or 1N914 diode
IC1, IC2—4013 dual flip-flop
IC3—4011 quad NAND gate
IC4—4049 hex inverter w/buffer
LED1, LED2, LED3—small, red LED
Q1—2N5129 transistor
R1, R3, R7—100,000-ohm, 1/4-watt resistor
R2, R4, R5—2,000,000-ohm, linear-taper potentiometer
R6, R9—10,000-ohm, 1/4-watt resistor
R8—470-ohm, 1/4-watt resistor
S1—DPDT slide switch
S2—1-pole, 3-position rotary switch
S3, S4—SPST momentary-contact pushbutton switch
S5—SPST slide switch
Misc.—battery clip, mounting case, hookup wire, knobs, etc.

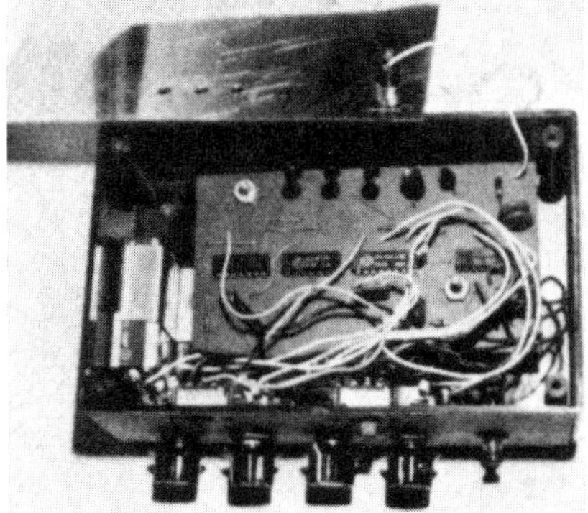

Fig. 4-14. The three LEDs must be carefully soldered to the PC board so that they will just fit through the holes in the project faceplate.

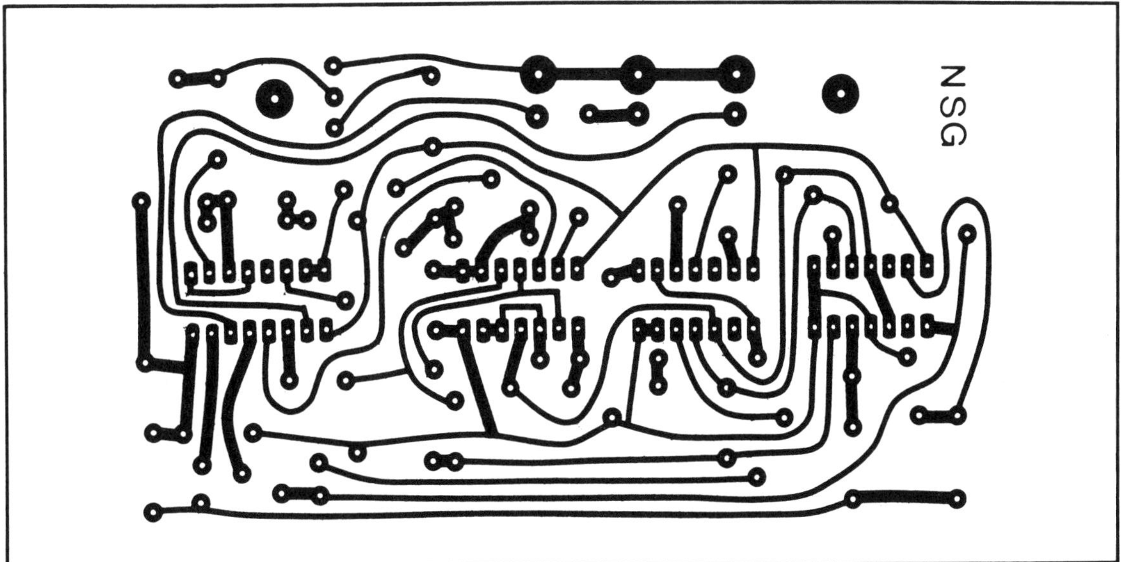

Fig. 4-15. This is the full-sized printed circuit board template for New Shell Game.

Initially, the operator should set a slow speed, medium interval and high odds. As the player becomes more confident, the control settings should be changed in an effort to fool the player. The controls can be set so that the last LED to illuminate does not appear to come on at all. With the odds control set to minimum, the speed and interval controls can be set so that the on-time of the last LED will be so short that (in a normally lighted room) it will not be seen. The proper settings will cause the interval to end during the low portion of the clock signal. Since this cannot be determined without monitoring the internal signals, the operator must develop a "feel" for the controls to obtain the desired effect. This effect should be used sparingly lest the player catch on. Although the game should not be used for gambling, non-monetary betting (with poker chips or the like) can make the game more entertaining. It is advisable to turn the unit off when not in use, to conserve battery life.

THE BALANCED BRIDGE GAME

HOW'S YOUR SENSE OF BALANCE? WE MEAN, YOUR ABILITY TO mentally balance our electronic bridge game. If it's good, you might find the key and unlock this fascinating puzzle's mystery in a few moments. But, we're warning you—even veteran mah jongg experts have been known to throw up their hands in utter disgust, after tying their skill at our little game of chance. Is it skill that rewards the player with the sweet sight of victory, or plain old-fashioned rabbi's-foot luck? Try our Balance Bridge game, and see for yourself!

Besides being great fun, this easy-to-build electronic game teaches you all about one of the most important electronic circuits yet devised: the Wheatstone Bridge. But, let's talk about fun first. The game is deceptively simple to play. The contestant starts out clutching a fistful of resistors (with their identifying color bands obliterated by painting them over). Four resistors will, when plugged in the correct terminals on the puzzle, cause the internal bridge circuit to be balanced.

So far, you'd figure that even your kid brother stands a winning chance. But, in order to complete the game and win points, he's got to make both "error" lamps go out. That's the hitch. If the wrong resistors are plugged in, or, if the right resistors are plugged into the wrong terminals, one of the error lamps will light. Better give your brash kid brother a healthy handicap!

The idea, of course, is to find the correct—or, winning—resistor combinations. And, then insert them into the correct terminals, so that both lamps remain unlit. You can make the puzzle as easy or hard as you wish. Just vary the number of resistors that the player has to work with! See our table of resistor values (Table 4-5) to get some idea of the several variations of puzzle complexity you can create.

The real trick, incidentally, to winning this puzzle is to set up a methodical approach by trying the various possible resistor combinations until you find one that works. Since most people don't work in a methodical fashion . . . well, we needn't say any more. And, to further confuse the head scratchers and nail biters even more, all

Table 4-5. Balanced Bridge Game Resistor Combinations.

A simple game for the kids: R1 = 47K, R2 = 100K, R3 = 22K, R4 = 47K **Slightly harder for your friends:** R1 = 1K, R2 = 10K, R3 = 47K, R4 = 100K, R5 = 5K (or 4.7K). There are many workable combinations in this group.	**Hardest yet, for MENSA types:** R1 = 10K, R2 = 100K, R3 = 68K, R4 = 33K, R5 = 220K Add as many additional odd-valued resistors as you like. The more, the merrier!

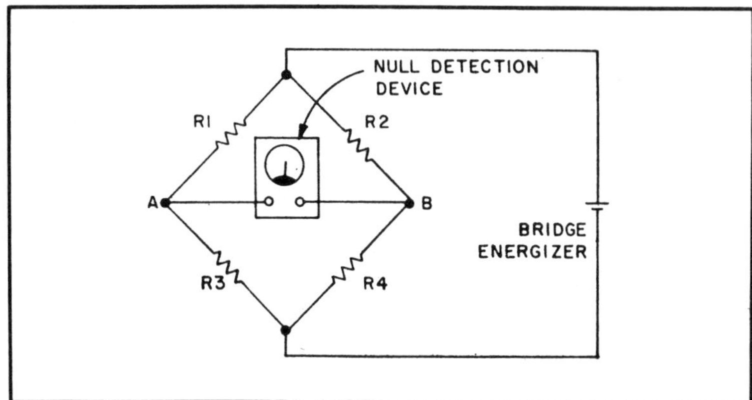

Fig. 4-16. The Wheatstone bridge, as it is usually drawn, in a diamond configuration. When R1/R3 = R2/R4, the meter will read zero volts.

the camouflaged resistors look alike, so it's impossible to memorize a solution to the puzzle. Luckily for you, though, head scratching isn't necessary in order to understand the Wheatstone Bridge.

Sir Charles' Bridge

The Wheatstone Bridge, as you probably guessed, is named after its inventor, the English physicist, Sir Charles Wheatstone. This basic circuit is used to measure electrical resistance with great accuracy. Figure 4-16 shows the drawing of Sir Charles' bridge in its most familiar form. It's traditionally drawn in the shape of a four-sided diamond, each leg representing a resistor element.

A voltage source connects to the "top" and "bottom" points of the diamond; a sensitive voltmeter (or, more often, a sensitive current-measuring instrument called a galvanometer) is hung across the diamond's side points A and B. Actually, the diamond configuration is a bit confusing, since it hides the fact that a Wheatstone Bridge is really only two voltage dividers connected back-to-back to a voltmeter or galvanometer.

We've redrawn the circuit in Fig. 4-17, showing how the Wheat-

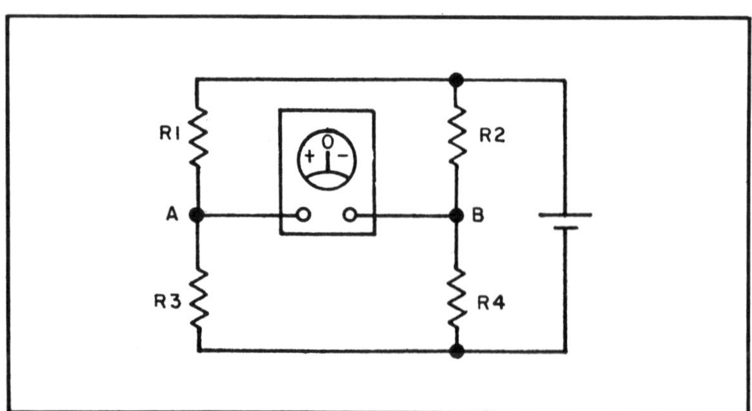

Fig. 4-17. The Wheatstone bridge, drawn to show that it is really a pair of voltage dividers with a voltmeter between the two.

stone Bridge works. Note that the voltmeter is simply indicating the voltage potential difference between the outputs of both dividers. Clearly—and this is an important point—if the outputs of the two voltage dividers are equal, the voltmeter will read zero volts.

Suppose the lefthand pair of dividers has a higher voltage output than the right-hand pair. Now the meter reads a positive voltage. If the right-hand pair's voltage output is higher than that of the left-hand set, then the meter will read a negative voltage.

Piecing the Puzzle Together

If you examine the schematic diagram (Fig. 4-18) of our electronic puzzle, you'll see that its heart is the basic Wheatstone bridge configuration—with one important difference. Instead of fixed resistances, the arms of our Balanced Bridge game consist of a pair of pin jacks. They're arranged so that leads of a resistor can be plugged into them. When the player inserts four appropriate resistors so that he produces a balanced bridge, he has solved the puzzle. More likely, though, he will create an unbalanced bridge, lighting one of the two error lamps.

These lamps are controlled by two Darlington amplifier transistors, each wired to the two side points of the bridge diamond. One lamp lights when the bridge is unbalanced on one side of the diamond. The other lamp lights when the bridge is unbalanced in its other side.

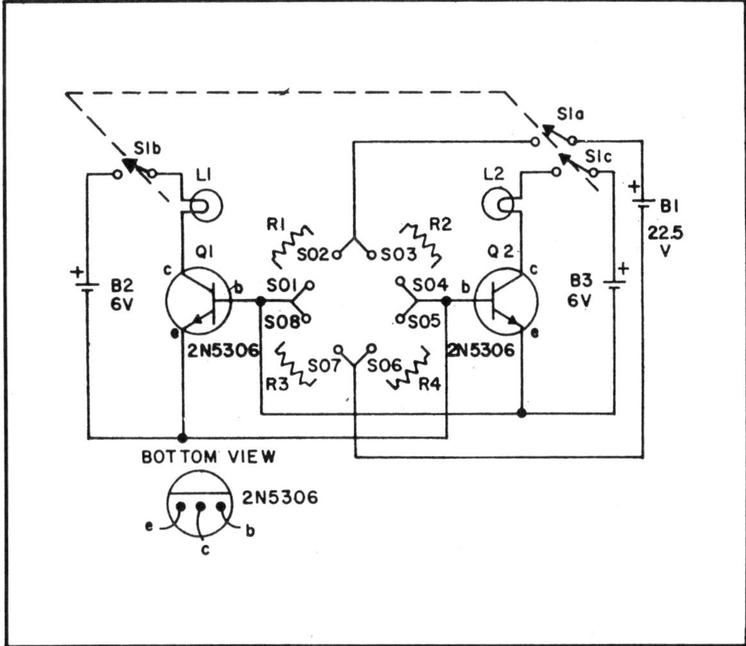

Fig. 4-18. Balanced bridge schematic.

Table 4-6. Parts List for The Balanced Bridge Game.

B1—22 1/2-Volt battery (RCA type VS084 or equiv.)
B2, B3—6-Volt battery (RCA type VS068 or equiv.)
L1, L2—6.3 Volt @ 1/4 amp pilot lamp—type 46 (Calectro E2-441 or equiv.)
Q1, Q2—darlington amplifier transistors (GE 2n5306 or Motorola HEP series S-9100). See text.
S1—4-pole, 2-position rotary switch (Calectro E2-167 or equiv.)
S01-S08—panel-mount pin jacks (Calectro F2-879 or equiv.)
1—pilot light socket assembly with red lens (Calectro E2-407 or equiv.)
1—pilot light socket assembly with green lens (Calectro E2-408 or equiv.
1—1 in. diameter knob (Calectro E2-720 or equiv.)
Misc.—3-in. × 5-in. × 7-in. aluminum minibox (Bud type CU-2108-A or equiv.), #22 stranded wire, pin plugs (Calectro F2-872 or equiv.), solder, etc.

Both lamps extinguish when the bridge is balanced, or when one or two resistors are inserted into pin sockets, but still don't provide electrical continuity within the bridge!

Groups of resisters can be plugged into the Balanced Bridge game in several "correct" ways. Reason is, the bridge is a symmetrical circuit. Left and right sets of bridge arms, as well as the upper and lower pairs, can be integrated without unbalancing the circuit.

Note that the lamp circuits are not sensitive to slight imbalances due to the nature of the driver transistors. If you decide to experiment and produce your own game resistance values, here is the general formula for bridge balance.

$$\text{At balance: } R1/R3 = R2/R4$$

Jigsaw Gyrations

Our Balanced bridge game is housed in a 3-in. × 5-in. × 7-in. aluminum minibox. As Figs. 4-19 and 4-20 show, both transistors and all associated interconnection wiring are mounted between the terminals on both pilot-lamp holders, the pin jacks, and S1. Parts placement is entirely non-critical; feel free to alter the layout if you wish. Keep one precaution in mind. Slip lengths of wire insulation over the transistor leads to eliminate any chance of accidental short circuits.

Three batteries are necessary for this project. Reason is, the bridge, itself, requires a "floating ground"; the 22 1/2-volt battery takes care of this. Next, two 6-volt voltage sources are needed to provide power for both lamp-driver transistor circuits. Special biasing techniques are used for both transistors; separate batteries perform this function. Cement all batteries in place on the top-half of the minibox with general-purpose cement. Solder connecting leads directly to the terminals. Construction of the Balanced Bridge ends after you've soldered pin plugs to the wire leads of each resistor needed to play the game.

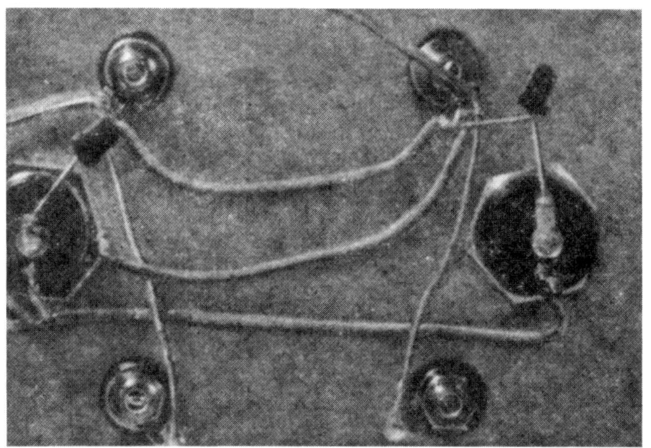

Fig. 4-19. Note that all the transistors are mounted between the pilot lamp holders and the nearest pin jacks.

To Find or Not to Find

Not everybody's parts collection has a pair of 2N5306 Darlington transistors floating around. Looking in Motorola's HEP Replacement Semiconductor catalog, you'll see that the nearest NPN Darlington amp listed is their type S-9100. Its characteristics are close enough to the author's original type specified.

And don't make the mistake of thinking that just any transistor will do in this circuit. A bipolar transistor's input bias current flow will upset the delicate balance of the bridge.

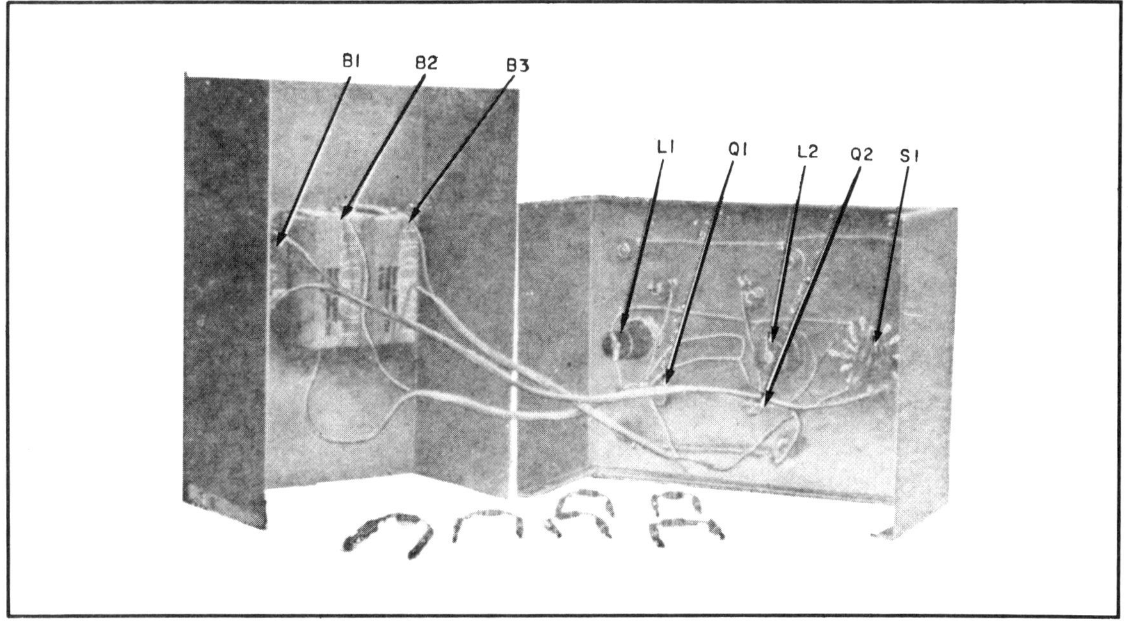

Fig. 4-20. This photo shows one possible layout of parts, but the placement isn't critical. Just be sure to put pieces of wire insulation on the transistor leads to prevent any chance of short circuits.

Darlington amps, have exceptionally high gain and very high input impedance; this solid-state configuration neatly fits the bridge's bill for a no-load, on-off transistorized switch.

One final point. If electronics buffs will be playing the game, paint all resistor bodies as suggested earlier. For your other friends, leave the resistors alone. The mysterious colored bands will probably add an additional note of confusion to the game.

WINKY-DINK

IF YOU'RE LOOKING FOR A USEFUL CONSTRUCTION PROJECT, which can help you test salvaged parts or log rarer DX, the Winky-Dink isn't for you. But if, like most of us, you enjoy a strictly fun gadget from time to time, then Winky-Dink is what you have been looking for.

Winky-Dink is a one-hour project leaving the remainder of the evening free to experiment with different blink rates. Only eight components are employed, and total cost should be under $3.00 (less if you're lucky and have some of the parts in your junkbox).

The completed Winky-Dink does nothing more than sit on the table and wink its two light-bulb eyes back and forth continually, but it's a conversation-stopper to non-electronic-minded visitors. In a home lab crammed with exotic (and expensive) equipment, Winky-Dink easily steals the show when anyone drops in.

If you must be practical, it makes a fine toy for a young child. To use it for this, perform simple surgery on a stuffed animal. Remove the sewn-on eyes and replace them with Winky-Dink's bulbs; then provide a zippered compartment for batteries and pack the tiny circuit board into the animal's interior.

Construction

Arrange the two transistors, the capacitors, and the resistors on the circuit board and solder the leads to a home-made printed circuit board. See Fig. 4-21. Use a small, hot iron and work rapidly; the transistors are rated to withstand soldering-iron heat for no more than 15 seconds at a distance of 1/16-inch from the case.

Rather than using the etched board, you may prefer to lay out the

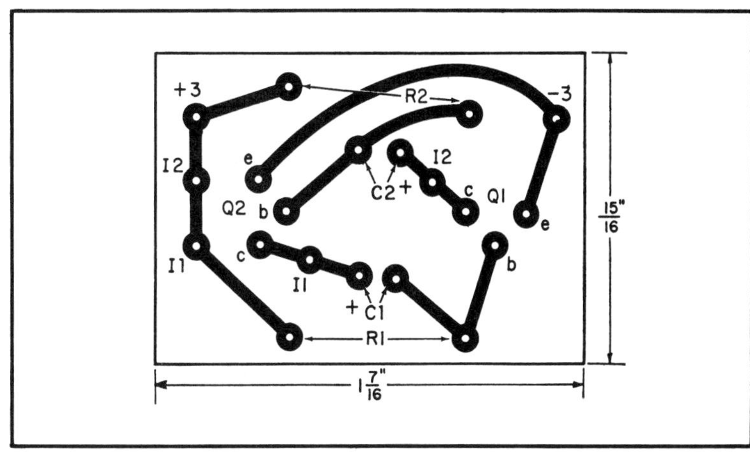

Fig. 4-21. Detailed diagram of underside of printed circuit board—be sure to copy to scale.

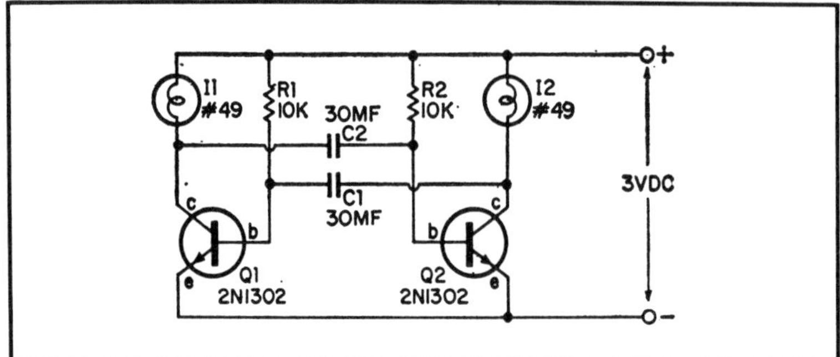

Fig. 4-22. Be sure to connect positive leads of electrolytic capacitors to Q1 and Q2 collectors.

components in similar arrangement on perforated hardboard. Stiff cardboard is also an excellent "chassis" material; necessary holes can be punched with the point of a drawing compass or with an ice-pick.

Leads to the bulbs can be connected either by soldering them directly to the bulb bases, or by using sockets. Since either #48 or #49 pilot lamps can be used (electrically they are identical), you can use either screw or bayonet-type lamp sockets—whichever you have in the junk box.

Battery connections are best made by using a battery holder, although with care you can solder directly to the two cells. The holder is recommended as Winky-Dink draws approximately 60 milliamperes from a fresh pair of D cells, which will require battery replacement from time to time. If the large ignition-type cells are used for power, they should last their shelf life.

Thumbnail Theory

Winky-Dink is an astable collector-coupled multivibrator, simplified to the most extreme degree possible. The transistors function as switches to turn the bulbs on and off, and the capacitors make one transistor stay "off" whenever the other is "on." See Fig. 4-22 and Table 4-7.

For instance, if transistor Q1 happens to be "on," its collector volt-

Table 4-7. Winky-Dink Parts List

C1, C2—30-μF, 6-v electrolytic capacitor, subminiature type for printed circuit boards (Lafayette 99G6076 or equiv.) I1, I2—#49 (screw type) or #49 (bayonet type) pilot lamp Q1, Q2—2N1302 transistor (RCA) (npn, average beta—100) R1, R2—10,000-ohm, 1/2 watt resistor	Misc.—Printed circuit board (optional), sockets for pilot lamps (optional), wire, solder, etc. Estimated cost: $3.00 Estimated construction time: 1 hour without printed circuit board

age will be nearly zero. This places the positive end of C2 at ground level. However, if Q2 is "off" at the same time, its collector voltage will be the same as that of the battery—3 volts. Thus C1 is charged to 3 volts, through bulb I2.

While C1 is charging, the current flowing to charge it passes through the base-emitter junction of Q1, keeping Q1 "turned on." When C1 reaches full charge, however, this current flow ceases, and Q1 tends to "turn off."

This raises the collector voltage of Q1 positive to ground, then the change in Q1's collector voltage is transferred through C2 to the base of Q2, tending to turn Q2 "on."

This action, in turn, causes the collector voltage of Q2 to drop. The change in collector voltage of Q2 is transmitted through C1 back to the base of Q1, further tending to turn Q1 "off." In addition, the 3-volt charge on C1 adds to the change, so that the base voltage of Q1 is 3 volts more negative than the collector voltage of Q2. This action is cumulative, and rapidly switches Q1 "off" and Q2 "on."

So long as the 3-volt charge remains on C1, Q1 will be held in cutoff and cannot conduct. C1 "reverse charges" through R1, until the base of Q1 becomes sufficiently positive to allow conduction to begin. Then Q1 begins to turn "on" again, turning Q2 "off" as just described. The process continues indefinitely—as long as the battery lasts.

Parts Substitutions

Almost any of the parts may be changed to fit your own availability situation. Npn transistors were used because they were on hand. Pnp's can be used by reversing polarity of the battery and thc capacitors. Resistor values for R1 and R2 can be anything between 4700 ohms and 33,000 ohms; the larger values will produce a slower wink rate. The capacitors can be larger but appreciably smaller ones are not recommended; the wink rate becomes so rapid the effect is lost. However, do not substitute the more common No. 47 pilot bulbs; they

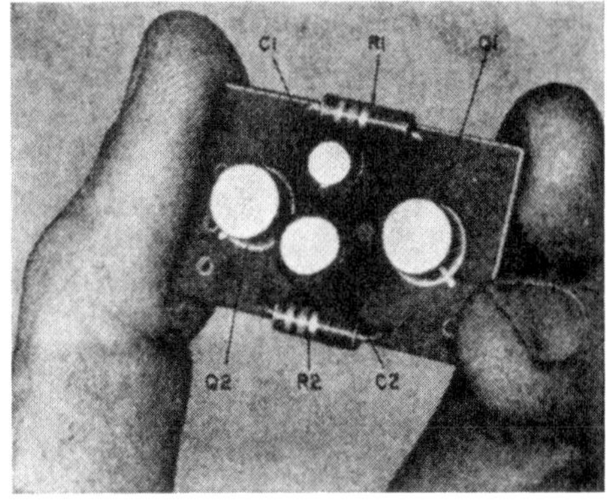

Fig. 4-23. Winky-Dink circuit board all wired and ready for lamp and battery connections. Be careful not to overheat transistor leads.

require 250 milliamperes for proper operation, which results in abnormally short battery life.

Should Winky-Dink fail to wink for you, the trouble should not be hard to find. If both lamps light dimly, you probably have a defective or disconnected capacitor. If one bulb lights brightly while the other is out, the capacitor connected to the same collector as the dark bulb is probably shorted. If both lamps light brightly, either both capacitors are shorted or your transistors are defective (either event is rare). If the bulbs wink, but dimly, you probably have weak batteries. See Fig. 4-23.

MAGIC LAMP

HERE'S A ONE EVENING SCIENCE FAIR PROJECT, GUARANTEED to mystify those household electronics experts-in-residence, and knock the socks off the novice who knows it all (or thought he did)! Even your kid sister is no doubt aware that when you take a pair of ordinary lamps and toggle switches, wire them all in series and connect them to the power line, nothing happens 'til both switches are closed. When they are, both lamps glow at reduced brilliance.

Not so with our Magic Lamp! Turn off both switches and hang our wonder box across the ac juice. The lamps remain off—whatdja expect, dancing girls? Throw one switch on and its corresponding lamp does a solo performance; throw the second switch on and both lamps glow. Reverse the sequence, and you'll see the same puzzling performance. Want to baffle your class Einstein? Remove one lamp from its socket and the other lamp's operation is unaffected. (They'll think you're onto some new and brain-boggling theory!)

What really stumps the experts is that Magic Lamp's method of construction makes all wiring clearly visible and a circuit diagram is provided to further confuse the issue. Given a really effective demonstration on your part, our Magic Lamp should turn you into a science project show-stopper par excellence.

Unraveling the Puzzle

A little basic theory of Magic Lamp's workings serves as a fascinating introduction to diode switching circuitry. Follow the action with our schematic diagram (Fig. 4-24 and Table 4-8).

With both switches S1 and S2 open, silicon diodes D3 and D4 are connected back-to-back. This setup effectively blocks both the positive and negative half-cycles of the applied ac voltage, so no current ever

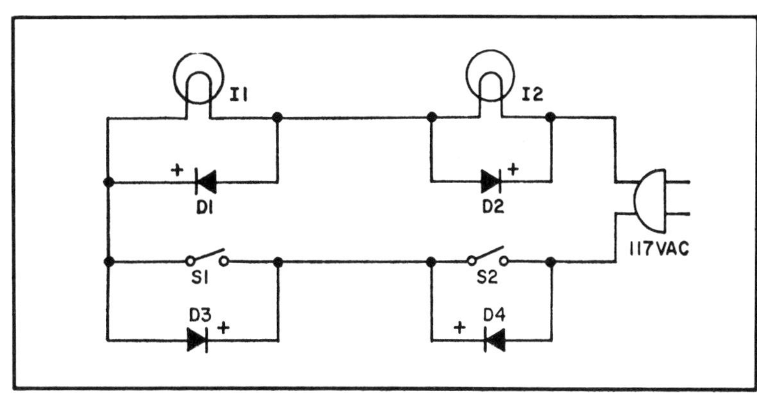

Fig. 4-24. Magic lamp schematic.

Table 4-8. Parts List for Magic Lamp.

D1-D4—Silicon diode (1N2070 or equiv.) I1, I2—Lamp, 25-watt, 115 Volt standard screw base, red frosted S1, S2—Spst toggle switch (Lafayette 99T 6150 or equiv.) 2—Lamp socket, medium screw base, keyless, brass shell 1—AC line cord, no. 18 zipcord, 6 ft. long	1—Instrument case, black plastic (Allied Radio no. 42 A 7886 or equiv.) 2—Threaded nipple, brass 3/8 × 1/2-in. long with lock nut Misc—Acrylic plastic panel, linecord strain relief, hookup wire, solder, etc.

reaches the lamp circuit. With switch S1 closed, diode D4 passes the positive half-cycles of the applied ac voltage to the series-connected lamps I1 and I2. Diode D1 thinks it's reverse-biased, so it doesn't conduct and current flows through lamp I1 to parallel-connected lamp I2 and diode D2.

Diode D2, on the other hand, conducts and completes the circuit to the other side of the ac line. Now you're beginning to see the light. Since the voltage drop across diode D2 is quite low (approximately 0.7 volt), current flows through D2 and lamp I2 remains extinguished. Lamp I1, however, glows at reduced brilliance cause we're feeding it with less than half its rated voltage.

Close switch S2 and, with switch S1 open, the reverse condition occurs. Lamp I2 glows while lamp I1 remains extinguished. With both switches S1 and S2 closed, full ac voltage hits both lamps. All this togetherness causes quite a family row, so diode D1 passes the negative half-cycle of the applied voltage and the positive half-cycle flows through the filament of I1. Not to be outdone by his sibling rival, diode D2 passes the positive half-cycle of the applied voltage and the negative half-cycle flows through the filament of I2. Both lamps are glowing at reduced brilliance. And if you've got our Magic Lamp at a science fair, a lot of guys are sure to be cracking a bunch of halfsmart remarks like "Only ML's constructor knows for sure!"

Construction

Magic Lamp may take any desired form just so long as there's no exposed wiring to provide a shock hazard. The method of construction we've shown in Figs. 4-25 through 4-27 is considered ideal because it provides a safe, shock-proof enclosure, permitting visual examination of the circuit wiring. It also allows silicon diodes D3 and D4 to be completely concealed behind the toggle switches while D1 and D2 hide in the bases of the lamp sockets.

Magic Lamp's housing is a black plastic instrument case measuring 6 13/16 × 5 9/32 × 2 5/32 in. Instead of employing the black

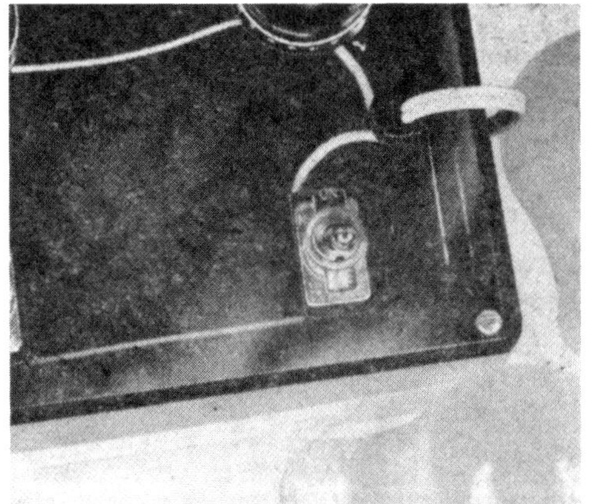

Fig. 4-25. Part of Magic Lamp's secret lies under base of toggle switch, hidden from viewer.

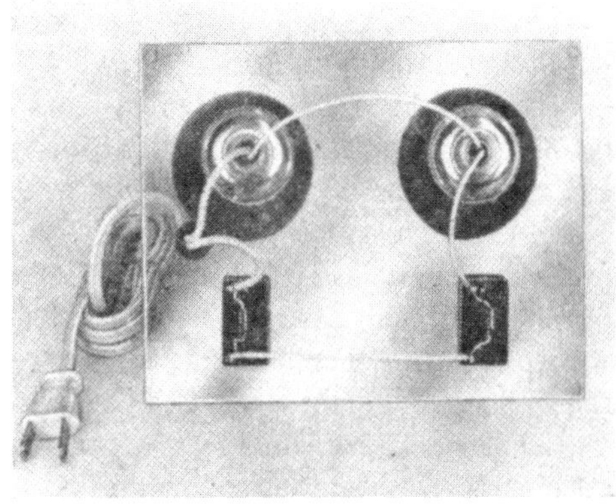

Fig. 4-26. Aladdin had easier time building his Magic Lamp 'cause he had fewer connections to solder. Note diodes lurking beneath both toggle switches.

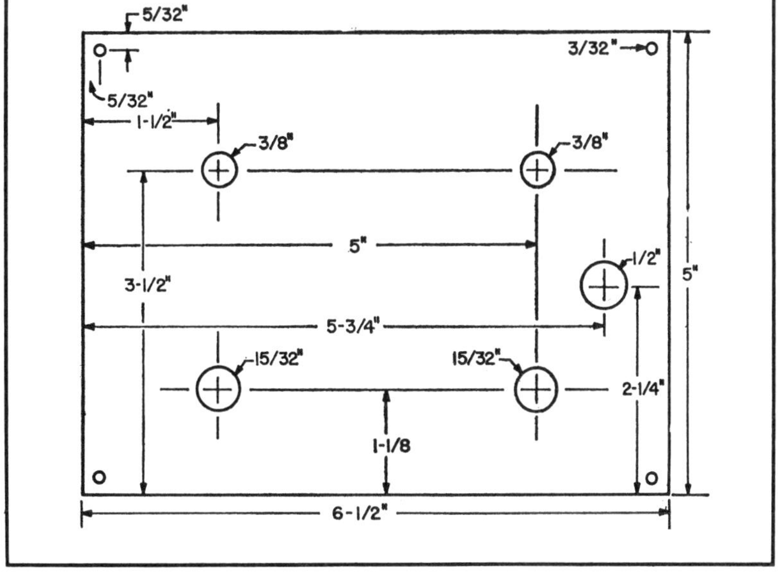

Fig. 4-27. Clear plastic top covers' dimensions, hole drilling data. Except for smallest holes, we suggest you start drill operations with smaller size bit, eventually working your way to specified hole diameter.

plastic cover normally found with such cases, substitute a 5 × 6 1/2-in. panel fabricated from 1/8-in. clear acrylic plastic stock. If you use the same case and components specified in the Parts List (Table 4-8), cut and drill the panel as shown. Your spare-parts box might yield different components; if that's the case modify the panel dimensions, layout, and hole sizes according to your needs. Only point we're emphasizing here is that it's important to keep Magic Lamp shock-free from prying hands.

Disassemble the lamp sockets and secure the base shells to the clear plastic panel with 1/2-in. long by 3/8-in. diameter threaded brass nipples and mounting nuts. You can find these items in a plumbing supply, or an electrical parts supply house. Drill holes for and mount toggle switches and on/off indicator plates using the supplied hardware. Next, install the line cord, making sure it passes through a strain relief bushing; leave approximately four inches of wire projecting through the panel.

The toggle switches specified in the Parts List permit silicon diodes D3 and D4 to be concealed against the back of their associated switch. Carefully observing diode polarity, solder the diode leads to the switch lugs, and dress the diodes flush against the back surfaces of the switches. Solder one lead of the line cord to the indicated lug of switch S2. You'll need a hank of stranded hookup wire (18 gauge will do). Solder a length of this wire between switches S1 and S2 and to lamp I1, feeding the wire through the lamp shell mounting bushing.

Diodes D1 and D2 are connected directly between the screw terminals of their lamp sockets. Carefully observe their polarity before you connect the diodes. Run another lead between the sockets of lamps I1 and I2. Connect your last-but-not-least-line-cord lead to the vacant terminal of lamp I2's socket. For safety's sake, keep this lead just long enough to permit connection to I2's terminal. Give your how-does-it-do-it a once-over, looking for short circuits and open solder joints. After all's said and done, replace the fiber insulators in the lamp socket shells.

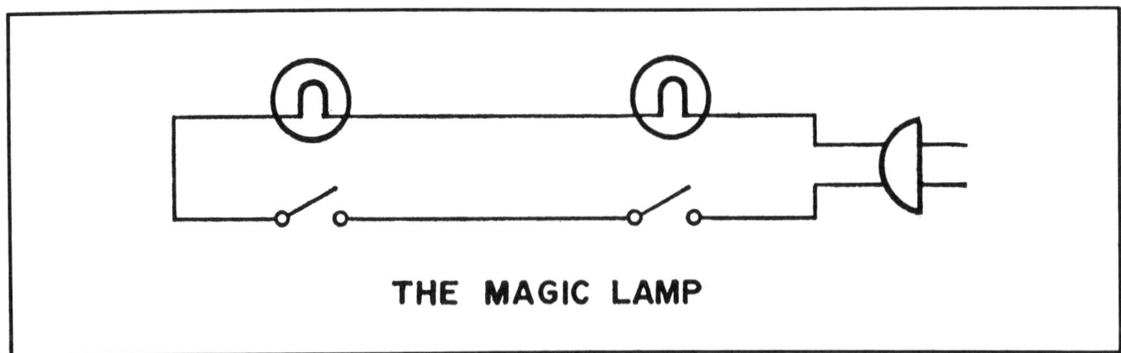

Fig. 4-28. Glue a copy of this schematic to the case.

After you've completed your Magic Lamp's wiring, redraw Fig. 4-28 and glue it to the case. Now mount the panel with the screws supplied with the case, and your Magic Lamp's ready for action. Okay, go out and fool the experts.

PUSHIE-BUTTON

To play this dueling game, two players sit opposite each other with the box in between. To start the game, the on-off-reset switch is closed and each player puts his hands in his lap. At the count of three each player hits his button. The first one to do so is the winner of the round as indicated by the lamp opposite his button. After each round, S3 must be turned off, then on to reset the lamps.

How It Works

Refer to the schematic diagram (Fig. 4-29); each of the two lamps is returned to the negative of the battery through a silicon controlled rectifier (SCR). Such rectifiers are special in that a positive voltage between gate to cathode must exist before current can flow from the anode to the cathode. One other feature of the SCR is that once anode-to-cathode current flows it continues to flow no matter what is done to the gate voltage. See Table 4-9.

Suppose S2 is pressed. Current will flow through L1, R3, and R4. While this current is far too low to light L1, it is sufficient to develop a voltage drop across R4. With SCR-2 turned on in this way, L2 will light.

If S1 is now pressed, very little current can flow through R1 and R2 because SCR-2 is turned on and represents, for all practical purposes, a short to ground. Therefore, not enough positive voltage can

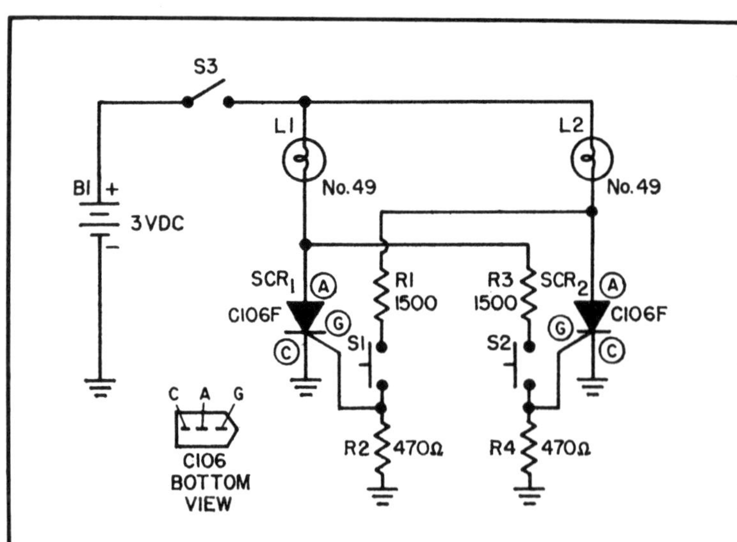

Fig. 4-29. Pushie-Button schematic.

Table 4-9. Parts List for Pushie-Button.

B1—3 volt battery (two D-cells in battery holder such as the Radio Shack 270-1439)
L1, L2—Low power #49 lamps (Radio Shack 272-1111 or equiv.)
R1, R3—1500-ohm, 1/2-watt resistor (Radio Shack 276-000 or equiv.)
R2, R4—470-ohm, 1/2-watt resistor (Radio Shack 276-000 or equiv.)
SCR1, SCR2—silicon controlled rectifier (General Electric C106F2 or equiv.)
S1, S2—Normally open pushbutton switch (Radio Shack 275-609 or equiv.)
S3—spst slide switch (Radio Shack 275-401 or equiv.)
Misc.—Utility box, lamp holders such as Radio Shack 272-318, wire, solder, etc.

be developed between gate and cathode to turn on SCR-1. Of course, if S1 had been pressed first, L1 would be on and L2 off.

Construction Details

The wiring layout is not at all critical. You can use perfboard or not, as you wish. Remember, the smaller the box, the more sporting the game. Dress up the metal front panel with self-adhesive shelf paper for good looks.

It's an exciting pushbutton gadget you can build for players of all ages. With a handful of parts and a few hours work anyone can construct this electronic game. By the way, the first player to achieve a ten-round win is the winner of the series and becomes eligible to participate in the annual Boardinghouse-Reach "grab-the-spuds" contest.

SOBRIETY TESTER

IT'S A CURIOUS AND UNFORTUNATE FACT, BUT MANY PEOPLE feel that a drink or two will improve their reflexes. Here's your chance to prove them wrong. Imagine for the moment that S1 is depressed (open circuited), S2 is closed, and C2 has been completely discharged. On command from someone acting as the tester, the person depressing S1 must remove his hand from that switch and use the same hand to open toggle switch S2. When S1 is released, charging current begins to flow into capacitor C2 through R1 and R2. This current is interrupted, however, as soon as S2 has been opened. C2 will have accumulated a voltage directly proportional to the reaction time, which is the interval between S1's release and the opening of S2. Longer times create higher voltages and cause higher-numbered

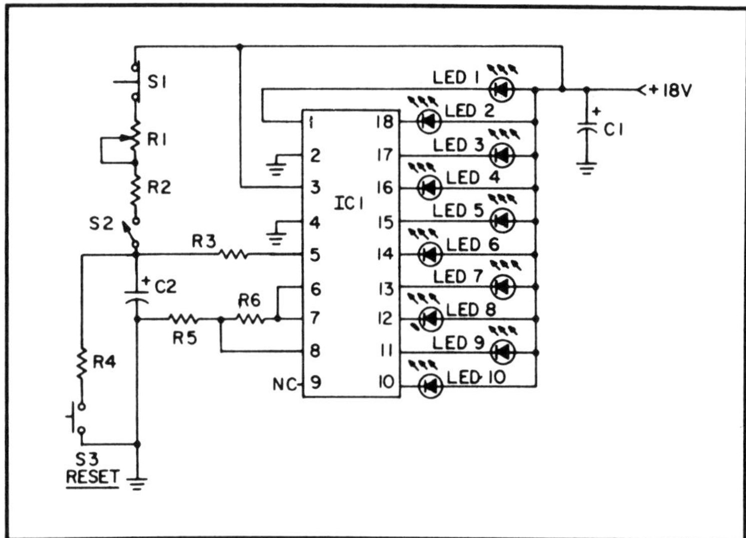

Fig. 4-30. Sobriety tester schematic.

Table 4-10. Parts List for Sobriety Tester.

C1—250-μF electrolytic capacitor, 35 Vdc
C2—50-μF electrolytic capacitor, 35 Vdc
IC1—LM3914 LED display driver
LED1 through LED10—light-emitting diode
R1—50K trimmer potentiometer
R2—5600-ohm 1/2-watt resistor, 10%
R3—33K-ohm 1/2-watt resistor, 10%
R4—47-ohm 1/2-watt resistor, 10%
R5—1800-ohm 1/2-watt resistor, 10%
R6—1000-ohm 1/2-watt resistor, 10%
S1—normally closed SPST pushbutton switch
S2—SPST toggle switch
S3—normally open SPST pushbutton switch

LEDs to light. For example, a sober person might react quickly enough to light LED 2 or LED 3, while someone truly sloshed will light up LED 10. To run another test, discharge C2 with S3, then press S1 and, finally, close S2 once more. R1 should be adjusted so that a sober person lights one of the low-numbered LEDs. See Fig. 4-30 and Table 4-10.

JOGGING PACESETTER

One of the problems faced by the beginning jogger, especially on city streets, is that of maintaining a constant pace. Tractor-trailer trucks, careening cars, and ill-mannered dogs can all interrupt your concentration. While there is little that can be done about these nuisances, this little pacesetter may make them less severe. A miniature earphone in your ear driven by a 555 timer produces regularly spaced "ticks" just like a metronome. The pace can be adjusted via R3 from a leisurely one stride per second to a sole-blistering six paces per second. The whole circuit complete with a 9-volt transistor radio battery weighs only a few ounces. See Fig. 4-31 and Table 4-11.

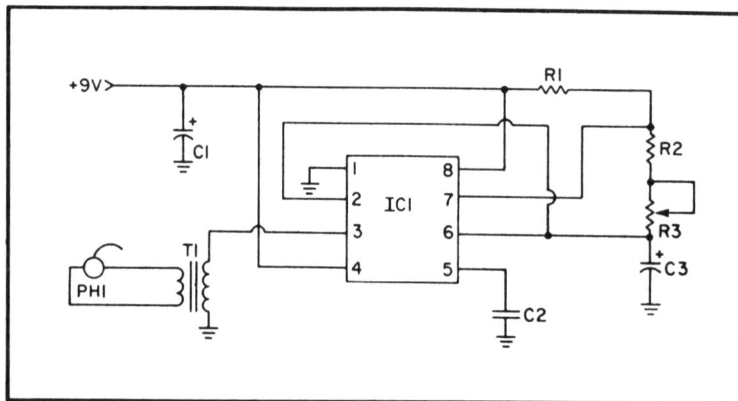

Fig. 4-31. Jogging pacesetter schematic.

Table 4-11. Parts List for Jogging Pacesetter.

C1—100-μF electrolytic capacitor, 16 Vdc
C2—0.1-μF ceramic disc capacitor, 35 Vdc
C3—1.0-μF tantalum electrolytic capacitor, 20 Vdc
IC1—555 timer
PH1—8-ohm miniature earphone
R1—10K, 1/2-watt resistor, 5%
R2—220K, 1/2-watt resistor, 5%
R3—1-Megohm trimmer potentiometer
T1—miniature audio output transformer—1,000-ohm primary/8-ohm secondary

TOUCH 'N FLIP

EVER WONDER HOW A TOUCH PLATE, LIKE THE KIND YOU SEE on some elevator buttons, works? This circuit will give you a good feel for how the touch plate works in a circuit and lets you experiment further. The plate can be just a small piece of metal or aluminum foil. Start by sliding S2 to "set" then back to R3. Now press S1. LED's D1 and D2 will flip. Now touch the plate to flip them back. The sensitivity of the touch plate will depend on humidity in the room and on R3 and C1. You can experiment with those in various ways. See Fig. 4-32 and Table 4-12.

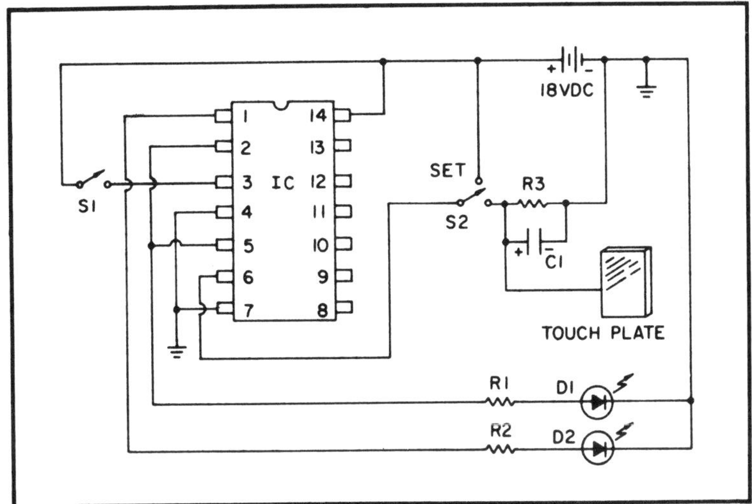

Fig. 4-32. Touch 'N Flip schematic.

Table 4-12. Parts List For Touch 'N Flip.

C1—4.7-μF electrolytic capacitor, 15 Vdc
D1, D2—large LED
IC1—4011 quad NAND gate
R1, R2, R3—2,000-ohm, 1/2 watt resistor
S1—SPST momentary contact push-button switch
S2—SPDT slide switch

HIGH PERFORMANCE TRANSISTOR RADIO

HERE'S A NEAT WAY TO UPDATE YOUR CRYSTAL SET, ASSUMING you can still find it. Or use these few inexpensive parts to build from scratch. Instead of using a cat's whisker or a diode, this radio uses the very sensitive junction of a junction FET as is detector. This makes it a very "hot," very sensitive high impedance detector. Then the JFET does double duty by converting the high input impedance to a lower output impedance—low enough and with enough drive to power a set of high impedance headphones or a high impedance earphone (about 1K or so).

The antenna coil is one of those simple loopsticks you've seen at the parts stores. (Or you might want to wind your own on an oatmeal box.) The broadcast variable capacitor is one of the tuning capacitors taken from an old, defunct radio. You can use any long wire for the antenna, but if you string it outdoors, be sure to use a lightning arrestor. You can also clip an alligator clip to your bedspring, a windowscreen, or the metal part of a telephone. See Fig. 4-33 and Table 4-13.

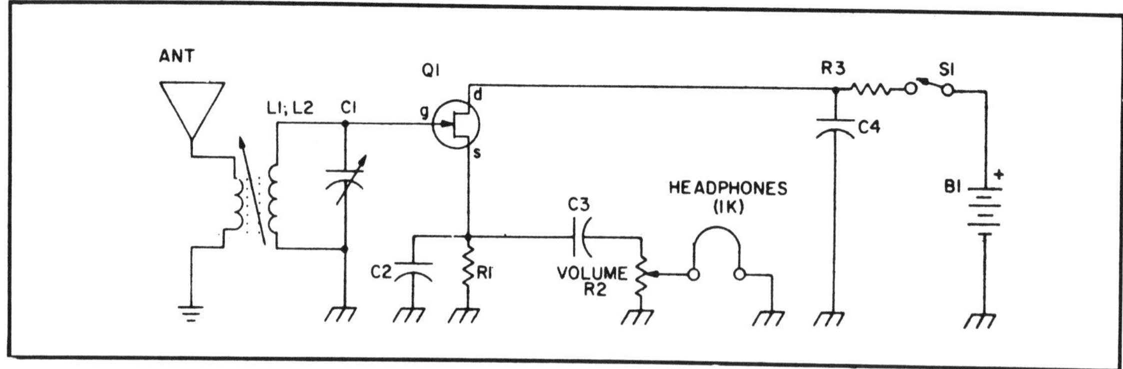

Fig. 4-33. High performance transistor radio schematic.

Table 4-13. Parts List for High Performance Transistor Radio.

B1—6-15 Vdc battery
C1—Approx. 356-pF broadcast-type variable capacitor
C2—300-600-pF capacitor
C3—0.5-.5μF capacitor
C4—.22-1.0-μF capacitor
L1/L2—Ferrite loopstick, or ferrite bar BCB antenna coil
Q1—N-channel JFET (Junction Field Effect Transistor) 2N-5458, MPF102 or equiv.)
R1—18,000-47,000-ohm resistor, 1/2-watt
R2—20,000-100,000-ohm potentiometer
R3—4700-10,000-ohm resistor, 1/2-watt

Chapter 5

Security Projects

MOBILE GAS ALARM

NOW—OUR MOBILE GAS ALARM MEANS SAFETY ON THE ROAD; it stands silently by—sniffing with an electronic nose for dangerous combustible gases. When just a small concentration accumulates around its solid-state nostrils . . . WHAMMO! The area is shattered. Not by a tragic explosion, but by a loud screaming alarm that keeps on sounding until you turn it off!

Best of all, this alarm can be conveniently powered by electrical systems found in cars, campers, trucks, travel trailers, motorhomes, houseboats, speedboats, electric-start outboard boats, airplanes, all terrain vehicles, even your electric-start lawn mower—virtually everywhere 12 volt dc power is available.

Although we don't always like to think of it, there is a danger associated with deoxidizing (combustible) gas such as propane-fired camper stoves, gasoline fumes in the bilge of a boat, exhaust fumes released by everything from diesel trucks to lawn mowers. There's even the possibility of flame-out and gas leakage with a plumber's soldering torch.

All these situations and many more can mean danger if gas is allowed to accumulate in confined areas. Though the special semiconductor gas sensor used in this project has been the basis for kits and construction projects in the past, none, to our knowledge,

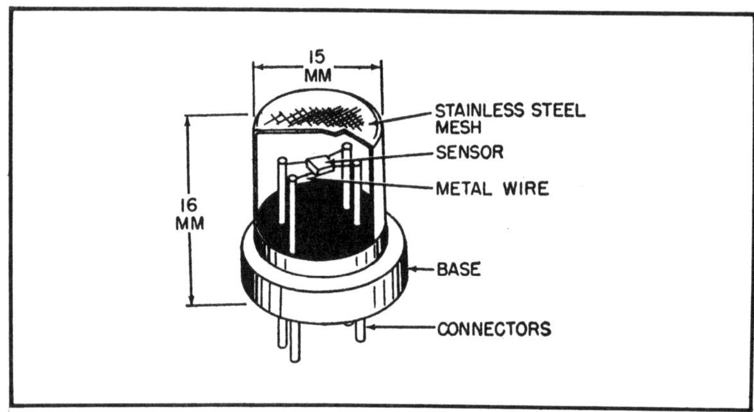

Fig. 5-1. This unit is electrically symmetrical. Either element can serve as the input or the output of this rugged detector.

made such efficient use of the power required to operate its sensor. OK. No problem when you're powered by your local electric company. It's when your power system is based on a storage battery that even 1/2-watt* becomes important. This project works anywhere 12-volt dc power is available.

You can have this modern gas sensor for use away from power lines that draws hardly more than one tenth of an amp at 12 volts—an average power of 1.2 watts. We've used the handy 555-type timer to power-pulse the detector at the 12-volt level, so the average power is similar to that provided by 1.2 volts dc.

How Does It Work?

Three basic parts of the circuit are a power-saving filament voltage supply for the sensor, the gas sensor device itself, and the alarm tripping circuit. Let us look at them one at a time.

□ The power supply for the gas sensor consists of pulse-generating integrated circuit IC1 and a PNP power transistor Q1. The integrated circuit sends periodic pulses which turn the power transistor on and off and thus gate the battery power. This approach saves approximately 80 percent of the battery power as compared to the conventional voltage dropping resistor or power transistor with heat sink methods. Zener diode D1 assures a constant filament supply for the sensor independent of changes in the battery voltage.

□ The gas sensor element (Fig. 5-1) is composed of bulk semiconductor material (mainly tin oxide) heated by a thin filament coil. The semiconductor material lowers its resistance when exposed

*With a series dropping resistor lowering 12 volts to the required 1.2, you can waste 9 times the power actually used by the gas detector element. This is pure power waste you can't afford when operating from battery power—even high power auto batteries. Multiply that power loss by the number of hours the unit is in operation (say, overnight) on a camping trip, and you come up with a hefty amount of wasted watt-hours.

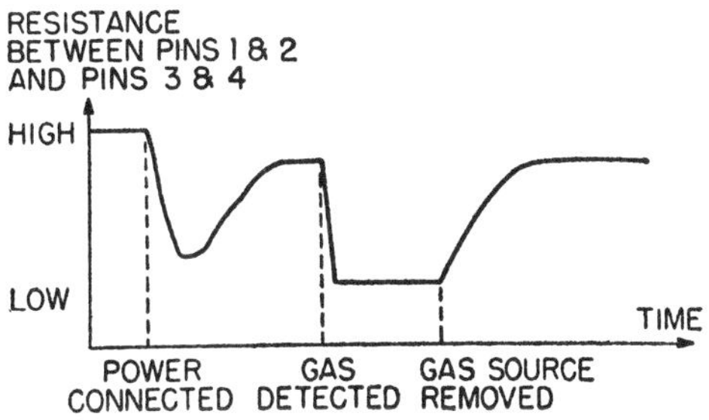

RESISTANCE
BETWEEN PINS 1 & 2
AND PINS 3 & 4
HIGH
LOW
TIME
POWER CONNECTED
GAS DETECTED
GAS SOURCE REMOVED

Fig. 5-2. Shows why you must warm up the heater element for a few minutes before making a sensitivity adjustment final.

to a variety of deoxidizing gases. The sensor reacts to hydrogen, carbon monoxide, propane, and organic solvent vapors in the alcohol, ketone, and benzol families. For example, the sensor can easily detect concentrations of only 100 ppm of carbon monoxide. The sensor restores itself to high resistance a few minutes after the gas source has been removed, and it has a life span of several years.

□ The alarm tripping circuit turns the buzzer on when the sensor resistance decreases so that the voltage at the gate of the SCR exceeds a value preset by R7, the sensitivity adjustment potentiometer. Once the SCR is triggered, the buzzer starts to operate. Then, switch S1 must be used to reset the SCR to stop the buzzer. Zener diode D2 prevents the circuit from sounding an alarm if a transient appears on the 12-volt power supply line.

Operation

The gas sensor element has a fair amount of thermal inertia as shown in Fig. 5-2. Therefore, after connecting the instrument to a 12-volt car or boat battery, wait for four to five minutes with S1 in off position and R7 at minimum (counterclockwise) resistance. After the time has elapsed, turn S1 on and start turning the sensitivity adjustment slowly clockwise. When the alarm sounds, switch S1 off, turn R7 slightly back, then switch S1 on again. To obtain maximum sensitivity you can repeat the sensitivity adjustment after a half hour.

When the buzzer sounds, the only way to turn it off is with S1 (not with the sensitivity adjustment). Check the circuit by rubbing a drop of gasoline or alcohol on your fingers near the sensor. The alarm should then sound. It then takes the sensor four to five minutes to restore itself to the same sensitivity.

Construction

The project is straightforward. Follow the layout shown (Figs. 5-3 and 5-4). All the components fit on a 3- by 4-in. perfboard. A 6- by 3- by 2-in. cabinet will house the entire project (Fig. 5-5). Mounting

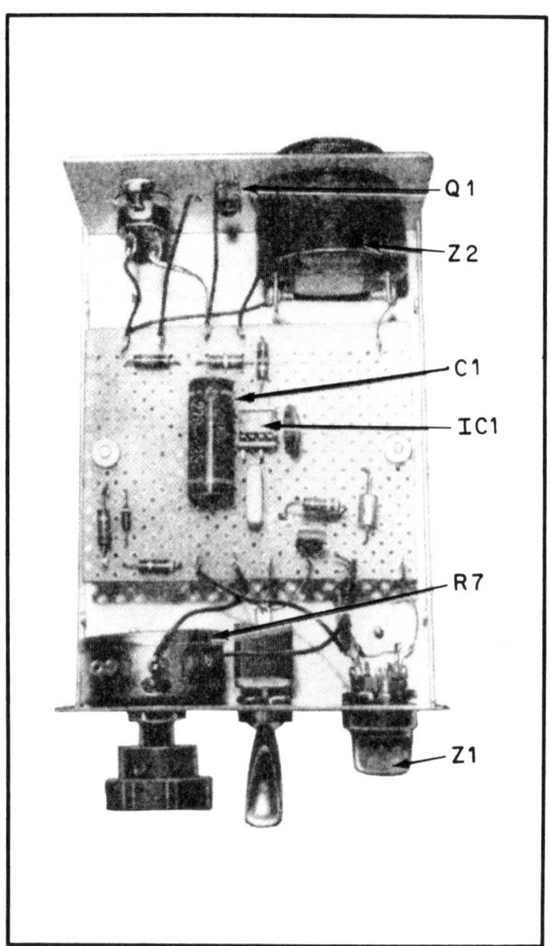

Fig. 5-3. You can follow this layout exactly making point-to-point wiring connections underneath the perfboard and to push-in clips. Take extra care to ensure that correct polarity is applied.

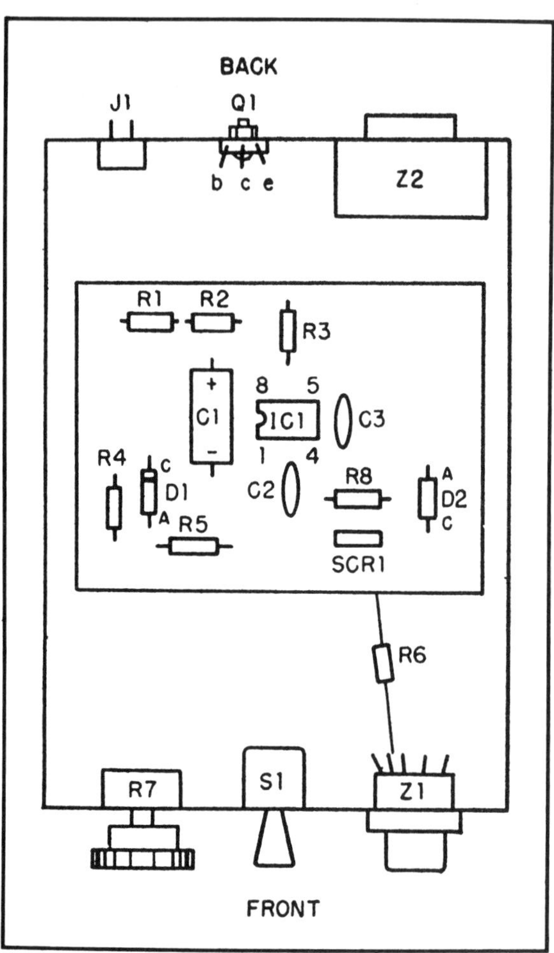

Fig. 5-4. Parts layout diagram.

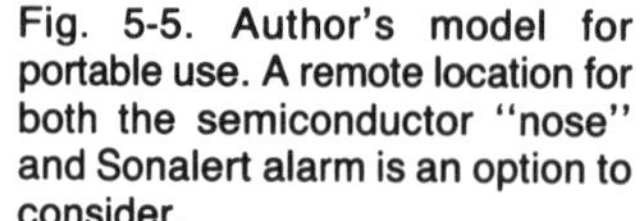

Fig. 5-5. Author's model for portable use. A remote location for both the semiconductor "nose" and Sonalert alarm is an option to consider.

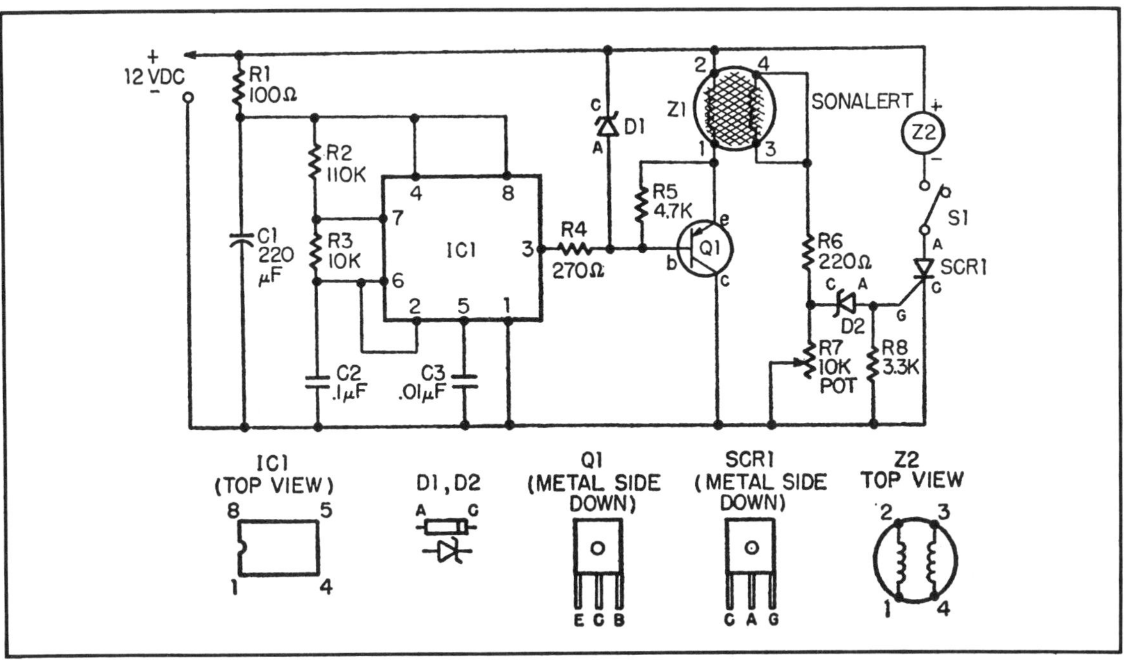

Fig. 5-6. Mobile gas alarm schematic.

Table 5-1. Parts List for Gas Alarm.

C1—220 μF electrolytic capacitor, 35 to 50 Vdc (Radio Shack 272-1017 or equiv.)
C2—0.1 μF capacitor, 25 Vdc or better (Radio Shack 272-1069 or equiv.)
C3—0.01 μF capacitor, 25 Vdc or better (Radio Shack 272-1065 or equiv.)
D1—Zener diode, 9-volt, 1/2-watt (Radio Shack 276-622 or equiv.)
D2—Zener diode, 4-volt, 1/2-watt (Radio Shack 276-620 or equiv.)
IC1—Integrated circuit, 555-type timer (Radio Shack 276-1723 or equiv.)
Q1—Transistor, HEP-700 or Radio Shack 276-2026
R1—100-ohm, 1/2-watt resistor (Radio Shack 271-000 or equiv.)
R2—110,000-ohm, 1/2-watt resistor (Radio Shack 271-000 or equiv.)
R3—10,000-ohm, 1/2-watt resistor (Radio Shack 271-000 or equiv.)
R4—270-ohm, 1/2-watt resistor (Radio Shack 271-000 or equiv.)
R5—4700-ohm, 1/2-watt resistor (Radio Shack 271-000 or equiv.)
R6—220-ohm, 1/2-watt resistor (Radio Shack 271-000 or equiv.)
R7—10,000-ohm potentiometer, linear taper (SENSITIVITY) (Radio Shack 271-1715 or equiv.)
R8—3300-ohm, 1/2-watt resistor (Radio Shack 271-000 or equiv.)
S1—Switch, spst, any style pushbutton or toggle you select (ALARM RESET) (author used Radio Shack 275-651)
SCR1—Silicon controlled rectifier, Radio Shack 276-1079, or General Electric C106.
Z1—Semiconductor gas detector model 105 (Available from Southwest Technical Products Co., 219 West Rhapsody, San Antonio, TX 78216 for $6.25 postpaid)
Z2—Sonalert model SC628 or equiv.
Misc.—Wire, solder, perf board, push-in clips, cabinet approx. 3-in. high by 4-in. wide by 6-in. deep (Radio Shack 270-252 shown), IC socket, knob, 7-pin miniature tube socket for Z1 (Radio Shack 274-1511 or equiv.), polarized socket for 12-volt input power (Calectro F3-170 shown), automotive-type cigar lighter accessary plug and cord for 12-volt input power (Radio Shack 270-021 or equiv.) etc.

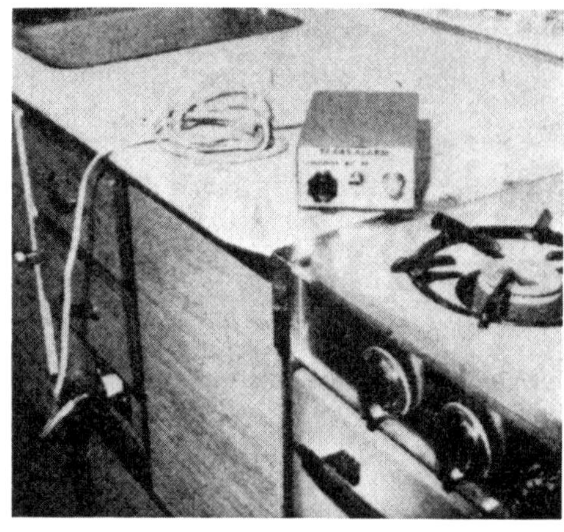

Fig. 5-7. Typical temporary installation in a pick-up camper. Recreational vehicles often have an electrical outlet supplying 12 volt power.

the gas sensor is easy, it fits into a 7-pin miniature tube socket. Pins 1 & 2 are interchangeable, as are pins 3 & 4 (see Fig. 5-6 and Table 5-1). Though we mounted the sensor in the same cabinet as the rest of the circuit, you may want to install it at some remote location in your boat or trailer and connect it via a 3-wire, No. 18 stranded cable to the alarm box. Use the cabinet as a heat sink for transistor Q1; it does not have to be insulated since the collector on the metallic transistor tab is at ground potential. You can pick the 12-volt supply from the cigarette lighter or by making a separate connection to your battery. Use a socket for the integrated circuit to avoid overheating the pins when soldering.

There is a strong possibility that a number of asphyxia-related camping tragedies could have been avoided if this simple gadget had been on the job. Of course, nothing takes the place of safety first! A propane-fired cooking stove should not be used to warm an enclosed camper or trailer while people sleep. Similarly, children should be taught the dangers of "haphazard" adjustment of kitchen knobs. See Fig. 5-7.

NIGHTLIGHT BLACKOUT ALARM

HEAVY RAINS, ELECTRICAL STORMS, DRIFTING SNOW, AND high winds and the energy shortage can cause a power failure to your home just when you urgently need electricity to operate your furnace, freezer, sump pump, clocks, etc. After I experienced a flooded basement due to a power failure during a heavy rain, I built this power failure alarm.

This small and inexpensive device will 1—sound a battery-operated buzzer to wake you up, 2—light a pilot lamp (flashlight bulb) so that you can locate the unit in a darkened room (you will want to shut off that darn buzzer!), 3—remind you to "reset" it after power is restored (the lamp stays on continuously until house current is applied to the device), and 4—provide you with a portable trouble-light (you can unplug the alarm and take it anywhere).

After you have built the alarm and installed it (under your bed is a good place), how do you know that it will work OK when that power failure hits? Testing its operation is quick and easy. Simulate a power failure by momentarily disconnecting the unit from the wall socket. If the buzzer and lamp both come on, plug it back in and rest assured that it's ready to alert you when a real power failure occurs.

The alarm is built into a ready-made box that measures 2 5/8-in. × 5 1/16-in. × 1 5/8-in. It costs about $10 to build, and about 10¢ per month to operate. It can be built for even less if you have on hand any parts that can be used, if you elect to fabricate your own box, or if you solder the batteries and lamp permanently into the circuit, thus eliminating the cost of a battery holder and lamp socket.

The gadget uses about 2 kilowatt-hours (kWh) of electrical power per month: in many localities electric power costs about 8¢ per kWh (most electric bills show the number of kilowatt-hours used per month—divide this figure into the amount of your bill to get your effective rate).

How It Works

As shown in the schematic diagram (Fig. 5-8) the buzzer and lamp are wired in parallel and are connected, through the switch and normally-closed relay contacts, to the battery (two C cells). When the power cord is plugged into any household outlet, the relay coil is energized and the contacts open to interrupt battery power to the buzzer and lamp. When a power failure occurs, the relay contacts close and complete the buzzer-lamp-battery circuit.

Section A of the DPDT switch opens the buzzer circuit to shut it off: simultaneously, section B applies battery power directly to the

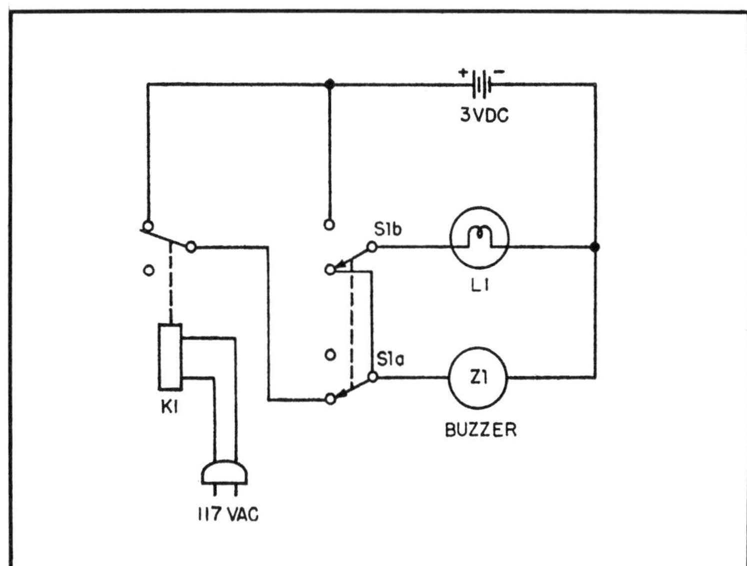

Fig. 5-8. Nightlight blackout alarm schematic.

lamp, which cannot be switched off. The lamp is wired in this manner to provide a reminder to switch the buzzer back to the on position after power is restored so that the alarm will be ready for the next power failure. If a switch were connected between the buzzer and lamp to turn just the buzzer off, you might forget to turn it back on after the emergency (the lamp would go out when the relay was energized again).

If parts are substituted for those shown in the parts list (Table 5-2) first check to see that all components will fit in the box or case to be used, including clearance for those parts that will be mounted on the cover. In the unit shown there is adequate room for everything, of course, but it's a reasonably tight squeeze and even a slightly larger part might give you a packaging problem. Also, if you've substituted parts it would be well to hay-wire everything together to see if the battery(s) you've chosen will deliver enough current to operate both

Table 5-2. Parts List for Power Lost.

B1—Batteries, two C cells in series (see text)

K1—Relay, normally closed or DPST contacts (Radio Shack 275-205 or equiv.)

L1—Lamp, PR-2 flashlight lamp (Radio Shack 272-1120 or equiv.) Note: You can also use a 222-type pre-focussed penlight lamp (Radio Shack 272-1124 or equiv.) in a Calectro E2-400 socket. It draws one-half the battery power of a PR-2 and beams the light for a flashlight effect.

S1—DPDT toggle switch (Radio Shack 275-666 or equiv.)

Z1—Buzzer for 3-volt operation (Radio Shack 273-004 or equiv.)

Misc.—Wire, case (Radio Shack 270-233), power cord, battery holder for C cells (Radio Shack 270-385), solder, etc.

the buzzer and lamp consistently and reliably. The buzzer in the parts list draws about 500 mA of current and the lamp about 50 mA less.

The buzzer selected may require some adjustment. As shown in the photo (Fig. 5-9), there are two adjustment screws on the back of its case. Tighten or loosen these screws as required for best operation (tightening the screws will raise the pitch of the note emitted, but if they are too tight the buzzer will not operate).

Put It Together

Start actual construction by drilling a 3/16-in. hole in one end of the box, threading the line-cord through the hole, trying a knot in the cord for strain relief, and soldering the conductors to the relay coil terminals. A diagram of the terminals comes with the relay. The box in the parts list is made of plastic and aluminum. The relay case and battery holder are plastic. Therefore the latter parts are best mounted by gluing them to the bottom of the box. With sandpaper, roughen up the bottom of the box, the bottom of the battery holder, and one side of the relay case to provide a better surface for the glue. Spread a couple of drops of Testors model cement (or Duco cement or Elmer's Glue) on the roughened surfaces, press into place in the positions shown in Fig. 5-9, and let them dry while mounting the other parts.

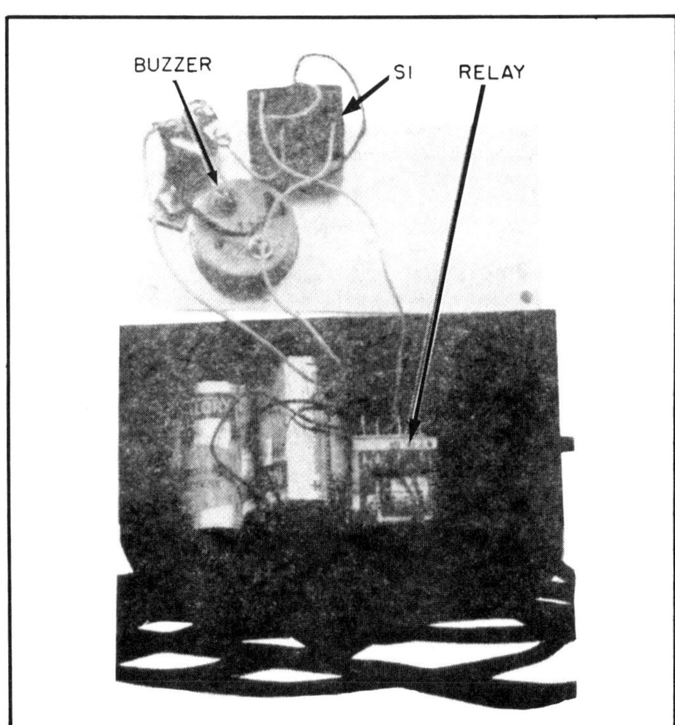

Fig. 5-9. Inside the black box a couple of parts can give you instant blackout warning. A buzz alerts sleepers during nighttime failures.

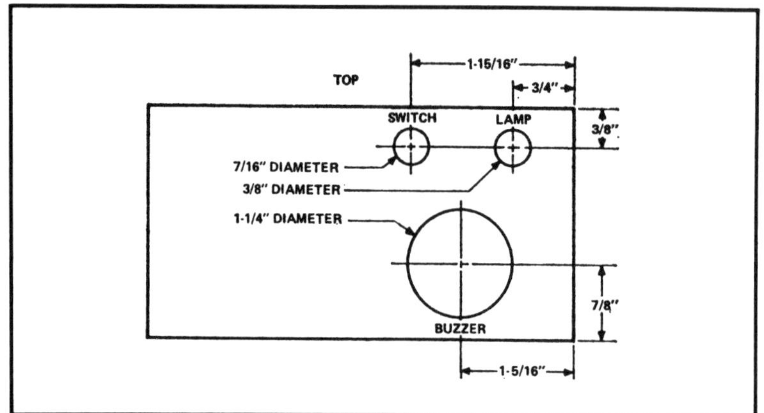

Fig. 5-10. Cut out the top metal plate of your box to these specifications. One additional hole is drilled in the side for the power cord.

You can put the batteries in the battery holder to help weight it down while the glue dries.

The buzzer, switch, and lamp are mounted in holes drilled in the aluminum cover, and are positioned as shown in the drilling template (Fig. 5-10). Then, interconnect all components as shown in the schematic diagram (Fig. 5-8). Wire those on the cover first, and make the 3 leads that go into the box long enough so that the cover can be moved well out of the way for replacing the batteries or lamp. The relay in the parts list is a 4PDT unit, although only one normally-closed set of contacts is used in the alarm circuit. The extra contacts can be used as convenient soldering lugs for some of the wires if desired.

LIGHT SENSOR

IF IT'S PROTECTION YOU NEED, DON'T PAY THE MOB! TAKE THE money and build the Light Sensor, an unusual burglar alarm you can construct in a few hours and which will give protection for years to come.

The Light Sensor is a solid-state, battery-operated, light-activated intrusion burglar alarm system that's different from other light-alarm systems in use today. As a starter, there isn't an obvious light-beam that a burglar might notice and try to avoid. Neither is a special light source required—any common 117-Vac lamp will do. And to top it off, the Light Sensor requires so little power that a single low-cost battery will operate it for months.

How it works

Perhaps the best way to explain the operation of the Light Sensor is to compare it to the human eye in a stationary position, looking at a light. All is fine as long as the light isn't interrupted, but let an object pass between the light source and the eye, and at that instant the light level reaching the eye is reduced, so the eye signals the brain to sound an alarm. Add to the alarm as many as three more such eyes and you have a system that compares to four tireless guards that cannot sleep or be diverted in any way.

Protection need not stop here. You can add as many closed-circuit protection switches as desired for both window and door protection, such as magnetic reed switches, pressure-sensitive switches, lead foil (used for glass-breakage detection), and any other suitable closed circuits, all of which must be wired in series and connected to one of the remote inputs, J1 through J4.

Putting it together

Today's burglar alarms need not have that typical "plain-Jane square-box" look as did the alarms of yesterday. You can go modern and build yours in a LMB CO-3 cabinet to match the author's model. Since housing or circuit layout isn't critical you can, if you wish, build your alarm in any suitable enclosure and use perfboard for the circuit wiring. See Figs. 5-11 and 5-12.

A printed-circuit board is available, with or without components, from Krystal Kits. See the parts list for the details (Table 5-3).

If a printed-circuit board is used, just follow the component layout diagram (Fig. 5-13) mount all parts on the board, and solder in place. Care should be taken when installing the semiconductors to insert the leads in the correct holes. Heat-sink each lead during soldering.

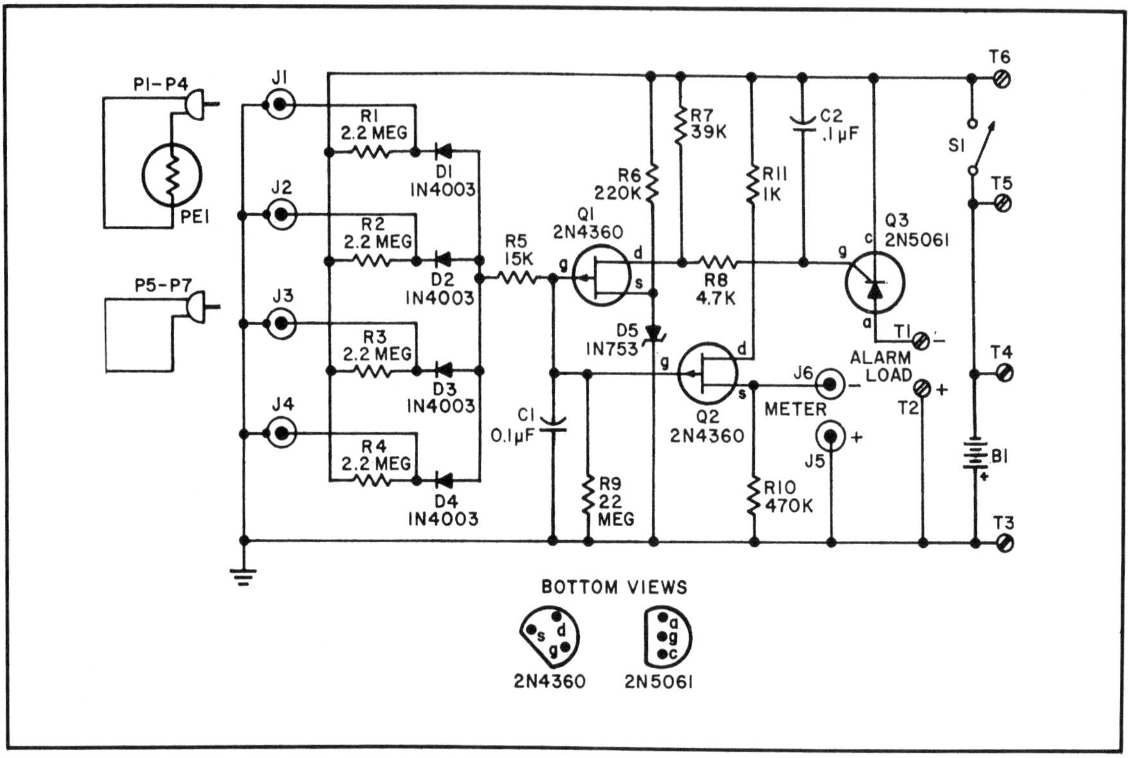

Fig. 5-11. Light sensor schematic.

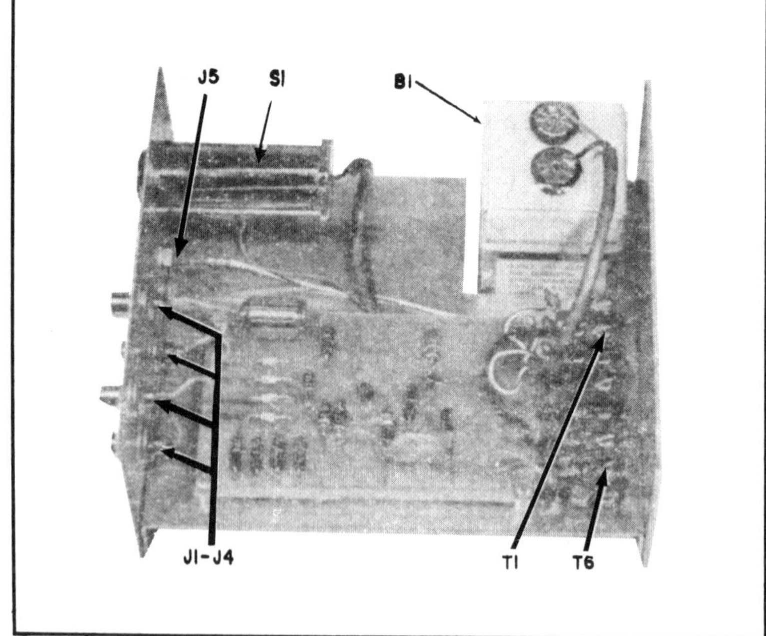

Fig. 5-12. The circuit layout isn't critical, so the components could be mounted on perfboard and put in any convenient housing. Jack J6 is hidden by lock switch S1.

Table 5-3. Parts List for Light Sensor.

B1—9-volt transistor battery (Eveready 276 or RCA VS306)
C1—.01-μF, 600-volt polystyrene capacitor (Mallory)
C2—.1-μF, disc capacitor
D1-D4—Silicon rectifier (Motorola IN4003 or HEP-156)
D5—Zener diode (Motorola IN753 or HEP-Z0214)
Q1, Q2—P-channel field-effect transistor (Fairchild 2N4360)
Q3—.8 amp 60 PIV silicon-controlled rectifier (Motorola 2N5061 or HEP-R1002)
R1-R4—2,200,000-ohm, 1/2-watt 10%
R5—15,000-ohm, 1/2-watt 10%
R6—220,000-ohm, 1/2-watt 10%
R7—39,000-ohm, 1/2-watt 10%
R8—4,700-ohm, 1/2-watt 10%
R9—22,000,000-ohm, 1/2-watt 10%
R10—470,000-ohm, 1/2-watt 10%
R11—1,000-ohm, 1/2-watt 10%
PE1—CL603AL or CL603A (see text) Clairex Photocell
P1-P4—Phono plugs
P5-P7—Phono plugs with shorting wire
J1-J4—Phono jacks, chassis-mount type
S1—Lock switch
Misc.—Six-terminal barrier strip, LMB type CO-3 cabinet, wire solder, hardware, PE-cell housing (see text), etc.

Lock switch S1 can be replaced by a lower cost switch, such as a standard toggle, hidden in an out-of-sight location so that it will not be obvious to an intruder.

Photocell Mounting

Remote pickup eyes PE1-PE4 can be constructed in a variety of shapes to meet almost any specific requirement. Constructing the eyes is easy—just glue the photocell in one end of a light tight paper or metal tube of the desired length, bring out the leads through spaghetti,

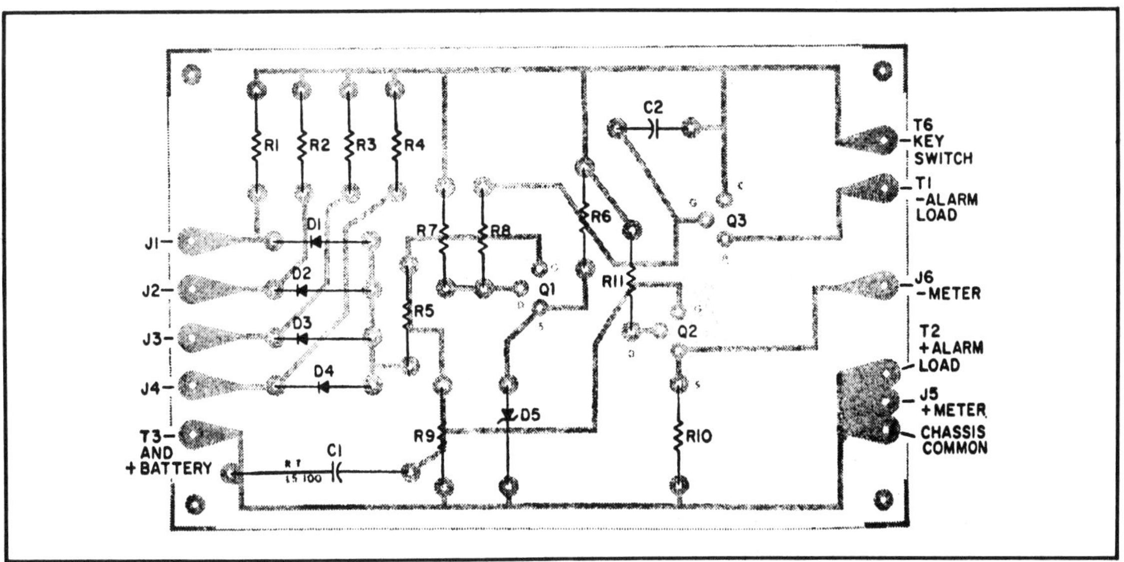

Fig. 5-13. Placement of parts on printed-circuit board. Drill holes in corners for mounting. The foil pattern is exact size, and can be used to make your own printed-circuit board.

and seal the end with either shrinkable tubing or electrical tape.

Sealing of the tubing is necessary to reduce the light leakage to the back end of the photocell that would cause a loss in sensitivity. It is very important that the dark resistance of the photocell be as high as possible for proper operation of the remote eye.

If the distance from the light source to the remote eye is great (over 25 feet) then the tubing should be 6 to 18 inches long. A 3- to 6-inch tube is suitable for shorter distances. The correct length of tubing can be determined by experimenting with different tube lengths and various light sources.

To simplify mounting of the remote eye, the photocell tubing can be assembled in a small mini-box with a two-wire cable connected to the photocell at one end and to a phono plug at the other.

If a low-wattage light source is used, or if the distance from the light to the photocell pickup is great, then the more sensitive CL603AL photocell should be used. If the distance is small, then use the less sensitive CL603A cell. These two photocells are far from being the only suitable ones. You may find that most similar types of cells will work just as well.

Setting up the Alarm System

The alarm unit can be placed in almost any convenient location, although it should not be placed in front of any of the remote eyes. See Figs. 5-14 through 5-17. Short all four input jacks J1-J4 and connect the battery to the alarm. Turn key switch S1 to the on position and monitor the voltage at the meter jacks J5 and J6, with a voltmeter set to the 10-Vdc range. The voltage reading will represent the

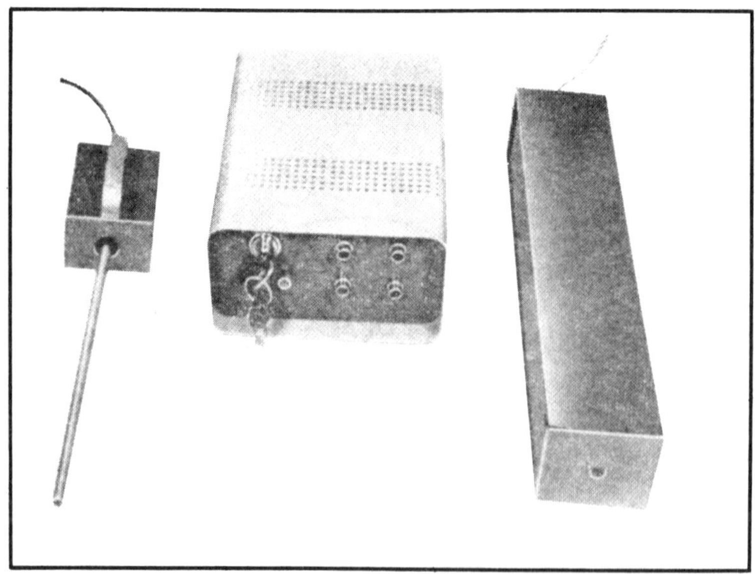

Fig. 5-14. The remote pickup "eyes" can be built in a variety of ways, with the tube exposed as at left, or enclosed in a casing as shown at right.

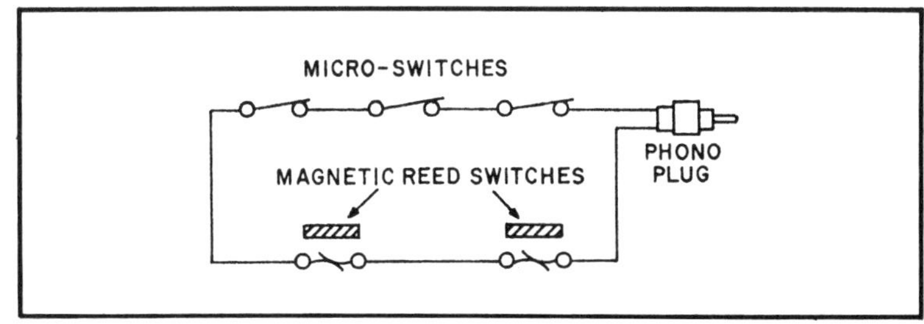

Fig. 5-15. Doors and windows can also be protected with the Light Sensor by wiring normally closed switches in a closed circuit.

minimum reading obtainable under a non-alarm condition, and should be between one and five volts with all inputs shorted. Remove one of the jumpers from ground, and plug a remote eye into the jack. Carefully adjust the remote eye at the selected light source for the minimum voltage reading. This voltage must be five volts or below. If the reading is too high, then increase the size of the light source or use a more sensitive photocell in the pickup. With the remote eye

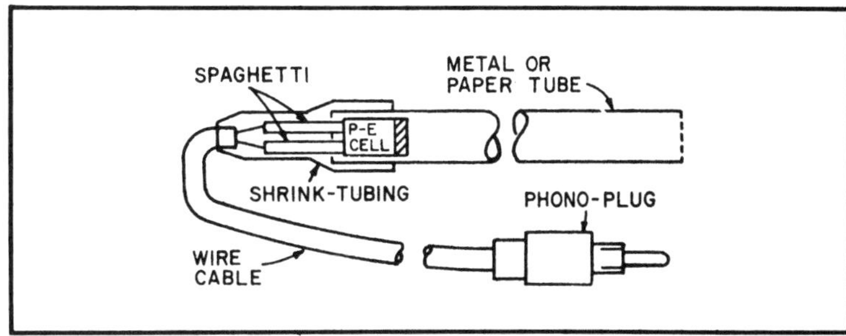

Fig. 5-16. Construction details for a remote eye. Electrical tape can be used instead of shrink tubing to seal the end.

plugged in and adjusted, blocking the light should cause the meter to indicate more than 6 volts. The alarm is now in alarm condition.

The remaining remote eyes must be adjusted in the same manner. If any of the J1-J4 input circuits are not used, then the unused inputs must have a shorting plug inserted in each jack. A shorting plug can be made from a phono plug by soldering a jumper wire between the two plug terminals.

Input Switches

One of the input circuits can protect all your doors and windows

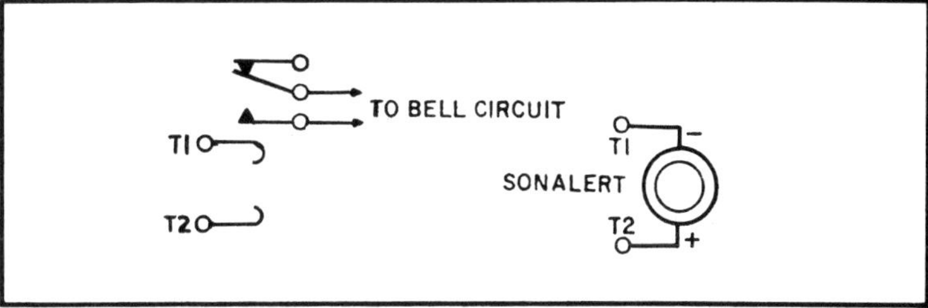

Fig. 5-17. For an audible alarm, connect a relay and bell circuit, or a Sonalert, to T1 and T2.

with either pressure-sensitive switches (such as microswitches) or magnetic-reed switches, all connected in series and wired to a phono plug. As long as all of the switches remained closed, the alarm is set. If only one of the switches opens, the alarm is then latched in the alarm condition and will remain so until reset with the key switch.

Alarm Sounder

When it comes to choosing the type of audible alarm that may be connected to the Light Sensor, it's dealer's choice. By far the cheapest and simplest alarm sounder to connect directly to the unit is a Mallory Sonalert solid-state audible warning device, which is just great for inhouse use. Low-voltage alarm bells may be connected to the unit by using a low-current relay, such as a Sigma 11F-1000-G SIL, to control the bell's current. Other types of alarm sounders could also be controlled by the relay—the choice is up to you!

HOBBYIST'S NIGHT LIGHT

A BEDSIDE LIGHT IS ALWAYS A NICE THING TO HAVE AROUND. It keeps you from falling over wastebaskets, shoes, and other obstacles that might be scattered around. It's even nicer when you build it yourself. The Hobbyist's Night Light is a lamp that responds to large changes in ambient light and switches itself on whenever the light level goes below a point that you select.

A Light Response

In this circuit, light is detected by a cadmium-sulphide photocell that varies its resistance in inverse proportion to the light striking it. This simply means that, in the evening when the light gets dimmer and dimmer, the photocell resistance slowly increases. When the resistance of the photocell becomes greater than the total resistance of R1 and R5, transistor Q1 will turn-on. Recalling basic transistor theory, an NPN transistor conducts (turns on) whenever the base is positive with respect to the emitter.

Whenever Q1 conducts, it makes Q2 conduct and turn on a small pilot lamp that serves as the night light. A night light need not be bright. We've chosen a common, inexpensive #47 pilot lamp for ours because a wide selection of sockets is available.

Quick Pick-Up

By conncting the lamp to the junction of PC1 and R4, the circuit is made to switch rapidly from off to on because lamp current flowing through R4 develops a small positive bias voltage to help Q1 turn on and remain on.

Most of the circuitry for this project can be wired on a small piece of perforated board about 2-in. × 3-in. in size. A suggested layout is shown in Fig. 5-18. Notice that connections are required for power, sensitivity control, photocell and lamp. See Fig. 5-19 and Table 5-4.

Night Light Construction

Mount the transformer and the rest of the power supply components in the box you are using and wire the power supply leaving 6-in. terminations for connection to the board. Wire the board. A heat sink for the power transistor is only necessary if you use a lamp rated over 300 milliamps. Mount the sensitivity pot on the box in a convenient location, secure the photocell in a hole with Duco cement where it will be exposed to room light, and screw the circuit board down on a couple of spacers. How you mount the lamp is up to you.

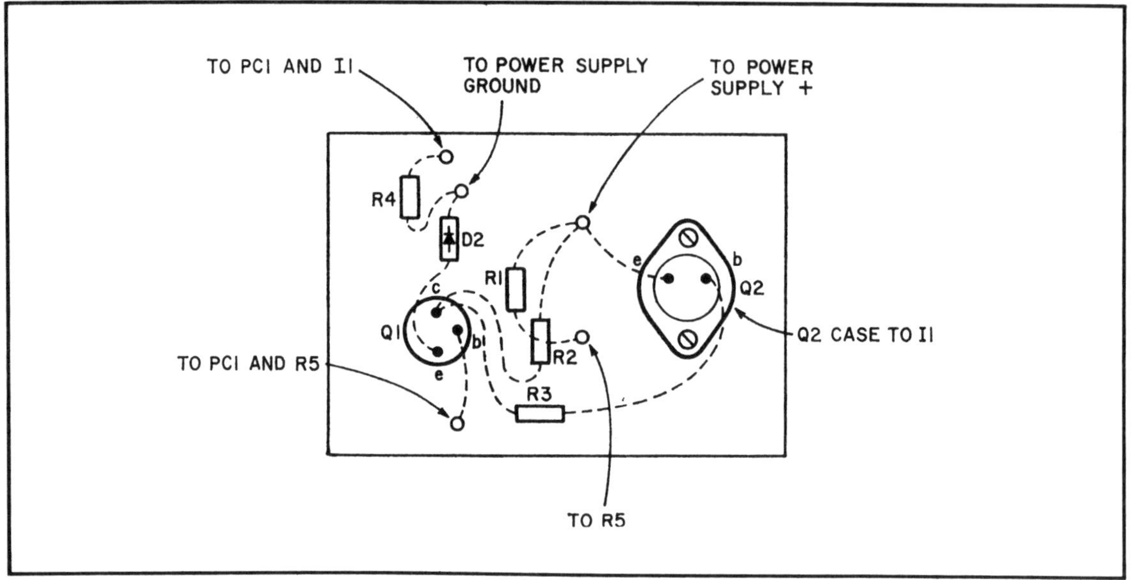

Fig. 5-18. Suggested perf board layout, top view. See Fig. 5-19 for complete wiring.

A plastic reflector on the author's model came from his junk box; everything was just glued in place.

In any case, just make sure that light from the pilot lamp doesn't get back to the photocell; it would lower your unit's light sensitivity. Finish wiring the unit by connecting the photocell, power supply, sensitivity pot, and the lamp to the board. Screw the cover on and your night light is ready for use.

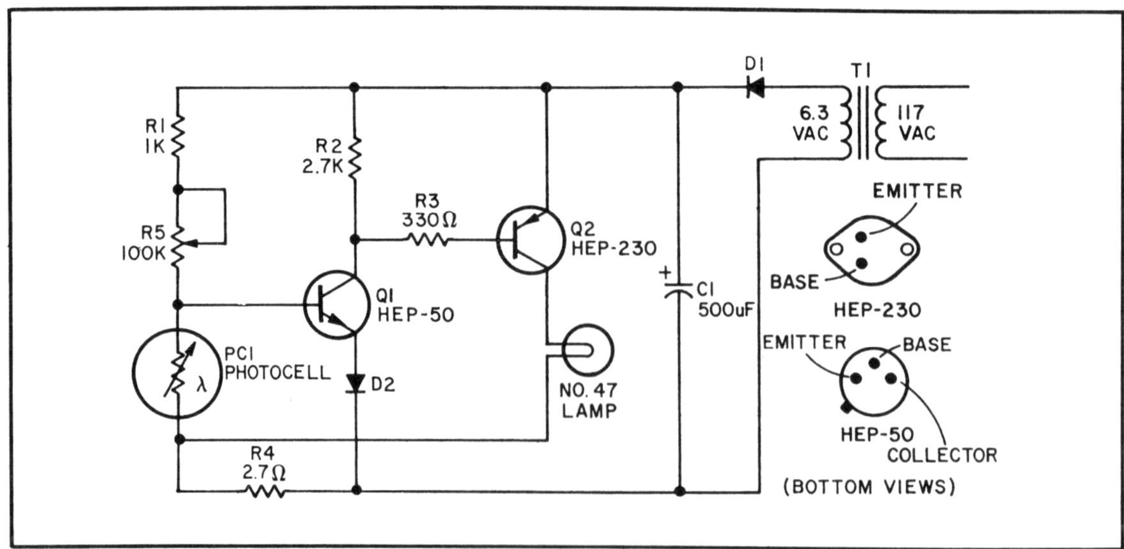

Fig. 5-19. Hobbyist's night light schematic.

Table 5-4. Parts List for Hobbyist's Nightlight.

C1—500 μF, 15-Vdc electrolytic capacitor
D1—Silicon rectifier diode, 2-amp, 50-V
D2—Diode, IN34 or any general purpose germanium (Lafayette 19-49015 or equiv.)
I1—Pilot lamp, #47
PC1—Photocell, Clairex CL703L
Q1—NPN transistor, Motorola HEP-50
Q2—PNP transistor, Motorola HEP-230
R1—1000-ohm, 1/2-watt resistor, 10%
R2—2,700-ohm, 1/2-watt resistor, 10%
R3—330-ohm, 1/2-watt resistor, 10%
R4—2.7-ohm, 1/2-watt resistor, 10%
R5—100,000-ohm, linear taper potentiometer
T1—Filament transformer, primary 117 Vac, secondary 6.3 Vac @ 1.2 amps (Stancor P-8190 or equiv.)

Adjustment is simple

Turn the unit on and set sensitivity pot R5 somewhat past the point at which the lamp goes out with the room lights on. It may be necessary to readjust things to account for ambient light conditions, but once set you'll be able to count on a light when you need it.

If you want to control an outside or porch light, substitute a 6-volt relay (Potter & Brumfield MR5D or equiv.) for the lamp and control the new lamp through its contacts.

AUDIO FIRE ALARM

THIS PORTABLE AUDIO FIRE ALARM IS ASSEMBLED FROM STANdard transistor-radio parts. It will protect lives and property from the ravages of fire. The alarm box can even be taken along on vacation trips to protect your summer cottage.

The alarm's warning sound is the amplified feed-back signal produced when a microphone and speaker, connected to their respective input and output terminals of an amplifier, are placed in close proximity to each other.

The heart of the device is the amplifier—a three-transistor subminiature unit—powered by a nine-volt transistor radio battery. A new battery will operate the alarm continuously for more than an hour.

To develop the signal, a speaker used as an input microphone and an output speaker are connected to the amplifier. Two miniature PM speakers will do the job nicely.

The unit's alarm sounds when its thermostatic switch closes. A preset detector switch closes the circuit when the surrounding air temperature reaches 135° F.

Construction

The fire alarm is housed in a plastic case measuring 2 × 3 3/4 × 6 1/4 inches. The case's predrilled cover serves as the back wall of the case. See Figs. 5-20, 5-21 and Table 5-5.

Drill a hole at a central point in the panel to permit hanging it from a nail on the wall. Then drill a 1/4-inch hole midway between the two sides of the panel and about one inch from one end of the panel. The two speakers will face out from the case. The back of the case serves as the front face of the alarm box, so drill two holes in it for the speakers.

To fasten the speakers to the inside bottom of the case, drill a 1/32-inch hole through each side of the afore-mentioned speaker holes and about 3/16 inch from the edge. Place the speakers in the case face down; fasten them to the case with at least one 4-40 × 1/2-inch machine screw, or with plastic cement applied around the rim of the speakers.

Fasten the amplifier flat against a side wall of the case. This will necessitate removing the amplifier's 30-μF capacitor by unsoldering the capacitor from the bottom of the amplifier's mounting board—being sure to first note its position and polarity in the circuit. Then resolder it to the top side of the mounting board.

Enlarge one of the holes at each end of the perforated mounting

Fig. 5-20. Alarm's shrill signal is started and maintained by feedback from the output to input speaker.

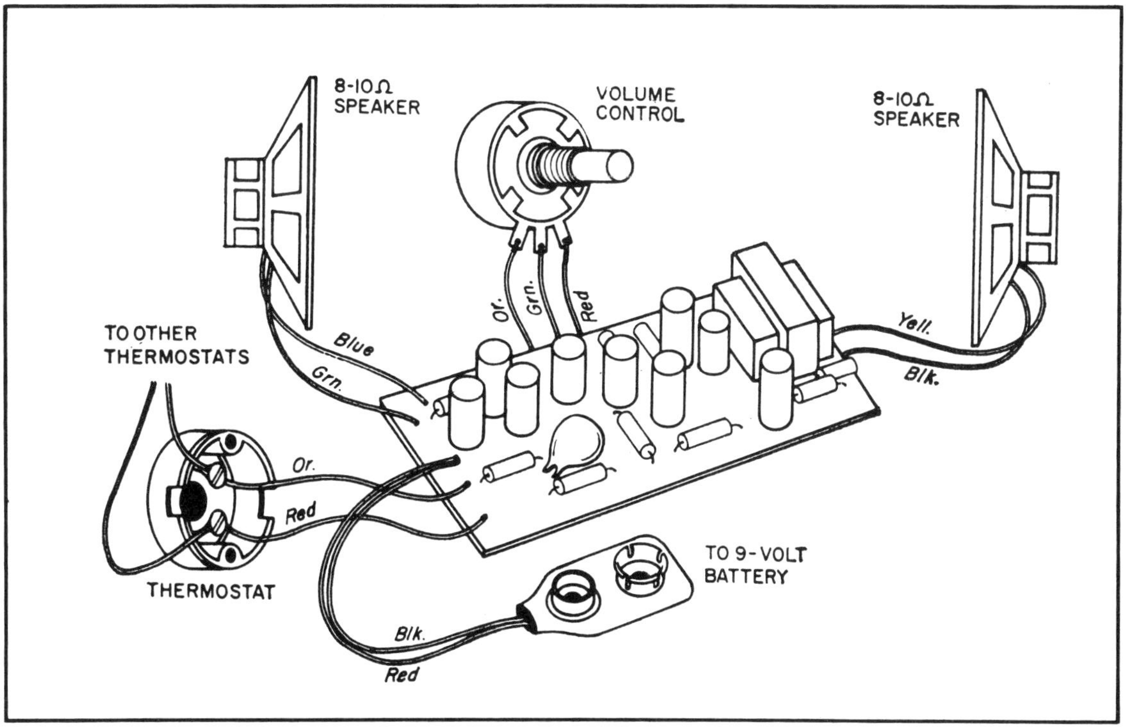

Fig. 5-21. Thermostat is connected as on-off switch, and control is adjusted for desired alarm signal.

Table 5-5. Parts List for Audio Fire Alarm.

1—Subminiature 3-transistor audio amplifier (Lafayette 99G9034 or equiv.)
1—2 1/2″-dia. PM miniature speaker, 10-ohms (Lafayette 99G6097 or equiv.)
1—5,000-ohm miniature potentiometer (Lafayette 99G6019 or equiv.)
1—9-volt transistor battery (Burgess 2U6 or equiv.)
1—Thermostatic switch (Lafayette EL-103)
1—Plastic case and panel (Lafayette 19G2001 and 19G3701 or equiv.)
Misc.—Hardware, washers, hook-up wire, solder, glue, etc.
Estimated construction time: 2 hours
Estimated cost: $10.75

board with a 1/32-inch drill to get the mounting holes for the amplifier. Using both holes as a template, locate the position of the fastening holes on the case wall and drill two corresponding 1/32-inch holes through the wall. Place the amplifier in the case and fasten it to the wall with two 4-40 × 1/2-inch machine screws.

Thermostatic Switch

The switch turns the alarm on and off; on by means of a bimetallic strip of heat-sensitive metal, which touches a contact point when the surrounding air temperature reaches 135°; off when, upon cooling, the strip and point separate.

This detector switch is housed in a plastic case that fastens to the bottom of the amplifier case with two 4-40 × 1/2-inch machine screws. Drill two 1/16-inch holes through the bottom of the upper case, using the holes in the detector-switch case as a template.

To provide for the two terminal wires that lead from the alarm switch, drill a 1/16-inch hole through the center of the amplifier case and detector-switch case where they join. The detector switch now must be wired before its case is tightened in place.

Added Versatility

Providing outside terminal connections makes it possible to connect alarm buttons in other rooms to the same alarm, and also permits the signal to be sounded by other types of contact switches connected to the terminals, so the device can be used for other purposes besides a fire alarm (burglar alarm, P.A. system, etc.)

The outside terminals (two Fahnestock clips) connect the two wires from any outside switch to the alarm circuit. They can be located at any point outside the case. We located them on the top center.

Drill two 1/16-inch holes about one inch apart. Then use two 4-40 × 1/2-inch machine screws—with two nuts for each screw—to hold the clips to the case.

Now for the Wiring

All hook-ups are made with No. 20 acetate-covered wire. Since the amplifier comes with its own leads, you'll need only two additional short wires to connect the outside terminals in parallel with the thermostat.

The amplifier comes from the supplier with an instruction sheet and diagrams showing the color of the lead provided at each of the amplifier terminals. We'll refer to these lead colors in describing the point at which each part hooks into the amplifier.

First solder the amplifier's green and blue leads to either of the speakers' terminals to connect the input microphone. Solder the amplifier's yellow and black leads to the other terminals to connect the output speaker.

The thermostatic switch is cut into the circuit at the point where an on-off switch would normally be located. Fasten the red and orange leads found at this point to the two thermostatic switch terminals.

The outside terminals are wired in parallel to the thermostatic switch with two six-inch lengths of hook-up wire. Connect each wire to an outside terminal, fastening their other ends to the corresponding thermo-switch terminals. (The connection at the outside terminals consists of the inner end of the machine screws holding the Fahnestock clips in place, and the extra nuts are used to tighten the wires down.) Finally, snap the nine-volt battery into the amplifier's battery clip.

Testing the Unit

Hold a lighted match under the case about an inch from the thermostatic switch button. When the temperature of the button reaches 135°, the switch will close to complete the circuit and the signal—a shrill whistle—will sound.

When the match is removed, the switch button will cool and automatically open the circuit.

More Than One Use

As mentioned before, this device can be used for a number of applications besides that of a fire alarm.

A pushbutton converts it to a call signal. A contact switch or mat turns it into a burglar alarm. Connect the outside terminals to a telegraph key and the device becomes loudspeaker signal for code practice.

BLACK BOX ALARM

EVER BEEN BOTHERED WITH A PEEPING TOM, A SHY BURGLAR, or an unwanted intruder? Then build the Black Box Alarm and be protected! Hang the Black Box on any metal door knob—in a hotel, motel, or your own home—and the alarm will sound the minute someone grabs the knob from the other side.

Place the Black Box in an open window and anyone approaching the window screen triggers the unit. Lay the capacity metal plate near your valuable possessions, and the alarm sounds off whenever an intruder draws near. The unit will cost you less than $15 to put together—a small price indeed for the positive protection it offers. See Fig. 5-22.

The Circuit

Basically, the alarm consists of three transistors: Q1 is an oscillator, while Q2 and Q3 act as amplifiers to drive the relay. Capacitor C1 is connected to jack J1 and couples the capacity plate to the base circuit of Q1. Jack J2 couples a common ground to the Black Box ground system. A trimmer capacitor (C3) and a choke (L2) in the emitter leg of Q1 control the point of oscillation.

Q2 and Q3 are conventional amplifiers with a sensitivity control (R3) in the collector circuit of Q2. The collector of Q2 and the base of Q3 are tied directly together, while an 8000-ohm relay appears in the output leg of Q3. Capacitor C5 is an electrolytic capacitor which

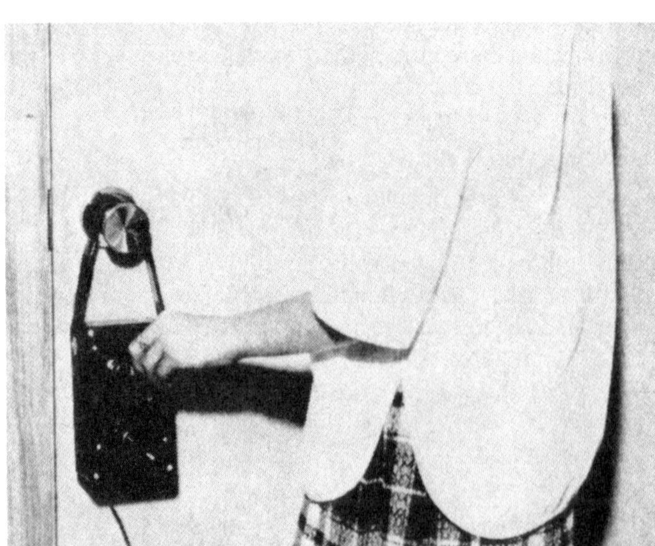

Fig. 5-22. Most traps and alarms are detected by the expert burglar, but he will be thwarted by the lack of wires or electric eyes in this capacity actuated alarm. A babysitter can hang it on a door knob and easily adjust it.

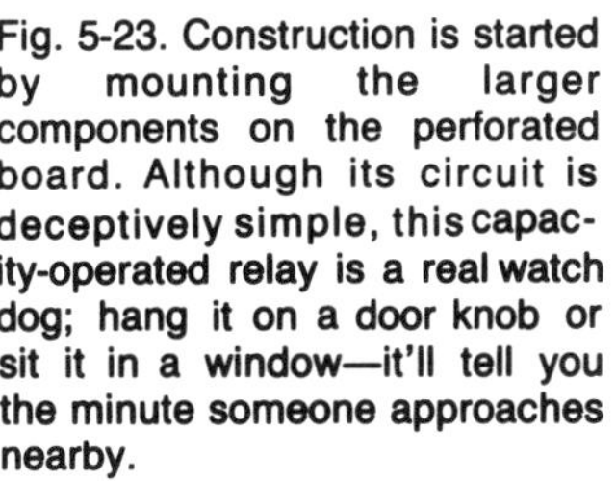

Fig. 5-23. Construction is started by mounting the larger components on the perforated board. Although its circuit is deceptively simple, this capacity-operated relay is a real watch dog; hang it on a door knob or sit it in a window—it'll tell you the minute someone approaches nearby.

eliminates relay chatter and provides smoother relay operation.

The whole unit is powered by one small 9-volt battery (B1). Whenever a person or a large animal comes near the capacity plate, Q1 is triggered into oscillation. Q1's output, meanwhile, is amplified by Q2 and Q3. The output of Q3 is fed into the relay, which will close and cause the buzzer to sound whenever the signal from Q3 is strong enough.

Construction

Start by mounting all of the larger parts as shown in Figs. 5-23, through 5-25; parts placement isn't at all critical. Wire the smaller

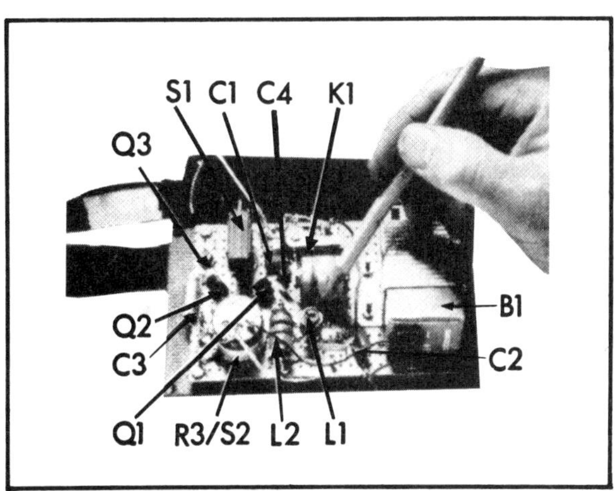

Fig. 5-24. Transistor oscillator coil L1 is the fixed coil in the oscillator circuit. L2 is adjustable to provide increased sensitivity.

Fig. 5-25. The trimmer screw of oscillator circuit capacitor C3 is conveniently located on the front panel to provide easy adjustment to bring on oscillation.

parts into the circuit as the unit is being put together. To avoid errors, it's always best to mark off on the diagram as the various components are wired in. See Fig. 5-26 and Table 5-6.

If you begin with the oscillator coil (L1), you can solder the small components to each terminal. Be sure that the bottom end of the coil (terminal 4) goes to a common ground point, and that the tap on L1

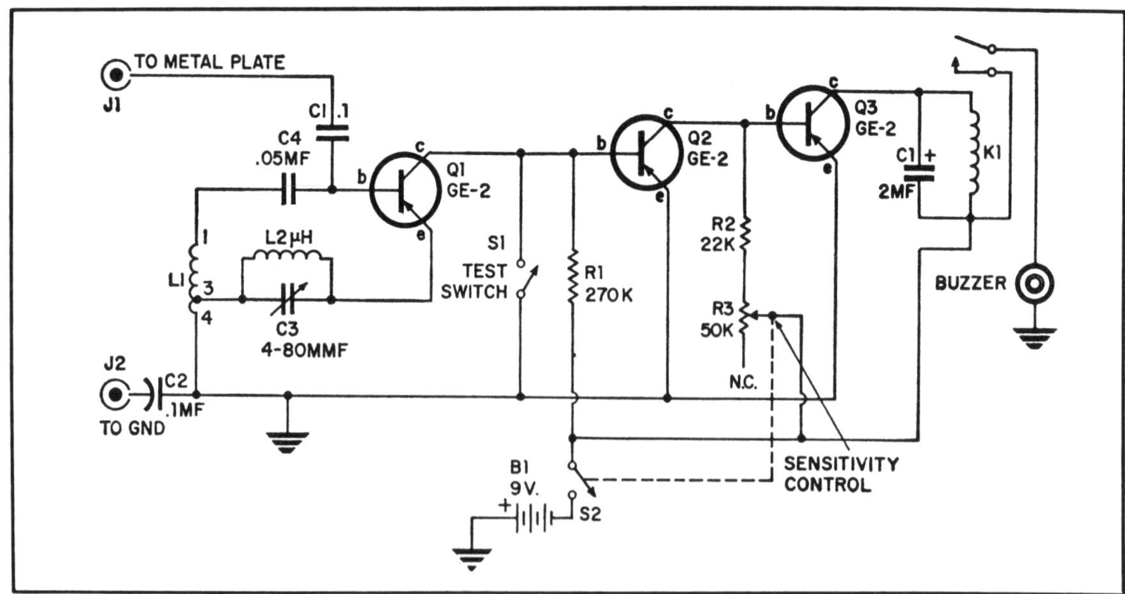

Fig. 5-26. Black Box Alarm schematic. Capacitance between an intruder and the metal plate or strap is coupled to oscillator transistor Q1 through jack J1 to trigger the circuit.

Table 5-6. Black Box Alarm Parts List.

B1—9 volt battery (Burgess 2N6 or equiv.)
C1, C2—.1-μF 75 volt ceramic capacitor
C3—4-80 pF trimmer capacitor
C4—.05-μF 75 volt ceramic capacitor
C5—2-μF wvdc electrolytic capacitor
J1, J2—Miniature tip jacks
L1—455-kc transistor oscillator coil (Miller 2020 or Stancor RTC-9079)
L2—1.5-millihenry iron-core r.f. choke (Miller 70F153AI or Stancor RTC-8524)
Q1, Q2, Q3—GE 2 or equivalent (see text)
R1—270,000-ohm, 1/2-watt resistor
R2—22,000-ohm, 1/2-watt resistor
R3—50,000-ohm potentiometer with s.p.s.t switch S2
K1—S.p.d.t. relay, 8000-ohm coil (Sigma 4F-8000-S/SIL)
S1—S.p.s.t. toggle switch
S2—S.p.s.t. switch (on R3)
1—Buzzer (Calrad CB-1.5 or Burstein-Applebee 22B51)
1—6 1/4″ × 3 3/4″ × 2″ bakelite case (Lafayette MS-216 with MS-217 cover, or equiv.)
Misc.—Pointer knob, battery plug, phenolic board, cloth belt, spare chassis bottom plate, wire, cable, connectors, hardware, solder, etc.
Estimated cost: $21.00
Estimated construction time: 4 hours

(terminal 3) is connected to L2 and C3. Take an ohmmeter, if handy, and measure the resistance between terminals 3 and 4 on the oscillator coil. This resistance will be extremely low in value, while the top half of the coil (between terminals 1 and 3) will measure around 4 ohms. Note that there are two terminals on the coil that aren't used; these are the ones from the primary winding.

Once you have the coil and the other oscillator components properly wired, you can install transistors Q2 and Q3 and their associated parts. These include the test switch (S1) and resistor R1 in the base circuit of Q2, as well as resistor R2 and potentiometer R3 in the base circuit of Q3.

It's always best to adjust the contact points on the relay coil before it's wired up. Unscrew the mounting bolts and remove the relay from the perforated board. Take a piece of typing paper, rip it in half, and insert one piece between the armature leaf and the coil magnet assembly. This done, insert the other piece of paper between the bottom adjustment control screw and the leaf contact point.

Now adjust both contact screws so the paper will just slide in and out easily. Next, remount the relay coil on the perforated board. Finish construction by soldering in the small electrolytic capacitor and the buzzer itself.

Testing the Black Box

After the alarm has been completely wired, go over your work again just to make sure there are no errors. Solder the battery plug to switch S2 and ground; note that the negative lead goes to S2. If a milliameter is handy, insert it in series with the negative battery lead and S2. The unit shouldn't pull over 1.5 ma. when it's operating unless there's a short or a wiring error.

Turn S2 on and rotate R3 until the relay closes and the buzzer sounds. Now turn R3 back until the buzzer quits, then throw S1 on. The buzzer will also buzz at this point. Now tighten C3 until its plates are as close together as possible. Run a lead from the free end of C2 to a water pipe or other suitable ground. In addition, attach a lead from a 1-ft. square metal plate (an old chassis bottom plate is ideal) to the free end of C1.

The buzzer should now sound whenever you put your hand near the metal plate. If necessary, back off C3 or adjust the slug on L2 to control the point at which Q1 goes into oscillation. You can also vary the setting of R3 to control the triggering of the relay coil.

Setting Up

After the unit has been tested to satisfaction, mount the perforated board on the front panel of the meter case. The top half of the front panel was sprayed red with a small can of spray paint to finish off the unit and cause the decals and the lettering to stand out.

Two small phone jacks are mounted in the back of the case. The top jack goes to one end of capacitor C1, while the bottom jack connects to the free end of capacitor C2. Its best to use long flexible wire leads when making these connections.

Next, cut a plastic or cloth belt to 12 inches in length and tape thin brass or copper stock to the inside of the belt material. Solder a length of flexible wire to one end of the slim stock metal and connect it to jack J1. Now when you wish to hang the alarm on a metal door knob, you can use this metal belt instead of the metal plate to set off the alarm.

Other Notes

The three transistors used in the alarm circuit are the type GE2. If you have a transistor tester, use the best of the three transistors in the oscillator circuit. Assuming you can't obtain the GE2's or don't have them in your junk box, you can use 2N215 for Q1 and Q2 and a 2N217 in the relay circuit (Q3).

L2 was a standard 1.5 millihenry choke in the author's model, although a homemade unit can be used. One can be made by taking 15 feet of No. 36 enameled wire, or smaller, and scramble-winding it over a 10-megohm, 1/2-watt resistor.

Sensitivity control R3 should always be turned up until the relay energizes and then backed off a little until the relay armature drops out. The buzzer will come on when the relay is energized and will quit as the point of drop out.

J2 is a ground jack that couples the alarm to a common ground. A metal radiator, a furnace duct, or a water pipe can all serve for this purpose. Naturally, the alarm works best with this lead connected to a good ground.

When the capacity plate is used, L2 may have to be adjusted for more sensitivity. It is easier to adjust the oscillator coil than C3. C3 will give a greater change, while the oscillator coil adjustment is finer and slower.

To find out whether the oscillator is working, turn on a small table radio near the unit. With capacitor C3 turned all the way in, an oscillator hum should be hear around 700 kHz on the dial.

If you still have trouble, throwing test switch S1 on grounds the output of the oscillator and thus enables you to check out the remainder of the circuit. If trouble does exist, you might check the resistances of the relay and oscillator coils for possible open windings. You might also try resetting the contact adjustment on the relay points to get a clean buzzer sound.

FOIL-A-BURGLAR ALARM

THIS PROFESSIONAL TYPE BURGLAR ALARM CAN BE USED TO protect windows or glass areas by using window foil that "breaks" a circuit as the glass is broken. It's an alarm that is triggered when the protective circuit is opened. All protective door and window circuits must be normally closed and series connected so that an opening of any protective device will trigger the alarm (see Fig. 5-27 and Table 5-7). Once the alarm is triggered it can be turned off only by opening master switch S1. The recommended power supply is an ac-powered 6 Vdc source or a lantern battery; standby current is about 100 μA. To adjust, connect a voltmeter (10 Vdc range) across resistor R1, open the protective circuit and adjust potentiometer R2 so the meter indicates a voltage rising towards 1 volt. The alarm bell should ring before 1 volt is reached on the meter. If it does not, there is a wiring error. Finally, set R2 for the 1-volt meter reading, remove the meter and restore the protective circuit.

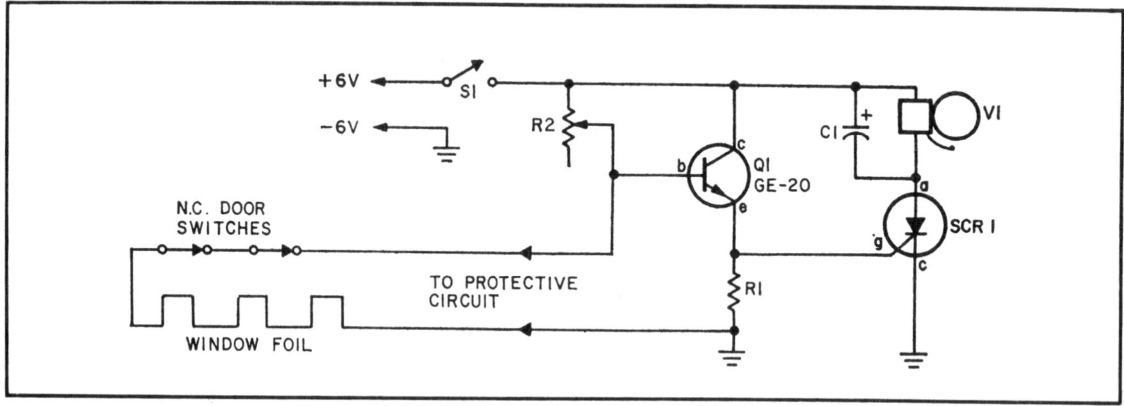

Fig. 5-27. Burglar alarm schematic.

Table 5-7. Parts List for Foil-A-Burglar Alarm.

C1—47 μF 12 Vdc electrolytic capacitor (Calectro A1-108 or equiv.)
Q1—NPN transistor, GE-20 or equiv.
R1—1000-ohm, 1/2 watt resistor
R2—500,000-ohm, pot (Calectro B1-687)
S1—SPST switch
SCR1—Silicon controlled rectifier rated 12 PIV or higher (G.E.C106 series or equiv.)
V1—6 Vdc alarm bell (Audiotex 30-9100)

INTRUDER DETECTOR

FOR LESS THAN $10—USING PARTS READILY AVAILABLE FROM Radio Shack stores—you can literally throw together an effective intruder alarm suitable for use around the house or as a portable alarm for use in hotels and motels.

How it works is best explained by following the schematic (see Fig. 5-28 and Table 5-8). The alarm itself consists of an extra-loud buzzer, battery B1, and normally-closed jack J1. Note that this is a series circuit that is normally closed so that the horn would sound (when it goes on) until you turn it off. These three items are housed in a small cabinet that is mounted adjacent to a door or window.

Plug P1 is a dummy plug to which a short wire or string is attached. When PL1 is inserted in jack J1, the series circuit is opened and the horn is turned off. The free end of the wire from P1 is affixed to the door or window (with a thumbtack). When an intruder attempts to force entry by opening the door or window, the wire pulls out of the jack, whose normally-closed contacts spring together, thereby completing the series circuit and sounding the horn.

Plenty of Sock!

The buzzer-horn specified in the parts list is marked for 1.5 to 3-volt operation. Dependable, loud operation is secured only with a 6-volt power supply, so do not substitute a 1.5-volt battery for the 6-volt battery specified in the parts list.

Jack J1 must be the miniature type specified in the parts list. Do not substitute a standard "phone" jack as it will not allow the plug to be conveniently pulled out. If you have an old transistor radio lying in the junk-box, simply salvage the headphone output jack.

When connecting the pull-wire to P1 take extreme care that you do not short circuit the two plug connections as this will cause the

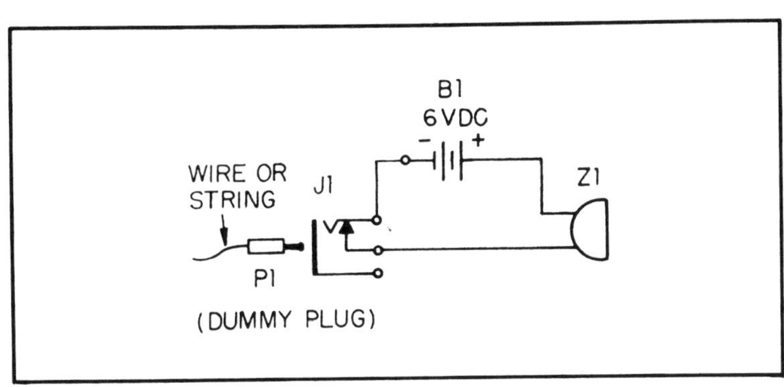

Fig. 5-28. Intruder detector schematic.

Table 5-8. Parts List For Simplex Detector.

B1—6-volt battery, Burgess Z4, RCA VS 068 or equiv.
J1—normally closed mini-jack (Radio Shack 274-292 or equiv.)
P1—plug to match J1 (see text)
Z1—1.5 to 3-volt buzzer, Radio Shack 273-004
Misc.—2 × 4 × 2 1/4-in. utility case (Radio Shack 270-231 used by author), "D" cell battery holder (Radio Shack 270-1438 or equiv.), wire, solder, etc.

alarm to sound continuously. Plug P1 is only a dummy used to open jack J1; it is not used as a connection.

The alarm can be secured adjacent to a door or window by a small screw passed through the back of the cabinet, or you can install a hanger bracket on top of the cabinet so the alarm can be slipped on and off a nail.

Since there is no standby current, the battery will last its shelf life. It's best to put a date sticker on the battery and replace it every year. To avoid soldering directly to the battery terminals the use of a "D" cell battery holder is suggested.

SIREN CIRCUIT

When switched on, this little screamer sounds like its official counterpart, with authentic-sounding rise and fall in pitch. Since the siren-sound is subjective to a large extent, plenty of variable components have been included in order to obtain the "perfect pitch." The circuit consists of a 555-type timer in astable mode, modulated by a varying dc, which is developed from a long-term multivibrator or clock. The high-low action of the clock causes capacitor C3 to charge and discharge through a resistance R4, the potential on the capacitor being applied to the "modulation input" (pin 5) of the 555. The long-period clock may be derived from another 555, or from the circuit shown. See Fig. 5-29 and Table 5-9.

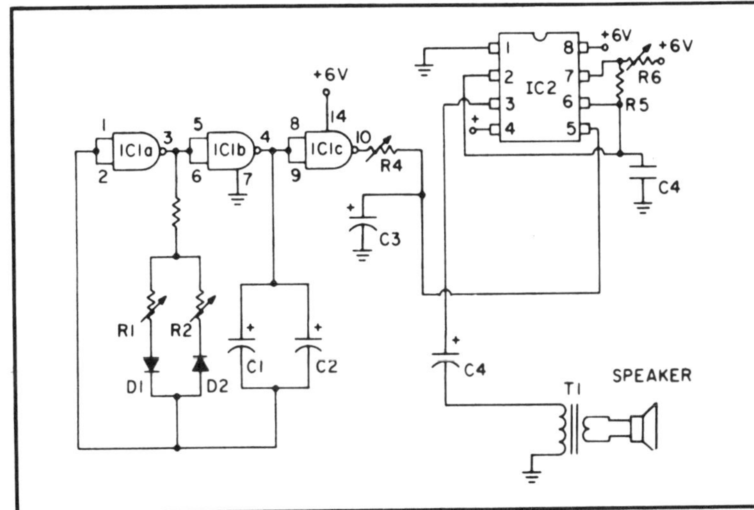

Fig. 5-29. Siren circuit schematic.

Table 5-9. Parts List for Siren Circuit.

C1, C2—4.7-μF tantalum capacitor, 25 Vdc
C3—500 to 1,000-μF electrolytic capacitor, 25 Vdc
C4—100-μF electrolytic capacitor, 25 Vdc
C5—0.1-μF ceramic capacitor, 15 Vdc
IC1—4011A quad NAND gate
IC2—555 timer
R1—500,000-ohm, 1/2-watt resistor
R2—500,000-ohm linear-taper potentiometer
R3—47,000-ohm, 1/2-watt resistor
R4—10,000-ohm linear-taper potentiometer
R5—4,700-ohm, 1/2-watt resistor
R6—25,000-ohm linear-taper potentiometer
SPKR—8-ohm PM type speaker
T1—audio output transformer 500-ohm primary/8-ohm secondary

AUTO BURGLAR ALARM

THIS BURGLAR ALARM WILL SOUND YOUR CAR HORN IF ANYONE opens your car door. The timers allow you to leave and enter the car without the horn sounding. To set, or arm, the alarm circuit, open S2. This will give you five seconds (R1, C1) to get out and shut the door behind you. If anyone opens a door for two seconds (R3, C2), the horn will sound and will stay locked on until S1 is opened. If you open the door to enter, you have two seconds to close S2, which is plenty of time if S2 is conveniently located. See Fig. 5-30 and Table 5-10.

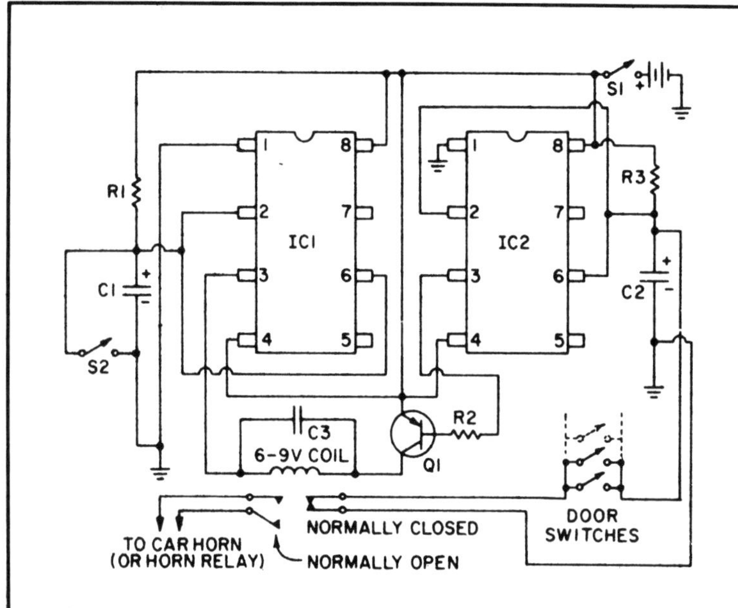

Fig. 5-30. Auto burglar alarm schematic.

Table 5-10. Parts List for Auto Burglar Alarm.

C1—10-μF electrolytic capacitor, 15 Vdc
C2—1-μF electrolytic capacitor, 15 Vdc
C3—0.1-μF ceramic disc capacitor, 15 Vdc
IC1, IC2—555 timer
Q1—2N4403

R1—500,000-ohm, 1/2-watt resistor
R2—270-ohm, 1/2-watt resistor
R3—2,000,000-ohm, 1/2-watt resistor
RELAY—6 to 9 Vdc coil with switch contacts rated at 15 VDC/30 amps; 1 set SPST normally open, 1 set SPST normally closed.

Chapter 6

Power Supply Projects

THE SMART POWER SUPPLY

WHEN WORKING WITH VARIOUS ELECTRONIC PROJECTS, IT'S easy to get carried away with too many current-eating components, which can overload a power supply. Our Smart Power Supply solves this problem with its built-in LED-ammeter, which always tells you what the current draw is.

The supply delivers a regulated 5 and 8-volt output at up to 1-amp, and you'll never be in the dark as to how much current is being drawn. Four LEDs display the amount of current being utilized by the load. Each LED lights respectively to show the level of current being drawn. For example, if 3/4 of an amp (.75) is being used, the first three LEDs (".25," ".50," and ".75") will all glow to show that a current of at least 3/4 of an amp is flowing. Best of all, the current measuring resistance is an unprecedented 0.1-ohm! What's more, the cost for the ammeter portion of the circuit is only about $5. That's way less than you'd pay for a good mechanical meter.

The 5-volt output is ideal for all of your TTL IC projects, while the 8-volt output may be selected for CMOS circuits, and other, higher-power requirements. The total cost for the whole supply, including the bargraph ammeter, is about $15-20, depending on your buying habits, and choice of parts suppliers.

How it Works

IC4 is supplied by an accurate reference voltage of 5-volts by IC3. IC4 is a quad op amp used in a quad comparator configuration.

The four op amps (comparators) in IC4 are each fed a separate reference voltage by the divider network made up of R1-R4 and R5-R8. These comparators in IC4 are very sensitive, and they can detect extremely small voltage differences and compare them.

Let's take the first op amp comparator as an example. Its inputs are pins 2 and 3, and its output is pin 1. The reference voltage appearing at pin 3 is compared to the voltage coming into the first comparator at pin 2. When 1/4 of an amp or more is flowing through R10, .025-volts or more (0.1-ohms times 0.25 A = .025 V) appears across R10, which is enough voltage to equal pin 3's reference voltage, thus turning on the first op amp. The output of this op amp is at pin 1, so LED1 turns on to signify that at least 1/4 of an amp is being drawn. In a like manner, the other LEDs turn on or off with the changing current. The rest of the circuitry makes up a basic voltage-regulated power supply.

Construction

All of the circuitry, except ICs 1 and 2, can be mounted on a small piece of perfboard. (See Figs. 6-1 through 6-4 and Table 6-1.) These two ICs must be mounted to the cabinet. In operation, IC1 and IC2 will get hot when the supply is run at higher currents, and they may shut down if the heat is not carried away. The back of the cabinet is the best place to mount ICs 1 and 2, for it allows a large heat dissipating area, while keeping the rest of the cabinet cool to the touch.

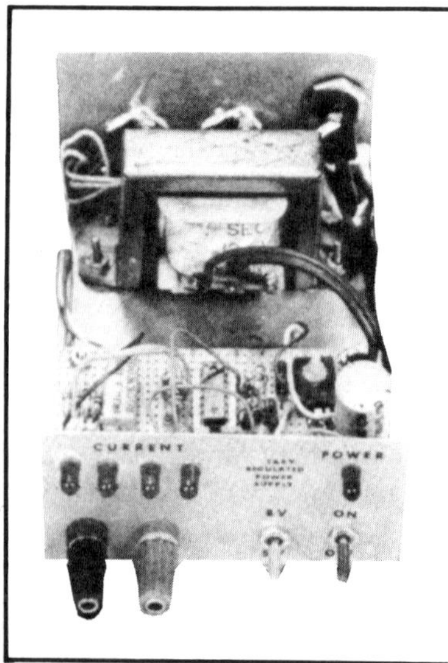

Fig. 6-1. As you can see, our prototype was assembled on breadboard, with plenty of room for the components. The parts layout isn't critical.

Fig. 6-2. This power supply keeps tabs automatically on current and voltage levels.

When mounting ICs 1 and 2, smear heatsink grease between the IC cases and the cabinet, then bolt the ICs down tightly. Connect three long wires to IC1 and 2. These will be connected to the main circuit board later.

If the transformer that you wish to use has a center tap, cut it off or tuck it away. You won't need it. Bolt T1 down to the cabinet. Use heavy gauge (#16) wire for all line voltage connections, and carefully wrap all ac line connections with electrical tape. Use a grommet around the line cord exit hole in the chassis to protect the cord from the heat that will be there due to ICs 1 and 2. Tie a knot in the line cord just inside the cabinet hole to prevent it from being pulled out.

IC3, unlike ICs 1 and 2, can be mounted on the perfboard because it will not get hot in operation. You should use a 14-pin socket for IC4. Install IC4 only after all of your wiring to the socket is complete.

Be careful not to make any solder "bridges" between socket pins, as they are close together. When you install IC4 in its socket, make sure that you observe the correct orientation with regard to pin 1.

After you've installed the circuit board, attach the wires from ICs 1 and 2 to their proper places on the board. Connect the wires to the

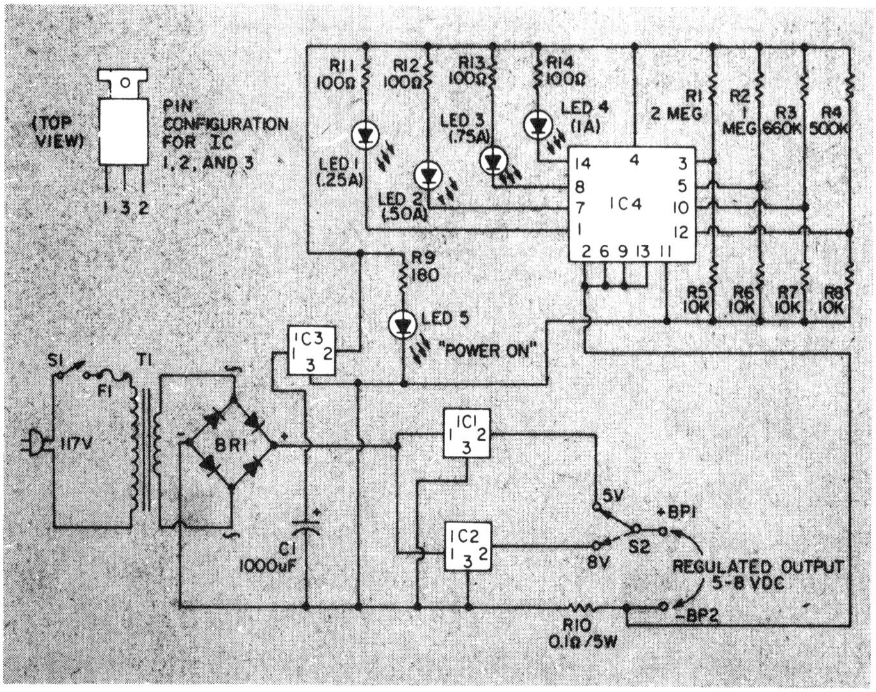

Fig. 6-3. The Smart Power Supply schematic.

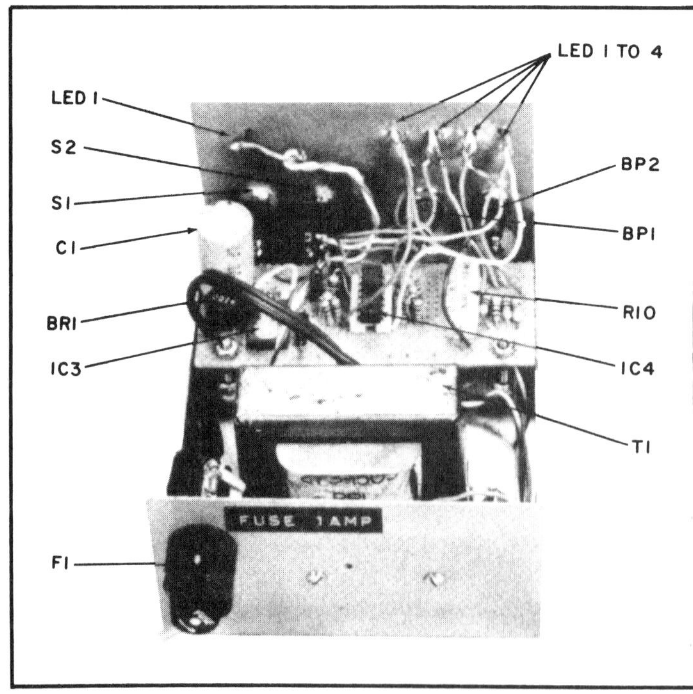

Fig. 6-4. Again, parts layout is not critical in this power supply, but feel free to use our idea of where things should go. It's always a good general design idea to keep the power transformer as far away from the rest of the circuitry as cabinet size or practicality permits. Suspend the board above chassis.

Table 6-1. Parts List for the Smart Power Supply.

BP1, BP2—5 way insulated binding post
BR1—bridge rectifier rated @ 50 PIV 2-Amperes
C1—1,000-μF, 24-Vdc electrolytic capacitor
F1—3AG 1-Amp fuse
IC1, IC3—7805 linear voltage regulator
IC2—7808 linear voltage regulator
IC4—LM324N quad op amp
LED1 through LED5—large, red LED rated @ 20 mA.
R1—2,000,000-ohm, 1/4-watt resistor
R2—1,000,000-ohm, 1/4-watt resistor
R3—660,000-ohm, 1/4-watt resistor
R4—500,000-ohm, 1/4-watt resistor
R5, R6, R7, R8—10,000-ohm 1/4-watt resistor
R9—180-ohm, 1/4-watt resistor
R10—0.1-ohm, 5-watt resistor (Radio Shack #271-128)
R11, R12, R13, R14—100-ohm, 1/4-watt resistor
S1—SPST switch
S2—SPDT switch
T1—transformer with primary rated @ 120-Vac/secondary @ 12.6-Vac, 2-Amperes

display LEDs last, and make sure that you observe polarity on each LED. Be careful not to let the LED leads short against the metal cabinet.

Operation

Carefully inspect your wiring on the circuit board, especially the wiring to IC4's pins. This is a very important step, as one misplaced wire here can produce some real odd-ball systems. If everything appears to be in order, turn the unit on. The "power" LED (LED5) should glow.

Connect a voltmeter to the output jacks. Depending on what position switch S2 is in, the voltmeter will read 5 or 8 volts. Throwing S2 to its other position should cause the voltmeter to read the other of the two voltages that the supply delivers.

To test the ammeter section, connect a circuit to the output jacks. With the supply set for 5-volts, a TTL IC circuit would be good for this test.

If the circuit that you hooked up draws more than 1/4 amp, then one or more of the display LEDs will go on to show you how much current is being drawn.

Conclusion

You shouldn't worry about overloading the power supply, as fuse F1 will limit current draw to a peak of about 1.3-amps momentarily, before acting, and we deliberately overloaded several times in a row, with no damage occurring to the circuitry.

You might wish to attach a solderless breadboard to the top of the cabinet, to act as a permanently-powered breadboard for your experiments, or to construct an output voltage switcher for powering several projects alternately.

THE JUNK BOX SPECIAL

BETWEEN 555 TIMERS, TTL, CMOS, OP AMPS AND RUN OF THE mill transistor projects, the average experimenter is often faced with the need for a regulated power supply with a range of about 5 to 15 volts—just to try out a breadboard project. If you've priced any regulated supplies lately you know they don't come cheap. Maybe, just maybe, you might get one for $30 or $35.

With a little careful shopping, a reasonably stocked junk box and one or two "brand new" components you can throw together a regulated supply costing less than $10 that will handle most of your experimenter power supply requirements. One of these Junk Box Specials is shown in Fig. 6-5. The range of this model is 5 to 15 volts dc at currents up to 1 ampere. One of the common, 3-terminal regulators which are now flooding the surplus market provides everything in the way of regulation. Depending on the source, the regulator will cost you from $1 to $2.50; the higher prices often include an insulated mounting kit (worth about 25-cents).

Five to 15 volts from one 3-terminal regulator? Correct. If regulator IC1's collector terminal is connected to a voltage divider across the output—R1 and R2—the output voltage will be that at the junction plus the voltage rating of the regulator, which in this instance is 5 volts. So, when potentiometer R2 is adjusted so its wiper is grounded the

Fig. 6-5. The Junk Box Special.

power supply's output is that of the regulator, 5 volts—perfect for TTL projects. As R2 is advanced, increasing the resistance from IC1's collector to ground, the voltage output increases. (See Figs. 6-6 through 6-9 and Table 6-2.)

Getting the Parts

There are plenty of parts around to build this supply for under $10. If you go out and round up "all new" components the cost is likely to go well over $30, so forget about new parts. Power transformer T1 can be 18 volts at 1 ampere (or rated at higher current, though the supply's maximum output is 1 ampere), or 36 volts center-tapped at 1 ampere or more. Both the 18 volt and 36 volt transformers are glutting the surplus market. If you get an 18 volt transformer use the bridge rectifier shown in Fig. 6-6. If you get a 36 volt C.T. transformer use the full-wave rectifier shown at the bottom of Fig. 6-6. The diode rectifiers SR1 through SR4, are type 1N4001, 1N4002, 1N4003, or 1N4004, which are also glutting the surplus market. Just to show you the savings possible, at the time this article is being prepared you can buy fifteen surplus 1N4001s for $1. Just one single "general replacement" for the 1N4001 from a national supplier is selling for over 40-cents. Get the idea how to save costs on this project?

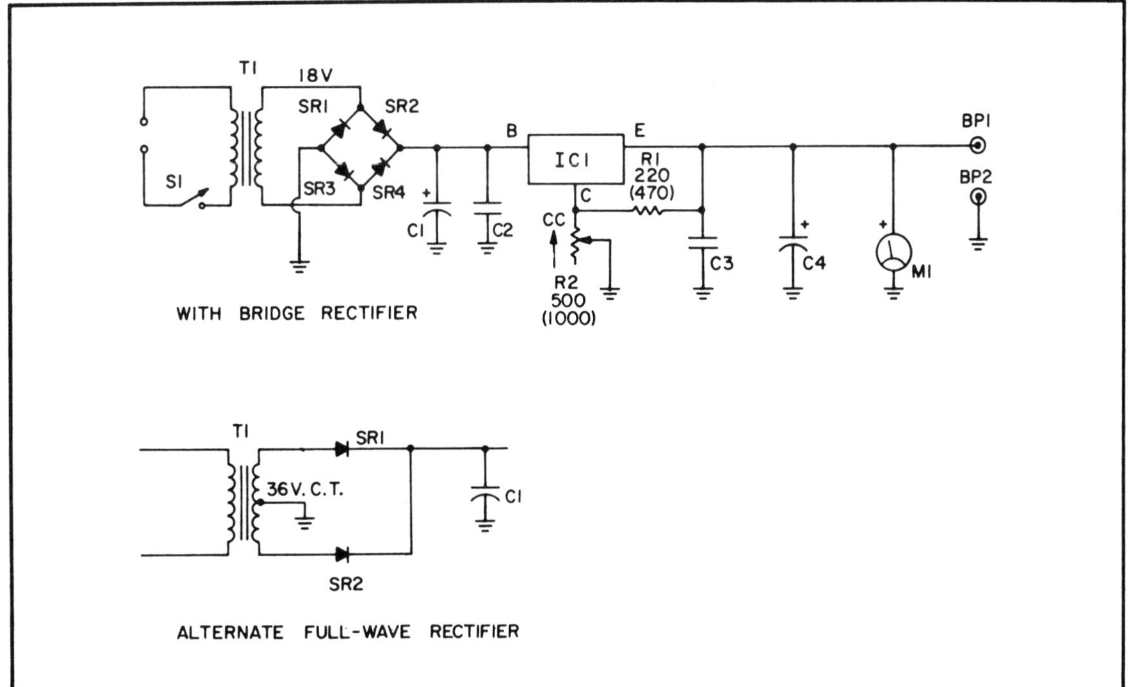

Fig. 6-6. Virtually any dc voltmeter that can display the range of 0 to 15 volts can be used. The surplus market is loaded with less-than-$5 meters that are suitable if you don't mind a little extra scale coverage.

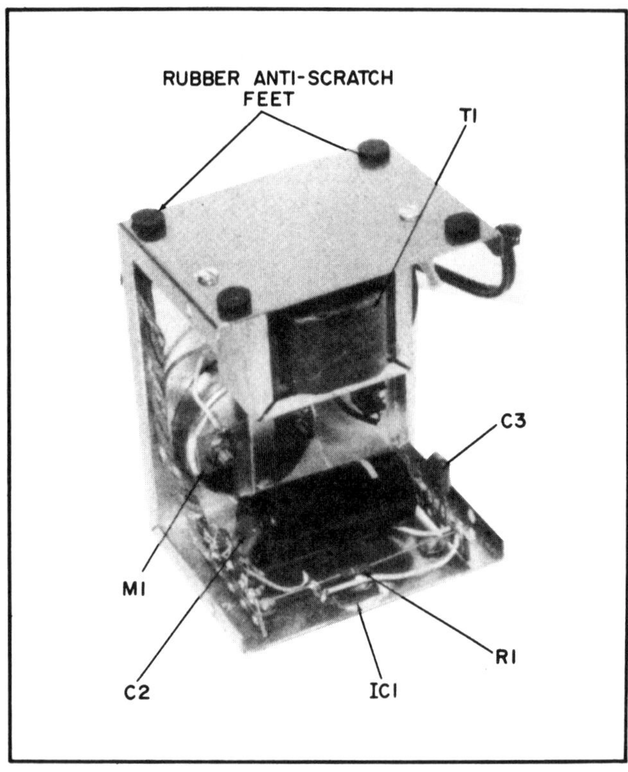

Fig. 6-7. To prevent scratching your workbench apply rubber anti-scratch feet or bumpers on the bottom of the cabinet. They are available in most hardware and houseware stores.

Capacitor C1 can be anything from 2000 to 4000 μF at 25 volts or higher. Look for an outfit selling surplus computer capacitors. If worse comes to worse you can get the value specified in the parts list in a Radio Shack store.

The 3-terminal, 5 volt regulator is another item easily found on the surplus market. With an adequate heat sink—such as the cabinet itself—the device can safely deliver 1 ampere. The unit shown is a Motorola MC7805 (though you can substitute any similar type) obtained for $2.50 from Circuit Specialists. We have seen similar devices from other manufacturers selling for $1. The terminals B, C, and E are indicated directly on the device or on the terminals—where they join the case. The collector (C) lead is connected to the IC's metal tab, and is normally grounded. Note that in this project, however, the collector terminal, and therefore the tab, is not grounded. You must use an insulated mounting kit consisting of a mica insulator and a shoulder washer. Place the insulator between the IC's body and the cabinet, or the tab and cabinet, and slip the shoulder washer into the opening (hole) in the body or tab. Pass the mounting screw from outside the cabinet through the mica washer, through the IC, and through the shoulder washer. Secure with a 1/4-inch (or smaller, not larger) nut hand-tightened against the shoulder washer. Before going

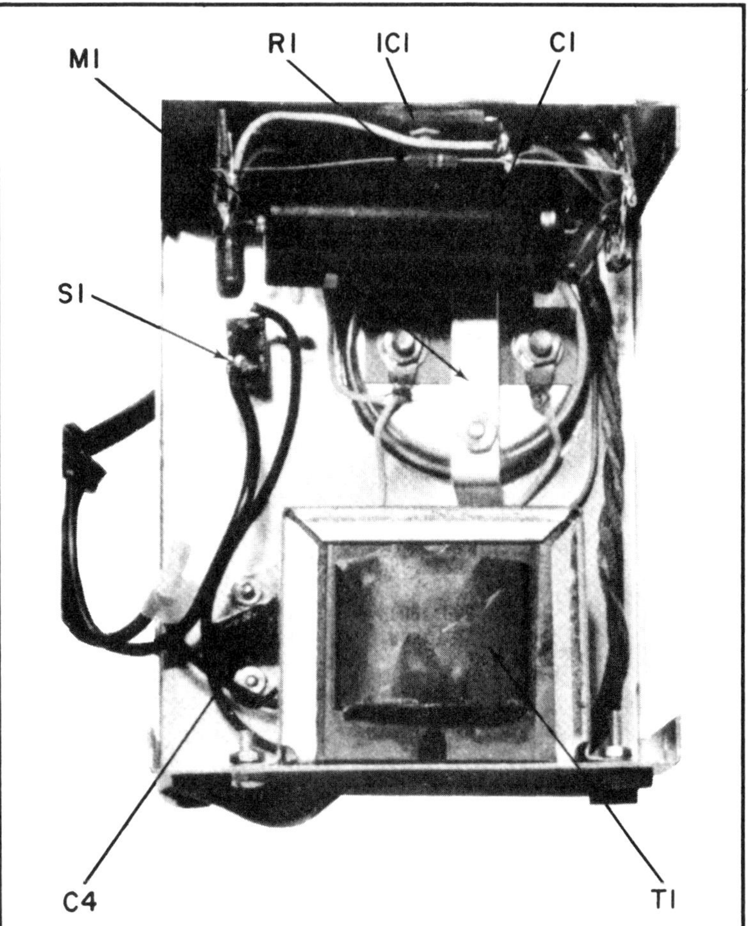

Fig. 6-8. If you've had experience with assembly in tight quarters, you can shoe-horn the power supply into a standard 3 × 4 × 5-inch Minibox. If your soldering iron is so big it burns adjacent wires when you make a connection, use a larger size cabinet.

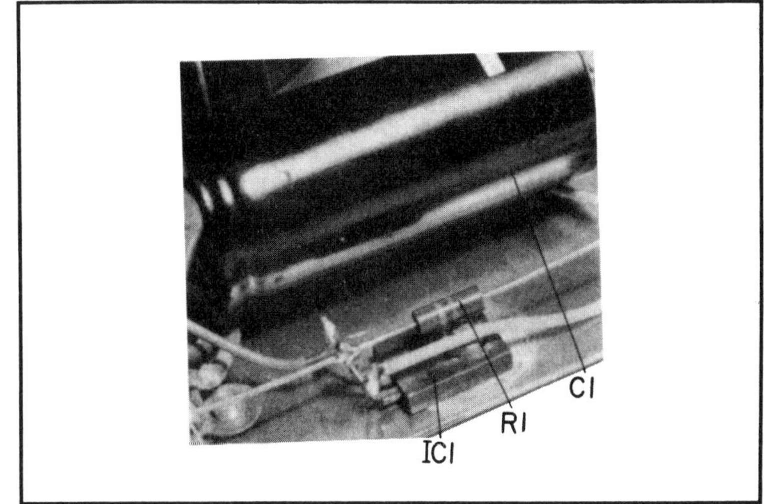

Fig. 6-9. In order to handle a full ampere, the IC regulator must be heat sinked to the cabinet. Make certain the collector and its attached sink tab (the back of the package) is insulated from the cabinet. Use silicon grease to ensure heat transfer from the IC to the cabinet.

Table 6-2. Parts List for Junk Box Special.

R1—220 or 470-ohms, 1/2 watt, 10% (see text)	terminal regulator (see text)
R2—Potentiometer, 500 or 1000-ohms (see text)	T1—Power transformer, secondary 1 ampere at 18 volts or 36 volts C.T. (see text)
C1—3300-μF, 35 Vdc (see text) (Radio Shack 272-1021 ore equivalent)	SR1, SR2, SR3, SR4—Silicon rectifiers (see text)
C2, C3—0.1 μ Mylar	S1—SPST switch
C4—25-μ, 25 VDC or higher	BP1, BP2—5-way binding posts
M1—DC voltmeter (see text)	Misc.—Cabinet, terminals strips, etc.
IC1—Motorola MC7805,5 volt 3-	

any further check with an ohmmeter to be certain the collector terminal is insulated from the cabinet.

Connecting wires are soldered directly to IC1's terminal leads; use a heat sink such as an alligator clip on each terminal if you have a large (greater than 40 watts) iron. Since the layout is not important, we suggest the arrangement shown, with IC1 positioned between two mounting strips so R1 can span across the strips and be soldered to IC1's collector terminal.

Finally, we come to the meter, a device that has become slightly more expensive than a barrel of Arabian oil. Any meter that can indicate at least the range of 0 to 15 Vdc is adequate. The EMICO 0-30 Vdc meter shown in Fig. 6-5 was selling in one local store for $7.95, while we bought ours almost down the block as "surplus" for $2.99. A good source for surplus meters is Fair Radio Sales. You might not end up with a meter case that looks suitable for NASA, but the output voltage doesn't care two hoots whether the meter is a modern $25 dollar model or a surplus-special for a buck ninety-nine.

Power switch S1 can be a separate SPST as shown in our project, or it can be part of R2. But keep in mind that a separate S1 allows you to turn the supply on and off without affecting voltage control R2's adjustment.

Finally, we come to R1 and R2. You will note that Fig. 6-6 shows two values for each. One value for each resistor is in brackets (parenthesis). You can use either set of values as long as they are matched. If R2 is 500 ohms R1 is 220 ohms; if R2 is 1000 ohms R1 is 470 ohms. The reason we show both sets of values is because 500 and 1000 ohm potentiometers appear on the surplus market from time to time, but usually not together. This way, you can use whatever is available at low cost.

Checkout

Set potentiometer R2 so the wiper shorts to the end connected to IC1's collector terminal, thereby connecting the collector directly to ground. If you wired R2 correctly it should be full counterclockwise.

Then set S1 to on. The meter should rise instantly to 5 volts dc. As R2 is adjusted clockwise the output voltage should increase to 15 Vdc or slightly higher. If R2 can adjust the output voltage only over the range of approximately 12 to 15 Vdc, or 12 to 15+ Vdc, IC1 is defective, or has been damaged.

TTL POWER SUPPLY

THIS IC PROJECT WILL PROVIDE YOU WITH A FLAT, RIPPLE-FREE, and locked-on 5 volts for any use around the house or on your work bench. It will prove to be very handy for the TTL projects using any IC that starts with the two numbers 74. The LM309 is a remarkable IC containing over a dozen transistors and several diodes. It can handle up to about 1 amp without a heat sink. If you mount it on a heat sink, a 4- by 4-inch piece of aluminum will do, it can supply up to 4 amps without dropping its 5 volt output. See Fig. 6-10 and Table 6-3.

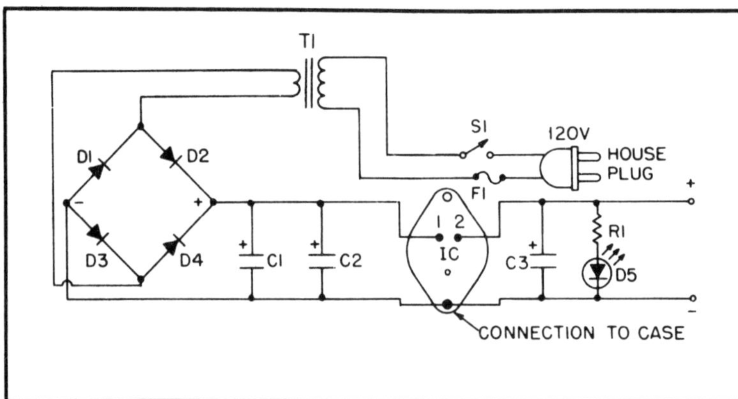

Fig. 6-10. TTL power supply schematic.

Table 6-3. Parts List for TTL Power Supply.

C1, C2, C3—1,000-μF electrolytic capacitor, 25 Vdc	IC1—LM309
D1, D2, D3, D4—1N4003 diode	R1—500-ohm, 2-watt resistor
D5—large LED	S1—SPST toggle switch rated at 120 Vac/15 amps
F1—120 VAC 1/2 amp fuse, fast acting type	T1—120 VAC to 12.6 Vac transformer

DUAL-POLARITY POWER SUPPLY

MANY OPERATIONAL AMPLIFIERS REQUIRE BOTH POSITIVE AND negative supplies for proper operation. With this simple circuit you can take a floating power supply and convert it into a dual-polarity supply. To provide ±15 volts as most op amps require, you will need a 30 volt supply to drive the circuit. The output voltage of this circuit are set by the voltage divider action of R1 and R2 and are well regulated. Current output is limited only by the unbalance between the loads on the positive and negative outputs, and should not exceed the rating of the transistors, 200 milliamperes. See Fig. 6-11 and Table 6-4.

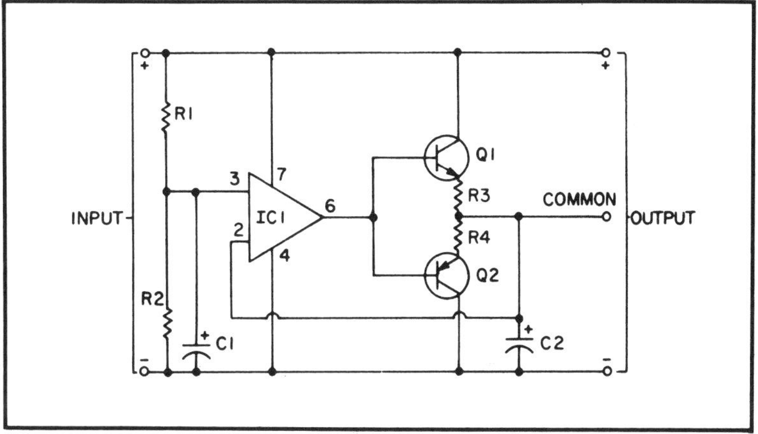

Fig. 6-11. Dual-polarity power supply schematic.

Table 6-4. Parts List for Dual-Polarity Power Supply.

C1, C2—15-μF electrolytic capacitor, 30n Vdc	Q2—2N4403
IC1—741 op amp	R1, R2—100,000-ohm, 1/2-watt resistor
Q1—2N4401	R3, R4—10-ohm, 1/2-watt resistor

VARIABLE REGULATED POWER SUPPLY

THERE ARE LOTS OF GOOD POWER SUPPLIERS ON THE MARKET, but why not build your own and save a bundle? This circuit can provide voltages between 5 and 15-volts dc at currents up to one ampere. Be sure to heat-sink the μA78GKC regulator by bolting it to either a commercial aluminum hat sink or to your supply's cabinet (if it's made of aluminum). Mount C2 and C3 as close as possible to pins 2 and 4 of IC1. If you cannot locate a 28 VCT transformer, go to something slightly higher, say 32 VCT. The same goes for the transformer's current rating; for example, you could use a 2-amp device. See Fig. 6-12 and Table 6-5.

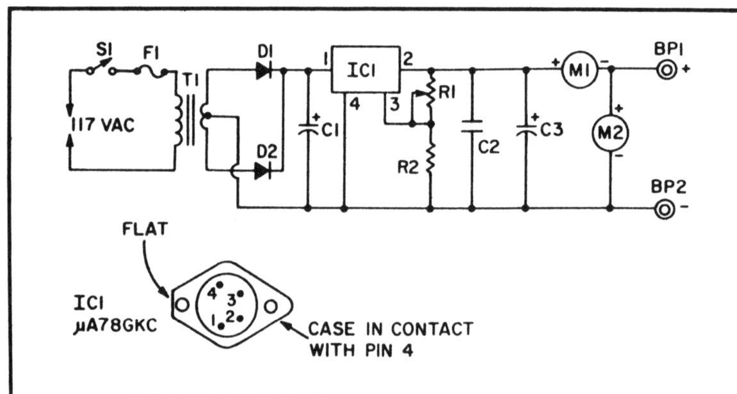

Fig. 6-12. Variable regulated power supply schematic.

Table 6-5. Parts List for Variable Regulated Power Supply.

BP1, BP2—binding post
C1—2200-μF electrolytic capacitor, 40 Vdc
C2—0.1-μF ceramic disc capacitor, 35 Vdc
C3—100-μF electrolytic capacitor, 25 Vdc
D1, D2—1N4003 (1A, 200 PIV) rectifier diode
F1—0.5-Ampere slow-blow fuse
IC1—μA78GKC adjustable voltage regulator
M1—0-to-1 Amp dc meter
M2—0-to-15-Volt dc meter
R1—10K-ohm linear-taper potentiometer
R2—4700-ohm, 1/2-watt resistor, 5%
S1—SPST toggle switch
T1—28VCT, 1.2-Amp power transformer (see text)

Index

A

A/D converter, 121
AND logic demonstrator, 147
anemometer, 57
antenna, underground, 80
antique radio, 95
armature, 23, 27
audio fire alarm, 214
auto burglar alarm parts list, 228
auto burglar alarm schematic, 228

B

balanced bridge game parts list, 176
balanced bridge game, 173
balanced bridge schematic, 175
black box alarm parts list, 221
black box alarm, 218
Blinkey game construction, 154
Blinkey game, 151
Blinkey parts list, 153
Blinkey schematic, 152
brushes, motor, 29
burglar alarm schematic, 224

C

capacitor, low-leakage, 17
carborundum, 96
charges, electrostatic, 4
chip-clip construction, 114
chip-clip, 113
CMOS NAND oscillator parts list, 140
CMOS NAND oscillator schematic, 140
CMOS NAND oscillator, 140
CMOS probe, 143
collector brush assembly, 7
commutator, 24, 27
corona gap, 1
crystal detector,98
crystal-controlled TTL, 144

D

digital voltmeter assembly, 124
digital voltmeter calibration, 125
digital voltmeter circuit, 122
digital voltmeter ICs, 121
digital voltmeter installation, 126
digital voltmeter parts list, 123
digital voltmeter schematic, 123
digital voltmeter troubleshooting, 126
digital voltmeter, dashboard, 121
DIP ICs, 113
do-it-yourself logic parts list, 146
double-ground hookup, 82
dual-polarity power supply parts list, 241
dual-polarity power supply schematic, 241
dual-polarity power supply, 241

E

Elec-tac-toe parts layout, 160
Elec-tac-toe parts list, 163
Elec-tac-toe pc board layout, 161
Elec-tac-toe schematic, 159
Elec-tac-toe, 156
Electro-Snoop parts list, 35
Electro-Snoop schematic, 32
Electro-Snoop, 30
electrode, hand,10
electronic pendulum circuit, 118
electronic pendulum construction, 118
electronic pendulum operation, 119
electronic pendulum parts list, 119
electronic pendulum, 118
electroscope materials list, 53
electroscope, 48
electroscope, experimenter's, 52
electrostatic charges, 4

F

field winding, 25
fire alarm parts list, 216
fire alarm, 214
foil-a-burglar alarm, 224
Franklin, Benjamin, 45, 52

G

gap, corona, 1
gas alarm parts list, 199
gas alarm schematic, 199
gas alarm, mobile, 195
germanium crystals, 102
Grandpa's whisker parts list, 100
Grandpa's whisker schematic, 99
Guericke, Otto, 45

H

hand electrode, 10
hobbyist's night light parts list, 213
hobbyist's night light schematic, 212
hobbyist's night light, 211

I

interrupter disc, 63
intruder detector schematic, 225
intruder detector, 225

J

Jogging Pacesetter, 192

L

LED displays, 121
Leyden jar, 45, 50
light sensor parts layout, 206
light sensor parts list, 207
light sensor schematic, 206
light sensor, 205
lightning generator parts list, 16
lightning, 1,000,000-volt, 13
logic probe, TTL, 141
logic, do-it-yourself, 146
logical probe parts list, 143
logical probe schematic, 143
logical probe, 143
low-leakage capacitor, 17

M

Magic-Lamp schematic, 183
Magic-Lamp, 183
magnetic field, 21
Maxiclock component connections, 133
Maxiclock construction, 130
Maxiclock operation, 135
Maxiclock parts layout, 129
Maxiclock schematic, 131
Maxiclock, 128
metal detector assembly and calibration, 92
metal detector parts list, 92
metal detector pc board layout, 93
metal detector schematic, 90
metal detector search head, 91
metal detector, 88
meter modification, 71
midget motor materials list, 29
midget motor, 2
mobile gas alarm, 195
motor, BOTDC, 38
motor, midget, 23

N

NAND logic demonstrator schematic, 148
NAND logic demonstrator, 148
new shell game construction, 169
new shell game parts list, 171
new shell game pc board template, 171
new shell game, 167
night light construction, 211
nightlight blackout alarm schematic, 202
nightlight blackout alarm, 201
NOR logic demonstrator parts list, 150
NOR logic demonstrator schematic, 150
NOR logic demonstrator, 150

O

Ohm's law, 12
OR logic demonstrator parts list, 149
oscillator, CMOS NAND, 140

P

pendulum, electronic, 118
photocell mounting, 62
plant polygraph, 77
plant skin resistance, 74
plant voice parts list, 78
plant voice schematic, 75
power supply, dual-polarity, 241
power supply, smart, 229
power supply, TTL, 240
power supply, variable regulated, 242
probe, CMOS, 143
pulse generator assembly, 68
pulse maker parts list, 145
pulse maker schematic, 145
pulse maker, 145
Pushie-Button game, 188
Pushie-Button parts list, 189
Pushie-Button schematic, 188

R

radio receiver circuit,95
radio receiver construction, 98
radio tuning coil, 97
radio, antique, 95
radio, transistor, 194
receiver, underground, 81
Roto-Stat layout, 47
Roto-Stat parts list, 47
Roto-Stat, 45

S

shell game schematic, 168
simplex detector parts list, 226
siren circuit parts list, 227
siren circuit schematic, 227
smart power supply parts list, 233
smart power supply, 229
Sobriety Tester game, 190
Sobriety Tester parts list, 190
Sobriety tester schematic, 190
solar swinger parts list, 108
solar swinger schematic, 108
solar swinger tube pin terminal connections, 107
solar swinger tube preparation, 106
solar swinger, 103
SonoPulse timer layout, 138
SonoPulse, 136
SonoPulse parts list, 137
SonoPulse schematic, 137
SonoPulse timer, 136
sounds from the ground, 79

T

thermistor thermometer bridge, 86
thermistor thermometer calibration, 87
thermistor thermometer design layout, 85
thermistor thermometer parts list, 87
thermistor thermometer, 84
timer, 555, 141
Touch 'N Flip, 193
transistor motor final adjustment, 44
transistor motor parts list, 42
transistor motor, 39
transistor radio, 194
TTL logic probe parts list, 142
TTL logic probe, 141
TTL power supply, 240
TTL, crystal-controlled, 144

U

underground antenna, 80
underground receiver, 81

V

Van de Graaff generator materials list, 9
Van de Graaff generator, 1
Van de Graaff, Dr. Robert J., 1
variable regulated power supply, 242
variable regulated power supply, 24p2
voltmeter, dashboard digital, 121
VTVM, 51, 55

W

Wheatstone bridge, 31, 174
wind cup assembly, 71
wind cup generator schematic, 63
wind cup pulse generator, 61
wind cups, 69
wind gauge, 57
wind guage parts list, 67
wind speed meter adjustment, 72
wind speed meter calibration, 72
Winkler, J.H., 45
Winky-Dink construction, 179
Winky-Dink parts list, 180

Other Bestsellers From TAB

☐ **BUILDING METAL LOCATORS: A Treasure Hunter's Project Book—Rakes**

With the metal detectors you'll build using this project guide, you'll be ready to get started in a hobby that is challenging and potentially PROFITABLE! Just some of the types of detectors covered include: frequency-shift metal locators, a simple beat frequency oscillator, balanced inductance locators, transmitter/receiver circuits, a VLF coin searcher, and a VLF deep searching locator! 126 pp., 102 illus.

Paper $9.95 **Hard $15.95**
Book No. 2706

☐ **BEGINNER'S GUIDE TO TV REPAIR—3rd Edition**

Now, anyone can locate and correct dozens of common TV problems quickly, easily, and inexpensively! You'll learn how to keep both black-and-white and color TV sets performing their best . . . to remedy problems that can cause loss of vertical, loss of picture, or loss of both sound and picture. Color set problems from burst amplifiers to color sync and color control circuits are also covered. 272 pp., 82 illus.

Paper $12.95 **Hard $18.95**
Book No. 1897

☐ **THE ILLUSTRATED DICTIONARY OF ELECTRONICS—3rd Edition—Turner and Gibilisco**

Identifies and defines over 27,000 vital electronics terms—more than any other electronics reference published! More than *2,000 new topics* have been added to this state-of-the-art 3rd Edition! *Every* term has been revised and updated to reflect the most current trends, technologies, and usage. Covers basic electronics, electricity, communications, computers, and emerging technologies! 720 pp., 395 illus.

Paper $21.95 **Book No. 1866**

☐ **EMERGENCY LIGHTING AND POWER PROJECTS—Graf & Graf**

Literally packed with practical advice and how-to-be-prepared solutions, it's a handbook that will not only make sure you're ready to handle any lighting emergency next time it occurs . . . but you may even be able to prevent them! Covers energy-efficient lighting, security systems for home and business, tips on commercially available products and plans for a build-your-own power project! 224 pp., 188 illus.

Hard $18.95 **Book No. 1788**

☐ **BASIC ELECTRONICS THEORY—WITH PROJECTS AND EXPERIMENTS—2nd Edition—Horn**

If you're looking for an introduction to modern electronics . . . or if you're an experienced hobbyist or technician in need of a quick-reference on the many facets of today's analog or digital electronics practice . . . there's simply no better sourcebook than this new second edition of *Basic Electronics Theory—with Projects and Experiments*! It includes all the basics plus the most recent digital electronics developments! 672 pp., 645 illus.

Paper $18.95 **Hard $29.95**
Book No. 1775

☐ **THE 555 IC PROJECT BOOK—Traister**

Now, with this exceptionally well-documented project guide, you can begin to use the 555 timer IC in a variety of useful projects that are both easy and fun to put together. From an IC metronome to a ten-second timer and even an electronic organ, this is an exciting collection of 33 different projects that even a novice at electronics can make easily, inexpensively, and in only a few hours time. Most important it provides the know-how to start you designing your own original 555 IC projects to suit your own special needs. 224 pp., 110 illus.

Paper $11.95 **Book No. 1996**

☐ **FUNDAMENTALS OF DIRECT CURRENT**

An essential guide for anyone who wants to learn the basics of electricity and electronics. Dc concepts are the easiest to grasp, making them the logical starting point for all electronics practice. This invaluable guide explains all of these basic concepts and gives you the strong foundation you need for more advanced work in electronics. Plus, the appendix contains indispensable dc formulas, electrical terms, abbreviations, and electronic symbols. 252 pp., 164 illus.

Paper $12.95 **Hard $19.95**
Book No. 1870

☐ **A BEGINNER'S GUIDE TO MAKING ELECTRONIC GADGETS—2nd Edition**

You can build a metal detector, light-operated control or alarm devices, a light beam radio, an inductive loop radio control . . . the list of practical, fun and easy-to-build projects goes on and on! If you're interested in electronics, but unsure of how to get started building projects that actually accomplish something, this is the ideal guide for you. It includes step-by-step how-to's and illustrations. 182 pp., 152 illus.

Paper $8.95 **Hard $14.95**
Book No. 1793

☐ **HANDBOOK OF REMOTE CONTROL AND AUTOMATION TECHNIQUES—2nd Edition**

From how-to's for analyzing your control needs to comping up with the electronic and mechanical systems to do the job, the authors provide a wealth of information on just about every kind of remote control system imaginable: temperature, light, and tone sensitive devices, pressure of gas sensors, radio controlled units, time controlled systems, and microcomputer interface systems, even robots. 350 pp., 306 illus.

Paper $13.95 **Book No. 1777**

☐ **THE COMPLETE BATTERY BOOK—Perez**

Here's the practical, money-saving information you need to choose the right batteries for any job you have in mind *and* how to get maximum performance and longer life from each and every battery you use. It even gives you complete schematics for constructing your own low-cost battery chargers and motor generator sets! If you're an electronics hobbyist, this book is packed with information that has immediate use. 192 pp., 111 illus.

Paper $16.95 **Hard $24.95**
Book No. 1757